OFFENSIVE WEAPONS

by
Robert S. Shiels,
M.A., LL.B., LL.M., Ph.D.
Solicitor in the Supreme Courts of Scotland

W. GREEN/Sweet & Maxwell
EDINBURGH
1996

First Published in 1992

© Robert S. Shiels 1996

ISBN 0 414 01171 6

A CIP catalogue record for this book
is available from the British Library

The moral rights of the author have been asserted

Typeset by Trinity Typesetting, Edinburgh
Printed in Great Britain by Redwood Books, Wiltshire

OFFENSIVE WEAPONS

SEVEN DAY LOAN

This book is to be returned on
or before the date stamped below

UNIVERSITY OF PLYMOUTH

PLYMOUTH LIBRARY

Tel: (01752) 232323
This book is subject to recall if required by another reader
Books may be renewed by phone
CHARGES WILL BE MADE FOR OVERDUE BOOKS

For Nicola and Alastair

PREFACE TO SECOND EDITION

Intense public concern at the carrying of knives has led to much activity in the courts and in Parliament within the last few years. The resulting case law and statutes justify a new edition which, it is hoped, will be of use to the legal profession and anyone else with an interest in the subject.

Robert Shiels
Edinburgh
August 1996

CONCURRENT -TOGETHER
CONSECUTIVE - ONE AFTER
THE OTHER

PREFACE TO FIRST EDITION

This purports to be a convenient collection of statutes and cases on the law of offensive weapons and similar items. It includes relevant matters from throughout the United Kingdom and recent legislation of interest from the Republic of Ireland.

I am grateful to David Kelly, Advocate, who read and commented on the draft of this work, although I alone am responsible for the end result. Any view expressed by me is mine and it is not to be taken as binding on any Government department or other body.

Robert Shiels
Edinburgh
September 1992

CONTENTS

TABLE OF CASES

[Reference is to paragraph numbers only.]

TABLE OF STATUTES

TABLE OF STATUTORY INSTRUMENTS

TABLE OF ABBREVIATIONS

A. Statutes

The 1953 Act: Prevention of Crime Act 1953 (c.14)
The 1959 Act: Restriction of Offensive Weapons Act 1959 (c.37)
The 1961 Act: Restriction of Offensive Weapons Act 1961 (c.22)
The 1979 Act: Customs and Excise Management Act 1979 (c.2)
The 1984 Act: Police and Criminal Evidence Act 1984 (c.60)
The 1988 Act: Criminal Justice Act 1988 (c.33)
The 1993 Act: Carrying of Knives etc. (Scotland) Act 1993 (c.13)
The 1994 Act: Criminal Justice and Public Order Act 1994 (c.33)
The 1995 Act: Criminal Law (Consolidation) (Scotland) Act 1995 (c.39)
The 1996 Act: Offensive Weapons Act 1996 (c.26)

B. Cases

The citation of individual cases follows the abbreviations set out in the *Scottish Current Law Case Citator*, to which reference can be made for additional citations.

ACKNOWLEDGEMENTS

Extracts from the following cases reproduced by kind permission of Butterworths:

Bates *v.* Bulman [1973] 3 All E.R. 170
Evans *v.* Hughes [1972] 3 All E.R. 412
Fisher *v.* Bell [1960] 3 All E.R. 731
Gibson *v.* Wales [1983] 1 All E.R. 869
Ohlson *v.* Hylton [1975] 2 All E.R. 490
R. *v.* Allamby and Medford [1974] 3 All E.R. 126
R. *v.* Dayle [1973] 3 All E.R. 1151
R. *v.* Jura [1954] 1 All E.R. 696
R. *v.* Petrie [1961] 1 All E.R. 466
R. *v.* Simpson [1983] 3 All E.R. 789
Woodward *v.* Koessler [1958] 3 All E.R. 557

Extracts from the following cases reproduced by kind permission of the Incorporated Council of Law Reporting for England and Wales:

Cawley *v.* Frost [1976] 1 W.L.R. 1207
Flack *v.* Baldry [1988] 1 W.L.R. 393
R. *v.* Cuguller [1961] 1 W.L.R. 858
R. *v.* Formosa and Upton [1990] 3 W.L.R. 1179
R. *v.* Kelt [1977] 1 W.L.R. 1365
R. *v.* Pawlicki and Swindell [1992] 1 W.L.R. 827
Wood *v.* Commissioner of Police of the Metropolis [1986] 1 W.L.R. 796

R. *v.* Edmonds [1988] 2 Q.B. 142

Extract from the following case reproduced by kind permission of the Incorporated Council of Law Reporting for Ireland.

Jardine *v.* Kelly [1985] 6 N.I.J.B. 96

Extract from the following case reproduced by kind permission of Justice of the Peace Ltd:

R. *v.* McCalla (1988) 152 J.P. 481

Extracts from the following cases reproduced by kind permission of the Law Society of Scotland:

Addison *v.* MacKinnon, 1983 S.C.C.R. 52
Barr *v.* MacKinnon, 1988 S.C.C.R. 561
Burke *v* . MacKinnan, 1983 S.C.C.R. 23
Campbell *v.* H.M. Advocate, 1986 S.C.C.R. 516

Extracts from the following cases reproduced by kind permission of Pageant Publishing:

Extract from the following case reproduced by kind permission of the Scottish Council of Law Reporting:

Extracts from the following cases reproduced by kind permission of © Times Newspapers Limited, October 1996:

PART A

LEGISLATION

CHAPTER ONE

The Principal Acts 1.0

Introduction 1.1
In this part consideration is given to the principal Acts dealing
with offensive weapons and to other statutes concerned in some
way with these weapons.

Prevention of Crime Act 1953 1.2

An Act to prohibit the carrying of offensive weapons in public
places without lawful authority or reasonable excuse.
[6th May 1953]

**Prohibition of the carrying of offensive weapons without lawful authority or
reasonable excuse**
1.—(1) Any person who without lawful authority or reasonable 1.3
excuse, the proof whereof shall lie on him, has with him in any
public place any offensive weapon shall be guilty of an offence,
and shall be liable—

(a) on summary conviction, to imprisonment for a term not
exceeding [six][1] months or a fine not exceeding [level 5
on the standard scale],[2] or both;
(b) on conviction on indictment, to imprisonment for a term
not exceeding [four] years or a fine.[3]

(2) Where any person is convicted of an offence under subsection
(1) of this section the court may make an order for the forfeiture or
disposal of any weapon in respect of which the offence was committed.
[4](3) ...
(4) In this section "public place" includes any highway and any
other premises or place to which at the material time the public have
or are permitted to have access, whether on payment or otherwise;
and "offensive weapon" means any article made or adapted for use
for causing injury to the person, or intended by the person having it
with him for such use by him [or by some other person.][5]

Short title, commencement and extent

1.4 **2.**—(1) This Act may be cited as the Prevention of Crime Act 1953. (2) This Act shall come into operation on the expiration of one month from the passing thereof.

(3) This Act shall not extend to Northern Ireland.[6]

NOTES
[1] See s.46(1) of Criminal Justice Act 1988.
[2] For penalty for England and Wales see s.32(2) of Magistrates Court Act 1980.
[3] Penalty amended by s.2(1) of the 1996 Act.
[4] Repealed for England and Wales by s.119(2) of Police and Criminal Evidence Act 1984.
[5] Words inserted by s.42(1) of Public Order Act 1986 for England and Wales.
[6] For the delegated legislation for Northern Ireland see *infra* at para. 2.3. The Scottish provisions are now in ss.47 *et seq* of the 1995 Act: see *infra* at para. 1.60. The 1953 Act now applies only to England and Wales.

1.5 **Restriction of Offensive Weapons Act 1959**

An Act to amend the law in relation to the making and disposing and importation of flick knives and other dangerous weapons. [14th May 1959]

Penalties for offences in connection with dangerous weapons

1.6 **1.**—(1) Any person who manufactures, sells or hires or offers for sale or hire, [or exposes or has in his possession for the purpose of sale or hire][1] or lends or gives to any other person—

> (*a*) any knife which has a blade which opens automatically by hand pressure applied to a button, spring or other device in or attached to the handle of the knife, sometimes known as a "flick knife" or "flick gun"; or
>
> (*b*) any knife which has a blade which is released from the handle or sheath thereof by the force of gravity or the application of centrifugal force and which, when released, is locked in place by means of a button, spring, lever, or other device, sometimes known as a "gravity knife,"

shall be guilty of an offence and shall be liable on summary conviction in the case of a first offence to imprisonment for a term not exceeding three months or to a fine not exceeding [level 5 on the standard scale][2] or to both such imprisonment and fine, and in the case of a second or subsequent offence to imprisonment for a term not exceeding six months or to a fine not exceeding [level 5 on the standard scale].[3]

(2) The importation of any such knife as is described in the foregoing subsection is hereby prohibited.

Short title, commencement and extent
2.—(1) This Act may be cited as the Restriction of Offensive **1.7**
Weapons Act 1959.

(2) This Act shall come into operation at the expiration of the period of one month beginning with the day on which it is passed.

(3) This Act shall not extend to Northern Ireland.[4]

NOTES
[1] Words inserted by s.1 of Restriction of Offensive Weapons Act 1961.
[2] See Criminal Justice Act 1988, s.46(2).
[3] *Ibid.*
[4] But see s.2 of Restriction of Offensive Weapons Act 1961, *infra* at para. 1.10.

Restriction of Offensive Weapons Act 1961   1.8

An Act to amend the law in relation to the exposure and possession for the purpose of sale or hire, and to the importation, of flick knives and other dangerous weapons.   [18th May 1961]
1.[1] ...   **1.9**

Prohibition of importation of dangerous weapons into Northern Ireland
2. Notwithstanding anything in subsection (3) of section two of **1.10**
the Restriction of Offensive Weapons Act 1959 (which restricts the operation of that Act to Great Britain), subsection (2) of section one of that Act (which prohibits the importation of flick knives and other knives described in subsection (1) of the said section one) *shall* extend to Northern Ireland.

Short title, citation and commencement
3.—(1) This Act may be cited as the Restriction of Offensive **1.11**
Weapons Act 1961.

(2) This Act and the Restriction of Offensive Weapons Act 1959 may be cited as the Restriction of Offensive Weapons Acts 1959 and 1961.

(3) This Act shall come into operation at the expiration of the period of one month beginning with the day on which it is passed.

NOTES
[1] The words in s.1 of the 1961 Act amend s.1(1) of the 1959 Act following the case of *Fisher* v. *Bell* [1960] 3 All E.R. 731; see *infra* at para. 3.9.1.

Theft Act 1968

. . . . .

Theft, robbery, burglary, etc.

. . . . . .

Burglary

1.13   **9.**—(1) A person is guilty of burglary if—

    (*a*) he enters any building or part of a building as a trespasser and with intent to commit any such offence as is mentioned in subsection (2) below; or

    (*b*) having entered any building or part of a building as a trespasser he steals or attempts to steal anything in the building or that part of it or inflicts or attempts to inflict on any person therein any grievous bodily harm.

(2) The offences referred to in subsection (1)(*a*) above are offences of stealing anything in the building or part of a building in question, of inflicting on any person therein any grievous bodily harm or raping any [person][1] therein, and of doing unlawful damage to the building or anything therein.

(3) References in subsections (1) and (2) above to a building shall apply also to an inhabited vehicle or vessel, and shall apply to any such vehicle or vessel at times when the person having a habitation in it is not there as well as at times when he is.

(4) A person guilty of burglary shall on conviction on indictment be liable to imprisonment for a term not exceeding fourteen years.

Aggravated burglary

1.14   **10.**—(1) A person is guilty of aggravated burglary if he commits any burglary and at the time has with him any firearm or imitation firearm, any weapon of offence, or any explosive; and for this purpose—

    (*a*) "firearm" includes an airgun or air pistol, and "imitation firearm" means anything which has the appearance of being a firearm, whether capable of being discharged or not; and

    (*b*) "weapon of offence" means any article made or adapted for use for causing injury to or incapacitating a person, or intended by the person having it with him for such use; and

    (*c*) "explosive" means any article manufactured for the purpose of producing a practical effect by explosion, or intended by the person having it with him for that purpose.

(2) A person guilty of aggravated burglary shall on conviction on indictment be liable to imprisonment for life.

NOTE
¹ Inserted by s.168(2) and Sched. 10 of the Criminal Justice and Public order Act 1994.

. . . . . .

Customs and Excise Management Act 1979   1.15

. . . . . .

Special penalty where offender armed or disguised
86. Any person concerned in the movement, carriage or   1.16
concealment of goods—

(a) contrary to or for the purpose of contravening any prohibition or restriction for the time being in force under or by virtue of any enactment with respect to the importation or exportation thereof ...

who, while so concerned, is armed with any offensive weapon or disguised in any way ... shall be liable on conviction on indictment to imprisonment for a term not exceeding three years... .

NOTE
This section was considered in *R. v. Jones* (1987) 85 Cr.App.R. 259 which is discussed *infra* at para. 3.4.3.

. . . . . .

Criminal Justice (Scotland) Act 1980   1.17

. . . . . .

Search for offensive weapons
4.—(1) Where a constable has reasonable grounds for suspecting   1.18
that any person is carrying an offensive weapon and has committed or is committing an offence under section 1 of the Prevention of Crime Act 1953 (prohibition of carrying of offensive weapons in public) the constable may search that person without warrant, and detain him for such time as is reasonably required to permit the search to be carried out; and he shall inform the person of the reason for such detention.

(2) Any person who—

   (*a*) intentionally obstructs a constable in the exercise of the constable's powers under subsection (1) above; or

   (*b*) conceals from a constable acting in the exercise of the said powers an offensive weapon,

shall be guilty of an offence and liable on summary conviction to a fine not exceeding £200.

(3) A constable may arrest without warrant any person who he has reason to believe has committed an offence under subsection (2) above.

(4) In this section, "offensive weapon" has the same meaning as in the said section 1.

· · · · · ·

NOTE

   Repealed from April 1, 1996; see s.48 of the Criminal Law (Consolidation) (Scotland) Act 1995 *infra* at para. 1.61.

Possession of fireworks etc. at sporting events.

1.19   **72A.**—(1) Any person who has entered the relevant area of a designated sports ground and is in possession of a controlled article or substance at any time during the period of a designated sporting event shall be guilty of an offence.

(2) Any person who, while in possession of a controlled article or substance, attempts to enter the relevant area of a designated sports ground at any time during the period of a designated sporting event at the ground shall be guilty of an offence.

(3) A person guilty of an offence under subsection (1) or (2) above shall be liable on summary conviction to imprisonment for a period not exceeding 60 days or to a fine not exceeding level 3 on the standard scale or both.

(4) It shall be a defence for a person charged with an offence under subsection (1) or (2) above to show that he had lawful authority to be in possession of the controlled article or substance.

(5) In subsection (1) and (2) above "controlled article or substance" means—

   (*a*) any article or substance whose main purpose is the emission of a flare for purposes of illuminating or signalling (as opposed to igniting or heating) or the emission of smoke or a visible gas; and in particular it includes distress flares, fog signals, and pellets and capsules intended to be used as fumigators or for testing pipes, but not matches, cigarette lighters or heaters; and (*b*) any article which is a firework.

. . . . . .

NOTE
Section 72A above was inserted into the 1980 Act by s.40(1) of and Sched. 1, para. 14 to the Public Order Act 1986.
Repealed from April 1, 1996; see s.20 of the Criminal Law (Consolidation) (Scotland) Act 1995 *infra* at para. 1.56.

Civic Government (Scotland) Act 1982   1.20

. . . . . .

Drunkenness
50.— ... (5) Any person who is drunk in a public place while in   1.21
possession of a firearm (including a crossbow, airgun, air rifle or
air pistol) shall be guilty of an offence and liable, on summary
conviction, to a fine not exceeding [level 2 on the standard scale][1]
(6) In this section, "public place" has the same meaning as in
section 133 of this Act but includes—

(*a*) any place to which at the material time the public are
permitted to have access, whether on payment or
otherwise; and
(*b*) any public conveyance other than a taxi or hire car within
the meaning of section 23 of this Act.

. . . . . .

NOTE
[1]See s.225 of the Criminal Procedure (Scotland) Act 1995.

Interpretation
133. In this Act, except where the context otherwise requires—   1.22
...
"public place" means any place (whether a thoroughfare or not) to
which the public have unrestricted access and includes—

(*a*) the doorways or entrances of premises abutting on any
such place; and
(*b*) any common passage, close, court, stair, garden or yard
pertinent to any tenement or group of separately owned
houses... .

NOTE
The definition of "public place" in s. 133, *supra*, is an explicit one but the phrase
must be construed in the context of a particular statute. The Road Traffic legislation is
particularly rich in case law on the point; see *e.g. R. v. Collinson* (1931) 23 Cr.App.R. 49;
R. v. Waters (1963) 47 Cr.App.R. 149; *Pugh v. Knipe* [1972] Crim.L.R. 247; *Sandy v. Martin*

[1974] R.T.R. 263; *Beattie* v. *Scott*, 1990 S.C.C.R. 435; *Young* v. *Carmichael*, 1991 S.C.C.R. 332 and *Alston* v. *O'Brien*, 4 92 S.C.C.R. 238. For public or der cases see *e.g. R.* v. *Edwards and Roberts* [1978] Crim.L.R. 564 and *Lawrenson* v. *Oxford* [1982] Crim.L.R. 185.

. . . . . .

1.23   **Roads (Scotland) Act 1984**

. . . . .

Interpretation

1.24   ¹**151.**—(1) In this Act, unless the context otherwise requires—

...

"classified road" shall be construed in accordance with section 11 of this Act;

...

"private road" means any road other than a public road;

"proposed road" means (without prejudice to the definition in this subsection of "proposed public road") a new road in course of construction, or proposed to be constructed, by or on behalf of any person;

"proposed public road" means either—

   (a) a new road in course of construction, or proposed to be constructed, by or on behalf of a roads authority; or

   (b) an existing road which is a prospective public road within the meaning of [Part IV of the New Roads and Street Works Act 1991]²

"public road" means a road which a roads authority have a duty to maintain; ...

"road" means, subject to subsection (3) below, any way (other than a waterway) over which there is a public right of passage (by whatever means) [and whether subject to a toll or not]³ and includes the road's verge, and any bridge (whether permanent or temporary) over which, or tunnel through which, the road passes; and any reference to a road includes a part thereof; ...

"special road" means a road provided or to be provided in accordance with a scheme under section 7 of this Act; ...

"trunk road" means a road which is a trunk road by virtue of section 5 of this Act or of an order or direction under that section or section 198(2) of the Town and Country Planning (Scotland) Act 1972.... .

⁴(1A) A way to which the public has access (by whatever means and whether subject to a toll or not) which passes over a bridge constructed in pursuance of powers conferred by, or by an order made under or confirmed by, a private Act shall, for the

purposes of the definition of "road" in subsection (1) above, be treated as if there were a public right of passage over it.".

(2) For the purpose of this Act, where over a road the public right of passage referred to in the definition of "road" in subsection (1) above—

  (*a*) is by foot only, the road is—
       (i)   where it is associated with a carriageway, a "footway"; and
       (ii) where it is not so associated, a "footpath";
  (*b*) is by pedal cycle only, or by pedal cycle and foot only, the road is a "cycle track";
  (*c*) includes such a right by vehicle, other than a right by pedal cycle only, the road is a "carriageway".

NOTE
  [1]The definition of "public place" in s.1(4) of the 1953 Act now includes, for Scotland, *any road* within the meaning of the Road (Scotland) Act 1984.
  [2]Inserted by the New Roads and Street Works Act 1991, Sched. 8.
  [3]*Ibid.*
  [4]Inserted by the Local Government etc. (Scotland) Act 1994.

. . . . . .

Police and Criminal Evidence Act 1984   1.25

PART I

POWERS TO STOP AND SEARCH

Power of constable to stop and search persons, vehicles etc.
  1.—(1) A constable may exercise any power conferred by this   **1.26**
section—

  (*a*) in any place to which at the time when he proposes to exercise the power the public or any section of the public has access, on payment or otherwise, as of right or by virtue of express or implied permission; or
  (*b*) in any other place to which people have ready access at the time when he proposes to exercise the power but which is not a dwelling.

  (2) Subject to subsection (3) to (5) below, a constable—

  (*a*) may search—
       (i)   any person or vehicle;
       (ii) anything which is in or on a vehicle;
            for stolen or prohibited articles [or any article to which subsection (8A) below applies][1]; and

(*b*) may detain a person or vehicle for the purpose of such a search.

(3) This section does not give a constable power to search a person or vehicle or anything in or on a vehicle unless he has reasonable grounds for suspecting that he will find stolen or prohibited articles [or any article to which subsection (8A) below applies].[2]

(4) If a person is in a garden or yard occupied with and used for the purposes of a dwelling or on other land so occupied and used, a constable may not search him in the exercise of the power conferred by this section unless the constable has reasonable grounds for believing—

(*a*) that he does not reside in the dwelling; and
(*b*) that he is not in the place in question with the express or implied permission of a person who resides in the dwelling.

(5) If a vehicle is in a garden or yard or other place occupied with and used for the purposes of a dwelling or on other land so occupied and used a constable may not search the vehicle or anything in or on it in the exercise of the power conferred by this section unless he has reasonable grounds for believing—

(*a*) that the person in charge of the vehicle does not reside in the dwelling; and
(*b*) that the vehicle is not in the place in question with the express or implied permission of a person who resides in the dwelling.

(6) If in the course of such a search a constable discovers an article which he has reasonable grounds for suspecting to be a stolen or prohibited article, [or any article to which subsection (8A) below applies,][3] he may seize it.

(7) An article is prohibited for the purposes of this Part of this Act if it is—

(*a*) an offensive weapon; or
(*b*) an article—
   (i) made or adapted for use in the course of or in connection with an offence to which this sub-paragraph applies; or
   (ii) intended by the person having it with him for such use by him or by some other person.

(8) The offences to which subsection (7)(*b*)(i) above applies are—

(*a*) burglary;
(*b*) theft;

(c) offences under section 12 of the Theft Act 1968 (taking motor vehicle or other conveyance without authority); and

(d) offences under section 15 of that Act (obtaining property by deception).

(8A) This subsection applies to any article in relation to which a person has committed, or is committing or is going to commit an offence under section 139 of the Criminal Justice Act 1988.[4]

(9) In this part of this Act—

"offensive weapon" means any article—

(a) made or adapted for use for causing injury to persons; or

(b) intended by the person having it with him for such use by him or by some other person... .

NOTES

[1,2] Words in square brackets inserted by s.140(1)(a) of the 1988 Act.

[3] Words in square brackets inserted by s.140(1)(b) of the 1988 Act.

[4] Section inserted by s.140(1)(c) of the 1988 Act.

. . . . . .

Reports of recorded searches and of road checks

5.—(1) Every annual report—   1.27

(a) [under section 22 of the Police Act 1996][1]

(b) made by the Commissioner of Police of the Metropolis,

shall contain information—

(i) about searches recorded under section 3 above which have been carried out in the area to which the report relates during the period to which it relates; and

(ii) about road checks authorised in that area during that period under section 4 above.

(2) The information about searches shall not include information about specific searches but shall include—

(a) the total numbers of searches in each month during the period to which the report relates—

(i) for stolen articles;

(ii) for offensive weapons [or articles to which section 1(8A) above applies][2]; and

(iii) for other prohibited articles;

(b) the total number of persons arrested in each such month in consequence of searches of each of the descriptions specified in paragraph (a)(i) to (iii) above.

(3) The information about road checks shall include information—

(*a*) about the reason for authorising each road check; and
(*b*) about the result of each of them.³

NOTES
¹ Amended by the Police Act 1996, Sched. 7.
² Words in brackets inserted by s.140(2) of the 1988 Act.
³ This section applies to England and Wales only; see s.120(1) of the 1984 Act. For the legislation for Northern Ireland see *infra* at para. 2.17.

. . . . . .

Arrest without warrant for arrestable and other offences

1.28 **24.**—(1) The powers of summary arrest conferred by the following subsections shall apply—

(*a*) to offences for which the sentence is fixed by law;
(*b*) to offences for which a person of 21 years of age or over (not previously convicted) may be sentenced to imprisonment for a term of five years (or might be so sentenced but for the restrictions imposed by section 33 of the Magistrates' Courts Act 1980); and
(*c*) to the offences to which subsection (2) below applies,

and in this Act "arrestable offence" means any such offence.
(2) The offences to which this subsection applies are—

(*a*) offences for which a person may be arrested under the customs and excise Acts, as defined in section 1(1) of the Customs and Excise Management Act 1979;
(*b*) offences under the Official Secrets Act 1920 that are not arrestable offences by virtue of the term of imprisonment for which a person may be sentenced in respect of them;
(*bb*) offences under any provision of the Official Secrets Act 1989 except section 8(1), (4) or (5)¹;
(*c*) offences under section … ²22 (causing prostitution of women) or 23 (procuration of girl under 21) of the Sexual Offences Act 1956;
(*d*) offences under section 12(1) (taking motor vehicle or other conveyance without authority etc.) or 25(1) (going equipped for stealing, etc.) of the Theft Act 1968; and
(*e*) any offence under the Football (Offences) Act 1991³;
(*f*) an offence under section 2 of the Obscene Publications Act 1959 (publication of obscene matter);
(*g*) an offence under section 1 of the Protection of Children Act 1978 (indecent photographs and pseudo-photographs of children)⁴;
(*h*) an offence under section 166 of the Criminal Justice and Public Order Act 1994 (sale of tickets by unauthorised persons)⁵;

(*i*) an offence under section 19 of the Public Order Act 1986 (publishing, etc. material intended or likely to stir up racial hatred)[6];

(*j*) an offence under section 167 of the Criminal Justice and Public Order Act 1994 (touting for hire car services).[7]

(*k*) an offence under section 1(1) of the Prevention of Crime Act 1953 (prohibition of the carrying of offensive weapons without lawful authority or reasonable excuse)[8];

(*l*) an offence under section 139(1) of the Criminal Justice Act 1988 (offence of having article with blade or point in public place)[8];

(*m*) an offence under section 139A(1) or (2) of the Criminal Justice Act 1988 (offence of having article with blade or point (or offensive weapon) on school premises)[8].

(3) Without prejudice to section 2 of the Criminal Attempts Act 1981, the powers of summary arrest conferred by the following subsections shall also apply to the offences of—

(*a*) conspiring to commit any of the offences mentioned in subsection (2) above;

(*b*) attempting to commit any such offence [other than an offence under section 12(1) of the Theft Act 1968][9];

(*c*) inciting, aiding, abetting, counselling or procuring the commission of any such offence,

and such offences are also arrestable offences for the purposes of this Act.

(4) Any person may arrest without a warrant—

(*a*) anyone who is in the act of committing an arrestable offence;

(*b*) anyone whom he has reasonable grounds for suspecting to be committing such an offence.

(5) Where an arrestable offence has been committed, any person may arrest without a warrant—

(*a*) anyone who is guilty of the offence;

(*b*) anyone whom he has reasonable grounds for suspecting to be guilty of it.

(6) Where a constable has reasonable grounds for suspecting that an arrestable offence has been committed, he may arrest without a warrant anyone whom he has reasonable grounds for suspecting to be guilty of the offence.

(7) A constable may arrest without a warrant—

    (*a*) anyone who is about to commit an arrestable offence;

    (*b*) anyone whom he has reasonable grounds for suspecting to be about to commit an arrestable offence.

NOTES

  ¹ Added by the Official Secrets Acts 1989, s.11(1).
  ² Words repealed by the Sexual Offences Act 1985, s.5(3).
  ³ Substituted by the Football (Offences) Act 1991, s.5(1).
  ⁴ Added by the Criminal Justice and Public Order Act 1994, s.85(2). See also s.85(4) and (5) which made an equivalent addition to the Northern Ireland PACE Order, s.26.
  ⁵ Added by the 1994 Act, s. 166(4).
  ⁶ Added by the 1994 Act, s.155.
  ⁷ Added by the 1994 Act, s.167(7).
  ⁸ Added by the 1996 Act, s.1.
  ⁹ The words in square brackets were added by the Criminal Justice Act 1988, Sched. 15, para. 98.

. . . . . .

1.29   **Sporting Events (Control of Alcohol etc.) Act 1985**

. . . . . .

Fireworks etc.

1.30   **2A.**—(1) A person is guilty of an offence if he has an article or substance to which this section applies in his possession—

    (*a*) at any time during the period of a designated sporting event when he is in any area of a designated sports ground from which the event may be directly viewed, or

    (*b*) while entering or trying to enter a designated sports ground at any time during the period of a designated sporting event at the ground.

(2) It is a defence for the accused to prove that he had possession with lawful authority.

(3) This section applies to any article or substance whose main purpose is the emission of a flare for purposes of illuminating or signalling (as opposed to igniting or heating) or the emission of smoke or a visible gas; and in particular it applies to distress flares, fog signals, and pellets and capsules intended to be used as fumigators or for testing pipes, but not to matches, cigarette lighters or heaters.

(4) This section also applies to any article which is a firework.

NOTE

    Section 2A was inserted into the 1985 Act by s.40(1) of and Sched. 1, para. 3 to the Public Order Act 1986.

. . . . . .

Crossbows Act 1987 1.31

An Act to create offences relating to the sale and letting on hire of crossbows to, and the purchase, hiring and possession of crossbows by, persons under the age of seventeen; and for connected purposes. [15th May 1987]

Sale and letting on hire

1. A person who sells or lets on hire a crossbow or a part of a 1.32 crossbow to a person under the age of seventeen is guilty of an offence, unless he believes him to be seventeen years of age or older and has reasonable ground for the belief.

Purchase and hiring

2. A person under the age of seventeen who buys or hires a 1.33 crossbow or a part of a crossbow is guilty of an offence.

Possession

3. A person under the age of seventeen who has with him— 1.34

(a) a crossbow which is capable of discharging a missile, or

(b) parts of a crossbow which together (and without any other parts) can be assembled to form a crossbow capable of discharging a missile,

is guilty of an offence, unless he is under the supervision of a person who is twenty-one years of age or older.

Powers of search and seizure etc.

4.—(1) If a constable suspects with reasonable cause that a person 1.35 is committing or has committed an offence under section 3, the constable may—

(a) search that person for a crossbow or part of a crossbow;

(b) search any vehicle, or anything in or on a vehicle, in or on which the constable suspects with reasonable cause there is a crossbow, or part of a crossbow, connected with the offence.

(2) A constable may detain a person or vehicle for the purpose of a search under subsection (1).

(3) A constable may seize and retain for the purpose of proceedings for an offence under this Act anything discovered by him in the course of a search under subsection (1) which appears to him to be a crossbow or part of a crossbow.

(4) For the purpose of exercising the powers conferred by this section a constable may enter any land other than a dwellinghouse.

Exception

1.36   **5.** This Act does not apply to crossbows with a draw weight of less than 1.4 kilograms.

Punishments

1.37   **6.**—(1) A person guilty of an offence under section 1 shall be liable, on summary conviction, to imprisonment for a term not exceeding six months, to a fine not exceeding level 5 on the standard scale, or to both.

(2) A person guilty of an offence under section 2 or 3 shall be liable, on summary conviction, to a fine not exceeding level 3 on the standard scale.

(3) The court by which a person is convicted of an offence under this Act may make such order as it thinks fit as to the forfeiture or disposal of any crossbow or part of a crossbow in respect of which the offence was committed.

Corresponding provision for Northern Ireland

1.38   **7.** An Order in Council under paragraph 1(1)(*b*) of Schedule 1 to the Northern Ireland Act 1974 (legislation for Northern Ireland in the interim period) which contains a statement that it is made only for purposes corresponding to the purposes of this Act—

(*a*) shall not be subject to paragraph 1(4) and (5) of that Schedule (affirmative resolution of both Houses of Parliament), but

(*b*) shall be subject to annulment in pursuance of a resolution of either House of Parliament.

Short title, commencement and extent

1.39   **8.**—(1) This Act may be cited as the Crossbows Act 1987.

(2) Sections 1 to 6 shall come into force at the end of the period of two months beginning with the day on which this Act is passed.

(3) Sections 1 to 6 shall not extend to Northern Ireland.

1.40   **Criminal Justice Act 1988**

· · · · · ·

Articles with blades or points and offensive weapons

Offence of having article with blade or point in public place

1.41   [1]**139.**—(1) Subject to subsections (4) and (5) below, any person who has an article to which this section applies with him in a public place shall be guilty of an offence.

(2) Subject to subsection (3) below, this section applies to any article which has a blade or is sharply pointed except a folding pocketknife.

(3) This section applies to a folding pocketknife if the cutting edge of its blade exceeds 3 inches.

(4) It shall be a defence for a person charged with an offence under this section to prove that he had good reason or lawful authority for having the article with him in a public place.

(5) Without prejudice to the generality of subsection (4) above, it shall be a defence for a person charged with an offence under this section to prove that he had the article with him—

(*a*) for use at work;
(*b*) for religious reasons; or
(*c*) as part of any national costume.

(6) A person guilty of an offence under subsection (1) above shall be liable—

(*a*) on summary conviction, to imprisonment for a term not exceeding six months, or a fine not exceeding the statutory maximum, or both;
(*b*) on conviction on indictment, to imprisonment for a term not exceeding two years, or a fine, or both.[2]

(7) In this section "public place" includes any place to which at the material time the public have or are permitted access, whether on payment or otherwise.

(8) This section shall not have effect in relation to anything done before it comes into force.

NOTES
[1] This section applies (a) by s.172(1) of the 1988 Act to England and Wales; and (b) by s.172(3) of the 1988 Act to Northern Ireland. Section 139 does not apply to Scotland; see s.172(2) of the 1988 Act. See also *Harris* v. *D.P.P.* and *Godwin* v. *D.P.P.*, both in *The Times* Law Reports, Aug. 14, 1992.
[2] Words in brackets substituted by s.3 of the 1996 Act.

Offence of having article with blade or point (or offensive weapon) on school premises

[1]**139A.**—(1) Any person who has an article to which section 139 **1.42** of this Act applies with him on school premises shall be guilty of an offence.

(2) Any person who has an offensive weapon within the meaning of section 1 of the Prevention of Crime Act 1953 with him on school premises shall be guilty of an offence.

(3) It shall be a defence for a person charged with an offence under subsection (1) or (2) above to prove that he had good reason

or lawful authority for having the article or weapon with him on the premises in question.

(4) Without prejudice to the generality of subsection (3) above, it shall be a defence for a person charged with an offence under subsection (1) or (2) above to prove that he had the article or weapon in question with him—

(*a*) for use at work,
(*b*) for educational purposes,
(*c*) for religious reasons, or
(*d*) as part of any national costume.

(5) A person guilty of an offence—

(*a*) under subsection (1) above shall be liable—
  (i) on summary conviction to imprisonment for a term not exceeding six months, or a fine not exceeding the statutory maximum, or both;
  (ii) on conviction on indictment, to imprisonment for a term not exceeding two years, or a fine, or both;
(*b*) under subsection (2) above shall be liable—
  (i) on summary conviction, to imprisonment for a term not exceeding six months, or a fine not exceeding the statutory maximum, or both;
  (ii) on conviction on indictment, to imprisonment for a term not exceeding four years, or a fine, or both.

(6) In this section and section 139B, "school premises" means land used for the purposes of a school excluding any land occupied solely as a dwelling by a person employed at the school; and "school" has the meaning given by section 14(5) of the Further and Higher Education Act 1992.

(7) In the application of this section to Northern Ireland—

(*a*) the reference in subsection (2) above to section 1 of the Prevention of Crime Act 1953 is to be construed as a reference to Article 22 of the Public Order (Northern Ireland) Order 1987; and
(*b*) the reference in subsection (6) above to section 14(5) of the Further and Higher Education Act 1992 is to be construed as a reference to Article 2(2) of the Education and Libraries (Northern Ireland) Order 1986.

Power of entry to search for articles with a blade or point and offensive weapons

1.43   [1]**139B.**—(1) A constable may enter school premises and search those premises and any person on those premises for—

(a) any article to which section 139 of this Act applies, or

(b) any offensive weapon within the meaning of section 1 of the Prevention of Crime Act 1953,

if he has reasonable grounds for believing that an offence under section 139A of this Act is being, or has been, committed.

(2) If in the course of a search under this section a constable discovers an article or weapon which he has reasonable grounds for suspecting to be an article or weapon of a kind described in subsection (1) above, he may seize and retain it.

(3) The constable may use reasonable force, if necessary, in the exercise of the power of entry conferred by this section.

(4) In the application of this section to Northern Ireland the reference in subsection (1)(b) above to section 1 of the Prevention of Crime Act 1953 is to be construed as a reference to Article 22 of the Public Order (Northern Ireland) Order 1987.

NOTE

[1] Inserted by s.4 of the 1996 Act. These provisions apply to England and Wales, and to Northern Ireland only. For the provisions for Scotland, see s.49A and s.49B of the 1995 Act as amended.

[1]**140.** ... **1.44**

NOTE

[1] This provision amended s.1 of the Police and Criminal Evidence Act 1984 and, by s.172(1) of the 1988 Act, applies to England and Wales only.

Offensive weapons

141.[1]—(1) Any person who manufactures, sells or hires or offers **1.45** for sale or hire, exposes or has in his possession for the purpose of sale or hire, or lends or gives to any other person, a weapon to which this section applies shall be guilty of an offence and liable on summary conviction to imprisonment for a term not exceeding six months or to a fine not exceeding level 5 on the standard scale or both.

(2) The Secretary of State may by order made by statutory instrument direct that this section shall apply to any description of weapon specified in the order except—

(a) any weapon subject to the Firearms Act 1968 [c.27]; and

(b) crossbows.

(3) A statutory instrument containing an order under this section shall not be made unless a draft of the instrument has been laid before Parliament and has been approved by a resolution of each House of Parliament.

(4) The importation of a weapon to which this section applies is hereby prohibited.

(5) It shall be a defence for any person charged in respect of any conduct of his relating to a weapon to which this section applies—

(*a*) with an offence under subsection (1) above; or

(*b*) with an offence under section 50(2) or (3) of the Customs and Excise Management Act 1979 [c.2] (improper importation),

to prove that his conduct was only for the purposes of functions carried out on behalf of the Crown or of a visiting force.

(6) In this section the reference to the Crown includes the Crown in right of Her Majesty's Government in Northern Ireland; and "visiting force" means any body, contingent or detachment of the forces of a country—

(*a*) mentioned in subsection (1)(*a*) of the Visiting Forces Act 1952 [c. 67]; or

(*b*) designated for the purposes of any provision of that Act by Order in Council under subsection (2) of that section,

which is present in the United Kingdom (including United Kingdom territorial waters) or in any place to which subsection (7) below applies on the invitation of Her Majesty's Government in the United Kingdom.

(7) This subsection applies to any place on, under or above an installation in a designated area within the meaning of section 1(7) of the Continental Shelf Act 1964 [c. 29] or any waters within 500 metres of such an installation.

(8) It shall be a defence for any person charged in respect of any conduct of his relating to a weapon to which this section applies—

(*a*) with an offence under subsection (1) above; or

(*b*) with an offence under section 50(2) or (3) of the Customs and Excise Management Act 1979,

to prove that the conduct in question was only for the purposes of making the weapon available to a museum or gallery to which this subsection applies.

(9) If a person acting on behalf of a museum or gallery to which subsection (8) above applies is charged with hiring or lending a weapon to which this section applies, it shall be a defence for him to prove that he had reasonable grounds for believing that the person to whom he lent or hired it would use it only for cultural, artistic or educational purposes.

(10) Subsection (8) above applies to a museum or gallery only if it does not distribute profits.

(11) In this section "museum or gallery" includes any institution which has as its purpose, or one of its purposes, the preservation, display and interpretation of material of historical, artistic or scientific interest and gives the public access to it.

(12) This section shall not have effect in relation to anything done before it comes into force.

(13) In the application of this section to Northern Ireland the reference in subsection (2) above to the Firearms Act 1968 [c. 27] shall be construed as a reference to the Firearms (Northern Ireland) Order 1981 [S.I. 1981/155 (N.I. 2)].

NOTE
This section applies (a) by s.172(1) of the 1988 Act to England and Wales; and (b) by s. 172(2) of the 1988 Act to Scotland; and (c) by s.172(3) of the 1988 Act to Northern Ireland. This section came into force by s.171(5) of the 1988 Act on the day this Act was passed.

Sale of knives and certain articles with blade or point to persons under sixteen
[1]**141A.**—(1) Any person who sells to a person under the age of 1.46 sixteen years an article to which this section applies shall be guilty of an offence and liable on summary conviction to imprisonment for a term not exceeding six months, or a fine not exceeding level 5 on the standard scale, or both.

(2) Subject to subsection (3) below, this section applies to—

(*a*) any knife, knife blade or razor blade,

(*b*) any axe, and

(*c*) any other article which has a blade or which is sharply pointed and which is made or adapted for use for causing injury to the person.

(3) This section does not apply to any article described in—

(*a*) section 1 of the Restriction of Offensive Weapons Act 1959,

(*b*) an order made under section 141(2) of this Act, or

(*c*) an order made by the Secretary of State under this section.

(4) It shall be a defence for a person charged with an offence under subsection (1) above to prove that he took all reasonable precautions and exercised all due diligence to avoid the commission of the offence.

(5) The power to make an order under this section shall be exercisable by statutory instrument which shall be subject to annulment in pursuance of a resolution of either House of Parliament.

NOTE
[1] Inserted by s.6 of the 1996 Act.

Power of justice of the peace to authorise entry and search of premises for offensive weapons
142.—(1) If on an application made by a constable a justice of 1.47 the peace (including, in Scotland, the sheriff) is satisfied that there are reasonable grounds for believing—

(a) that there are on premises specified in the application—
    (i) knives such as are mentioned in section 1(1) of the Restriction of Offensive Weapons Act 1959 [c. 37]; or
    (ii) weapons to which section 141 above applies; and
(b) that an offence under section 1 of the Restriction of Offensive Weapons Act 1959 or section 141 above has been or is being committed in relation to them; and
(c) that any of the conditions specified in subsection (3) below applies,

he may issue a warrant authorising a constable to enter and search the premises.

(2) A constable may seize and retain anything for which a search has been authorised under subsection (1) above.

(3) The conditions mentioned in subsection (1)(b) above are—

(a) that it is not practicable to communicate with any person entitled to grant entry to the premises;
(b) that it is practicable to communicate with a person entitled to grant entry to the premises but it is not practicable to communicate with any person entitled to grant access to the knives or weapons to which the application relates;
(c) that entry to the premises will not be granted unless a warrant is produced;
(d) that the purpose of a search may be frustrated or seriously prejudiced unless a constable arriving at the premises can secure immediate entry to them.

(4) Subsection (1)(a)(i) shall be omitted in the application of this section to Northern Ireland.

NOTE

    This section applies (a) by s.172(1) of the 1988 Act to England and Wales; and (b) by s.172(2) of the 1988 Act to Scotland; and (c) by s.172(3) of the 1988 Act to Northern Ireland. This section came into force by s.171(5) of the 1988 Act on the day this Act was passed.

1.48   **Carrying of Knives etc. (Scotland) Act 1993**

An Act to provide, as respects Scotland, for it to be an offence to have in a public place an article with a blade or point; and for connected purposes.   **[27th May 1993]**

Offence of having in public place article with blade or point
1.49   **1.**—(1) Subject to subsections (4) and (5) below, any person who has an article to which this section applies with him in a public place shall be guilty of an offence and liable—

(a) on summary conviction, to imprisonment for a term not exceeding six months or a fine not exceeding the statutory maximum or both; and

(b) on conviction on indictment, to imprisonment for a term not exceeding two years or a fine or both.

(2) Subject to subsection (3) below, this section applies to any article which has a blade or is sharply pointed.

(3) This section does not apply to a folding pocketknife if the cutting edge of its blade does not exceed three inches.

(4) It shall be a defence for a person charged with an offence under subsection (1) above to prove that he had good reason or lawful authority for having the article with him in the public place.

(5) Without prejudice to the generality of subsection (4) above, it shall be a defence for a person charged with an offence under subsection (1) above to prove that he had the article with him—

(a) for use at work;

(b) for religious reasons; or

(c) as part of any national costume.

(6) Where a person is convicted of an offence under subsection (1) above the court may make an order for the forfeiture of any article to which the offence relates, and any article forfeited under this subsection shall (subject to section 443A of the Criminal Procedure (Scotland) Act 1975 (suspension of forfeiture etc, pending appeal)) be disposed of as the court may direct.

(7) In this section "public place" includes any place to which at the material time the public have or are permitted access, whether on payment or otherwise.

Extension of constable's power to stop, search and arrest without warrant

2.—(1) Where a constable has reasonable grounds for suspecting **1.50** that a person has with him an article to which section 1 of this Act applies and has committed or is committing an offence under subsection (1) of that section, the constable may search that person without warrant and detain him for such time as is reasonably required to permit the search to be carried out.

(2) A constable who detains a person under subsection (1) above shall inform him of the reason for his detention.

(3) Where a constable has reasonable cause to believe that a person has committed or is committing an offence under section 1(1) of this Act and the constable—

(a) having requested that person to give his name or address or both—

(i) is not given the information requested; or

(ii) is not satisfied that such information as is given is correct; or

(b) has reasonable cause to believe that it is necessary to arrest him in order to prevent the commission by him of any other offence in the course of committing which an article to which that section applies might be used,

he may arrest that person without warrant.

(4) Any person who—

(a) intentionally obstructs a constable in the exercise of the constable's powers under subsection (1) above; or

(b) conceals from a constable acting in the exercise of those powers an article to which section 1 of this Act applies,

shall be guilty of an offence and liable on summary conviction to a fine not exceeding level 3 on the standard scale.

(5) Where a constable has reasonable cause to believe that a person has committed or is committing an offence under subsection (4) above he may arrest that person without warrant.

Citation, commencement and extent

1.51　　**3.**—(1) This Act may be cited as the Carrying of Knives etc. (Scotland) Act 1993.

(2) This Act shall not have effect in relation to anything done before it comes into force.

(3) This Act extends to Scotland only.

NOTE

The 1993 Act was in force from May 27, 1993 (when it received Royal Assent) and March 31, 1995 (when it was repealed by s.6 and Sched. 5 to the Criminal Law (Consequential Provisions) (Scotland) Act 1995).

1.52　　　　　　**Criminal Justice and Public Order Act 1994**

.　　.　　.　　.　　.

Powers of police to stop and search

Powers to stop and search in anticipation of violence

1.53　　**60.**—(1) Where a police officer of or above the rank of superintendent reasonably believes that—

(a) incidents involving serious violence may take place in any locality in his area, and

(b) it is expedient to do so to prevent their occurrence,

he may give an authorisation that the powers to stop and search persons and vehicles conferred by this section shall be exercisable at any place within that locality for a period not exceeding twenty-four hours.

(2) The power conferred by subsection (1) above may be exercised by a chief inspector or an inspector if he reasonably believes that incidents involving serious violence are imminent and no superintendent is available.

(3) If it appears to the officer who gave the authorisation or to a superintendent that it is expedient to do so, having regard to offences which have, or are reasonably suspected to have, been committed in connection with any incident falling within the authorisation, he may direct that the authorisation shall continue in being for a further six hours.

(4) This section confers on any constable in uniform power—

    (a) to stop any pedestrian and search him or anything carried by him for offensive weapons or dangerous instruments;

    (b) to stop any vehicle and search the vehicle, its driver and any passenger for offensive weapons or dangerous instruments.

(5) A constable may, in the exercise of those powers, stop any person or vehicle and make any search he thinks fit whether or not he has any grounds for suspecting that the person or vehicle is carrying weapons or articles of that kind.

(6) If in the course of a search under this section a constable discovers a dangerous instrument or an article which he has reasonable grounds for suspecting to be an offensive weapon, he may seize it.

(7) This section applies (with the necessary modifications) to ships, aircraft and hovercraft as it applies to vehicles.

(8) A person who fails to stop or (as the case may be) to stop the vehicle when required to do so by a constable in the exercise of his powers under this section shall be liable on summary conviction to imprisonment for a term not exceeding one month or to a fine not exceeding level 3 on the standard scale or both.

(9) Any authorisation under this section shall be in writing signed by the officer giving it and shall specify the locality in which and the period during which the powers conferred by this section are exercisable and a direction under subsection (3) above shall also be given in writing or, where that is not practicable, recorded in writing as soon as it is practicable to do so.

(10) Where a vehicle is stopped by a constable under this section, the driver shall be entitled to obtain a written statement that the

vehicle was stopped under the powers conferred by this section if he applies for such a statement not later than the end of the period of twelve months from the day on which the vehicle was stopped and similarly as respects a pedestrian who is stopped and searched under this section.

(11) In this section—

"dangerous instruments" means instruments which have a blade or are sharply pointed;

"offensive weapon" has the meaning given by section 1(9) of the Police and Criminal Evidence Act 1984; and

"vehicle" includes a caravan as defined in section 29(1) of the Caravan Sites and Control of Development Act 1960.

(12) The powers conferred by this section are in addition to and not in derogation of, any power otherwise conferred.

1.54   **Criminal Law (Consolidation) (Scotland) Act 1995**

. . . . . .

PART II

SPORTING EVENTS: CONTROL OF ALCOHOL ETC.

Designation of sports grounds and sporting events

1.55   **18.**—(1) Subject to subsection (2) below, the Secretary of State may for the purposes of this Part of this Act by order designate—

(*a*) a sports ground or a class of sports ground;

(*b*) a sporting event, or a class of sporting event, at that ground or at any of that class of ground;

(*c*) a sporting event, or a class of sporting event, taking place outside Great Britain.

(2) An order under this section shall not apply to a sporting event at which all the participants take part without financial or material reward and to which all spectators are admitted free of charge; but this subsection is without prejudice to the order's validity as respects any other sporting event.

(3) The power to make an order under subsection (1) above shall be exercisable by statutory instrument which shall be subject to annulment in pursuance of a resolution of either House of Parliament.

. . . . . .

Sporting events: controls

20.—(1) Any person who—   **1.56**

(*a*) is in possession of a controlled container in; or

(*b*) while in possession of a controlled container, attempts to enter,

the relevant area of a designated sports ground at any time during the period of a designated sporting event shall be guilty of an offence and liable on summary conviction to imprisonment for a period not exceeding 60 days or to a fine not exceeding level 3 on the standard scale or both.

(2) Any person who—

(*a*) is in possession of alcohol in; or

(*b*) while in possession of alcohol, attempts to enter,

the relevant area of a designated sports ground at any time during the period of a designated sporting event, shall be guilty of an offence and liable on summary conviction to imprisonment for a period not exceeding 60 days or to a fine not exceeding level 3 on the standard scale or both.

(3) Any person who has entered the relevant area of a designated sports ground and is in possession of a controlled article or substance at any time during the period of a designated sporting event shall be guilty of an offence.

(4) Any person who, while in possession of a controlled article or substance, attempts to enter the relevant area of a designated sports ground at any time during the period of a designated sporting event at the ground shall be guilty of an offence.

(5) A person guilty of an offence under subsection (3) or (4) above shall be liable on summary conviction to imprisonment for a period not exceeding 60 days or to a fine not exceeding level 3 on the standard scale or both.

(6) It shall be a defence for a person charged with an offence under subsection (3) or (4) above to show that he had lawful authority to be in possession of the controlled article or substance.

(7) Any person who—

(*a*) is drunk in; or

(*b*) while drunk, attempts to enter,

the relevant area of a designated sports ground at any time during the period of a designated sporting event shall be guilty of an offence and liable on summary conviction to a fine not exceeding level 2 on the standard scale.

(8) In this section—

"controlled article or substance" means—

(*a*) any article or substance whose main purpose is the emission of a flare for purposes of illuminating or signalling (as opposed to igniting or heating) or the emission of smoke or a visible gas; and in particular it includes distress flares, fog signals, and pellets and capsules intended to be used as fumigators or for testing pipes, but not matches, cigarette lighters or heaters; and
(*b*) any article which is a firework.
"controlled container" means any bottle, can or other portable container, whether open or sealed, which is, or was, in its original manufactured state, capable of containing liquid and is made from such material or is of such construction, or is so adapted, that if it were thrown at or propelled against a person it would be capable of causing some injury to that person; but the term does not include a container holding a medicinal product for a medicinal purpose.
"medicinal product" and "medicinal purpose" have the meanings assigned to those terms by section 130 of the Medicines Act 1968.

Police powers of enforcement

1.57   **21.** For the purpose of enforcing the provisions of this Part of this Act, a constable shall have the power without warrant—

(*a*) to enter a designated sports ground at any time during the period of a designated sporting event;
(*b*) to search a person who he has reasonable grounds to suspect is committing or has committed an offence under this Part of this Act;
(*c*) to stop and search a vehicle where he has reasonable grounds to suspect that an offence under section 19 of this Act is being or has been committed;
(*d*) to arrest a person who he has reasonable grounds to suspect is committing or has committed an offence under this Part of this Act;
(*e*) to seize and detain—
   (i) with its contents (if any), a controlled container as defined in section 20(8) of this Act; or
   (iii) with its contents, any other container if he has reasonable grounds to suspect that those contents are or include alcohol.

1.58   **22.** ...

Interpretation of Part II

1.59   **23.** In this Part of this Act, unless the context otherwise requires—
"advertised" means announced in any written or printed document or in any broadcast announcement;

"alcohol" means alcoholic liquor as defined in section 139 of the Licensing (Scotland) Act 1976;

"designated" means designated by the Secretary of State by order under section 18 of this Act, and "designated sporting event" includes a sporting event designated under section 9(3)(a) of the Sporting Events (Control of Alcohol) Etc. Act 1985;

"keeper", in relation to a vehicle, means the person having the duty to take out a licence for it under section 1(1) of the Vehicles Excise and Registration Act 1994;

"period of a designated sporting event" means the period commencing two hours before the start and ending one hour after the end of a designated sporting event, except that where the event is advertised as to start at a particular time but is delayed or postponed it includes, and where for any reason an event does not take place it means, the period commencing two hours before and ending one hour after, that particular time;

"public service vehicle" has the same meaning as in the Public Passenger Vehicles Act 1981 and "operator" in relation to such a vehicle means—

(a) the driver if he owns the vehicle; and

(b) in any other case the person for whom the driver works (whether under a contract of employment or any other description of contract personally to do work);

"railway passenger vehicle" has the same meaning as in the Licensing (Scotland) Act 1976;

"relevant area" means any part of a sports ground—

(a) to which spectators attending a designated sporting event are granted access on payment; or

(b) from which a designated sporting event may be viewed directly;

"sporting event" means any physical competitive activity at a sports ground, and includes any such activity which has been advertised as to, but does not, take place; and

"sports ground" means any place whatsoever which is designed, or is capable of being adapted, for the holding of sporting events in respect of which spectators are accommodated.

Offensive weapons

Prohibition of the carrying of offensive weapons

47.—(1) Any person who without lawful authority or reasonable **1.60** excuse, the proof whereof shall lie on him, has with him in any public place any offensive weapon shall be guilty of an offence, and shall be liable—

(*a*) on summary conviction, to imprisonment for a term not exceeding six months or a fine not exceeding the statutory maximum, or both;

[1](*b*) on conviction on indictment, to imprisonment for a term not exceeding [four] years or a fine, or both.

(2) Where any person is convicted of an offence under subsection (1) above the court may make an order for the forfeiture or disposal of any weapon in respect of which the offence was committed.

(3) A constable may arrest without warrant any person whom he has reasonable cause to believe to be committing an offence under subsection (1) above, if the constable is not satisfied as to that person's identity or place of residence, or has reasonable cause to believe that it is necessary to arrest him in order to prevent the commission by him of any other offence in the course of committing which an offensive weapon might be used.

(4) In this section "public place" includes any road within the meaning of the Roads (Scotland) Act 1984 and any other premises or place to which at the material time the public have or are permitted to have access, whether on payment or otherwise; and "offensive weapon" means any article made or adapted for use for causing injury to the person, or intended by the person having it with him for such use by him [or by some other person][2].

NOTE
[1] As amended by s.2(2) of the 1996 Act.
[2] As amended by s.5 of the 1996 Act.

Search for offensive weapons

1.61 **48.**—(1) Where a constable has reasonable grounds for suspecting that any person is carrying an offensive weapon and has committed or is committing an offence under section 47 of this Act, the constable may search that person without warrant, and detain him for such time as is reasonably required to permit the search to be carried out; and he shall inform the person of the reason for such detention.

(2) Any person who—

(*a*) intentionally obstructs a constable in the exercise of the constable's powers under subsection (1) above; or

(*b*) conceals from a constable acting in the exercise of those powers an offensive weapon,

shall be guilty of an offence and liable on summary conviction to a fine not exceeding level 4 on the standard scale.

(3) A constable may arrest without warrant any person who he has reason to believe has committed an offence under subsection (2) above.

(4) In this section "offensive weapon" has the same meaning as in the said section 47.

Offence of having in public place article with blade or point

49.—(1) Subject to subsections (4) and (5) below, any person who has an article to which this section applies with him in a public place shall be guilty of an offence and liable— **1.62**

- (*a*) on summary conviction, to imprisonment for a term not exceeding six months or a fine not exceeding the statutory maximum or both; and
- (*b*) on conviction on indictment, to imprisonment for a term not exceeding two years or a fine or both.

(2) Subject to subsection (3) below, this section applies to any article which has a blade or is sharply pointed.

(3) This section does not apply to a folding pocketknife if the cutting edge of its blade does not exceed three inches (7.62 centimetres).

(4) It shall be a defence for a person charged with an offence under subsection (1) above to prove that he had good reason or lawful authority for having the article with him in the public place.

(5) Without prejudice to the generality of subsection (4) above, it shall be a defence for a person charged with an offence under subsection (1) above to prove that he had the article with him—

- (*a*) for use at work;
- (*b*) for religious reasons; or
- (*c*) as part of any national costume.

(6) Where a person is convicted of an offence under subsection (1) above the court may make an order for the forfeiture of any article to which the offence relates, and any article forfeited under this subsection shall (subject to section 193 of the Criminal Procedure (Scotland) Act 1995 (suspension of forfeiture etc, pending appeal)) be disposed of as the court may direct.

(7) In this section "public place" includes any place to which at the material time the public have or are permitted access, whether on payment or otherwise.

Offence of having article with blade or point (or offensive weapon) on school premises

49A.—(1) Any person who has an article to which section 49 of this Act applies with him on school premises shall be guilty of an offence. **1.63**

(2) Any person who has an offensive weapon within the meaning of section 47 of this Act with him on school premises shall be guilty of an offence.

(3) It shall be a defence for a person charged with an offence under subsection (1) or (2) above to prove that he had good reason or lawful authority for having the article or weapon with him on the premises in question.

(4) Without prejudice to the generality of subsection (3) above, it shall be a defence for a person charged with an offence under subsection (1) or (2) above to prove that he had the article or weapon in question with him—

    (*a*) for use at work,
    (*b*) for educational purposes,
    (*c*) for religious reasons, or
    (*d*) as part of any national costume.

(5) A person guilty of an offence—

    (*a*) under subsection (1) above shall be liable—
        (i) on summary conviction to imprisonment for a term not exceeding six months, or a fine not exceeding the statutory maximum, or both;
      (ii) on conviction on indictment, to imprisonment for a term not exceeding two years, or a fine, or both;
    (*b*) under subsection (2) above shall be liable—
        (i) on summary conviction, to imprisonment for a term not exceeding six months, or a fine not exceeding the statutory maximum, or both;
      (ii) on conviction on indictment, to imprisonment for a term not exceeding four years, or a fine, or both.

(6) In this section and section 49B of this Act, "school premises" means land used for the purposes of a school excluding any land occupied solely as a dwelling by a person employed at the school; and "school" has the meaning given by section 135(1) of the Education (Scotland) Act 1980.

Power of entry to search for articles with a blade or point and offensive weapons
1.64   **49B.**—(1) A constable may enter school premises and search those premises and any person on those premises for—

    (*a*) any article to which section 49 of this Act applies, or
    (*b*) any offensive weapon within the meaning of section 47 of this Act,

if he has reasonable grounds for suspecting that an offence under section 49A of this Act is being, or has been, committed.

(2) If in the course of a search under this section a constable discovers an article or weapon which he has reasonable grounds

for believing to be an article or weapon of a kind described in subsection (1) above, he may seize it.

(3) The constable may use reasonable force, if necessary, in the exercise of the power of entry conferred by this section.

NOTE
Sections 49A and 49B inserted by section 4(3) of the 1996 Act.

Extension of constable's power to stop, search and arrest without warrant
[1]**50.**—(1) Where a constable has reasonable grounds for **1.65** suspecting that a person has with him an article to which section 49 of this Act applies and has committed or is committing an offence under subsection (1) of that section, the constable may search that person without warrant and detain him for such time as is reasonably required to permit the search to be carried out.

(2) A constable who detains a person under subsection (1) above shall inform him of the reason for his detention.

(3) Where a constable has reasonable cause to believe that a person has committed or is committing an offence under section 49(1) [or section 49A (1) or (2)][2] of this Act and the constable—

   (a) having requested that person to give his name or address or both—
       (i) is not given the information requested; or
       (ii) is not satisfied that such information as is given is correct; or
   (b) has reasonable cause to believe that it is necessary to arrest him in order to prevent the commission by him of any other offence in the course of committing which an article to which that section applies might be used,

he may arrest that person without warrant.

(4) Any person who—

   (a) intentionally obstructs a constable in the exercise of the constable's powers under subsection (1) above; or
   (b) conceals from a constable acting in the exercise of those powers an article to which section 49 of this Act applies,

shall be guilty of an offence and liable on summary conviction to a fine not exceeding level 3 on the standard scale.

(5) Where a constable has reasonable cause to believe that a person has committed or is committing an offence under subsection (4) above he may arrest that person without warrant.

NOTE
[1] The foregoing sections of the Consolidation Act came into force on April 1, 1996 by reason of s.53(2) of that Act.
[2] Inserted by s.1 of the 1996 Act.

[REPUBLIC OF IRELAND]

1.66   **Firearms and Offensive Weapons Act 1990**

An Act to amend and extend the Firearms Act, 1925 to 1971, to control the availability and possession of offensive weapons and other articles and to provide for certain other matters connected with the matters aforesaid.

[12th June 1990]

PART I

Preliminary

Short title and commencement
1.67   **1.**—(1) This Act may be cited as the Firearms and Offensive Weapons Act 1990.

(2) This Act (other than Part II) shall come into operation on the date of its passing.

(3) Part II of this Act shall come into operation on such day or days as may be fixed thereof by order or orders of the Minister either generally or with reference to any particular provision, and different days may be so fixed for different provision of that Part.

Interpretation
1.68   **2.**—(1) In this Act "the Minister" means the Minister for Justice.

(2) In this Act a reference to a section is a reference to a section of this Act unless it is indicated that reference to some other enactment is intended and a reference to a subsection is a reference to the subsection of the section in which the reference occurs, unless it is indicated that reference to some other section is intended.

(3) A reference in this Act to any enactment shall be construed as a reference to that enactment as amended or adapted by or under any subsequent enactment.

PART II

Amendments to Firearms Acts

Collective citative and construction
1.69   **3.**—(1) The Firearms Acts, 1925 to 1971, and this Part may be cited together as the Firearms Acts, 1925 to 1990.

(2) The Firearms Acts, 1925 to 1971 (other than the Firearms (Proofing) Act, 1968) and this Part shall be construed together as one.

Extension of Firearms Acts to crossbows and stun guns
4.—(1) In the Firearms Acts, 1925 to 1990, "firearm" means—   **1.70**

(a) a lethal firearm or other lethal weapon of any description from which any shot, bullet or other missile can be discharged;

(b) an air gun (which expression includes an air rifle and an air pistol) or any other weapon incorporating a barrel from which metal or other slugs can be discharged;

(c) a crossbow;

(d) any type of stun gun or other weapon for causing any shock or other disablement to a person by means of electricity or any other kind of energy emission;

(e) a prohibited weapon as defined in section 1(1) of the Firearms Act, 1925;

(f) any article which would be a firearm under any of the foregoing paragraphs but for the fact that, owing to the lack of a necessary component part or parts, or to any other defect or condition, it is incapable of discharging a shot, bullet or other missile or of causing a shock or other disablement (as the case may be);

(g) save where the context otherwise requires, any component part of any article referred to in any of the foregoing paragraphs and, for the purposes of this definition, the following articles shall be deemed to be such component parts as aforesaid:

  (i) telescope sights with a light beam, or telescope sights with an electronic light amplification device or an infrared device, designed to be fitted to a firearm specified in paragraph (a), (b) or (e), and

  (ii) a silencer designed to be fitted to a firearm specified in paragraph (a), (b) or (e).

(2) the following provisions are hereby repealed:

(a) the definition of "firearm" in section 1(1) of the Firearms Act, 1925, and in section 1 of the Firearms (Proofing) Act, 1968, and

(b) section 2 of the Firearms Act, 1964, and section 2 of the Firearms Act, 1971.

. . . . . .

Part III

Offensive Weapons

Possession of knives and other articles

1.71   **9.**—(1) Subject to subsections (2) and (3), where a person has with him in any public place any knife or any other article which has a blade or which is sharply pointed, he shall be guilty of an offence.

(2) It shall be a defence for a person charged with an offence under subsection (1) to prove that he had good reason or lawful authority for having the article with him in a public place.

(3) Without prejudice to the generality of subsection (2), it shall be a defence for a person charged with an offence under subsection (1) to prove that he had the article with him for use at work or for a recreational purpose.

(4) Where a person, without lawful authority or reasonable excuse (the onus of proving which shall lie on him), has with him in any public place—

(a) any flick-knife, or

(b) any other article whatsoever made or adapted for use for causing injury to or incapacitating a person,

he shall be guilty of an offence.

(5) Where a person has with him in any public place any article intended by him unlawfully to cause injury to, incapacitate or intimidate any person either in a particular eventuality or otherwise, he shall be guilty of an offence.

(6) In a prosecution for an offence under subsection (5), it shall not be necessary for the prosecution to allege or prove that the intent to cause injury, incapacitate or intimidate was intent to cause injury to, incapacitate or intimidate a particular person; and if, having regard to all the circumstances (including the type of the article alleged to have been intended to cause injury, incapacitate or intimidate, the time of day or night, and the place), the court (or the jury as the case may be) thinks it reasonable to do so, it may regard possession of the article as sufficient evidence of intent in the absence of any adequate explanation by the accused.

(7) (a) A person guilty of an offence under subsection (1) shall be liable on summary conviction to a fine not exceeding £1,000 or to imprisonment for a term not exceeding twelve months or to both.

(b) A person guilty of an offence under subsection (4) or (5) shall be liable—

(i) on summary conviction, to a fine not exceeding £1,000 or to imprisonment for a term not exceeding twelve months or to both, or

(ii) on conviction on indictment, to a fine or imprisonment for a term not exceeding five years or to both.

(8) In this section "public place" includes any highway and any other premises or place to which at the material time the public have or are permitted to have access, whether on payment or otherwise, and includes any club premises and any train, vessel or vehicle used for the carriage of persons for reward.

(9) In this section "flick-knife" means a knife—

(*a*) which has a blade which opens when hand pressure is applied to a button, spring, lever or other device in or attached to the handle, or

(*b*) which has a blade which is released from the handle or sheath by the force of gravity or the application of centrifugal force and when released is locked in an open position by means of a button, spring, lever or other device.

Trespassing with a knife, weapon of offence or other article

10.—(1) Where a person is on any premises as defined in subsection (2) as a trespasser, he shall be guilty of an offence if he has with him— 1.72

(*a*) any knife or other article to which section 9(1) applies, or

(*b*) any weapon of offence (as defined in subsection (2)).

(2) In this section—

"premises" means any building, any part of a building and any land ancillary to a building;

"weapon of offence" means any article made or adapted for use for causing injury to or incapacitating a person, or intended by the person having it with him for such use.

(3) A person guilty of an offence under this section shall be liable—

(*a*) on summary conviction, to a fine not exceeding £1,000 or to imprisonment for a term not exceeding twelve months or to both, or

(*b*) on conviction on indictment, to a fine or to imprisonment for a term not exceeding five years or to both.

Production of article capable of inflicting serious injury

11.—Where a person, while committing or appearing to be about to commit an offence, or in the course of a dispute or fight, produces in a manner likely unlawfully to intimidate another person any 1.73

article capable of inflicting serious injury, he shall be guilty of an offence and shall be liable—

(*a*) on summary conviction, to a fine not exceeding £1,000 or to imprisonment for a term not exceeding twelve months or to both, or

(*b*) on conviction on indictment, to a fine or to imprisonment for a term not exceeding five years or to both.

Power to prohibit manufacture, importation, sale, hire or loan of offensive weapon

1.74   **12.**—(1) Any person who—

(*a*) manufactures, sells or hires, or offers or exposes for sale or hire, or by way of business repairs or modifies, or

(*b*) has in his possession for the purpose of sale or hire or for the purpose of repair or modification by way of business, or

(*c*) puts on display, or lends or gives to any other person,

a weapon to which this section applies shall be guilty of an offence.

(2) Where an offence under subsection (1) is committed by a body corporate and is proved to have been so committed with the consent or connivance of or to be attributable to any neglect on the part of a director, manager, secretary or other officer of the body corporate, the director, manager, secretary or other officer or any person purporting to act in such capacity shall also be guilty of an offence.

(3) A person guilty of an offence under this section shall be liable—

(*a*) on summary conviction, to a fine not exceeding £1,000 or to imprisonment for a term not exceeding twelve months or to both; or

(*b*) on conviction on indictment, to a fine or to imprisonment for a term not exceeding five years or to both.

(4) The Minister may by order direct that this section shall apply to any description of weapon specified in the order except any firearm subject to the Firearms Acts, 1925 to 1990.

(5) The Minister may by order amend or revoke an order made under this section.

(6) The importation of a weapon to which this section applies is hereby prohibited.

(7) Every order made under this section shall be laid before each House of the Oireachtas as soon as may be after it is made and, if a resolution annulling the order is passed by either such House within the next 21 days on which that House has sat after the order

is laid before it, the order shall be annulled accordingly, but without prejudice to the validity of anything previously done thereunder.

Forfeiture of weapons and other articles

13.—(1) Where a person is convicted of an offence under this **1.75** Part, the court by or before which he is convicted may order any article in respect of which the offence was committed to be forfeited and either destroyed or otherwise disposed of in such manner as the court may determine.

(2) An order under this section shall not take effect until the ordinary time for instituting an appeal against the conviction or order concerned has expired or, where such an appeal is instituted, until it or any further appeal is finally decided or abandoned or the ordinary time for instituting any further appeal has expired.

Power of arrest without warrant

14.—A member of the Garda Siochána may arrest without **1.76** warrant any person who is, or whom the member, with reasonable cause, suspects to be, in the act of committing an offence under section 9, 10 or 11.

Search warrants

15.—If a justice of the District Court or a Peace Commissioner is **1.77** satisfied on the sworn information of a member of the Garda Siochána that there are reasonable grounds for suspecting that an offence under section 12 has been or is being committed on any premises, he may issue a warrant under his hand authorising a specified member of the Garda Siochána, accompanied by such other members of the Garda Siochána as the member thinks necessary, at any time or times within one month from the date of the issue of the warrant, on production if so requested of the warrant, to enter, if need be by force, and search the premises specified in the warrant and to seize anything found there that he believes on reasonable grounds may be required to be used in evidence in any proceedings for an offence under section 12 or an offence under the Customs Acts in relation to the importation into the State of a weapon to which section 12 applies.

Power of search without warrant

16.—(1) This section applies to a situation where a number of **1.78** people are congregated in any public place (within the meaning of section 9(8)) and a breach of the peace is occurring, or a member of the Garda Siochána has reasonable grounds for believing that a breach of the peace has occurred, or may occur, in that place when the people were or are congregated there.

(2) If in a situation to which this section applies a member of the Garda Síochána suspects with reasonable cause that a person has with him any article in contravention of section 9, he may search him in order to ascertain whether this is the case.

(3) If in a situation to which this section applies a member of the Garda Síochána suspects with reasonable cause that some one or more of the people present has or have with him or them an article or articles in contravention of section 9, then, even if the member has no reason to suspect that any particular one of the people present has with him any such article, the member may search any of those people if he considers that a search is necessary in order to ascertain whether any of them has with him any such article or articles.

Extension of section 8 of Criminal Law Act 1976

1.79   **17.**—Section 8 of the Criminal Law Act 1976, is hereby amended by the insertion in subsection (1) after paragraph (i) of the following paragraph:

"(j) an offence under section 12(1) of the Firearms and Offensive Weapons Act 1990."

Repeal of portion of section 4 of Vagrancy Act, 1824

1.80   **18.**—Section 4 of the Vagrancy Act, 1824 (as extended to Ireland by section 15 of the Prevention of Crimes Act, 1871), is hereby amended by the deletion of "or being armed with any gun, pistol, hanger, cutlass, bludgeon, or other offensive weapon," and "and every such gun, pistol, hanger, cutlass, bludgeon, or other offensive weapon."

CHAPTER TWO

Delegated legislation   2.0

Introduction   2.1
The relevant legislation for Northern Ireland, and some important
aspects for the remainder of the United Kingdom, is contained in
delegated legislation which is set out below.

1987 No. 463 (N.I. 7)   2.2
The Public Order (Northern Ireland) Order 1987

[1]**1.**—(1) This Order may be cited as the Public Order (Northern 2.3
Ireland) Order 1987.
(2) This Order shall come into operation on the expiration of
two weeks from the day on which it is made.

Carrying of offensive weapon in public place
2.—(1) A person who, without lawful authority or reasonable   2.4
excuse (proof of which lies on him), has with him in any public
place any offensive weapon shall be guilty of an offence.
(2) In paragraph (1) "offensive weapon" means any article made
or adapted for use for causing injury to the person, or intended by
the person having it with him for such use by him or by some
other person.
(3) A person guilty of an offence under paragraph (1) shall be
liable—

    (*a*) on summary conviction, to imprisonment for a term not
        exceeding six months or to a fine not exceeding the
        statutory maximum, or to both; or
    [2](*b*) on conviction on indictment, to imprisonment for a term
        not exceeding [four] years or to a fine, or to both.

NOTES
[1] See also s.170 of and Sched. 15, para. 118 to the Criminal Justice Act 1988.
[2] As amended by s.2(3) of the 1996 Act.

2.5

1988 No. 2019
The Criminal Justice Act 1988
(Offensive Weapons) Order 1988

In exercise of the powers conferred upon me by section 141(2) of the Criminal Justice Act 1988 [c. 33], a draft of this instrument having been laid before Parliament and having been approved by each House of Parliament, I hereby make the following Order:

2.6 **1.** This Order may be cited as the Criminal Justice Act 1988 (Offensive Weapons) Order 1988 and shall come into force two months after the day on which it is made.

2.7 **2.** The Schedule to this Order shall have effect.

Article 2

SCHEDULE

2.8 **1.** Section 141 of the Criminal Justice Act 1988 (offensive weapons) shall apply to the following descriptions of weapons, other than weapons of those descriptions which are antiques for the purposes of this Schedule:

(*a*) a knuckleduster, that is, a band of metal or other hard material worn on one or more fingers, and designed to cause injury, and any weapon incorporating a knuckleduster;

(*b*) a swordstick, that is, a hollow walking-stick or cane containing a blade which may be used as a sword;

(*c*) the weapon sometimes known as a "handclaw," being a band of metal or other hard material from which a number of sharp spikes protrude, and worn around the hand;

(*d*) the weapon sometimes known as a "belt buckle knife," being a buckle which incorporates or conceals a knife;

(*e*) the weapon known as a "push dagger," being a knife the handle of which fits within a clenched fist and the blade of which protrudes from between two fingers;

(*f*) the weapon sometimes known as a "hollow kubotan," being a cylindrical container containing a number of sharp spikes;

(*g*) the weapon sometimes known as a "footclaw," being a bar of metal or other hard material from which a number of sharp spikes protrude, and worn strapped to the foot;

(*h*) the weapon sometimes known as a "shuriken," "shaken" or "death star," being a hard non-flexible plate having three or more sharp radiating points and designed to be thrown;

(*i*) the weapon sometimes known as a "balisong" or "butterfly knife," being a blade enclosed by its handle, which is designed to split down the middle, without the operation of a spring or other mechanical means, to reveal the blade;

(*j*) the weapon sometimes known as a "telescopic truncheon," being a truncheon which extends automatically by hand pressure applied to a button, spring or other device in or attached to its handle;

(*k*) the weapon sometimes known as a "blowpipe" or "blow gun," being a hollow tube out of which hard pellets or darts are shot by the use of breath;

(*l*) the weapon sometimes known as a "kusari gama," being a length of rope, cord, wire or chain fastened at one end to a sickle;

(*m*) the weapon sometimes known as a "kyoketsu shoge," being a length of rope, cord, wire or chain fastened at one end to a hooked knife;

(*n*) the weapon sometimes known as a "manrikigusari" or "kusari," being a length of rope, cord, wire or chain fastened at each end to a hard weight or hand grip;

2. For the purposes of this Schedule, a weapon is an antique if it was **2.9** manufactured more than 100 years before the date of any offence alleged to have been committed in respect of that weapon under subsection (1) of the said section 141 or section 50(2) or (3) of the Customs and Excise Management Act 1979 [c. 2] (improper importation).

1988 No. 794 (N.I. 5)   **2.10**
The Crossbows (Northern Ireland) Order 1988

Title and commencement

1.—(1) This Order may be cited as the Crossbows (Northern **2.11** Ireland) Order 1988.

(2) This Order shall come into operation on the expiration of two months from the day on which it is made.

Interpretation

2. The Interpretation Act (Northern Ireland) 1954 [c. 33] shall **2.12** apply to Article 1 and the following provisions of this Order as it applies to a Measure of the Northern Ireland Assembly.

Sale and letting on hire

3. A person who sells or lets on hire a crossbow or a part of a **2.13** crossbow to a person under the age of 17 is guilty of an offence, unless he believes him to be 17 years of age or older and has reasonable ground for the belief.

Purchase and hiring

2.14   4. A person under the age of 17 who buys or hires a crossbow or a part of a crossbow is guilty of an offence.

Possession

2.15   5. A person under the age of 17 who has with him—

   (*a*) a crossbow which is capable of discharging a missile, or
   (*b*) parts of a crossbow, which together (and without any other parts) can be assembled to form a crossbow capable of discharging a missile,

is guilty of an offence, unless he is under the supervision of a person who is 21 years of age or older.

Powers of search and seizure etc.

2.16   6.—(1) If a constable suspects with reasonable cause that a person is committing or has committed an offence under Article 5, the constable may—

   (*a*) search that person for a crossbow or part of a crossbow;
   (*b*) search any vehicle, or anything in or on a vehicle, in or on which the constable suspects with reasonable cause there is a crossbow, or part of a crossbow, connected with the offence.

(2) A constable may detain a person or vehicle for the purpose of a search under paragraph (1).

(3) A constable may seize and retain for the purpose of proceedings for an offence under this Order anything discovered by him in the course of a search under paragraph (1) which appears to him to be a crossbow or part of a crossbow.

(4) For the purpose of exercising the powers conferred by this Article a constable may enter any land other than a dwelling-house.

Exception

2.17   7. This Order does not apply to crossbows with a draw weight of less than 1.4 kilograms.

Punishments

2.18   8.—(1) A person guilty of an offence under Article 3 shall be liable, on summary conviction, to imprisonment for a term not exceeding six months, to a fine not exceeding level 5 on the standard scale, or to both.

(2) A person guilty of an offence under Article 4 or 5 shall be liable, on summary conviction, to a fine not exceeding level 3 on the standard scale.

(3) The court by which a person is convicted of an offence under this Order may make such order as it thinks fit to the forfeiture or disposal of any crossbow or part of a crossbow in respect of which the offence was committed.

1989 No. 1341 (N.I. 12)   2.19
The Police and Criminal Evidence (Northern Ireland) Order 1989

Title and commencement
2.—(1) This Order may be cited as the Police and Criminal   2.20
Evidence (Northern Ireland) Order 1989.

(2) This Article and Articles 2, 29(4), 60(a), 65, 66 and 89 shall come into operation on the expiration of one month from the day on which the Order is made.

(3) The other provisions of this Order shall come into operation on such day or days as the Secretary of State may by order appoint..

NOTE
The Articles in the 1989 Order all came into effect on January 1, 1990 by virtue of Article 2 of the Police and Criminal Evidence (1989 Order) (Commencement No. 2) Order (Northern Ireland) 1989 (S.R. 441/89).

Power of constable to stop and search persons, vehicles etc.
3.—(1) A constable may exercise any power conferred by this   2.21
Article—

(*a*) in any place to which at the time when he proposes to exercise the power the public or any section of the public has access, on payment or otherwise, as of right or by virtue of express or implied permission; or

(*b*) in any other place to which people have ready access at the time when he proposes to exercise the power but which is not a dwelling.

(2) Subject to paragraphs (3) to (5), a constable—

(*a*) may search—
(i) any person or vehicle;
(ii) anything which is in or on a vehicle,
for stolen or prohibited articles or any article to which paragraph (9) applies; and

(*b*) may detain a person or vehicle for the purpose of such a search.

(3) This Article does not give a constable power to search a person or vehicle or anything in or on a vehicle unless he has reasonable

grounds for suspecting that he will find stolen or prohibited articles or any article to which paragraph (9) applies.

(4) If a person is in a garden or yard occupied with and used for the purposes of a dwelling or on other land so occupied and used, a constable may not search him in the exercise of the power conferred by this Article unless the constable has reasonable grounds for believing—

(*a*) that he does not reside in the dwelling; and

(*b*) that he is not in the place in question with the express or implied permission of a person who resides in the dwelling.

(5) If a vehicle is in a garden or yard occupied with and used for the purposes of a dwelling or on other land so occupied and used, a constable may not search the vehicle or anything in or on it in the exercise of the power conferred by this Article unless he has reasonable grounds for believing—

(*a*) that the person in charge of the vehicle does not reside in the dwelling; and

(*b*) that the vehicle is not in the place in question with the express or implied permission of a person who resides in the dwelling.

(6) If in the course of such a search a constable discovers an article which he has reasonable grounds for suspecting to be a stolen or prohibited article or an article to which paragraph (9) applies, he may seize it.

(7) An Article is prohibited for the purposes of this Part if it is—

(*a*) an offensive weapon; or

(*b*) an article—

(i) made or adapted for use in the course of or in connection with an offence to which this sub-paragraph applies; or

(ii) intended by the person having it with him for such use by him or by some other person.

(8) The offences to which sub-paragraph (b) of paragraph (7) applies are—

(*a*) burglary;

(*b*) theft;

(*c*) offences under section 12(2) of the Theft Act (Northern Ireland) 1969 [c. 16 (N.I.)] (taking of vehicles and other conveyances without authority);

(*d*) offences under section 15 of that Act (obtaining property by deception); and (*e*) offences under Article 172 of the Road Traffic (Northern Ireland) Order 1981 [1981 N.I. 1] (taking of motor vehicle, etc. without owner's consent or authority).

(9) This paragraph applies to any article in relation to which a person has committed, or is committing or is going to commit an offence under section 139 of the Criminal Justice Act 1988 [c. 33] (offence of having article with blade or point in public place).

(10) In this Part "offensive weapon" means any article—

(*a*) made or adapted for use for causing injury to persons; or
(*b*) intended by the person having it with him for such use by him or by some other person.

Provisions relating to search under Article 3 and other powers

4.—(1) A constable who detains a person or vehicle in the exercise— **2.22**

(*a*) of the power conferred by Article 3; or
(*b*) of any other power—
    (i) to search a person without first arresting him; or
    (ii) to search a vehicle without making an arrest,

need not conduct a search if it appears to him subsequently—
    (i) that no search is required; or
    (ii) that a search is impracticable.

(2) If a constable contemplates a search, other than a search of an unattended vehicle, in the exercise—

(*a*) of the power conferred by Article 3; or
(*b*) of any other power, except a power conferred by any of the provisions referred to in paragraph (3)—
    (i) to search a person without first arresting him; or
    (ii) to search a vehicle without making an arrest,

it shall be his duty, subject to paragraph (5), to take reasonable steps before he commences the search to bring to the attention of the appropriate person—

    (i) if the constable is not in uniform, documentary evidence that he is a constable; and
    (ii) whether he is in uniform or not, the matter specified in paragraph (4);

and the constable shall not commence the search until he has performed that duty.

(3) The provisions referred to for the purposes of paragraph (2)(*b*) are—

(*a*) Article 8,

(*b*) section 15, section 16 (in so far as the powers under that section are exercisable by a constable) and section 20 of the Northern Ireland (Emergency Provisions) Act 1968 [c. 5], and

(*c*) section 27(2) of the Aviation Security Act 1982 [c. 36].

(4) The matters referred to in paragraph (2)(ii) are—

(*a*) the constable's police number and the name of the police station to which he is attached;

(*b*) the object of the proposed search;

(*c*) the constable's grounds for proposing to make it; and

(*d*) the effect of Article 5(7) or (8), as may be appropriate.

(5) A constable need not bring the effect of Article 5(7) or (8) to the attention of the appropriate person if it appears to the constable that it will not be practicable to make the record in Article 5(1).

(6) In this Article "the appropriate person" means—

(*a*) if the constable proposes to search a person, that person; and

(*b*) if he proposes to search a vehicle, or anything in or on a vehicle, the person in charge of the vehicle.

(7) On completing a search of an unattended vehicle or anything in or on such a vehicle in the exercise of any such power as is mentioned in paragraph (2), other than a search under any of the provisions mentioned in paragraph (3), a constable shall leave a notice—

(*a*) stating that the vehicle has been searched by the police;

(*b*) giving his police number and the name of the police station to which he is attached;

(*c*) stating that an application for compensation for any damage caused by the search may be made to that police station; and

(*d*) stating the date on which the search was carried out and the effect of Article 5(8).

(8) The constable shall leave the notice inside the vehicle unless it is not reasonably practicable to do so without damaging the vehicle.

(9) The time for which a person or vehicle may be detained for the purposes of such a search is such time as is reasonably required to permit a search to be carried out either at the place where the person or vehicle was first detained or nearby.

(10) Neither the power conferred by Article 3 nor any other power to detain and search a person without first arresting him or

to detain and search a vehicle without making an arrest is to be construed—

- (*a*) as authorising a constable to require a person to remove any of his clothing in public other than an outer coat, jacket, headgear or gloves; or
- (*b*) as authorising a constable not in uniform to stop a vehicle.

(11) This Article and Article 3 apply to vessels, aircraft and hovercraft as they apply to vehicles.

Duty to make records concerning searches
5.—(1) Where a constable has carried out a search in the exercise 2.23 of any such power as is mentioned in Article 4(2), other than a search under a power conferred by any of the provisions mentioned in Article 4(3), he shall make a record of it in writing unless it is not practicable to do so.

(2) If—

- (*a*) a constable is required by paragraph (1) to make a record of a search; but
- (*b*) it is not practicable to make the record on the spot,

he shall make it as soon as practicable after the completion of the search.

(3) The record of a search of a person shall include a note of his name, if the constable knows it, but a constable may not detain a person to find out his name.

(4) If a constable does not know the name of a person whom he has searched, the record of the search shall include a note otherwise describing that person.

(5) The record of a search of a vehicle shall include a note describing the vehicle.

(6) The record of a search of a person or a vehicle—

- (*a*) shall state—
    - (i) the object of the search;
    - (ii) the grounds for making it;
    - (iii) the date and time when it was made;
    - (iv) the place where it was made;
    - (v) whether anything, and if so what, was found;
    - (vi) whether any, and if so what, injury to a person or damage to property appears to the constable to have resulted from the search; and
- (*b*) shall identify by reference to his police number the constable making it.

(7) If a constable who conducted a search of a person made a record of it, the person who was searched shall be entitled to a copy of the record if he asks for one before the end of the period specified in paragraph (9).

(8) If—

    (*a*) the owner of a vehicle which has been searched or the person who was in charge of the vehicle at the time when it was searched asks for a copy of the record of the search before the end of the period specified in paragraph (9); and

    (*b*) the constable who conducted the search made a record of it,

the person who made the request shall be entitled to a copy.

(9) The period mentioned in paragraphs (7) and (8) is the period of 12 months beginning with the date on which the search was made.

(10) The requirements imposed by this Article with regard to records of searches of vehicles shall apply also to records of searches of vessels, aircraft and hovercraft.

Road checks

2.24   **6.**—(1) This Article shall have effect in relation to the conduct of road checks by police officers for the purpose of ascertaining whether a vehicle is carrying—

    (*a*) a person who has committed an offence other than a road traffic offence or a vehicles excise offence;

    (*b*) a person who is a witness to such an offence;

    (*c*) a person intending to commit such an offence; or

    (*d*) a person who is unlawfully at large.

(2) For the purposes of this Article a road check consists of the exercise in a locality of the power conferred by Article 180(1) of the Road Traffic (Northern Ireland) Order 1981 in such a way as to stop during the period for which its exercise in that way in that locality continues all vehicles or vehicles selected by any criterion.

(3) Subject to paragraph (5), there may only be such a road check if a police officer of the rank of superintendent or above authorises it in writing.

(4) An officer may only authorise a road check under paragraph (3)—

    (*a*) for the purpose specified in paragraph (1)(*a*), if he has reasonable grounds—

      (i) for believing that the offence is a serious arrestable offence; and

    (ii) for suspecting that the person is, or is about to be, in the locality in which vehicles would be stopped if the road check were authorised.

  (*b*) for the purposes specified in paragraph (1)(*b*), if he has reasonable grounds for believing that the offence is a serious arrestable offence;

  (*c*) for the purpose specified in paragraph (1)(*c*), if he has reasonable grounds–

    (i) for believing that the offence would be a serious arrestable offence; and

    (ii) for suspecting that the person is, or is about to be, in the locality in which vehicles would be stopped if the road check were authorised;

  (*d*) for the purpose specified in paragraph (1)(*d*), if he has reasonable grounds for suspecting that the person is, or is about to be, in the locality.

(5) An officer below the rank of superintendent may authorise such a road check if it appears to him that it is required as a matter of urgency for one of the purposes specified in paragraph (1).

(6) If an authorisation is given under paragraph (5), it shall be the duty of the officer who gives it—

  (*a*) to make a written record of the time at which he gives it; and

  (*b*) to cause an officer of the rank of superintendent or above to be informed that it has been given.

(7) The duties imposed by paragraph (6) shall be performed as soon as it is practicable to do so.

(8) An officer to whom a report is made under paragraph (6) may, in writing, authorise the road check to continue.

(9) If such an officer considers that the road check should not continue, he shall record in writing—

  (*a*) the fact that it took place; and

  (*b*) the purpose for which it took place.

(10) An officer giving an authorisation under this Article shall specify the locality in which vehicles are to be stopped.

(11) An officer giving an authorisation under this Article, other than an authorisation under paragraph (5)—

  (*a*) shall specify a period, not exceeding seven days, during which the road check may continue; and

  (*b*) may direct that the road check—

    (i) shall be continuous; or

    (ii) shall be conducted at specified times, during that period.

(12) If it appears to an officer of the rank of superintendent or above that a road check ought to continue beyond the period for which it has been authorised he may, from time to time, in writing specify a further period, not exceeding seven days, during which it may continue.

(13) Every written authorisation shall specify—

(a) the name of the officer giving it;

(b) the purpose of the road check; and

(c) the locality in which vehicles are to be stopped.

(14) The duties to specify the purposes of a road check imposed by paragraphs (9) and (13) include duties to specify any relevant serious arrestable offence.

(15) Where a vehicle is stopped in a road check, the person in charge of the vehicle at the time when it is stopped shall be entitled to obtain a written statement of the purpose of the road check if he applies for such a statement not later than the end of the period of 12 months from the day on which the vehicle was stopped.

(16) Nothing in this Article affects the exercise by police officers of any power to stop vehicles for purposes other than those specified in paragraph (1).

Reports of recorded searches and of road checks

2.25   **7.**—(1) Every annual report under section 15 of the Police Act (Northern Ireland) 1970 [c. 9 (N.I.)] shall contain information—

(a) about searches recorded under Article 5 which have been carried out during the period to which it relates; and

(b) about road checks authorised during that period under Article 6.

(2) The information about searches shall not include information about specific searches but shall include—

(a) the total numbers of searches in each month during the period to which the report relates—

(i)   for stolen articles;

(ii) for offensive weapons or articles to which Article 3(9) applies; and

(iii) for other prohibited articles;

(b) the total number of persons arrested in each such month in consequence of searches of each of the descriptions specified in sub-paragraph (a)(i) to (iii).

(3) The information about road checks shall include information—

(a) about the reason for authorising each road check; and

(b) about the result of each of them.

1995 No. 1804
The Units of Measurement Regulations 1995   **2.26**

Citation and commencement
1. These Regulations may be cited as the Units of Measurement   **2.27**
Regulations 1995 and shall come into force on 1st October 1995.

Interpretation
2. In these Regulations—   **2.28**
"Act" includes a local and personal or private Act, an Act of the
Parliament of Northern Ireland and a Measure of the Northern
Ireland Assembly;
"the commencement date", subject to regulation 4 below, means
1st October 1995;
"corresponding metric unit", in relation to a relevant imperial
unit, means the unit of measurement specified in relation to
the relevant imperial unit in the second column of the Schedule
to these Regulations;
"existing provision" means any of the following, namely—
   (*a*) a provision of any Act passed, or of any subordinate
   legislation made, before the commencement date;
   (*b*) a provision of any contract, agreement, licence, authority,
   undertaking or statement made or given before that date;
   and
   (*c*) a provision of any deed, instrument or document made
   before that date;
"relevant imperial unit" means a unit of measurement specified
in the first column of the Schedule to these Regulations;
"subordinate legislation" means Orders in Council, orders, rules,
regulations, schemes, warrants, byelaws and other instruments
made under any Act; and
"the Units of Measurement Directive" means the Directive of
the Council of the European Communities dated 20th
December 1979 (No. 80/181/EEC) on the approximation of the
laws of member States relating to units of measurement.

Conversion of imperial units of measurement
3.—(1) Subject to the following provisions of these Regulations,   **2.29**
where—

   (*a*) an existing provision authorises or requires a measurement to be made, or an indication of quantity to be expressed, in a relevant imperial unit,
   (*b*) the provision has effect for economic, public health, public
   safety or administrative purposes, and

(c) the provision has legal effect on or after the commencement date,

the provision shall, unless the context otherwise requires, be construed on or after that date as authorising or requiring the measurement to be made, or the indication of quantity to be expressed, in the corresponding metric unit.

(2) Subject to the following provisions of these Regulations, where—

(a) an existing provision contains a reference to an indication of quantity expressed in a relevant imperial unit,

(b) the provision has effect for economic, public health, public safety or administrative purposes, and

(c) the provision has legal effect on or after the commencement date,

the provision shall, unless the context otherwise requires, be construed on or after that date as if the indication of quantity concerned were expressed in the corresponding metric unit.

(3) Subject to paragraph (4) below, any conversion of an indication of quantity expressed in a relevant imperial unit which is required to be made by virtue of paragraph (2) above shall be made by using the metric equivalent specified in relation to the relevant imperial unit in the third column of the Schedule to these Regulations.

(4) Any conversion of an indication of quantity expressed in degrees Fahrenheit which is required to be made by virtue of paragraph (2) above shall be made by subtracting thirty-two and multiplying the result by five-ninths.

RELEVANT IMPERIAL UNITS, CORRESPONDING METRIC UNITS
AND METRIC EQUIVALENTS

Relevant imperial unit	Corresponding metric unit	Metric equivalent
Length		
inch	centimetre	2.54 centimetres
hand	metre	0.1016 metre
foot	metre	0.3048 metre
yard	metre	0.9144 metre
fathom	metre	1.8288 metres
chain	metre	20.1168 metres
furlong	kilometre	0.201168 kilometre
mile	kilometre	1.609344 kilometres
nautical mile (UK)	metre	1853 metres
Area		
square inch	square centimetre	6.4516 square centimetres
square foot	square metre	0.09290304 square metre
square yard	square metre	0.83612736 square metre
rood	square metre	1011.7141056 square metres
acre	square metre	4046.8564224 square metres
square mile	square kilometre	2.589988110336 square kilometres

PART B

CASES

CHAPTER THREE

General Principles	3.0

Introduction—Part One: 1953 Act Cases   **3.1**
In this part the relevant cases will be considered, in the first instance in relation to the parts of the various Acts and thereafter in relation to the types of weapon.

Section 1(1) of the 1953 Act: "without lawful authority"	**3.1.1**

R. v. Brown	**3.1.2**

(1971) 55 Cr.App.R. 478

B. was charged with conspiracy to rob and having with him in a public place several offensive weapons. He was convicted of the latter and appealed. The facts were that two detectives were patrolling in a police car in the East Ham area. They said that they saw three men together walking along Barking Road. The appellant was in the middle carrying a holdall. K. was one of the other two. The third man was not identified. The police officers continued patrolling, and about five or ten minutes later they saw the three men turn into a road called Abbey Road. As they were nearing the entrance to a factory estate in that road, K. dropped slightly behind the other two, and those two walked into the factory entrance. K. remained at the entrance. The police officers pulled outside the entrance and got out of their car. K. shouted and made off down Abbey Road, the appellant quickened his pace and the third man ran away and was never seen again. One of the police officers stopped the appellant and the other one went after K. and stopped him.

The appellant was asked what he had in the holdall. He shrugged his shoulders and handed it over. It was then found to contain two iron bars and a pickaxe handle sawn off to a convenient length. On being asked what he was doing with them, he said: "I am taking them to Phapps, it's down here, ain't it?" Phapps was apparently a metal dealer or car breaker who lived near at hand. On being further questioned, the appellant said that he had found those things in the alley at the side of his house the previous night, he did not know who left them there, and he was getting rid of them because he did not want to get caught with them at his house. He also maintained that he had been on his own that morning.

At the police station a pair of gloves was found on him and, on being further questioned, he repeated his explanation about why he was carrying the iron bars and the handle and continued to maintain that he had been on his own. He later said that he happened to meet the third man in Barking Road, but had no idea where the man was going, though they both walked into the factory entrance together. He continued to maintain that he had not been with K. at all. K. told a story which was inconsistent with the appellant's in some respects. The police officers checked the different routes from the appellant's house to Phapps' premises and found that there were several such routes, but that the one which the appellant was taking, if he had indeed been on that journey, would have been the longest.

The appellant gave evidence. He said that quite early that morning he had seen the holdall with its contents near his house and that he had never seen them before. He thought that they might have been planted at the back door by his enemies, or that they might have informed the police. He said that, when being questioned by the police, he told them that the articles might have been planted in that way. He said that he decided to get rid of them before the police came, thought he would take them to Bill Phapps, a car breaker, and he went off alone. In Barking Road he met Fred, the third man. They walked along together. They saw K. in front of them and passed him. K. was a mere acquaintance and they only said "Hello" and walked on. At the factory estate entrance he told Fred "This is where I go in" and Fred said "So do I." The appellant maintained that he was going through the estate as a short cut to Phapps. He said that he was some five or six yards from the gate when there was a call of "Just a minute" by the police, he stopped, did not quicken his pace and Fred just carried on walking. K. also gave evidence and he said among other things that he had seen the appellant walking along with another man and joined them and walked with them for some time, but afterwards had separated from them.

Cairns, L.J. (at p. 481)
"The grounds of appeal are as follows: as to conviction, that the learned judge failed to give a proper direction on the burden of proof on the defendant in relation to the possession of offensive

weapons in that he at no time told the jury that the onus on the defendant was merely to satisfy the jury on the balance of probabilities; as to sentence, that the judge failed to give effect to the verdict of the jury, and misdirected himself as to the proper considerations to take into account and that the sentence was in all the circumstances excessive and wrong in principle.

"The indictment contained three counts charging the appellant and a man called Kemp—count 1 for conspiracy to rob, count 2 for having articles for theft and count 3 for having in their possession offensive weapons, the articles referred to in count 2 and the weapons referred to in count 3 being the same, namely, two iron bars and a pickaxe handle. The two men were arraigned on the second and third counts only, and they were duly tried, having pleaded Not Guilty. They were found Not Guilty on the count of having articles for theft and Kemp was found Not Guilty on the remaining count, but on the count of having in his possession offensive weapons, the appellant was convicted.

"In the course of his summing-up the judge dealt with what constitutes an offensive weapon, and there was no contention in the court below, nor has there been any contention here, that these were anything other than offensive weapons. The judge then went on to deal with the onus of proof. He referred in unexceptionable terms to the general burden of proof, and the duty on the prosecution to satisfy the jury so that they felt sure of the guilt of the accused, and the judge indicated that a similar burden of proof was of full application in relation to the count for having articles for the purpose of theft.

"He then went on to deal with the situation in relation to offensive weapons. He said: 'There is this distinction between [the two] counts, however, that the law has laid down what we lawyers call the onus of proof shifts. There is a section of the Prevention of Crime Act 1953 which lays down the prohibition of the carrying of offensive weapons without lawful authority or reasonable excuse. The wording (section 1) is this: "Any person who, without lawful authority, or reasonable excuse, the proof whereof shall lie on him, has with him in any public place any offensive weapon shall be guilty of an offence... ." So there, because it is so difficult to say why a man is carrying something in the way of an offensive weapon, the law unkindly puts the onus on him to show that he had some lawful authority or reasonable excuse for carrying it. If, therefore, the police stop a man carrying a cosh, or a weapon such as these, which are at least extremely suspicious as such, they can say "What is your excuse?" He might say, of course, "I am a police officer taking them to the station," which would be a very good excuse and there he would have lawful authority. But what here is the lawful authority or reasonable excuse? The defendants are called upon to give their lawful authority or excuse. They say, in the one case [Kemp], "I did not know they were there, in spite of what the police say I said"; in the other, "I have an excellent explanation and I said at the time that I found them near my house and I was taking them to sell as a good way of getting rid of them."' A little later the judge said, by way of summary: 'That is the difference between the two counts, (1) as to theft; (2) as to violence of the person, the one where the onus is fair and square on the prosecution, and the other where the onus passes to some extent to the defendants to show that they had lawful excuse for being in possession... .'

"Later still he said 'Now, what is the explanation put forward by the defence? They do not have to put an explanation on the first count, they do on the second, they have got to give some explanation.' Next he said this: 'He has got to give you a reason. He did give a reason at the time. Therefore, it is for you to say, can you possibly believe it, or do you think that it is sheer impertinence as an invention for the defence?' Finally near the end of the summing-up: 'Do you believe Brown's excuse? If you do not, then you are not believing the lawful authority or excuse put forward by Brown, and equally that of Kemp because he knew nothing about it, and there, as I told you, the onus of proof shifts, and you are entitled to convict him.'

"Now, it is clear law that the accused has to satisfy the jury only on a balance of probabilities and not beyond a reasonable doubt as to his having a reasonable excuse for having with him offensive weapons. There was certainly no express direction that it was for the accused to prove beyond reasonable doubt that he had reasonable excuse for carrying the weapons. [Counsel for the appellant] argues that that was the implication of at least one of the passages that I have read, where the learned judge said that the onus shifts from the prosecution to the defence. It is suggested that that meant that the standard of proof the defence would have to satisfy would be the same standard as the prosecution have to satisfy where the onus is on them.

"This Court is not satisfied that there was any such definite implication at all. We note the passage in which the judge said the onus *to some extent passed* to the accused, and we note also the passage in which he said 'It is for you to say, can you possibly believe it?' which might be said to be a direction more favourable to the accused than he was entitled to under the provisions of the Act.

"Nevertheless, the Court is of the opinion that there was an incompleteness of direction here, and that it is a case where it should be considered whether the proviso to section 2(1) of the Criminal Appeal Act 1968 should be applied."

Appeal against conviction
dismissed.

NOTE
The trial judge in his charge to the jury referred, using the words of the section, to "lawful authority or reasonable excuse." On appeal, the court proceeded to apply the statutory proviso. In doing so the court held that if a reasonable jury had been directed that it was for the accused to satisfy them on the balance of probabilities of his explanation then that jury would not have accepted the explanation. The court, however, did vary the sentence imposed.

In construing the meaning of "lawful authority or reasonable excuse" one must bear in mind the observation of Lord Hewart, C.J., in *R. v. Collinson* (1931) 23 Cr.App.R. 49 (at p.50), that "cases must be read and statutes must be construed with regard to the evils that they are expected to avert." Thus, for example, in *Wong v. Public Prosecutor* [1955] A.C. 93, the deliberations of the Judicial Committee of the Privy Council on a conviction of carrying without lawful excuse a firearm without lawful authority must be seen in the context of a capital offence arising out of Malayan Regulations at a time of acute political tension.

Section 1(1) of the 1953 Act: "reasonable excuse" **3.2.1**

(i) R. v. Jura **3.2.2**

[1954] 1 All E.R. 696

J. went to a shooting gallery at a fair in a public park. He had possession of an air rifle to shoot at a target. In a moment of anger he turned and fired the air rifle at a woman and hit her on the hip. There was a "very slight" wound as a result.

J. was charged with the offence of having with him an offensive weapon without lawful authority or reasonable excuse in a public place. The trial judge directed the jury that if the incident was an accident then J. was not unlawfully in possession of an air rifle. His possession only became unlawful if he turned the rifle deliberately on the woman. Then immediately his possession of it became unlawful and he was in possession of an offensive weapon in a public place.

J. was convicted and sentenced to eighteen months' imprisonment. He appealed.

Lord Goddard, L.C.J. (at p. 697)
"The appellant was not carrying his rifle without lawful excuse because he was at a shooting gallery where for the payment of a few pence people could amuse themselves by firing at a target

and was carrying the rifle for that purpose. He had an obvious excuse for carrying the rifle. He made use of the rifle in a way which was unlawful, for which he might have been convicted of a felony. If a person having a rifle in his hand for lawful purpose suddenly uses the rifle for an unlawful purpose, the Offences Against the Person Act, 1861, provides appropriate punishment for doing that, but the Act of 1953 is meant to deal with a person who, with no excuse whatever, goes out with an offensive weapon, it may be a 'cosh', or a knife, or something else, without any reasonable excuse. If, with all respect to the learned judge, his direction were right in this case, it would mean that anybody who was found in possession of a shotgun going to a shooting party and used his gun for an unlawful purpose would be guilty of an offence under this Act. He would be guilty of an offence under the Offences Against the Person Act, 1861, but not under the Act of 1953.

"In my opinion, there is no evidence that the man was carrying the weapon without reasonable excuse, and, therefore, the learned judge ought to have directed the jury to acquit on that count."

Appeal allowed.

NOTE

The editors of Archbold (44th ed., 1992) observe (at para. 24–124) that "this approach [in *R. v. Jura*] to the 1953 Act which had been undermined by observations in *R. v. Powell* [*infra*, at para. 4.33.1] and in *Woodward* v. *Koessler* [*infra*, at para. 3.7.2] has been reaffirmed in *R. v. Dayle* [*infra*, at 3.14.2]. In *Dayle* the Court observed that s.1 of the 1953 Act applies not only to the case of a person going out with an offensive weapon without lawful authority or reasonable excuse but also to the case of a person who deliberately while out selects an article with the intention of using it without such authority or excuse." It was the latter point in the reasoning that justified a conviction for picking up a stone in *Harrison* v. *Thornton* (*infra*, at para. 4.28.1).

However the editors also proceed to indicate that the facts in *Bates* v. *Bulman* (*infra*, para. 3.4.4) "could not realistically be distinguished from those in *Ohlson* v. *Hylton* [*infra*, at para. 3.14.5] and *R. v. Humphreys* [*infra*, at para. 3.14.7]. To distinguish between a weapon carried innocently by the defendant being subsequently used by him with the intention of an assault and a similar article which is acquired either by borrowing from somebody else or fortuitously being picked up in the street 'would be a rather academic and over-analytical approach.' Inevitably this decision [in *Bulman* v. *Bates*] means that the decision in *Harrison* v. *Thornton* (stone throwing) must for all practical purposes be regarded as one which is unlikely to be followed even though it appeared to receive the blessing of Kilner Brown J. in *Dayle*."

It is submitted that some of this difficulty arises from the accused being charged with the wrong offence: the long title of the 1953 Act is "An Act to prohibit the *carrying* of offensive weapons in public places without lawful authority or reasonable excuse" [emphasis added]. The 1953 Act is a preventative one. To throw a stone at another or to hold a knife at another's face is, in Scotland at any rate, an assault and it should be charged as such. A very careful consideration of the evidence is required before alleging a contravention of the 1953 Act.

(ii) Evans v. Wright

[1964] Crim.L.R.466

E. was stopped while driving his car; a knuckleduster was found in his pocket and a truncheon in the car. He was charged with having these offensive weapons without lawful authority or reasonable excuse in a public place contrary to s.1 of the 1953 Act.

E.'s defence was that he was a partner in a business and that he used the car to collect large sums of money for wages for employees; the weapons had been carried to guard against possible attempts to rob him of the wages.

E. was not collecting wages on the occasion of the arrest, having last done so a few days before; but the truncheon had been left in the car and he was wearing the suit which he had worn when last collecting the wages.

E. was convicted and he appealed. On appeal it was held that the question was whether E.'s explanation was a reasonable one. "Reasonable excuse" was intended to cover the particular moment at which the weapon was carried. If, the moment E. had returned from the bank, the weapons were found on him, the excuse might still be reasonable. But it was necessary to look at the actual moment of time of carrying the weapons. On the facts, the conviction was correct.

Appeal dismissed.

NOTE

Knuckledusters seem now to be comparatively rare, but in *Wright v. Lees*, 1995 G.W.D. 17–951 the appellant having one with him attracted a fine of £1,000.

(iii) Grieve v. Macleod

1967 S.L.T. 70

G., a taxi-driver in Edinburgh, had with him in his taxi cab a piece of rubber hose about two feet long with a piece of metal inserted at one end. He was charged with and convicted of a contravention of s.1(1) of the 1953 Act.

It was found as a fact in the stated case that "Taxicab drivers are from time to time assaulted in Edinburgh, sometimes to their severe injury, especially during the night hours, when violent passengers are more frequent than during the day: this fact is well known to taxi drivers and in particular to the appellant."

G. argued at trial and on appeal that he had a reasonable excuse for having the offensive weapon with him as he had a reasonable explanation of being compelled to use it for the legitimate purpose of self-defence.

Lord Justice-Clerk (Grant) (at p. 71)

"The charge upon which the appellant was convicted is that, on 19th February 1966, without lawful authority or reasonable excuse, he had with him in a public place an offensive weapon, contrary to s.1(1) of the Prevention of Crime Act 1953. It is not disputed that at the time and in the public place libelled the appellant had with him in the taxicab of which he is the owner-driver, a piece of rubber hose about two feet long with a piece of metal inserted at the end and that this article is an offensive weapon within the meaning of s.1 of the above-mentioned Act. The sole issue is whether he had reasonable excuse for doing so, the proof whereof lies, in terms of s.1(1), upon the person accused.

"In rejecting the defence of 'reasonable excuse', the learned sheriff-substitute made it clear that he had in mind the fact that, although the danger of being attacked at night is one which is shared by both taxi drivers and other members of the public, the former by reason of the conditions of their employment, are more frequently exposed to the danger than others. 'Nevertheless', he says, 'I did not consider that taxi drivers were entitled to carry offensive weapons as a general defence against possible attack any more than other members of the public'. He adds that no question arose of the weapon having been carried on this occasion against a specific threat of danger.

"The appellant does not suggest that there is any general rule under which ordinary members of the public could successfully plead that, if they carry offensive weapons as a general defence against possible attack, they have 'reasonable excuse' for so doing. It is said, however, that taxi drivers (at any rate in particular cities or areas) are in a special position. The learned sheriff-substitute has found as a fact in finding (9) that 'taxicab drivers are from time to time assaulted in Edinburgh, sometimes to their severe injury especially during the night hours, when violent passengers are more frequent than during the day; this fact is well known to taxi drivers and in particular to the appellant.' It is upon this finding that the appellant's basic argument is founded. His contention is that reasonable excuse for having an offensive weapon is established where the person concerned has a reasonable anticipation of being compelled to use it for a legitimate purpose–that purpose being, in essence, self-defence—and that that is the situation in regard to all taxicab drivers (including the appellant) who operate in conditions such as are described in finding (9).

"Appellant's counsel laid very considerable stress on the word 'compelled' but I must say that I have some difficulty in seeing what greater degree of 'compulsion' was likely in the case of the taxicab driver than in the case of the ordinary citizen. However that may be, no such general proposition, as is contended for by the appellant, is in my opinion justified. Indeed, I think that the only general proposition which can be laid down in regard to 'reasonable excuse' is that each individual case must be judged on its own particular facts and circumstances. I do not think it is possible to lay down ab ante general rules applicable to classes of persons, whether they be taxicab drivers, bank messengers, security guards or vulnerable shopkeepers with a cosh below the counter. Thus, as the appellant's counsel frankly admitted, one must for example have regard to the nature of the offensive weapon. There may be circumstances where there is reasonable excuse for carrying a wooden truncheon, but none for carrying a sawn-off shotgun or a butcher's knife. Equally one must keep in mind that, quite apart from dealing with what I might call the 'professional' weapon-carrier, one object of the 1953 Act, as I read it, is to ensure that ordinary citizens do not, unless in exceptional circumstances, take the law into their own hands.

"In the present case the learned sheriff-substitute has considered very carefully the whole facts and circumstances as disclosed to him including in particular the nature of the weapon and the risks to which the appellant might be exposed—by night. Looking at those facts and circumstances, and having considered the reasons given by the learned sheriff-substitute for his decision, I am satisfied that he was fully justified in holding that the defence of reasonable excuse had not been established. I would accordingly answer the question in the affirmative and refuse the appeal. I should add that, as the issue raised here is one on which previous authority is lacking and as the appellant may well have been under a misapprehension as to his rights (a matter which was recognised in the Court below), it would, in my opinion, be unfortunate if this conviction were to place in jeopardy his licence as a taxicab operator."

Appeal refused.

NOTE

J. B. Hill in *Weapons Law* (2nd ed., 1995) opines (at p. 148) that "a car is an object, not a place and if the car is in a public place so is the weapon in it." The authority is a dangerous dog case: *Bates v. DPP* [1993] J.P.N. 457.

In *Mok Chi-ho* [1979] H.K.L.R. 118 it was held that a private car on a public road was a public place for the purpose of the Hong Kong law on offensive weapons.

3.2.5 <center>**(iv) Evans v. Hughes**</center>

[1972] 3 All E.R. 412

H. was seen in a public place to have with him a 6-inch long metal bar. Policemen asked H. what the bar was for. After some prevarication H. said that he carried it for protection. He said that he knew that the metal bar was an offensive weapon. Later, in a statement to the police, he said that a week earlier he had been assaulted by three boys. He said that he had carried the bar for self-protection and if the boys attacked him again he would have used the bar on them.

The magistrate acquitted H. on the ground that, first, the metal bar being a defensive weapon was not an "offensive weapon" within the meaning of s.1(4) of the 1953 Act. Secondly, that even if the bar was an offensive weapon H. had a reasonable excuse for having it with him. The prosecutor appealed.

Lord Widgery, C.J. (at p. 415)

"[I]t may be a reasonable excuse for the carrying of an offensive weapon that the carrier is in anticipation of imminent attack and is carrying it for his own personal defence, but what is abundantly clear to my mind is that this Act never intended to sanction the permanent or constant carriage of an offensive weapon merely because of some constant or enduring supposed or actual threat or danger to the carrier. People who are under that kind of continuing threat must protect themselves by other means, notably by enlisting the protection of the police, and in order that it may be a reasonable excuse to say, 'I carried this for my own defence,' the threat for which the defence is required must be an imminent particular threat affecting the particular circumstances in which the weapon was carried."

Appeal dismissed.

NOTE

The rule in *Evans* v. *Hughes, supra,* was applied in *R.* v. *Peacock* [1973] Crim.L.R. 639 where, on the particular facts, a judge directed a jury that there was no reasonable excuse. The Court of Appeal agreed with the trial judge and said that "it must be very rare that someone not under immediate fear of attack could claim to be entitled to carry a weapon for self-defence on the off-chance of being attacked. No currency should be given to the proposition that the law permitted people to arm themselves and fight it out if they encountered trouble."

The commentary on *Peacock's* case, *ibid,* includes the observation that the phrase "without ... reasonable excuse" gives the courts a very wide discretion in deciding what is and what is not reasonable. The policy adopted, of construing "reasonable excuse" strictly seemed to the commentator to be very sound.

(v) Geraghty v. Skeen 3.2.6

Skeen v. Gemmell

Skeen v. Smith

(1974) 38 J.C.L. 79

In the late evening of Saturday July 8, 1972 there was some sort of adolescent gang disturbance in Netherlee, near Glasgow. Shortly afterwards, about 10.30 p.m., in nearby Clarkston Road, Netherlee, police officers saw three youths walking along the pavement. There was no one else about. The police approached the youths. One of them, Geraghty, was carrying the top of a broken milk bottle which had a protruding glass spike. Another, Gemmell, was carrying a broken milk bottle. The third, Smith, was carrying an 18-inch long piece of wood. As the police approached, Geraghty threw his broken bottle top into a hedge and the other two dropped what they were carrying. The youths were all arrested although, as the sheriff pointed out at Gemmell's trial, it was at least doubtful whether the arrest was justified under the Act. On being charged each replied to the effect that he had been chased by boys from Clarkston, the "Touns," who were armed, and that as he, the accused, came from the rival area of Castlemilk, he had run away. Smith said specifically, "We've got to defend ourselves."

For reasons which do not appear on the record, each youth was tried separately before a different sheriff. There was no charge of acting in concert.

The first sheriff who tried Geraghty found that taking into account the time of day, the fact that his implement "was peculiarly suited for causing injury, if not specifically adapted with that in mind," the implements carried by his companions, his attempt to conceal the implement when the police arrived, and "that the implement was, in a very general way, carried against a background of gang activity," he was carrying an offensive weapon. He added that he might have picked up the bottle from among some nearby broken glass "as a safeguard," having been chased not long before. The sheriff held that Geraghty "did not begin" to discharge the onus of proving reasonable excuse, and convicted him. There was no evidence as to how he came by the weapon, his own evidence at the trial having been a denial that he ever had it at all.

The second sheriff who tried Gemmell had doubts as to whether the broken bottle was an offensive weapon, but held that Gemmell's reply to the caution and charge ("We were chased by about five 'Touns' with choppers and blades and we started running away") constituted on a balance of probabilities a reasonable excuse. He concluded, "I could find nothing in the circumstances of this case to satisfy me beyond a reasonable doubt that the respondent had offensive rather than defensive intentions." He found the charge not proven.

The third sheriff who tried Smith was inclined to believe his evidence that he and his companions had been chased away from Clarkston Halls about five minutes before their arrest, and that he had picked up the wood in case he needed it to defend himself. Accordingly, far from proving that the wood was being carried for offensive purposes the Crown had shown merely, and even that only by the accused's admission, that the wood was intended for a defensive purpose. Evidence of the milk bottles was irrelevant in the absence of a charge of concert. The charge was found not proven.

Geraghty appealed against his conviction and the Crown appealed against the acquittals of the other two. The High Court of Justiciary, without delivering any opinions, dismissed the appeal of Geraghty and upheld the appeals by the Crown. That Court indicated none of the accused had proved that he had a reasonable excuse for carrying a weapon.

Geraghty's appeal dismissed,
Crown appeals allowed.

3.2.7   **(vi) R. v. Leer**

[1982] Crim.L.R. 310

L. was in a public house late one evening. He was searched by the police. They found a knife in his pocket. It was by agreement described as a fishing knife.

L. was asked why he was carrying the knife. He said that he was going fishing the following morning and he would require the knife for that purpose. L. said that he had chosen not to leave it with the rest of his fishing gear at home.

L. was questioned further by the police about why he had the knife with him then. L. was alleged by the police to have said that he had the knife "in case someone had a go at me." L. added that he would have used the knife only in self-defence.

L. was charged with possessing an offensive weapon contrary to s.1 of the 1953 Act. At trial the defence took issue with the police evidence concerning the intended use of the knife as stated following the additional questions.

L. submitted at the end of the prosecution case that the matter should be withdrawn from the jury since the prosecution had not established by evidence that he had the knife with him with intent to cause injury. The submission was rejected.

L. submitted further that there were four issues that should be left to the jury, even in the absence of any defence evidence, viz. (i) why he was carrying the knife; (ii) whether he intended to use it to injure anyone; (iii) whether the police were honest and accurate in the account they gave of the conversations with him, particularly during the further questioning; and (iv) whether, if he did give the second reason in answer to the further questioning, it amounted to an admission that the knife was held by him as a weapon of offence, the onus being on the prosecution to show that the fishing knife, not an offensive weapon *per se*, was in fact in the circumstances an offensive weapon.

The judge directed the jury that the answers to the police did not amount to a reasonable excuse and so L. had no defence to put forward and the jury were directed to convict.

L. appealed against conviction on the ground that, as the jury had to determine four issues, it was not one of the rare cases in which the judge was entitled to direct the jury to convict. The Crown sought application of the proviso to s.2(1) of the Criminal Appeal Act 1968.

It was held on appeal that, standing certain authorities in English law, such a direction as the judge gave was possible. However, there were matters for the jury's decision and, although it might have been surprising if they had decided in the appellant's favour on a proper direction, their decision would not have been perverse. The case was not one for application of the proviso for, once a direction to convict was given to a jury, it was impossible to say that the eventual verdict of guilty was safe or satisfactory.

Appeal allowed.

(vii) Bryan v. Mott   3.2.8

(1976) 62 Cr.App.R. 71

B. was found to have with him in a public place a broken end of a milk bottle. The surrounding facts and circumstances and the procedural history of the subsequent prosecution are set out in the case stated by the Magistrates, *viz.*—On October 10, 1974, an information was preferred by the prosecutor, John Mott, a chief inspector of the Thames Valley Police Force, that on September 2, 1974, the defendant, David Rickman Bryan, at Amersham, in the county of Buckingham, without lawful authority or reasonable excuse had with him in a public place, Chiltern Avenue, a broken milk bottle, being an offensive weapon, contrary to section 1 of the Prevention of Crime Act 1953. The information was heard by Amersham Magistrates' Court on November 14, 1974, which Court found the information proved and convicted the defendant. The defendant appealed to the Crown Court against that conviction.

The facts found by the Crown Court are these. On the evening of September 1, 1974, the defendant had quarrelled with his brother, knocked him out and left home in a suicidal mood. He telephoned the "Samaritans" at about midnight, but no terms of the conversation ensuing are disclosed in the case.

He then went for assistance to the police, calling at a police station asking for advice as to the best method of committing suicide. Whether his inquiry was treated seriously or not one does not know because it is not dealt with in the case.

But eventually we come to 12.34 a.m. on the following day, September 2. The defendant stopped in a public street in Amersham, and after a short conversation between the police constable who stopped him and the defendant, the defendant produced from his jacket pocket a broken end of a milk bottle, which he raised above his head but immediately threw away. He did not threaten the police officer with the bottle.

He said he had found the bottle a short distance away from the place where he was stopped, and it was then in the broken condition in which it was produced to the police officer.

The Crown Court heard the appeal on January 17, 1975, and reserved their judgment until January 24, 1975. They found, *inter alia*, that the defendant's reason for possessing the broken milk bottle was to inflict personal injury on himself or attempt to commit suicide, and that was a reasonable excuse with section 1(1) of the Act of 1953. Accordingly, they allowed the appeal and quashed the conviction.

The prosecutor appealed.

Lord Widgery, C.J. (at p. 72)
"The Crown Court found that the defendant intended to use the said broken bottle to commit suicide by slashing his wrists. Before the Crown Court there was consideration in the first instance of whether this broken bottle was to be regarded as an offensive weapon *per se* or not.

"An offensive weapon *per se* means an article made or adapted for use for causing injury to the person. The Crown Court took the view that this broken milk bottle was an article adapted for use for causing injury to the person, and consequently the offence was necessarily made out unless the defendant below had been able to discharge the burden of showing that he had the weapon in his possession with lawful authority or reasonable excuse.

"The Crown Court therefore went on to consider the question of reasonable excuse. They were advised that it is no longer an offence to attempt to commit suicide. They took the view therefore that the purpose for which they had found this bottle had been pocketed by the defendant was a lawful purpose, and they decided that the offence was not made out on that account.

"The prosecutor brings the matter here, and the case does not raise the first issue, namely, whether this was an offensive weapon *per se.* It was so held by the Crown Court, as I have said, and that conclusion is not reviewed in the Case Stated or in argument before us, so we must approach the problem on the footing that it was an offensive weapon *per se.*

"Then, as I say, one comes to the second question, which is whether the defendant discharged the onus of showing lawful authority or reasonable excuse. He certainly did not have lawful authority. The reference to lawful authority in the section is a reference to those people who from time to time carry an offensive weapon as a matter of duty—the soldier and his rifle and the police officer with his truncheon. They are all carrying offensive weapons, but they do so normally under lawful authority. That is not this case because no such authority covered the possession of this broken bottle.

"So, getting the matter down to the final point on which everything must turn: was there a reasonable excuse? The Crown Court seems to have thought that the only inquiry on this issue was whether the purpose was lawful. Had the offensive weapon been required for a purpose in itself lawful, it seems the Crown Court would say that reasonable excuse existed; whereas if the offensive weapon was possessed for a purpose which was itself unlawful, a contrary conclusion would be reached.

"It seems to me that this is not really the proper way to approach this question. That for which a reasonable excuse is required is the possession of the weapon in a public place. The whole purpose of this section, and valuable it is, is to discourage people from being in public places 'tooled up,' as is the expression sometimes heard,' with weapons of this kind, and when a man is found in possession of such a weapon without lawful authority then the question is: has he got a reasonable excuse for having it in a public place?

"That is not necessarily a matter which turns on the legality or illegality of his ultimate purpose. Has he got a reasonable excuse for having it in a public place? It seems to me that in deciding that question one has to introduce the element of the reasonable man.

"In deciding whether there is a reasonable excuse one has to ask oneself whether a reasonable man would think it excusable to carry an offensive weapon in a public place merely in order to have it available to commit suicide. Frankly I am bound to say the reasonable man in my view might regard the whole story as being so unconvincing and irrational as not to accept it at all; but that is not necessarily the end of the matter.

"It is for the tribunal of fact in the first instance to inquire whether a reasonable man would accept that this was a proper occasion for having the weapon in a public place. It seems to me, I must confess, that if the Crown Court had looked at the matter that way, they would have been bound to hold that no reasonable excuse had been established. The whole story of the intended suicide, though accepted by the justices, is so remote from the carriage of the offensive weapon in the public place that it seems to me that properly instructed, any reasonable Bench or reasonable Crown Court must have come to the conclusion that this excuse, although honestly put forward, was not a reasonable excuse. If one comes to that view, it is necessary to say that the appeal will be allowed and the case will be sent back with a direction to restore the conviction of the justices."

Appeal allowed.

3.2.9　　(viii) Houghton v. Chief Constable of Greater Manchester

(1987) 84 Cr.App.R.319

H. was a former police officer. He went to a fancy dress party dressed in a police constable's uniform. As part of that uniform he had a police truncheon. In the early hours of the morning H. made his way home from the party. He was stopped by two policemen who asked H. if he was a member of a police force. H. replied that he was, then explained that he was a former police officer.

H. was arrested, taken to a police station where he was detained and then charged with carrying an offensive weapon contrary to s.1 of the 1953 Act and then released on bail. After committal for trial, the prosecution did not proceed and H. was acquitted and awarded costs.

H. brought a civil action against the Chief Constable of Greater Manchester for damages for unlawful arrest, false imprisonment and malicious prosecution. H.'s claim was dismissed by the court of first instance and he appealed. The questions arising on appeal included *inter alia* whether H., the plaintiff, had reasonable excuse for having the truncheon with him.

May, L.J. (at p. 323)

"On the facts as I have outlined them, it is quite clear why he [H.] had it [the truncheon] on him, namely as a theatrical prop to support the verisimilitude of his fancy dress. [Counsel], on behalf of the respondent, submits that that is not enough, that that cannot be said to be a reasonable excuse for carrying an offensive weapon *per se* in a public place, particularly at one o'clock in the morning in the middle of an urban area. In the course of argument he canvassed the situation of someone who, for instance, goes to a fancy dress party dressed as an ancient Briton, carrying with him a club into the head of which nails have been knocked so that, if used, it will cause substantial damage to the person against whom it is used. Clearly that would be an offensive weapon *per se*. But if the facts are merely that a person, somewhat inadequately clad in a goatskin, is walking along a street carrying such a weapon as part of his fancy dress, is that a reasonable excuse for him to have it in his possession? I stress that the only facts which are proved are that it is being carried as a prop for his fancy dress. The situation would be different if there was other evidence, for instance as to the amount of drink taken, or as to the presence of opposing factions at the particular party to which the accused had been, or that the weapon had been used in a threatening way. But where the weapon, offensive *per se*, is carried merely as a theatrical property, as part and parcel of a fancy dress worn by a person going to a fancy dress party, I think that that does constitute a reasonable excuse for carrying that particular prop. I ask myself rhetorically, what other reason has he got for carrying that particular article at that time? The only answer that one can give is that he has it to add, as I say, verisimilitude to his fancy dress. That, as I think, is a reasonable excuse in itself. Nevertheless I wish to stress that to wear fancy dress with appropriate props should not be used as an excuse unlawfully to carry through urban areas articles which are *per se*, or can very rapidly be turned into offensive weapons. I am dealing with the facts as found in this particular case and which I have outlined. No others were deposed to in evidence nor found by the learned judge. Consequently I have reached the conclusion that the truncheon was an offensive weapon *per se* but that the plaintiff had reasonable excuse at the time for carrying it."

Appeal allowed in part.

NOTE
This case is considered further *infra*, at para. 4.34.2.

3.2.10   **(ix) McGovern v. Allan**

High Court of Justiciary, October 22, 1987

M. and a friend were chased by a crowd of men on New Year's Day.
The crowd followed M. and the friend to the front door of their
house and began kicking the door and shouting and swearing. After
the kicking had ceased, M. took a sword from a wall where it was
hanging. M. chased the crowd of men. He was screaming at them
while he had the sword. The crowd of men also threw things at M.
Policemen attended and saw the crowd of men running off. M.
was seen standing on a grassed area near houses. He had the sword
which had its point stuck into the grass. M. was muttering loudly
and incoherently and he was agitated. He was arrested but he could
not be cautioned and charged because of his drunkenness.

The blade of the sword was two feet and six inches in length
and it was pointed. The sword was fairly sharp along its cutting
edge. It was heavy and had little pliancy.

M. was charged with a contravention of s.1(1) of the 1953 Act
and after trial was convicted. He appealed. The sheriff noted in
the stated case that on his own evidence M. had denied himself
the defence of "reasonable excuse". He accepted that the kicking
of the door had ended even before he removed the sword from the
wall. M. agreed that when he left the house the crowd ran off
downstairs and out of the building. He had no need to follow them
into a public place holding the sword.

At the hearing of the appeal in the High Court their Lordships
did not give a formal opinion and simply refused the appeal.

Appeal refused.

NOTE
This case illustrates well the principle that a reasonable excuse may be such at
one moment and not so at the next: much turns on the facts and circumstances of
each case. M. may have had a reasonable excuse initially but he over reacted. He
ceased to have a reasonable excuse from the time he left the building and was in a
public place. A briefer report of this case is at 1987 G.W.D. 40–1470.

3.2.11   **(x) Miller v. Douglas**

1988 S.C.C.R. 565

M. and a friend were attacked by some boys carrying staves or
batons. M., after initially seeking to defend himself, had to run on
to a beach and then to his home. As he ran off he heard his friend
being assaulted and shouting out as a result.

M. phoned for an ambulance. Meanwhile the boys left. Two others came across the injured friend and assisted him into a passing ambulance. M. returned to the scene to find only the two others referred to.

M. mistakenly believed the two others to have been assailants and he began arguing with them. Matters reached the stage where one of the two came close to punching M.

M. was seen to have a knife handle protruding from his jacket at chest height. The police attended and removed the knife. It was a kitchen knife with a seven-inch blade.

M. was charged with contravening s.1 of the 1953 Act. He was convicted and appealed. It was found as a fact in the stated case that at the moment M. was under threat from being punched, he pulled back and made no attempt to handle the knife.

Lord Justice-Clerk (Ross) (at p. 570)

"The second matter which [counsel for the appellant] raised was whether the appellant had succeeded in establishing reasonable excuse for having this weapon in his possession. It was not disputed that the onus was upon him to establish that reasonable excuse."

And (at p. 571):

"The question for us must be whether the sheriff was entitled to arrive at the view that there was no reasonable excuse established in this case. Although it is certainly to the credit of the appellant that even when he was under threat of being punched, he pulled back from confrontation and made no attempt to handle the knife, we have come to the conclusion that the sheriff was fully entitled on the facts of this case to hold that there was not reasonable excuse made out for the appellant's having with him the knife at the time and place libelled."

Appeal refused.

NOTE

It was again made clear in *Normand* v. *Saunders*, 1991 G.W.D. 27–1577 that the onus of establishing reasonable excuse is on the accused. The absence of an explanation may be eloquent of guilt: in *Nairn* v. *Lees*, 1991 G.W.D. 32–1910 the appellant did not or could not explain his return to a place "in a strange town" where he himself had previously been assaulted. No explanation was offered in *Bradley* v. *Annan*, 1993 G.W.D. 27–1670.

(xi) Malnik v. D.P.P.   3.2.12

[1989] Crim.L.R. 451

M. had an offensive weapon with him in a public place. The weapon was a rice flail. That consisted of two pieces of wood joined by a chain. Such weapons were sometimes used in connection with martial arts. M. had a long-standing interest, and some expertise in martial arts.

M. had been acting as an adviser to X. and in that capacity he had investigated alleged over-invoicing by a company which supplied chauffeurs for X.'s fleet of cars.

One day M. discovered that two of X.'s valuable cars had been taken without authority. It was thought that one of the cars had been taken by J. who was known to have a tendency to violent and irresponsible behaviour.

M. and three others set out to visit J. M. armed himself with a rice flail for the purpose of self-defence: it was tucked into the waistband of his trousers. As he was approaching J.'s house, he was arrested.

At a trial, on a contravention of s.1 of the 1953 Act, it was conceded that flails were offensive weapons *per se* but it was argued that M. had proved, on a balance of probabilities, that he had a reasonable excuse for having the flail with him at the material time, namely because he had reasonable cause to believe that he was in imminent danger of being subject to violent attack.

The stipendiary magistrate concluded that, while M. had reasonable cause to believe that he was involved in an operation which carried an imminent risk of violent attack, by searching out a person of violent disposition, J., then M. had voluntarily assumed the risk and, in such circumstances, he had no reasonable excuse for arming himself to resist attack.

On appeal by stated case it was argued by M., who had been convicted, that a man should not be disqualified from protecting himself in the course of carrying out a lawful activity of seeking the repossession of property which had wrongfully been taken. An imminent particular threat affecting the particular circumstances in which a weapon had been carried might provide a reasonable excuse; it was necessary to look at the actual moment of time when the weapon was carried: *Evans v. Hughes* [1972] 3 All E.R. 412.

Moreover, there was the element of self-defence: *R. v. Field* [1972] Crim.L.R. 435. It had been unreasonable to deprive M. of the means of self-defence, even though he had assumed the risk by going to a place where he might be attacked by the person he was seeking.

Counsel for the D.P.P. argued that the correct test was whether or not it was reasonable in all the circumstances for the weapon to be carried in a public place, which did not necessarily turn on the legality or illegality of the ultimate purpose: *Bryan v. Mott* (1976) 62 Cr.App.R. 71. A reasonable man who anticipated attack in the pursuit of the recovery of property should call the police instead of arming himself against the potential attacker—*R.* v. *Peacock* [1973] Crim.L.R. 639.

Held, that the stipendiary magistrate had correctly concluded that as a matter of law the defence of reasonable excuse was not available to M. The cases of *Evans* v. *Hughes* and *R.* v. *Field* were distinguishable.

Ordinarily, individuals could not legitimately arm themselves with an offensive weapon in order to repel unlawful violence which such individuals had knowingly and deliberately brought by creating a situation in which violence was liable to be inflicted. It was quite different where those concerned with security and law enforcement were concerned.

If private citizens set out on expeditions such as this, armed with offensive weapons, the risk of unlawful violence and serious injury was great and obvious. The policy of the law must therefore be against such conduct, which conclusion was consistent with the very narrow limits which previous decisions had imposed on the freedom of the citizen to arm himself against attack. It had been rightly concluded that the risk of violence could have been avoided and thus the need to carry weapons, by inviting the appropriate agency to repossess the cars by the usual means.

Appeal dismissed.

NOTE

Professor J. C. Smith in his commentary on the above case, see *ibid.*, at p. 452, observes that "reasonable excuse" is given a restricted meaning by the courts in the interests of policy. The effectiveness of the Prevention of Crime Act in keeping offensive weapons off the streets might be seriously impaired if everyone who reasonably feared that he might at some time be attacked was allowed to carry an "offensive weapon"—for a weapon may, of course, be "offensive" though the accused intends to use it only for self-defence.

(xii) McCulloch v. Normand 3.2.13

High Court of Justiciary, November 3, 1993

M. was convicted in Glasgow District Court of a contravention of s.1(1) of the 1953 Act in that he was found in a public place with a sword. M. appealed.

The stipendiary magistrate found the following facts admitted or proved:

> "1. The appellant is a member of the White Cockade Society. The society re-enacts mock battles and promotes the Jacobean era.

2. On 11 September 1991 the appellant attended the Botanic Gardens in Glasgow together with other members of the White Cockade Society where a mock battle was re-enacted and this was filmed by the British Broadcasting Corporation. Thereafter the appellant attended hospitality facilities provided by the BBC and later he socialised in a public house with friends. Thereafter the appellant spent the night at the home of a [woman friend]. The appellant remained at [his friend's home] until approximately 10 am on 12 September 1991.

3. Around 10.35 a.m. on 12 September 1991 Murdo Nicolson and Peter Scougall, both constables of Strathclyde Police, stationed at Maryhill were on uniform mobile patrol in Cromwell Street, Glasgow. The said officers observed a male person, identified by both officers as the appellant, wearing a plaid and round his waist he had a scabbard and at his left side could be seen the handle of a sword. Crown Label No. 1 Sword and Scabbard was identified by both police officers in court as being the production seized from the appellant at the material time.

4. The appellant was cautioned at common law by Constable Nicolson. He was asked why he had the sword and the appellant stated that he was a member of the White Cockade Society and took part in mock battles. The appellant stated he had not been to nor was going to any re-enactment that day.

5. The appellant was cautioned and charged with a contravention of s.1(1) of the Prevention of Crime Act 1953 and made no reply.

6. Cromwell Street is in the Maryhill district of Glasgow and is a public place.

7. The sword was approximately two feet long and was made for the appellant to enable him to participate in mock battles. The cost of having the sword made was in the region of £200–£250.

8. The sword was capable of causing personal injury and indeed James McPhail Wilson, a defence witness, stated in cross examination that the 'Dirk' (Crown Production No. 1 described as a Sword and Scabbard) 'would cause you a great deal of damage if someone stabbed you with it.'

9. Any sword, and thus this sword, is an item made for use for causing personal injury and is *per se* an offensive weapon.

10. Rifles are also used by the White Cockade Society at re-enactments. The rifles are kept under lock and key and

are conveyed to venues in a vehicle. Firearm certificates are held in respect of the rifles. "The evidence was in short compass. The appellant was seen by two police officers in a public street wearing a scabbard and sword. The appellant was not attending any re-enactment on the day in question.

"The appellant maintained that the sword was a toy that was used by himself in re-enactments when he attended functions of the White Cockade Society.

"I repelled a submission made in terms of s.354(A) of the Criminal Procedure (Scotland) Act 1975 to the effect that there was no evidence that the weapon was a Class A weapon. In my humble view the Crown had led evidence which showed the sword was prima facie a Class A weapon and as a result the onus lay on the appellant to show that he had it 'with lawful authority or reasonable excuse.'

"The fact that the appellant had been at a re-enactment the previous day did not permit him to carry the sword or dirk in a public street the following day.

"I found the appellant guilty on the charge as libelled. The procurator fiscal depute then made a motion for the sword to be forfeited in terms of the penalty notice and the agent for the appellant stated that he could not oppose the motion. Accordingly I granted the motion and ordered forfeiture of the sword/dirk."

The Lord Justice-General (Hope)
"The application for stated case raised three points. First, that there was no evidence to entitle the magistrate to find that the article was an offensive weapon; second, that there was evidence which was a sufficient basis to show that the appellant had a reasonable excuse for having this article with him in a public place; and, third, that in the exceptional circumstances of the case forfeiture should not have been ordered.

"The findings tell us that the appellant is a member of the White Cockade Society which re-enacts mock battles and promotes the Jacobean era. On the day prior to the alleged offence the appellant had attended, with other members of the Society, a re-enactment of a mock battle which had been filmed by the BBC. Later that day he took part in various social occasions and then spent the night in Glasgow with a friend. It was on the following morning that he was seen by two police officers in Cromwell Street, Glasgow wearing a plaid and having round his waist a scabbard from which was protruding the handle of a sword. When he was asked why he had the sword, he explained that he was a member of the society and took part in mock battles. But he also said that he had not been to nor was going to any re-enactment that day. That response led to him being cautioned and charged with the contravention of s.1(1) of the Act, to which he made no reply.

"The magistrate has made the following findings about the article which was taken into possession by the police."

[Lord Hope then referred to findings 7 to 9 inclusive.]

"The first point which [counsel for the appellant] took in the light of what we have described so far was that this article was not shown to have been an article made for causing personal injury. The whole basis upon which the Crown had proceeded against the appellant was that this was an article falling within the first of the three classes described in s.1(4) of the 1953 Act. Finding 7, however, made it clear that this sword had been made for the appellant to enable him to participate in mock battles. We were invited to infer from that finding that this sword was not made for causing personal injury. Against that background finding 9 was said to be too sweeping, because it was going too far to say that any sword, and thus this sword was an item made for such use.

"So far as this point is concerned, we observe that the appellant's position in evidence was that the sword was a toy which was used by himself in re-enactments when he attended functions of the White Cockade Society. No doubt an article which appears to be a sword may not truly be a sword. If the article is a toy or some other kind of replica it may then not be accurate to describe it as a sword at all. And if it is not a sword at all then it cannot be said to be a weapon, and it cannot be said to have been made for use for causing personal injury.

"In the present case however, although the findings are perhaps not entirely consistent with each other, the magistrate was satisfied that the article was a sword. It is said to have been capable of causing personal injury, and it is said that it was an article which was capable of causing a great deal of damage if it was used to stab someone. In the light of these findings it seems to us inevitable that the article, having been properly described as a sword, was not a toy at all but was a weapon made for use for causing personal injury. For these reasons we do not find it possible to accept the first argument that the magistrate was not entitled to conclude that this was an article within the first of the three relevant categories.

"The second point was that the appellant had a reasonable excuse for having the sword with him in all the circumstances. It was pointed out that he had been at a re-enactment of a mock battle the previous day. He had been spending the night in Glasgow and was apparently on his way home when he was seen by the police. That in itself might support the argument, but the way in which he was behaving tends to negative it. What he was doing was going through the streets wearing the scabbard with the sword in it round his waist. That in our opinion provides an answer to the point that he had a reasonable excuse for having the article with him, because the circumstances in which the person has the article with him fall to be taken into account in considering whether there was such an excuse. In this case he was carrying the sword in the way it would be carried if it were to be available for use as a weapon, when he had no reasonable excuse for carrying it in that way.

"So far as the third point is concerned, the magistrate decided to grant the motion and to order forfeiture of the sword. In our view he went further than was necessary in the circumstances of this case. The findings are perfectly clear, that the use to which the appellant put this article was in the re-enactment of mock battles and that the sword had been made for him for that express purpose. As [counsel for the appellant] pointed out, there was no deliberate criminal purpose in this case. It appears to have been more an oversight or act of foolishness on his part that he had the article with him as he did when he committed the offence.

"In all the circumstances we consider that forfeiture of the sword was not justified in the exceptional circumstances here, and we shall quash that part of the sentence which the magistrate imposed. So far as the questions relating to conviction are concerned, however, we shall answer these two questions in the affirmative and refuse the appeal against conviction."

Appeal refused.

NOTE
    First, reference to "Class A" follows from the terms of the appellant's application for a Stated Case although he gives no authority for such a classification. Secondly, the appellant appealed the order of forfeiture although the motion by the Crown was unopposed at first instance. Thirdly, there is a brief report of this case at 1994 G.W.D. 8–470.

Section 1(1) of the 1953 Act: "the proof whereof shall lie on him"   3.3.1

(i) R. v. Petrie   3.3.2

[1961] 1 All E.R. 466

P. was a passenger in a motor car. That car collided with a motor scooter. The pillion passenger was thrown off the scooter and as a result he went to speak to the car driver about the collision and the consequent injuries sustained by the driver of the scooter. A fracas of some sort ensued. The police attended.

When the police attended P. was seated in the car. The police searched that car and found a cut-throat razor under the passenger seat on which P. had been sitting. P. was charged *inter alia* with a contravention of s.1 of the 1953 Act. P. was convicted and he appealed.

Salmon, J. (at p. 468)

"It is clear that the definition section of the Act [s.1(4) of the 1953 Act] contemplates offensive weapons of, at any rate, two classes, namely (a) an article which per se is an offensive weapon, that is to say, an article made or adapted for use for causing injury to the person; and (b) an article which, though it is not made or adapted for such use, is carried with the intent so to use it. A cosh, a knuckleduster, and a revolver are examples of articles in the first class. A sandbag and a razor are examples of articles in the second class. No jury could find that a sandbag was in the first class because there would be no evidence to support such a finding. It seems to this court that the same is true about an ordinary razor. There are some articles which are equivocal, for example, knives. It would always be for a jury to say whether a knife was made or adapted for use for causing injury to the person. It would depend on the view the jury took of the knife.

"It is absolutely essential in summing-up to the jury in a case of this sort not to muddle up the definition of 'offensive weapon' because, if the article in question is an offensive weapon, per se, once possession in a public place is proved, the onus shifts to the defence to prove on a balance of probability that there was lawful authority or reasonable excuse for carrying the weapon. If the accused fails to discharge this onus the jury must convict him. On the other hand, if the article is something like a sandbag or a razor, the onus is on the prosecution to show that it was carried with the intention of using it to injure. The onus remains on the prosecution throughout, and if at the end of the day the jury are left in doubt about the intent of the accused, he is entitled to be acquitted."

Appeal allowed.

(ii) R. v. Whitman

[1962] Crim.L.R. 394

W. and three other men conspired to rob a wages clerk. They went to the scene of the proposed robbery by car. After their arrest there was found in the car a club (a rounders bat) and a piece of metal tubing (the extension for a funnel) wrapped in a newspaper.

W. was charged with conspiracy to rob and possessing an offensive weapon. The trial judge left it to the jury that it was for the prosecution to prove that W. knew that these articles were in the car.

The judge failed to draw the jury's attention to the definition of "offensive weapon" in s.1(4) of the 1953 Act. The judge had directed the jury that: "The prosecution have to prove in this instance that they [W. and the others] had in their possession with them offensive weapons in a public place; but once the prosecution have proved to your satisfaction that they are in a public place and that those things are offensive weapons it is then for the defendants to show you that they were carrying these things with reasonable excuse or other authority." W. was convicted of both charges and appealed.

Held, if so far as an offensive weapon *per se* is concerned it is shown by the prosecution that an accused knowingly had it in his possession then it is for him to prove that he had lawful authority or reasonable excuse for such possession.

In the case of offensive weapons which are not offensive weapons *per se*, it is always for the prosecution to prove that they were intended to be used to cause an injury to a person.

The trial judge, in the direction cited above, considered the implements to be offensive weapons *per se*. It was admitted that they were not, and they would not be offensive until the prosecution proved that they were intended to be used for an offensive purpose.

Appeal *quoad* offensive
weapon charge allowed.

(iii) Davis v. Alexander 3.3.4

(1970) 54 Cr.App.R. 398

A. had what appeared to be a walking stick with him in a street in the early hours of the morning. Policemen saw A. wave the stick in the air. They examined the walking stick and they found it to be a swordstick. When A. was charged with a contravention of s.1 of the 1953 Act he said that he had just picked the stick up from being mended.

At trial the magistrates found three matters: (1) that the swordstick was an offensive weapon *per se*; (2) that A. had no reasonable excuse for having it with him at the time, they having disbelieved his story that he was just taking it home from having it repaired; and (3) that A. had no intention of using the stick to cause injury to any person. A. was acquitted and the prosecutor appealed.

Lord Parker, C.J. (at p. 399)

"[Offensive] weapons may be of two classes; either an article which is an offensive article *per se* made or adapted for causing injury to the person, or an article which can have a purely innocent purpose which will only be an offensive weapon for the purposes of the Act if it is intended for use to cause injury to the person. The justices, in my judgment, came to an entirely correct conclusion in saying that the swordstick was an offensive weapon *per se*, being clearly made for the purpose of causing injury to the person. They seemed to think, however, that not only was it necessary to find that it was an offensive weapon *per se*, but also that the respondent had it with him with the intention of using it to cause injury to a person. That, of course, is a very vital ingredient if the offensive weapon is not an offensive weapon *per se*, and only becomes one if it is carried with the intent to cause injury. But once they found that it was an offensive weapon *per se*, and I think they were clearly right in so finding, and found further that there was no lawful authority or reasonable excuse for the respondent having it with him, then it automatically followed that he was guilty of an offence."

Appeal allowed.
Magistrates directed
to convict.

3.3.5   **(iv) R. v. Brown**

(1971) 55 Cr.App.R. 478

Policemen saw B. and others acting suspiciously. B. was stopped by the police and a holdall he was carrying was found to contain two iron bars and a pickaxe handle sawn off to a convenient length. B. was charged with conspiracy to rob and possessing offensive weapons.

At his trial B. was convicted of the charges of possessing offensive weapons and sentenced to a term of imprisonment. He appealed on the ground that the trial judge, it was said, had erred in his direction to the jury where the burden of proof lay on the defence, on the standard of proof required.

Cairns, L.J. (at p. 483)

"[I]t is clear law that the accused has to satisfy the jury only on a balance of probabilities and not beyond a reasonable doubt as to his having a reasonable excuse for having with him offensive weapons."

> Appeal against conviction
> dismissed, but appeal
> against sentence allowed
> and sentence reduced.

Section 1(1) of the 1953 Act: "has with him" **3.4.1**

(i) R. v. Cugullere **3.4.2**

[1961] 1 W.L.R. 858

Policemen saw C. driving a stolen van. The vehicle was stopped and C. got out and ran away. He was caught by the police. In the back of the van were found three pickaxe handles bound with adhesive tape. C. was charged *inter alia* with a contravention of s.1 of the 1953 Act.

At his trial C. said that he had no idea that the van was stolen and that he did not know that the three pickaxe handles were in the back of the van. He was convicted and he appealed on the ground of misdirection.

Salmon, J. (at pp. 860–1)
"This court is clearly of the opinion that the words 'has with him in any public place,' must mean 'knowingly has with him in any public place.' If some innocent person has a cosh slipped into his pocket by an escaping rogue, he would not be guilty of having it with him within the meaning of the section because he would be quite innocent of any knowledge that it had been put into his pocket. In the judgment of this court, the section cannot apply in circumstances such as those. It is, therefore, extremely important in any case under this section [s.1] for the judge to give a careful direction to the jury on the issue of possession. The first thing the jury have to be satisfied about—and it is always a question for the jury—is whether the accused person knowingly had with him the alleged offensive weapon.

"... The real question for the jury here was: Did the appellant know that these pickaxe handles were in the back of the van?

"... [A]s far as the question of possession was concerned the onus remained throughout on the Crown to prove that the appellant knew that the pickaxe handles were in the van."

> Appeal allowed.

(ii) R. v. Kelt

[1977] 1 W.L.R. 1365

The police searched K.'s house while he was there. In the kitchen they found a holdall containing a robber's kit which included a sawn-off shotgun. K. said that he was looking after the kit for a friend.

K. was arrested and charged, *inter alia*, with having with him a firearm with intent to commit an indictable offence contrary to s.18 of the Firearms Act 1968.

The trial judge rejected a submission that there was no case to go to the jury, holding that "having with him a firearm" within the meaning of s.18 was not confined to carrying a firearm but, in summing up to the jury, he did not direct them that possession of a firearm was insufficient to establish the offence.

K. was convicted and appealed against conviction.

Scarman, L.J. (at p. 1366)

"The defendant appeals against his conviction under section 18 of the Firearms Act 1968, of the offence of having with him a firearm with intent to commit an indictable offence. He submits through [counsel] that that section is to be interpreted upon the basis that 'having with him' means 'carrying': alternatively, in case that should be wrong, that 'having with him' is to be distinguished from 'possession' and that the judge in summing up the case to the jury failed to give an adequate or indeed any direction as to the distinction between possessing a firearm and having a firearm with him.

"The defendant appeared at the Central Criminal Court on June 21, 1976, when he pleaded guilty to robbery, a firearms offence, and to being carried in a motor vehicle which had been taken without the authority of the owner. He pleaded not guilty however to a section 18 offence. On July 1 after a trial before Judge Clarke and a jury, he was convicted of the section 18 offence, and on that day was sentenced, on the various counts to which he had either pleaded or in respect of which he had been convicted, to a total term of 10 years' imprisonment. Upon the count under section 18, having a firearm with intent, he was given two years' imprisonment concurrent with the total of 10 years for the robbery. His appeal therefore has a certain academic flavour, since, even if he is successful, the term of 10 years' imprisonment will remain unimpaired and undiminished.

"The offences were these. On October 14, 1975, the defendant and another man robbed a Securicor Guard of £7,900 outside the

National Westminster Bank Ltd. in the Barking Road. On that adventure the defendant carried a sawn-off shotgun, while his companion had bolt cutters with which he snipped the chain attaching the money bag to the guard's wrist.

"A few days later police went to the address of a man called Mohan, where they found a robber's kit, comprising among other things a sawn-off shotgun and a pair of bolt croppers. The defendant subsequently admitted that the sawn-off shotgun then found had been used on the robbery. There was forensic evidence to show that the bolt cutters then discovered in that kit had been used to cut the guard's chain.

"Some months later, on January 15, 1976, the police went to the defendant's home, arrested him and searched the premises. It is not absolutely clear, but it would appear that the defendant was in bed and got out of bed when the police arrived and it would appear that he was arrested in the kitchen. When the police searched the kitchen, they found a holdall containing a robber's kit, a kit which in the course of the trial was called kit no. 2. This holdall contained a sawn-off shotgun, some bolt croppers, some ammunition, some woollen hats and gloves and a squeezy bottle containing ammonia. When the defendant was asked about this kit he agreed that it was a complete robber's kit, but said that he was looking after it for a friend. There was no evidence other than that to which I have already briefly referred.

"At the conclusion of the prosecution case, on the count charging the defendant with having with him on January 15 a firearm with intent to commit an indictable offence, his counsel submitted that there was no case to go to the jury. On the basis that no more could be proved than the matters to which I have referred, he submitted that there was here no evidence that the defendant was carrying a firearm with criminal intent. The judge ruled that there was a case to go to the jury, and it is that ruling which is the subject matter of [counsel's] first submission in this appeal.

"[Counsel] submits that upon this evidence there was no 'carrying of the firearm', and that 'having a firearm with him', where those words are used in the section, means carrying. The submission was overruled and the matter was left to the jury. In the course of summing up the judge, as it seems to this court, allowed the jury to think that there was no distinction between possession and 'having a firearm with him.'

"[Counsel's] second submission was that if such were the direction which the judge gave to the jury, then that also was wrong in law. We look first at the submission that the offence created by section 18 is one of carrying with criminal intent.

"Section 18 appears in that part of the Firearms Act 1968 concerned with the prevention of crime and the preservation of public safety. A number of sections in that part of the Act create a number of offences and in order to construe section 18 properly, it is necessary, in our judgment, to have in mind the scheme of those offence-creating sections. They are sections 16 to 24 inclusive. It will be observed in regard to these sections that the draftsman had in mind throughout that there was a clear distinction between possession and having a firearm with one.

"Section 16 makes it an offence for a person to have in his possession a firearm with intent by means thereof to endanger life. Section 17 makes it an offence for a person to make or attempt to make any use whatever of a firearm with intent to resist or prevent arrest. Section 18, to which I have already referred, makes it an offence for a person to have with him a firearm with intent to commit an indictable offence. Section 19 makes it an offence for a person, without lawful authority or reasonable excuse, to have with him in a public place a loaded shotgun or a weapon. Section 20 makes it an offence if a person who has a firearm with him enters a building as a trespasser. Section 21 makes the possession of a firearm by a person who has been sentenced to imprisonment an offence. Section 22 deals with the acquisition and possession of a firearm by minors. It is an offence for a person under the age of 14 to have in his possession a firearm in certain circumstances. Under subsection (3) it is an offence for a person under the age of 15 to have with him an assembled shotgun. It is clear that the legislature has drawn a distinction in this collection of offence-creating sections between possessing a firearm and having a firearm with one.

"There is an indication that the sections which make it an offence to 'have a firearm with him' in certain circumstances were intended to deal with carrying firearms. As [counsel] submits, the indication comes from the marginal notes. Each section which creates an offence for a person to have a firearm with him has a marginal note which includes the word 'carrying.' Where this phrase is used in other criminal statutes, one finds also the same marginal note. For example, in the Prevention of Crime Act 1953, it is an offence for a person without lawful authority or reasonable excuse to have with him in a public place an offensive weapon and the marginal note reads 'Prohibition of the Carrying of Offensive Weapons.'

"It used to be thought that one could have no regard to marginal notes in studying the meaning of an Act of Parliament. It is still law that one may not use a marginal note for the purpose of interpreting an Act, but the House of Lords made it clear in a case which was referred to the judge by counsel in the course of argument, *Reg.* v. *Schildkamp* [1971] A.C. 1, that regard may be had to a marginal note, not to interpret the Act of Parliament, but as an indication of the mischief with which the Act is dealing. It is well put if I may say so with respect, both by Lord Reid and by Viscount Dilhorne in their speeches. Lord Reid, having said that the strict view as to marginal notes should no longer be followed, gives, however, a clear warning as to the limit of their value. He said, at p. 10:

'A cross-heading ought to indicate the scope of the sections which follow it but there is always a possibility that the scope of one of these sections may have been widened by amendment. But a side-note is a poor guide to the scope of a section, for it can do no more than indicate the main subject with which the section deals.'

"There can be no doubt but that the main subject with which a section such as section 18 of the Firearms Act 1968 deals is that of carrying firearms with criminal intent, and the presence of a marginal note is a useful indication that this is the main subject. But that does not mean that the marginal note is of any value in determining the scope of the section, which is the problem with which the court at this moment is concerned. Viscount Dilhorne said much the same thing in the course of his speech and I quote only one sentence from p. 20: 'A marginal or side-note is inserted by the draftsman as an indication, but not as a definition, of the contents of the section.' Though therefore the marginal note is a convenient indication as to the main intention or main purpose of a section, it is of no assistance in distinguishing the scope of the section.

"If one therefore puts on one side the marginal notes, one is left with some ordinary English words appearing in a statutory context, where they are plainly contrasted with the word 'possession' and there is, as far as we know, no judicial decision as to the scope of those words in this context.

"[Counsel], for the Crown, submitted that the section cannot be confined merely to carrying a firearm. He indicates that section 18 is very general in the way it is drafted. It is not limited for instance to having a firearm in a public place, and it is wide enough to cover any situation, whether it be on private premises or a public place, where the man may properly be said to have a firearm with him.

"We think that this submission of [counsel] is sound, and that it must be a matter of fact and degree for a jury to determine whether, in all the circumstances, the accused person does have with him a firearm. This firearm was found in the kitchen of the house where the defendant was living. The defendant was arrested in the kitchen and it was in the kitchen that this gun was found. Plainly therefore there was evidence here which, subject to a proper direction of the judge when summing up, could have formed the basis of a verdict of guilty of the offence charged.

"But one thing is clear in our judgment: the legislature has drawn a distinction between a person who has a firearm with him and a person who is in possession of a firearm. Some of the offences created by the sections to which I have referred are offences of possession, others are offences of having with one a firearm. This cannot be merely a semantic distinction, it must be a distinction of substance. The legislature must have had in mind that, in regard to those offences where it is an offence for the person to have with him a firearm, there must be a very close physical link and a degree of immediate control over the weapon by the man alleged to have the firearm with him.

"Certainly it is necessary to warn the jury, when summing up in a case under section 18, that the mere fact of possession would not be enough to establish the offence. The evidence must take the matter one stage further and be such that they are satisfied that the person charged was not only in possession but had with him the firearm with intent to commit an indictable offence while he had the firearm with him.

"How then did the judge deal with this vital distinction? In our judgment he did not draw it to the attention of the jury at all. There was, therefore, a misdirection. His directions as to having a firearm were these:

'I direct you that by having [the firearm] to his knowledge, in the kitchen, where he could have control of it, that is sufficient to satisfy you that he had it with him.'

"There the judge has allowed, as we read the words, the jury to think that the mere fact that the firearm was in the kitchen was sufficient to satisfy the requirements of the section. A little later in the summing up the judge says:

'Your task in respect of [the defendant] who, after all, and do not count this in a prejudicial way against him, had already admitted a serious robbery, is to decide as to whether the prosecution are right when they ask you to say that those articles, namely, the coat, the cartridges and the bolt cutters were part of a robber's kit, and this gun, which he had with him on that day, were not being looked after for friends, as he says; he may have been looking after it for friends, but he also,'—here come the crucial words–'and this is what must be proved, had it with him with the intention of committing robbery in the near future; in other words, if the police had not arrived and found it, when they arrested him, he and his companions would be out on a robbery within the next few days or weeks, with that lethal weapon. If you are not satisfied of that suggestion, and that those ingredients have been proved against [the defendant] you will acquit him. If you are satisfied that he had it with him, namely, under his control, and to his knowledge, and that he intended to use it in the future for robbery, well then count 6 is established ...'

"The judge in that passage passes swiftly to intention without making clear what are the ingredients of the external fact, i.e. having a gun with him, and without drawing any distinction between possessing the gun and having it with him.

"We have come to the conclusion that it is necessary when summing up a case in which an offence under section 18 is alleged, for the judge to make it clear to the jury that possession is not enough, that the law requires the evidence to go a stage further and to establish that the accused had it with him. Of course the classic case of having a gun with you is if you are carrying it. But, even if you are not carrying it, you may yet have it with you, if it is immediately available to you. But if all that can be shown is possession in the sense that it is in your house or in a shed or somewhere where you have ultimate control, that is not enough.

"For these reasons we have come to the conclusion that, though the judge was right to leave the question to the jury, by failing to distinguish in his charge to the jury between possession and 'having a gun with him,' he misdirected them on the essential question of law covering the external facts that would have to be proved to establish the offence under the section. Accordingly we think that the appeal should be allowed and the conviction under section 18 quashed."

Appeal allowed.

NOTE
The *ratio decidendi* of *Kelt's* case was applied to *R. v. Jones* (1987) 85 Cr.App.R. 259. The latter case is concerned with s.86 of the 1979 Act which makes it a crime to be armed with any offensive weapon while smuggling. It was held (*ibid.*, at p. 266) that "the expression 'armed' is an ordinary English word. Normally, it will involve either physically carrying arms, or it will involve proof that, to his knowledge, a defendant knows that they are immediately available. In our judgment, it is not necessary to prove an intent to use those arms if the situation should require it, though clearly if a defendant does use them, or has used them, then that is an obvious indication that he is armed. However, in our judgment, it is not necessary for the prosecution under this section to prove an intention to use them." For further discussion see *R. v. Pawlicki* [1992] 1 W.L.R. 827, *infra* at para. 3.4.9.

3.4.4   **(iii) Bates v. Bulman**

[1979] 3 All E.R. 170

Bates, B., assaulted A. in a street by slapping and punching him. B. then asked C. to hand him an unopened clasp knife which B. intended to use to injure A. That knife was not made or adapted for use for causing injury. B. received the knife and opened it and he held the knife against A.'s head. The knife was not used, it seems, to cause any injury to A.

B. was charged with a contravention of s.1 of the 1953 Act. After trial B. was convicted and he appealed. On appeal counsel for B. submitted that the nature of the offence in s.1 of the 1953 Act was the carrying and not the use of a weapon. Thus, a person who borrowed from another an article not offensive *per se*, with the immediate intention of using it as an offensive weapon, was not guilty of an offence under s.1(1) for in such a case there was not possession of the weapon for a long enough period to say that the accused had the weapon with him in a public place.

Stocker, J. (at p. 176)

"In my judgment, the facts of this case cannot be distinguished from those in [*Ohlson* v. *Hylton* [1975] 2 All E.R. 490 and *R.* v. *Humphreys* [1977] Crim.L.R. 225] without resort to what, in my view, would be a rather academic and over-analytical approach by making a distinction between an innocent weapon subsequently used with the intention of an assault and which is being carried innocently by the defendant in the case, and a similar article which is acquired either by borrowing from somebody else or fortuitously by being picked up in the street.

"For my part also, it seems to me that the purport of the 1953 Act, as revealed by its long title, is to cover the situation where an accused person, a defendant, has with him and is carrying an offensive weapon intending that it shall be used, if necessary, for offensive purposes. Where an assault in fact takes place, whether it amounts to an assault causing actual bodily harm or a lesser or greater criminal substantive offence, and the only circumstances in which the weapon used is converted or could be converted into an offensive weapon for the purposes of the definition are its use itself in the assault concerned, then an alternative or second charge under the 1953 Act would be more likely to confuse than to resolve the situation.

"Therefore, in my judgment, the real purpose of the 1953 Act is to prevent the carrying of offensive weapons. Their use would almost inevitably be better dealt with by a substantive offence."

Appeal allowed.

(iv) R. v. Russell 3.4.5

(1985) 81 Cr.App.R. 315

A cosh was found in R.'s car. He was charged with a contravention of s.1(1) of the 1953 Act. His defence at trial was that although he had put the cosh under the seat he had forgotten all about it. He was convicted. He appealed on the ground that the trial judge had failed to direct the jury that the onus was on the prosecution to prove that R. had the cosh with him "knowingly."

Jupp, J. (at p. 317)

"Raymond Russell pleaded not guilty at the Inner London Crown Court on an indictment containing two counts of having with him in a public place an offensive weapon.

"On March 27, 1984, he was convicted by the jury on the second count. He now appeals, by leave of the single judge, against that conviction.

"In the first count, the offensive weapon was a knife; in the second count a cosh.

"The Crown's case was that the appellant was stopped by police officers as he drove his car in Evelyn Street, S.E.8. They searched the car and found the knife taped to the inside of the compartment under the dashboard. The cosh consisted of a piece of rubber hose, filled at one end with metal. This they found under the driver's seat.

"The appellant's explanation about the knife was that he had taped it there so it would not rattle about and damage his cassettes. It was not intended as a weapon, but for ordinary use as a tool. This explanation was accepted by the jury, and they acquitted the appellant on Count 1.

"The appeal relates to Count 2, on which the jury convicted.

"The prosecution evidence was that on finding the cosh under the driver's seat, one of the three police officers asked the appellant: 'What's this for then?' According to the police officer the appellant said: 'That's for my protection'. He asked: 'Why have you got it in your car?' and he was told: 'I've had a couple of people come up to me, you know what it's like around here, I just didn't want to get hurt' and [counsel] told you he then said: 'What does a bloke of your size need to carry weapons like that around for?' and he said: 'I know, it's silly'.

"Later at the police station the appellant was questioned by different officers. The appellant, they said, told them he had the cosh 'in case someone has a go at me. Someone's had a go at me a couple of times, and I need to defend myself'. 'Is that why you've got it, to defend yourself?' Answer: 'Yeah, for protection'.

"The defendant gave evidence at the trial. The judge summarised it as follows: '... he told you that he was interested in cars, that he was capable of looking after himself, as he appears to be, and that the circumstances in which he found the cosh was that he was doing repairs to his car. He pulled the carpet up at the back, and he found the cosh underneath, and he said "I didn't think anything about the cosh", he said "but I thought the metal in it might be useful, because it is difficult to get small pieces of metal", and he said "I threw it under the front seat and then", he said, "I forgot about it"'.

"The appellant's version of the police questioning in the street when they found the cosh was that it was the police, not he, who said it was for protection.

"The appellant's version of the interview at the police station was that he did not remember any question being asked him about a cosh, although later on in his evidence he said there was mention of protection, but not by him.

"The nub of the appellant's case is succinctly summarised on p. 26C of the summing-up: '... as far as the cosh was concerned he said, "I never made any of the admissions, never told the police that I was using it for my protection because", he said, "I was never consciously aware of having it in the car ..." He said he realised when he found out what it was, that his purpose in keeping it was because he thought the metal would be useful, and that once he had put it under the driver's seat he forgot all about it and went around driving with it'.

"The charge laid against the appellant was under section 1 of the Prevention of Crime Act 1953, which reads: 'Any person who without lawful authority or reasonable excuse, the proof whereof shall lie on him, has with him in any public place any offensive weapon shall be guilty of an offence'.

"The learned judge listed correctly the matters which had to be proved by the Crown:

(1) That it was in a public place;
(2) That the cosh was an offensive weapon;
(3) That the appellant had it with him;
(4) That he, the appellant, had not proved any lawful authority or reasonable excuse.

"There was no real dispute as to the first two matters, although the judge did leave the second to the jury. What is complained of in the notice of appeal (it is put in three different ways) is that the learned judge did not leave the third matter to the jury as an issue to be decided by them, namely, whether or not the appellant 'had it with him'.

"The judge said (p. 7B): 'Now, it is not denied that the defendant had a cosh with him. Remember what he agrees is that the cosh was something he found, the cosh was something he put under the driver's seat, and that the police officers were telling you the truth when they say that that was where they found it and the circumstances in which they found it, so there is no dispute about those; but the prosecution has to go on, the allegation does go on to say that that cosh, being with him in a public place in a public street, was an offensive weapon'.

"We were referred to the case of CUGULLERE (1961) 45 Cr.App.R. 108; [1961] 1 W.L.R. 858, brought under the same section of the Prevention of Crime Act 1953, in which the Court of Criminal Appeal said, at the bottom of p. 110 and p. 860 respectively: 'This court is clearly of the opinion that the words "has with him in any public place" must mean "knowingly has with him in any public place". If some innocent person has a cosh slipped into his pocket by an escaping rogue, he would not be guilty of having it with him within the meaning of the section, because he would be quite innocent of any knowledge that it had been put into his pocket. In the judgment of this court, the section cannot apply in circumstances such as those. It is, therefore, extremely important in any case under this section for the judge to give a careful direction to the jury on the issue of possession. The first thing the jury have to be satisfied about, and it is always a question for the jury, is whether the accused person knowingly had with him the alleged offensive weapon.'

"The facts in CUGULLERE were that three pick-axe handles were found in the back of a stolen motor van the appellant was driving. His defence was that he had no idea the van had been stolen, and had no idea that the implements were in the back of the van, implying that someone had put them there without his knowledge.

"The appellant's defence in the present case is not that, having had a cosh slipped under his driving seat by some third party, he was innocent of any knowledge that it had been put there. It is that he himself put the cosh under the driving seat, but until the police found and showed it him, he had forgotten all about it. Whether or not the jury would have accepted it, this defence should have been properly left to the jury, but it was not.

"It was submitted on behalf of the Crown in this Court that there is a distinction between 'not knowing' and 'having forgotten'. The appellant, it is said, always knew how he came to put the cosh under the driving seat, although he only recalled it when the police confronted him with the cosh, and asked him to explain it.

"In our judgment, the Court in CUGULLERE, in saying that the words in the statute must be construed as 'knowingly had with him', were not merely dealing with the situation where a defendant has an offensive weapon put within his reach by a stranger without his knowing it. They were applying the general responsibility principle of criminal responsibility which makes it incumbent on the prosecution to prove full *mens rea*. The well-known observations of Lord Reid in *Sweet* v. *Parsley* (1969) 53 Cr.App.R. 221, 225, [1970] A.C. 132, are relevant here: 'It is firmly established by a host of authorities that *mens rea* is an essential ingredient of every offence unless some reason can be found for holding that it is not necessary. It is also firmly established that the fact that other sections of the Act expressly require *mens rea*, for example because they contain the word "knowingly", is not in itself sufficient to justify a decision that a section which is silent as to *mens rea* creates an absolute offence. In the absence of a clear indication in the Act that an offence is intended to be an absolute offence, it is necessary to go outside the Act and examine all relevant circumstances in order to establish that this must have been the intention of Parliament. I say "must have been" because it is a universal principle that if a penal provision is reasonably capable of two interpretations, that interpretation which is most favourable to the accused must be adopted'.

"It would in our judgment be wrong to hold that a man knowingly has a weapon with him if his forgetfulness of its existence or presence in his car is so complete as to amount to ignorance that it is there at all. This is not a defence which juries would in the ordinary way be very likely to accept, but if it is raised it should be left to them for their decision.

"In this case it was not, and having regard to their verdict on Count 1 we cannot speculate on what conclusion they would have reached if it had been. We accordingly feel bound to allow this appeal, and quash the appellant's conviction on Count 2."

Appeal allowed.

NOTE
   The decision in *R.* v. *Russell* was *per incuriam* and it must be read in the context of *R.* v. *McCalla*, *infra* at para. 3.4.8.

3.4.6   (v) Wood v. Commissioner of Police of the Metropolis

[1986] 1 W.L.R. 796

Two police officers went to W.'s house to deal with a domestic dispute but were refused entry by W. who slammed the door shut, breaking the glass in the door panel. He then lunged at the officers with a piece of broken glass.

W. was convicted in the magistrates' court of being armed with an offensive weapon with intent to commit an arrestable offence contrary to s.4 of the Vagrancy Act 1824. He appealed to the Crown Court. That Court held that the piece of glass was an offensive weapon and dismissed the appeal. W. then appealed to the Court of Appeal (Criminal Division).

Nolan, J. (at p. 798)

"This is an appeal by way of case stated against a decision of the Knightsbridge Crown Court given on 10 February 1984. By that decision the Crown Court dismissed the appeal of the defendant against his conviction at the Camberwell Green Magistrates' Court on 12 May 1983 upon two charges of assaulting a police officer in the execution of his duty, contrary to section 51(1) of the Police Act 1964 and one charge of being armed with an offensive weapon, viz., a piece of broken glass, with intent to commit an arrestable offence at 61, Grove Hill Road, London S.E.5, contrary to section 4 of the Vagrancy Act 1824. The charges against the defendant arose out of an incident involving the defendant and two police officers at the door of 61, Grove Hill Road which was his home. Having reheard the case by way of appeal, the Crown Court found the following facts:

'The officers had been called to 61, Grove Hill Road on the basis that there was a domestic disturbance. They heard raised voices including a female voice and knocked at the door which was opened by the defendant who appeared aggressive and under the influence of drink. He said "I don't want you [people] here," and closed the door. The officers knocked again at the door, which this time was opened by an elderly lady who was almost immediately pushed out of the way by the defendant. He then slammed the door shut and in so doing caused the glass in the door panel to break into pieces. While the door was open one of the officers heard the sounds of a distressed female. Before the officers could take further action, the defendant came out of the house and lunged at the officers with a piece of the broken glass approximately six to seven inches long and three inches wide, leading the police officers to think that he intended to attack them with it. This constituted an assault. We found that the officers were acting in good faith in the execution of their duty in coming onto the defendant's property in order to investigate an alleged breach of the peace; that they had reasonable grounds to believe that such a breach had just occurred or was occurring;

that the defendant himself was a party to the disturbance, and that they had reasonable grounds for apprehending that such a breach was about to reoccur or continue. Nothing the defendant said or did terminated the implied licence of the officers to be on the premises: they were entitled to investigate the matter, and events had happened too quickly after the second knock for them to leave.'

"It was contended by the defendant before the Crown Court, first, that the officers were not acting in the execution of their duty, as the defendant had revoked their implied licence to enter his premises and, secondly, that the piece of broken glass in the defendant's possession could not be an offensive weapon within the meaning of section 4 of the Vagrancy Act 1824. The Crown Court rejected both of these contentions, saying:

'We were of the opinion that the officers had told the truth as to what had happened and that the defendant and his witnesses had not told the truth. We were satisfied that there had been a domestic disturbance, that the defendant had been drinking, and that the officers were fully justified in going onto the premises. We were of the opinion that the defendant had not revoked the officers' implied licence after the first knock, and matters after the second knock happened too quickly for the licence to be revoked so that the officers never became trespassers. We were of the opinion that the piece of glass was an offensive weapon within the meaning of the Act.'

"The Crown Court dismissed the appeal against conviction and as there was no appeal against sentence the fines of £50 upon each of the two charges of assaulting a police officer in the execution of his duty, the £30 upon the charge under section 4 of the Vagrancy Act 1824, and the order to pay £120 towards the costs of the prosecutor imposed at the magistrates' court were allowed to stand. The question of law for this court, shortly stated, is whether the Crown Court acted rightly in rejecting the contentions of the defendant to which I have referred. At an early stage in his argument on behalf of the defendant, [counsel for the appellant] accepted that the first of his contentions could not be sustained on the basis that the defendant had revoked the implied licence of the officers to come upon his property. As Watkins L.J. observed, having been called to the house and having reason to anticipate a breach of the peace, the officers were entitled, if not bound, to enter the property in the execution of their duty, with or without the licence of the owner. [Counsel for the appellant] then sought to make good his contention on the footing that the officers had remained on the property for longer than was needed to investigate any possible breach of the peace. But this submission derives no support from the findings of fact in the stated case. On the contrary, those findings, and the conclusions of the Crown Court about the sequence and pace of events, seems to me to make it clear that the officers remained upon the premises for no longer than the execution of their duty required. I would therefore reject the first contention of the defendant.

"The second contention of the defendant carries greater weight. Section 4 of the Vagrancy Act 1824, as amended, covers a wide range of offences. It provides that every person convicted of one of those offences

> 'shall be deemed a rogue and vagabond, within the true intent and meaning of this Act; and … it shall be lawful for any justice of the peace to commit such offender … to [imprisonment] for any time not exceeding three calendar months;'

"Most of the offences to which the section applies are of a kind which one would associate with wandering or vagrant offenders who are to be deemed to be rogues and vagabonds. The offence with which the defendant is charged, however, does not, in express terms at least, fall within that category. It comprises

> 'every person being armed with any gun, pistol, hanger, cutlass, bludgeon, or other offensive weapon, or having upon him or her any instrument, with intent to commit an arrestable offence.'

"[Counsel for the appellant] relied upon the ejusdem generis rule in support of his argument that the piece of broken glass was not an offensive weapon within the meaning of the section. He submitted, in effect, that the specific articles mentioned in the section (that is to say, gun, pistol etc.) were all articles made or adapted for use for the purpose of causing injury, or in other words were offensive weapons per se. A piece of glass accidentally broken did not fall within that genus and so could not be covered by the words 'or other offensive weapon.' Nor did it constitute an 'instrument.' [Counsel] for the prosecutor submitted that the section covered the possession of any weapon or instrument with the intent to commit an arrestable offence, in this case assault. On this view of the matter, the piece of broken glass clearly came within the section, if not as an offensive weapon then as an instrument, because of the defendant's intent to use it in assaulting the police officers. The word 'instrument' in the ordinary dictionary sense bears a wide and general meaning and includes any article intended for use in the commission of the relevant arrestable offence. It will be apparent that where the relevant arrestable offence is assault [counsel's] submission involves construing the material words in section 4 in the same sense as the definition of offensive weapon in section 1(4) of the Prevention of Crime Act 1953, that is to say, 'any article made or adapted for use for causing injury to the person, or intended by the person having it with him for such use by him.' [Counsel] accepted that this was so. He observed that the defendant could not have been charged under section 1(1) of the Act of 1953, because the incident did not occur in a public place. He submitted that section 4 of the Act of 1824 fulfilled the same role in relation to offences on private property as that of section 1(1) of the Act of 1953 in relation to public places and stated that section 4 was commonly relied upon by those instructing him for that purpose.

"At first sight, it seems remarkable that a prohibition against the carrying of weapons enacted in 1824 in the context of a Vagrancy Act should find its current fulfilment in the realm of offences on private property and should make it possible for a householder's behaviour upon his own doorstep to result in his being deemed both a rogue and a vagabond. The part of section 4 under which the defendant was charged is not, however, the only part whose terms can be applied to offences upon private property. For example, the section also applies to

> 'every person pretending or professing to tell fortunes, or using any subtle craft, means, or device, by palmistry or otherwise, to deceive and impose on any of His Majesty's subjects; ...'

"These words fell to be considered by the Exchequer Division in *Monck* v. *Hilton* (1877) 2 Ex.D. 268. The defendant in that case had been convicted of offences covered by the words 'by palmistry or otherwise' which had occurred in a private house in Huddersfield. It was proved on behalf of the defendant that he had had rooms at a house in Bristol for the previous four years and it was contended that the Vagrancy Act 1824 could not apply to him because 'it was intended to apply to gipsies and other wandering and homeless vagabonds.' Rejecting this contention, Cleasby B. said, at p. 277:

> 'Palmistry was at one time practised by gipsies and persons leading a vagabond life, and the legislation was directed against them. But the idea of leading a wandering and vagabond life is not now at all an ingredient in the description of a rogue and vagabond, as is obvious by reading the enumeration in section 4. The statute 5 Geo. 4, c. 83'—that is, the Vagrancy Act 1824—'repeals all the former statutes relating to rogues and vagabonds, and forms itself the

legislation on the subject, and enacts in substance that by doing certain things, or neglecting certain duties, a man shall be in the same predicament as rogues and vagabonds and dealt with as such. Whatever an offender's position may be under other Acts of Parliament not relating to rogues and vagabonds, if he comes within the enumeration in section 4 he is properly punished as a rogue and vagabond.'

"In more recent years charges of indecent exposure, to which section 4 also applies, have commonly been brought in respect of offences committed on private premises by their occupiers. It is true that this is only possible as the result of the repeal by section 42 of the Criminal Justice Act 1925 of words in section 4 which had confined the offence to acts occurring in a public place: see *Ford* v. *Falcone* [1971] 1 W.L.R. 809. But the Divisional Court in that case clearly did not regard the general context of the Vagrancy Act 1824 as affecting the meaning of the charging words in their amended form. The original wording of the part of section 4 under which the defendant in the present case was charged began:

> 'every person having in his or her custody or possession any picklock, key, crow, jack, bit or other implement, with intent feloniously to break into any dwelling house, warehouse, coach house, stable or outbuilding or being armed ...'

"The words between 'every person' and 'being armed' might have supported the proposition that this part of the section was concerned only with itinerant offenders, but those words were repealed by section 33(3) of and Part 1 of Schedule 3 to the Theft Act 1968. Consequently, in the present case, as in *Ford* v. *Falcone* [1971] 1 W.L.R. 809 there is nothing in the language of the relevant part of the section in its amended form to prevent it from applying to those occupying or present upon private property. In the light of *Monck* v. *Hilton*, 2 Ex.D. 268 I regard it as settled law, whatever first impressions might otherwise suggest, that section 4 even as originally enacted was confined to vagrants in the ordinary sense of that word. Further, it seems to me clear from that case and from *Ford* v. *Falcone* ... that the section in its currently amended form can properly be applied to an occupier of premises in respect of offences on those premises, if he falls within the language of the relevant charging provision.

"It is interesting to note that in 1976 a working party set up by the Home Office recommended that the part of section 4 under which the defendant in the present case is charged should be repealed. While doing so, however, they cited the argument of two commentators that 'without a provision of this kind the police could find themselves in difficult circumstances, e.g. if a weapon is produced in the course of a domestic dispute': see the Report of the Working Party on Vagrancy and Street Offences, May 1976. The working party felt nonetheless that the relevant part of the section could safely be repealed on the ground that the law of assault probably provided an adequate remedy against domestic disturbances. In the circumstances of the present case at least, I should be inclined to share that view. The section remains unrepealed, however, and the issue raised in the present case remains to be resolved. I, for my part, would resolve the general issue of construction on the lines submitted by [counsel for the appellant]. If the section is intended by the legislature to be applicable to domestic disturbances, then it would naturally embrace not only offensive weapons per se but also the numerous articles commonly found in private houses, such as knives and glasses, which can be used to inflict injury. Acknowledging the force of [counsel for the appellant's] contention upon the ejusdem generis rules, I would construe the relevant words 'other offensive weapon' as being confined to articles made or adapted for use for causing injury to the person, but would construe the words 'any instrument' as including any article intended by the person having it with him for such use. In other words, I would interpret the relevant words as producing the same result mutatis mutandis as section 1(4) of the Prevention of Crime Act 1953 ...

"But was the defendant rightly convicted? The Crown Court upheld the conviction on the basis of the defendant 'being armed with' an offensive weapon, as distinct from 'having upon him' an instrument. The words 'having upon him' are to be compared with 'has with him' in section 1(1) of the Prevention of Crime Act 1953. In my judgment, there is nothing to choose between these three phrases; each is to the same effect. It follows that in the relevant part of section 4 of the Act of 1824, no less than in section 1(1) of the Act of 1953, what is contemplated is not the use of a weapon or other article for offensive purposes but the premeditated carrying of the article for those purposes: see *Ohlson v. Hylton* [1975] 1 W.L.R. 724. In the last sentence of his judgment in that case Lord Widgery C.J. said, at p. 730:

> 'To support a conviction under the Act the prosecution must show that the defendant was carrying or otherwise equipped with the weapon, and had the intention to use it offensively before any occasion for its actual use had arisen.'

This point was not argued before the Crown Court. I have considered whether the case should be remitted to the Crown Court for further findings upon it, but the existing findings seem to me to be sufficiently clear to make remission unnecessary. It seems plain that the defendant's seizure and use of the piece of broken glass, like the seizure and use of the hammer in *Ohlson v. Hylton* [1975] 1 W.L.R. 724, were all part and parcel of the assault and were not premeditated. Therefore, the charge against him under section 4 of the Vagrancy Act 1824 is not made out. For these reasons I would dismiss the appeal of the defendant against his convictions under section 51(1) of the Police Act 1964, but would allow his appeal against his conviction under section 4 of the Vagrancy Act 1824."

Watkins, L.J. (at p. 803)

"I agree. This is an appeal without any merit whatsoever. Police officers called to the scene of domestic disputes have a difficult and often delicate duty to discharge. This is especially so when they have somehow to calm a wholly irresponsible, crude and violent party to it such as this defendant undoubtedly was in order not only to restore peace but to remove the fear felt by, as is more often than not, his wife or the woman with whom he lives.

"The issues involved here are entirely technical but nevertheless of importance. The question as to whether or not in any given circumstances a defendant had with him or upon him or was armed with an offensive weapon or instrument is essentially one of fact, providing it is appreciated that the relevant law involves the notion of a premeditated carrying of a weapon or instrument and not a sudden seizure and use of something readily to hand. There may be little time involved in the carrying of an offensive weapon or instrument in order to offend. In that event it is from the whole of the other circumstances that the court may be entitled to find premeditation. It is possible that the findings of fact here—they have not been fully explored—could not have been disturbed if the justices and the Crown Court had properly directed themselves in law. That they do not appear to have done. Accordingly, I too see no alternative but to quash the conviction under section 4 of the Vagrancy Act 1824. That conviction will be quashed. As to the other conviction, the appeal is dismissed."

Appeal allowed in part.

(vi) Glendinning v. Guild 3.4.7

1987 S.C.C.R. 304

Glendinning [G.] was seen in a public place. The policemen who saw him also saw him wave a flail about. That flail was

formed with two pieces of lightweight wooden stick joined by
a chain.

G. was on his way to a class in the martial arts. His training in
martial arts involved the use of such items. G. had purchased the
item at a specialist shop two years earlier. The flail is an offensive
weapon *per se*.

G. was charged with a contravention of s.1(1) of the 1953 Act.
The sheriff took the view that although G. had an offensive weapon
in a public place with a reasonable excuse, the fact that he waved
it about and utilised it in some way extricated him from the category
of being a person with a reasonable excuse. G. was convicted and
he appealed.

Lord Justice-Clerk (Ross) (at p. 306)
    "[Counsel for the appellant] has drawn attention to the fact
that although there is no express finding to this effect it is plain
from the terms of the sheriff's note that he concluded that the
appellant had a reasonable excuse for having the flail with him.
In the findings he has held that the appellant at the time was on
his way to a class in the martial arts and that the flail ... was
used in the practice of the martial arts. Reading the findings
and the note together it is accordingly plain that the sheriff was
satisfied as matter of fact that the appellant at the material time
had a reasonable excuse for having the flail with him. That being
so we are clearly of the opinion that the offence under section
1(1) could not have been committed by him. The evidence
showed that he had the flail with him with reasonable excuse
and that being so he could not be convicted of the contravention
of section 1(1).

    "The learned sheriff in his note goes on to explain that at the
material time the appellant was apparently waving the flail about
and utilising it in some way in this public place and the argument
which was advanced before the sheriff by the Crown was that the
fact that he was using the weapon in this way took him out of the
category of being a person with a reasonable excuse. With that
argument we cannot agree. Section 1(1) is concerned with the
possession of an offensive weapon in a public place. It is not
concerned with the use of such a weapon in that place. If the
appellant did utilise the weapon and wave it about as the sheriff
suggests he might, of course, thereby be committing another offence
but no other offence has been libelled against him and the only
charge which was before the sheriff was the contravention of section
1(1) of the Act of 1953."

Appeal allowed.

(vii) R. v. McCalla 3.4.8

(1988) 152 J.P. 481

A cosh was found in M.'s car by policemen. The prosecution alleged that M. had told the police that he kept it to use to defend himself. M. gave evidence at his trial and denied that. He said that he had told the truth to the police, namely that he had picked up the cosh on the building site where he worked and that he had put it in the car about a month before and had forgotten about it. M. was convicted and appealed.

May, L.J. (at p. 482)

"On November 27, 1987 in the Crown Court at Inner London Sessions House the appellant was convicted after a three-day trial on count 2, attempted wounding, count 3, carrying an offensive weapon, and count 4, reckless driving. He was sentenced respectively to 12 months' imprisonment, three months' imprisonment consecutive, three months' imprisonment concurrent and to be disqualified from driving for three years, a total sentence of 15 months' imprisonment. He appeals against conviction on the count of carrying an offensive weapon on a point of law referred to the full court by the single Judge, who so determined it to be and therefore needing no leave.

"The incident giving rise to the offences began when plainclothes police officers, travelling in an unmarked Fiesta motor car, remonstrated with the appellant, who had double-parked his Saab motor car in a side street off Stockwell Road in London. The Fiesta was able to get past, but with difficulty.

"Unfortunately, instead of leaving the matter there, as would have been wiser, the appellant, who alleged during the trial that the police officers had made racially offensive remarks, followed the Fiesta, overtaking another vehicle in Stockwell Road as he went, coming in behind the Fiesta and then bumping it twice from behind. He overtook the Fiesta, passed a pedestrian crossing on the wrong side of the road, and went into a side turning, causing an oncoming car to swerve. He then stopped his car at the next junction with the Fiesta alongside it.

"The police officer who had been in the passenger's seat of the Fiesta went over to the driver's window of the Saab, told the driver, who was the appellant, that they were police officers and to stay where he was, and tried to take the ignition key from the Saab. The appellant pushed the door against the officer and produced a knife. He moved his hand holding the knife in what was described as a slashing movement towards the officer's face and shouted: 'I don't joke, I'm going to kill.' The officer fell backwards to avoid the knife. The appellant then shut the door and accelerated off once again. He was arrested not long afterwards on a nearby estate. He was taken to the police station with the Saab. It was not disputed that when that vehicle was searched there was found in the glove compartment a cosh, the subject of the count with which this appeal is concerned. The appellant accepted that it was in the car. According to the prosecution, when he was asked why it was there he replied: 'Well, some of my mates have been attacked before and I don't want that to happen to me.' He was asked: 'If someone attacked you, would you use the cosh?', and he said: 'Yes, but only to defend myself.'

"During his evidence the appellant denied that the conversation had taken place. He said that he had told the police the truth, which was that he had picked up the cosh on a building site where he worked, that he had put it in the car about a month before the incident with the Fiesta, and that he had forgotten about it.

"Against that background two criticisms are made of the Judge's summing-up. First, it is submitted that there was a misdirection on the question whether or not the appellant had had the cosh with him for the purposes of the relevant statute in the context that, although he had picked up the cosh on the building site, at the time when he was stopped by the police officers and the cosh was found he had forgotten that it was in the car.

"The Judge's summing-up on this point (p. 9) reads:

'Did the defendant have it with him? That is a question for you to answer. You may come to the conclusion that if, as is not in dispute, it was in the glove compartment of his Saab motor car, then when he was driving the motor car he certainly had it with him, in the same way that he had everything else in the car with him. But that begs one question which arises in this case. What is the significance, if you accept it, of the defendant's evidence to the effect that he had forgotten that the cosh was in the glove compartment? Members of the jury, I am going to direct you as a matter of law that if you come to the conclusion—which, as I say, is not in dispute—that the defendant himself put the cosh into the glove compartment, he had it with him at the time he put it in, and he continued to have it with him whenever he was in the car, whether or not he remembered it was there. Having something with you in this legal sense does not depend upon the powers of memory of the person who put the article where it was. Possession of the article, if I can use that particular expression, does not come and go as memory revives or fades. It would be ridiculous to say, as he drives along the road, so, if he remembers that he has got the cosh in the glove compartment, he is guilty of an offence, and if at the next traffic lights he forgets, he ceases to be guilty of the offence, and then becomes guilty again next time he thinks about the cosh. That would be absurd.'

"It has been submitted that that was a misdirection in respects to which we will come in a moment, and that the Judge ought not to have withdrawn from the jury consideration of whether the appellant knew at the material time that he had the cosh with him.

"The other aspect of the summing-up which is criticized is the direction on reasonable excuse, viz.:

'There is one other requirement' (under the statute). 'If the defendant himself proves that he had some lawful authority or reasonable excuse for having the offensive weapon with him, he is to be acquitted. I say if he proves it, because the Act of Parliament says that the proof of that particular lawful authority or reasonable excuse lies on him. It does not mean that he has to prove it as the prosecution have to prove, beyond reasonable doubt or so that you are sure. It means that he has to prove lawful authority or reasonable excuse on the balance of probabilities; in other words, it is more likely than not that facts exist which constitute lawful authority or reasonable excuse. I am going to direct you again as a matter of law that there is no evidence before you which could justify you in coming to the conclusion that the defendant has proved lawful authority or reasonable excuse.'

"Briefly, the contention on behalf of the appellant is that his absence of recollection of the presence of the cosh in the glove compartment could be a reasonable excuse for the appellant having the offensive weapon with him, if indeed he had, and that in any event that ought to have been left to the jury; further, that the Judge was wrong to say that there was no evidence before the jury upon which they could come to the conclusion that the defendant had proved lawful authority or reasonable excuse.

"Consideration of those two points—which if we may say so have been advanced to the court succinctly, cogently and attractively by [counsel] on the appellant's behalf—involves the examination of at least four earlier decisions. We start with *R. v. Cugullere* (1961) 125 J.P. 414; [1961] 45 Cr.App.R. 108. The prosecution there was under s.1(1) of the Prevention of Crime Act in respect of an offensive weapon. On the facts the appellant was found driving a stolen motor van in the back of which there were three pickaxe handles which the prosecution said were offensive weapons. The appellant's defence was that he did not know, and never had known, that the implements were in the back of the van. At the trial the chairman directed the jury that the appellant had been in possession of the implements and that it was for him to prove that he had a lawful excuse for that possession. "When the matter came before the Court of Criminal Appeal the judgment was delivered by Salmon, J. (as he then was). The only passage that need be read is at p. 110 where, having cited the relevant provisions of the 1953 Act, the Judge continued:

> 'This court is clearly of the opinion that the words "has with him in any public place" must mean "knowingly has with him in any public place". If some innocent person has a cosh slipped into his pocket by an escaping rogue, he would not be guilty of having it with him within the meaning of the section, because he would be quite innocent of any knowledge that it had been put into his pocket. In the judgment of this court, the section cannot apply in circumstances such as those. It is, therefore, extremely important in any case under this section for the Judge to give a careful direction to the jury on the issue of possession. The first thing the jury have to be satisfied about, and it is always a question for the jury, is whether the accused person knowingly had with him the alleged offensive weapon.'

"In that case the appeal was allowed and the conviction quashed. "Chronologically we mention *R. v. Buswell* (1972) 136 J.P. 141; [1972] 1 All E.R. 75. It is, we think, unnecessary to deal in any detail with the facts. They concerned the alleged unlawful possession of drugs. The judgment of the court on appeal was delivered by Phillimore, L.J. A substantial portion of it appears in the judgment in the later case of *R. v. Martindale* (1986) 150 J.P. 548; [1986] 84 Cr.App.R. 32 to which we will refer in a moment, and accordingly that part need not be quoted here. We take in *Buswell* merely on the way, as it were, because chronologically it comes in that place. "Then there was *R. v. Russell* [1985] 81 Cr.App.R. 315, which was concerned with an alleged offensive weapon and having it contrary to s.1(1) of the 1953 Act. Police officers stopped a car which was being driven by the appellant. Inside it there was a knife taped to the inside of the compartment under the dashboard, and a cosh consisting of a piece of rubber hose filled at one end with metal was found under the driver's seat. The appellant was charged with possessing both of those offensive weapons in a public place, one count relating to the knife and the other to the cosh. He was acquitted on the count relating to the knife and convicted on that relating to the cosh. His defence to the second count had been that, although he had put the cosh under the seat, he had forgotten all about it. On appeal it was contended that the trial Judge had failed to direct the jury that the onus was on the prosecution to prove that the appellant had knowingly had the cosh with him.

"In the reserved judgment of this court in *Russell*, delivered by Jupp, J. reference was made to *Cugullere* (*supra*). The court quoted the passage from that judgment which we have already read. At the foot of p. 318 of the report Jupp, J. said:

> 'In our judgment, the court in *Cugullere*, in saying that the words of the statute must be construed as "knowingly had with him", were not merely dealing with the situation where a defendant has an offensive weapon put within his reach by a stranger without his knowing it. They were applying the general principle of criminal responsibility which makes it incumbent on the prosecution to prove full *mens rea*.'

"In those circumstances the court in that case allowed the appeal and quashed the conviction on the second count, relating to the cosh.

"Finally, we turn to the most recent decision in this quartet of cases, that is, *Martindale*, which we have already mentioned. There the allegation was made under the Misuse of Drugs Act and the offence charged was possession of drugs. The facts were that during a police operation the applicant (as he then was) was stopped by police officers and a very small quantity of cannabis resin was found in a wallet in his pocket. When he was interviewed at the police station he said that the cannabis resin had been given to him in Canada two years previously, that he did not smoke cannabis, and that he had forgotten that it was in his wallet. He was charged with contravening s.5(2) of the Misuse of Drugs Act 1971.

"At the trial the Judge ruled *inter alia* that, as the applicant knew what the substance was and had kept it in his possession, even though he had forgotten its existence he had no defence to the charge. On that ruling the applicant changed his plea to one of guilty and was convicted. He applied for leave to appeal on the ground that there could be no possession of the wallet containing the drug if he, the possessor of it, had completely forgotten that he had it.

"It is unnecessary to read the whole of the judgment of the Lord Chief Justice in that case, but it is appropriate to read a substantial part of it, particularly at p. 33:

> 'In the judgment of this court that argument (that lack of memory or knowledge negatives possession) is fallacious. It

is true that a man does not necessarily possess every article which he may have in his pocket. If for example some evil minded person secretly slips a portion of cannabis resin into the pocket of another without the other's knowledge, the other is not in law in possession of the cannabis. That scarcely needs stating. But the present situation is different. Here the applicant himself put the cannabis into his wallet knowing what it was and put the wallet into his pocket. In our judgment, subject to the authorities, to which reference will have to be made in a moment, he remained in possession, even though his memory of the presence of the drug had faded or disappeared altogether. Possession does not depend upon the alleged possessor's powers of memory. Nor does possession come and go as memory revives or fails. If it were to do so, a man with a poor memory would be acquitted, he with the good memory would be convicted.'

"In the summing-up in the instant case one can hear the echo of that part of the judgment of the Lord Chief Justice in *Martindale*.

"The Lord Chief Justice then went on to refer to *Russell* (*supra*), which we have already quoted, and to the submissions on behalf of the Crown; because it was difficult to see how the contention in *Martindale* could be upheld if the decision in *Russell* were to stand.

"The Lord Chief Justice continued:

'We do not pause to consider the matter on that basis, because what was not drawn to the attention of the court in *Russell* was an earlier decision of this court, namely, *Buswell*. It is only necessary for me to read a passage on p. 78 and p. 67 of the respective reports to illustrate how, had the decision been brought to the attention of the court in *Russell*, the decision in *Russell* would almost certainly have gone the other way.'

"The Lord Chief Justice then quoted a substantial passage from the judgment of Phillimore, LJ, in *Buswell*, to which we have in passing referred. It is unnecessary to set it out in full. However, the last few sentences of the relevant passage merit quotation, viz.:

'But if you have got it in your custody and you put it in some safe place, and then forget that you have got it, and discover a year or two later, when you happen to look in that particular receptacle that it is still there, it seems to this court idle to suggest that during those two years it has not been in your possession. It has been there under your hand and control. If it has not been in your possession, in whose possession has it been? Presumably it has not been in a state of limbo.'

"The Lord Chief Justice continued the substantive judgment in *Martindale* in these terms:

'As I say, had that judgment been brought to the attention of the court in *Russell*, the decision in that case would almost certainly have been different. In any event, as far as the two cases are inconsistent, we follow the earlier case, namely, *Buswell*. It is in accordance with the views which we ourselves have formed. In our judgment the Judge in the present case was right to take the course which he did, and this application is accordingly refused.'

"As to the law as stated in those four cases one comment must first be made. In those concerning drugs the consideration is that of possession. In those concerning offensive weapons it is having them in a public place. To have something with one necessarily requires, we think, closer contact, as it were, than mere possession. Every case of 'having' is one of 'possessing', but it does not necessarily follow that every case of 'possessing' is one of 'having' within the meaning of the relevant statutory provisions. However, for the purpose of the instant case, and having regard to the earlier decisions to which we have referred, in our view the relevant considerations as to recollection and forgetfulness are the same.

"Having said that, we are driven to the conclusion that the decisions in *Buswell* and *Martindale* cannot be reconciled with the decision in *Russell*. As the Lord Chief Justice pointed out in *Martindale*, *Russell* was decided without the court having been referred to *Buswell*. We think that we must hold that, as in effect the Lord Chief Justice said in *Martindale*, the decision in *Russell* was given *per incuriam*. This does not detract from the authority of *Cugullere (supra)*, which on its facts is clearly distinguishable, in that from the outset there had been no knowledge of possession. It was not a matter of possession having been gained and forgotten; the pickaxe handles had been put into the back of the van, unknown to the appellant, by a third party. The situation in which a packet of cannabis resin is slipped secretly into the pocket of the defendant by another was adverted to in *Martindale*. The decision in *Cugullere* can therefore stand perfectly properly and easily alongside *Buswell* and *Martindale*.

"We think that the basic principle underlying those cases is that once one has or possesses something, be it an offensive weapon or a drug, one continues to have or possess it until one does something to rid oneself of having or possessing it; that merely to have forgotten that one has possession of it is not sufficient to exclude continuing to have or possess it. As Phillimore, L.J. said in *Buswell*, there is no limbo into which the article can go if recollection dims.

"Accordingly, in our judgment there was no misdirection by the Judge in the instant case about the appellant's knowledge that he had the cosh with him. There was no need to leave to the jury the question whether he had forgotten that he had it with him. He knew that he had it, because he had picked it up at the building site and continued to have it with him in his car; and by the statutory provisions he had it with him in a public place.

"As to the second alleged misdirection, we are quite satisfied that to have forgotten that one had an offensive weapon in the car that one is driving is not in itself a reasonable excuse under the Act. But when such forgetfulness is coupled with particular circumstances relating to the original acquisition of the article the combination of the original acquisition and the subsequent forgetfulness of possessing it may, given sufficient facts, be a reasonable excuse for having the offensive weapon with one.

"For instance, to take an example that was adverted to in the course of argument: if someone driving along a road where earlier there had been a demonstration were to see and pick up a police truncheon which had obviously been dropped there and were to put it in the boot of his car, intending to take it to the nearest police station, and then were to be stopped within a few minutes, he would have a reasonable excuse for having the truncheon with him in the boot of the car. If he were to forget that it was there and two years later were to be stopped and the truncheon were then found in the boot of the car, the circumstances of the original acquisition of the truncheon and the time for which that person had completely forgotten that it was in the car could constitute a reasonable excuse for possessing the truncheon two years after its acquisition.

"Thus we do not think that here was a misdirection by the Judge on the question of reasonable excuse, as contended by [counsel]. In our judgment, the summing-up was full, it covered every aspect of the case that required to be dealt with, and no criticism can be made of it."

Appeal dismissed.

NOTE
For further discussion on forgetfulness, see *R. v. Wright* [1992] Crim.L.R. 596 and *D.P.P. v. Gregson* (1993) 96 Cr.App.R. 240.

3.4.9   **(viii) R. v. Pawlicki and Swindell**

[1992] 1 W.L.R. 827

The appellant P. drove to an auctioneer's showroom, parked outside, locked the car, leaving three sawn-off shotguns inside, and went into the auction room and stood a few feet from the appellant S. Police officers, who had been alerted to the possibility of a robbery, arrested both appellants. A search of P.'s car revealed the sawn-off shotguns. Both appellants were convicted, *inter alia*, of having firearms with intent to commit an indictable offence, namely, robbery, contrary to s.18(1) of the Firearms Act 1968. *Held*, dismissing the appeals, that "to have with him a firearm" within the meaning of s.18(1) of the Firearms Act 1968 imported an element of propinquity which was not required for mere possession; that in considering that element the emphasis was on the accessibility of the guns to those embarking on committing an indictable offence rather than on the exact distance between them and the guns; that, in the circumstances, the guns were readily accessible to the appellants at the time they were about to commit a robbery; and that, therefore, there were no grounds for interfering with the conviction for an offence under s.18(1) of the Act of 1968.

Steyn L.J. (at p. 828)

"At the hearing of these appeals by two men against their conviction an important question arose as to the meaning of the words 'have with him a firearm' in s.18 of the Firearms Act 1968. That was why we reserved judgment. Section 18(1) of the Act of 1968, in so far as it is relevant, provides: 'It is an offence for a person to have with him a firearm ... with intent to commit an indictable offence ...'

"The two appellants were jointly charged, on the basis that they had been involved in a joint enterprise to commit an offence under s.18(1). The particulars of the offence asserted that the appellants:

'on 20 October 1988 had with them firearms namely three shortened double-barrelled shotguns with intent to commit an indictable offence, namely robbery.'

"That was count 1 on the indictment. Count 2 arises from the same events and involves an additional charge that the appellants possessed shortened shotguns without a certificate, contrary to ss. 1 and 4 of the Act of 1968. The latter count is only of marginal relevance to this appeal.

"On 20 February 1990 in the Crown Court at Newcastle-upon-Tyne the appellants were convicted of both offences. The appellant Pawlicki was sentenced to eight years' imprisonment on the first count and three years' imprisonment on the second count. The appellant Swindell was sentenced to five years' on the first count and two years' imprisonment on the second count.

"The prosecution case was that Pawlicki and Swindell agreed to commit a robbery at the premises of a firm of auctioneers in

Bradford on 20 October 1988. Pawlicki drove a car to the auctioneers' premises and parked outside. There were three sawn-off shotguns in the car. He locked the car, leaving the shotguns in the car. He then went into the auction room. The police had been alerted to the possibility of a robbery and there were five police officers in the building. Pawlicki was seen standing a few feet from Swindell. The police arrested both men. They searched the car in which Pawlicki arrived and they searched the homes of both men. What the police found during these searches eventually became the foundation of the prosecution case.

"The case against Pawlicki was strong. The police evidence was that in the car, in which Pawlicki drove to the auction room, they found three sawn-off shotguns, two sets of handcuffs, masking tape and a keyring with seven keys. When Pawlicki was asked questions in interview about the guns he said that he did not want to answer questions. Pawlicki testified in his own defence. He denied that the weapons and other items found in the car were a robbery kit. He said it was a chance collection. The guns he had for the purposes of restoration and resale. The handcuffs were intended to liven up sexual intercourse with his wife. The masking tape he had used to dress a wound to his dog.

"The prosecution case against Swindell was as follows. He was a friend and associate in legitimate dealings with Pawlicki. He had been in the company of Pawlicki shortly before 20 October. On 20 October he was seen in the auction room next to Pawlicki shortly before the arrests. The search of Swindell's flat revealed in a locked cupboard two shotguns: one 16-bore and the other 20-bore. In Pawlicki's car the police found a key which could unlock the cupboard in Swindell's flat where the two guns were found. In Pawlicki's house and car the police found cartridges for a 20-bore shotgun. These cartridges could be fired in the 20-bore shotgun found in Swindell's flat. The police found a key on Swindell which fitted the handcuffs found in Pawlicki's car. The prosecution relied on inferences to be drawn from Swindell's statement in interview that he did not recognise the keys found in Pawlicki's car which fitted a number of locks in Swindell's flat. The prosecution argued that Swindell was lying to hide his involvement. Swindell did not testify. His account had to be gathered from his interview. When he was interviewed he denied knowledge of the guns in Pawlicki's car and he denied involvement in a planned robbery. But he repeatedly refused to answer questions on matters of detail.

"On behalf of both appellants it was submitted that the judge erred in allowing evidence to be led of the two shotguns found in a cupboard in Swindell's flat. The evidence, together with the evidence that Pawlicki had a key to unlock the cupboard, as well as ammunition for one shotgun, was logically probative of a link in respect of guns between the two appellants. It was relevant and admissible evidence. The alternative submission was that the judge should, in the exercise of his discretion, have excluded this evidence on the basis that the prejudicial effect of the evidence outweighed its probative value. In our judgment this submission is not well founded. In any event, there is no basis on which this court could interfere with the exercise of the trial judge's discretion on this particular point.

"Counsel for Swindell submitted to the trial judge at the end of the prosecution case that there was no evidence, or insufficient evidence, of a joint criminal enterprise between Pawlicki and Swindell. The judge rejected this submission. The correctness of his ruling is now challenged. Looking at the cumulative effect of the factors which linked Swindell and Pawlicki in relation to the guns, Swindell's presence at the scene and Swindell's implausible explanation that he did not recognise the keys found in the car, it is, in our judgment, clear that there was ample evidence to support Swindell's eventual conviction.

"That brings us to the main point of this appeal, namely, the submission of [counsel] on behalf of Pawlicki, which was adopted by [counsel] on behalf of Swindell, that there was no evidence that Pawlicki and Swindell *had with them* the three guns at the time of their arrest inside the auction room. Pawlicki had, of course, driven to the auction room and during the journey plainly had the guns with him. But it is emphasised on his behalf that Swindell was not in the car; that the two were first seen together in the auction room; and that they were charged on the basis of a joint enterprise. Accordingly, it was submitted that the critical time is when Pawlicki and Swindell were first seen together inside the auction room. Without further examination of the validity of this proposition in the case of Pawlicki ... it is emphasised on behalf of both appellants that when they were arrested the guns were in the locked car, outside in the street some 50 yards away, while the appellants were at the far end of a crowded auction room.

"It is submitted that within the meaning of s.18(1) of the Act of 1968 a person will only 'have with him' a firearm if the firearm is immediately available to him. While it is conceded that the question is one of fact, it is submitted that no reasonable jury properly directed could find that the appellants had the gun with them. In support of the test of immediate availability counsel cited *Reg.* v. *Kelt* [1977] 1 W.L.R. 1365. In that case the appellant was arrested in the kitchen of his house. The police found a sawn-off shotgun in the kitchen. The appellant was charged with an offence under s.18 of the Act of 1968. A submission of no case to answer on the ground

that the appellant was not 'carrying' the firearm—the word which
appears in the marginal note to s.18—was overruled. The appellant
was convicted of an offence under s.18. On appeal the court ruled
that the section cannot be confined merely to carrying a firearm.
Accordingly, it was held that there was evidence on which a jury
could properly have convicted. But the judge had in his summing
up wrongly equated possessing the gun and having it with him.
Scarman L.J. giving the judgment of the court, said, at p. 1369:

> 'But one thing is clear in our judgment: the legislature has
> drawn a distinction between a person who has a firearm with
> him and a person who is in possession of a firearm. Some of
> the offences created by the sections to which I have referred
> are offences of possession, others are offences of having with
> one a firearm. This cannot be merely a semantic distinction,
> it must be a distinction of substance. The legislature must
> have had in mind that, in regard to those offences where it is
> an offence for the person to have with him a firearm, there
> must be a very close physical link and a degree of immediate
> control over the weapon by the man alleged to have the
> firearm with him. Certainly it is necessary to warn the jury,
> when summing up in a case under [s].18, that the mere fact
> of possession would not be enough to establish the offence.
> The evidence must take the matter one stage further and be
> such that they are satisfied that the person charged was not
> only in possession but had with him the firearm with intent
> to commit an indictable offence while he had the firearm with
> him.'

Scarman L.J. then referred to the summing up in that case and
continued, at p. 1370:

> 'We have come to the conclusion that it is necessary when
> summing up a case in which an offence under s. 18 is alleged,
> for the judge to make it clear to the jury that possession is not
> enough, that the law required the evidence to go a stage
> further and to establish that the accused had it with him. Of
> course the classic case of having a gun with you is if you are
> carrying it. But, even if you are not carrying it, you may yet
> have it with you, if it is immediately available to you. But if
> all that can be shown is possession in the sense that it is in
> your house or in a shed or somewhere where you have
> ultimate control, that is not enough.'

"This passage is the foundation for counsel's submission that
the governing criterion is whether the guns are immediately
available.

"*Reg.* v. *Kelt* is a decision which helpfully established two propositions. The first is that it is necessary in summing up in such cases to distinguish between possession and having the firearm under s.18. A man who leaves a shotgun at home while he proceeds to the next town to rob a bank is still in possession of the shotgun but he does not 'have it with him' when he commits the robbery at the bank. Under s.18 the words 'have it' import an element of propinquity which is not required for possession. The second, and for present purposes, more important point is that it was established that 'having with him a firearm' is a wider concept than carrying the firearm.

"We do not, however, consider that the court in *Reg.* v. *Kelt* intended to lay down that for the words 'to have with him a firearm' should be read as 'to have immediately available a firearm'. The risk of substituting different words for words in a statute was explained by Lord Reid in *Cozens* v. *Brutus* [1973] A.C. 854, 861:

> 'No doubt the court could act as a dictionary. It could direct the tribunal to take some word or phrase other than the word in the statute and consider whether that word or phrase applied to or covered the facts proved. But we have been warned time and again not to substitute other words for the words of a statute. And there is very good reason for that. Few words have exact synonyms. The overtones are almost always different. Or the court could frame a definition. But then again the tribunal would be left with words to consider. No doubt a statute may contain a definition—which incidentally often creates more problems than it solves—but the purpose of a definition is to limit or modify the ordinary meaning of a word and the court is not entitled to do that.'

"One can be confident that Scarman L.J. in *Reg.* v. *Kelt* did not have in mind such a substitution. Read in context, and particularly in the light of the examples given, the court was merely intending to highlight the element of propinquity which is a necessary ingredient of s.18(1) but not of offences of possession under the Act of 1968.

"A satisfactory definition of the words 'to have with him a firearm' in s.18 is unattainable but there are a few reflections which we would mention. A literalist approach may have led to s.18(1) being interpreted as applying only to the carrying of firearms. That approach was rejected in *Reg.* v. *Kelt* [1977] 1 W.L.R. 1365. It seems to us implicit in that decision that the words 'to have with him a firearm' must derive their colour from the purpose of the Firearms Act 1968. That purpose, in broad terms, is to combat the use of the firearms in and about the commission of crime and to protect public safety. The legislative technique, in so far as it is relevant, involves prohibitions on possession of firearms, and prohibitions on having a firearm. It was intended to be a relatively comprehensive statute. It is submitted that a distance of 50 yards between the men and the guns placed the men beyond the ambit of s.18(1). If that proposition is accepted, the Act of 1968 is less effective than one would have expected. It seems to us that a court ought to try to make sense of the statute and its purpose. If this purposive approach is adopted, it will still be necessary to consider the element of propinquity. But the emphasis must be not so much on exact distances between the criminals and their guns but rather on the accessibility of those guns, judged in a common sense way in the context of criminals embarking on a joint enterprise to commit an indictable offence.

"In our judgment the terms of separation in terms of space of Pawlicki and Swindell from the guns, which they agreed to bring on the planned robbery, does not mean that for the purpose of s.18(1) they did not have the guns with them. It is sufficient that the guns were readily accessible to them at a time when they were about to commit the robbery. The ruling of the judge was right. On this issue of fact there was no basis for a challenge to the jury's verdict."

Appeals dismissed.

3.4.10   **(ix) R. v. Morgan**

[1993] Crim.L.R.870

The five appellants, one co-accused and two others were stopped by the police in a Ford Sierra motor car. They behaved furtively, reaching and bending down as though placing objects on the floor of the car. In the front of the car, on the floor, the police found a large penknife, a gun holster and a chair leg. In the back, under the rear front passenger seat was a pistol loaded with a magazine: there were three blank rounds and a further round in the chamber. The pistol was a realistic imitation of a Colt 45, designed to fire blanks; the action was cocked and the safety catch was off. There was a large butcher's knife between the driver's seat and the door. When the car was searched, more potential weapons were found, including the butt of a snooker cue and another wooden chair leg between the front seats. In the centre of the rear seats was a metal pipe. Along the length of the rear seat there was a two-and-a-half foot iron bar and on the rear seat there was a knuckleduster. Tucked into a division in the back seat was a Stanley knife; on the parcel shelf there was another half snooker cue and a pair of jeans in the pockets of which were 11 rounds of blank ammunition. Under the driver's seat was a beer bottle and in the glove compartment there was a small iron bar.

The appellants and their co-accused were convicted of conspiracy to commit an affray. On appeal, it was argued on their behalf that the evidence of the close of the prosecution case had been insufficient to be left to the jury because an inference of guilt could not properly be drawn from presence in the car. It was further argued that the judge had wrongly ruled against the submission of no case and that none of the defendants having given evidence, the jury ought not to have convicted.

Held, dismissing the appeal, the appeal turned on whether the judge was right to rule against the defence submission. That question could be answered shortly; there was quite clearly a case to go to the jury. There was no evidence to contradict the inference of guilty which could properly be drawn and there was clear evidence to justify the convictions. It was properly open to the jury to draw the following inferences:

(i) that having regard to where they were in the car, this collection of implements had been put in the car for the purpose of using them as weapons of offence;

(ii) that the use of such weapons would constitute an affray;

(iii) that each appellant had got into the car when at least some of these implements were already there, or that some or all of them were brought into the car after he or she had got into it;

(iv) that anyone in the car must have been aware of the presence of at least some of the implements;

(v) that anyone getting into or remaining in the car had lent himself to and agreed to the purpose referred to in the first inference. If these five inferences were drawn, then in the absence of any explanation from an appellant, and there had been none from any of the appellants, it was open to the jury to conclude that he was party to a conspiracy to commit an affray.

(x) Murdoch v. Carmichael 3.4.11

1993 S.C.C.R. 444

M., an appellant, was a passenger in a car which was stopped by the police late at night as it drove into the driveway of the driver's house in a residential area. He was seen making erratic movements as the car stopped. A large knife was found lying unsheathed with its handle in the passenger footwell. The car was searched and the police found neither a sheath for the knife nor any hunting or fishing equipment. When the police wanted to search the appellant and the driver of the car, they ran into the driver's house. The appellant was convicted of a contravention of the 1953 Act in respect of the knife and sentenced to six months' imprisonment. He appealed to the High Court by stated case.

Held (1) that the sheriff was entitled to hold that the appellant had the knife with him; (2) that the sheriff was entitled to hold that the knife was an offensive weapon; and appeal against conviction refused.

In his note to the stated case the sheriff stated, *inter alia*:

"At the conclusion of the Crown case [the solicitor for the appellant] advanced a submission of no case to answer. His first point was that this was a 'class 3' weapon, i.e., one which was 'intended by the person having it with him for such use by him', the use in question being 'causing injury to the person' (section 1(4) of the 1953 Act). He referred me to *Woods* v *Heywood*, 1988 S.L.T. 849 and *Coull* v *Guild*, 1986 S.L.T. 184. In the light of these authorities the procurator fiscal depute very properly conceded that this was, if anything, a class 3 weapon and that she required to prove the intent already referred to.

"[The solicitor for the appellant] went on to submit that there was no evidence from which I could infer the guilty intention which was essential to the proof of the charge. He appreciated that each case required to be looked at in the light of its own circumstances; but he said that the circumstances were not capable of bearing the inference for which the Crown contended. As an example he cited *Barr* v *MacKinnon*, 1988 S.C.C.R. 561, and submitted, fairly, that there was no background of disturbance or violence occurring nearby in the present case. There was no evidence of other persons being in the vicinity. The knife was there in the car with the men and that was all.

"For the Crown it was submitted that the nature of the knife, the lack of a sheath, the position of the knife in the car, the absence of hunting or fishing equipment, the time of night, the locus, which was a residential area, and the fact that the two men ran for the house were all factors of varying weight which, taken together, could justify a finding of guilt. She referred me to *Kane* v *H.M. Advocate*, 1988 S.C.C.R. 585, but I did not find that case to be of much relevance because it concerned a Stanley knife which could have been made safe but had not been. In that case reference is made to *Ralston* v *Lockhart*, 1986 S.C.C.R. 400, a case with points of similarity to the present case. However, a mere modelling knife was involved in that case and a question of car theft rendered the appellant's flight from the police ambiguous.

"In my opinion, although the evidence was clearly very thin, the submissions for the Crown were to be preferred and I allowed the trial to proceed against both accused. No defence evidence was led and, after hearing further submissions, I convicted the appellant and found Strang [the car driver] not guilty.

"At this stage of the case the fact that there were two men in the car caused some difficulty for the Crown. The procurator fiscal depute was unable to refer me to any case in which two people had been found guilty under this section in respect of one weapon. She submitted that I could convict both but that, in view of the passenger's movements and the position of the knife, the case was stronger against the passenger than against the driver.

"For both accused [the solicitor for the appellant] submitted that it was impossible to say which of the two men had the knife and that, without concert, for which there was no evidence, it would be impossible to convict either accused. He also repeated his submissions regarding the inadequacy of the evidence pointing to the necessary guilty intention ... .

"It appears to me that the phrase in section 1(1) 'has with him' should be construed in a non-technical way (vide Gordon (2nd edn), paragraph 30–46). Looking at it that way, I considered that both men had this knife with them. The streets were public places, so there was no difficulty there. The words of section 1(4), 'for such use by him', suggest to me that the usual rules of concert are not available to the Crown in attributing guilt to an accomplice in respect of a class 3 weapon. It seems to me that, in the case of a class 3 weapon, the person must have the weapon with him in public without reasonable excuse and that he must intend to use it himself to cause personal injury. It appeared to me that the position of the knife in the car, together with the appellant's movements described in finding 3, pointed to him as the putative user of the knife. I inferred that the appellant, when moving about in the front of the car, was seeking to dissociate himself from the knife in the knowledge that the police wanted to stop the car. The various factors founded on by the Crown satisfied me that he intended to use the knife for causing personal injury. I laid some stress on the nature of the weapon. It was a particularly vicious-looking object and I could imagine no legitimate purpose for having it—at least in Larkhall. Different considerations would doubtless apply in the heart of the Grampians. I observe that the nature of the weapon was considered to be a material factor in

Lopez v *Macnab* [1978 J.C. 41]. In these circumstances, I was satisfied beyond reasonable doubt of the guilt of the appellant and so I convicted him ... .

"In respect of charge (1), I imposed a sentence of six months' imprisonment on the appellant because of the nature of this weapon, taken with his record. Far too many weapons are carried in Lanarkshire, as elsewhere in Scotland, and this leads to numerous affrays becoming much more serious than they need to. In my view, the maximum sentence was appropriate and so I imposed it."

The questions for the opinion of the High Court were:

"1. Should I have sustained the submission of no case to answer advanced on behalf of the appellant?
2.   Was I entitled to make finding in fact 13?
3.   Was I entitled to make finding in fact 14?
4.   On the facts stated, was I entitled to convict the appellant?
5.   Was the sentence imposed in respect of charge (1) excessive?"

Lord Justice-Clerk (Ross) (at p. 446)

"This is an appeal at the instance of Alan Watson Murdoch. He was found guilty in the sheriff court at Hamilton of two charges on a complaint. The first charge was a charge of contravening section 1(1) of the Prevention of Crime Act 1953 and the second charge was a charge under the Bail etc. (Scotland) Act 1980. He was sentenced to six months' imprisonment in respect of charge (1). He has appealed against conviction and sentence by means of stated case. The sheriff in his note records that, at the conclusion of the Crown case, the solicitor for the appellant had made a submission of no case to answer. The sheriff repelled that submission and no evidence was led by the appellant. Today on his behalf [counsel] has maintained that the sheriff had erred in repelling the submission of no case to answer which he submits ought to have been sustained. Under reference to the questions in the case [counsel] pointed out that the appellant is challenging findings 13 and 14 in the case, which are really statements of inferences which the sheriff drew from the facts.

"So far as the facts are concerned, putting the matter shortly, two police officers were on mobile patrol in a marked police vehicle around 10.50 p.m. when they observed a Ford Escort car with two occupants. They decided to stop it and they observed it pulling into a driveway in Larkhall. They followed the Escort into the driveway which was the driveway of the appellant's co-accused. Finding 3 is in the following terms.

'After the klaxon and light had been put out and before the vehicle pulled into Strang's driveway, the officers could see that the front-seat passenger was making erratic movements with his shoulders going up and down.'

"The subsequent findings disclose that the appellant was the front-seat passenger and his co-accused the driver. Finding 6 is in the following terms.

'Sergeant Niezynski looked about the vehicle. He could see something in the passenger footwell from outside the car. Leaning in the driver's door he found Crown Label No. 1, a large knife, lying unsheathed with its handle in the passenger footwell and its blade pointing up and at an angle supported by the gear stick housing. He removed the knife from the car.'

"There follows a description of the knife, which was about eight inches long, had two edges, one of which was partially serrated and the other of which was a cutting edge. Both edges were shut. There was a handle with finger guards across the junction of the handle and the blade. The knife was well balanced and quite heavy and there is a finding that it was well capable of inflicting severe personal injury. The findings then record the procedures followed by the police. When first called on for an explanation, the co-accused maintained that he did not know there was a knife in the vehicle and the appellant apparently replied something to the effect that he had never seen any knife in the vehicle. The car was searched and no hunting or fishing equipment was found nor any sheath for the knife. When the appellant was charged with a contravention of section 1(1) of the Act of 1953 he replied, 'Offensive weapon. Aye.' Findings 13 and 14 which are challenged are in the following terms.

'13. The appellant had Crown Label No. 1 with him in the streets named in the charge and in the driveway of 69 Robert Smillie Crescent, all public places, with the intention that he should use it to cause injury to the person. He had no lawful authority or reasonable excuse for having the knife with him.

14. When the appellant was moving about in the front seat of the car, he was adjusting the position of the knife with a view to dissociating himself from it, in the knowledge that the car was about to be stopped by the police.'

"In seeking to advance the appellant's appeal [counsel] made two principal submissions. His first submission was that the evidence which the sheriff referred to in the findings of fact was not such as to yield any reasonable inference of possession of the knife on the part of the appellant. The advocate-depute, however, pointed out that for the offence under section 1(1) of the Act of 1953 it is not possession which requires to be established but what requires to be established is that the accused had with him an offensive weapon, namely a knife. Accordingly, the question must be whether the evidence was such as to entitle the sheriff to infer that the appellant had this knife with him at the material time. The sheriff in his note records the matters relied on by the Crown. Having regard to where the knife was found, with its handle in the passenger footwell, and the description of the appellant's movements while he was in the front passenger seat before he left the car, we are satisfied that the sheriff was entitled to conclude that the appellant did have the knife with him at the material time. There were two persons in the car, but when the knife was found, it was in the passenger's side at the front of the car with the handle in the passenger footwell and, when that fact is combined with the description of the appellant's movements shortly before, we are satisfied that the sheriff was entitled to conclude that he had the knife with him at that time.

"[Counsel]'s second submission was that, even if it was held that the appellant had the knife with him at the material time, none the less there was no evidence to justify the inference that he had any intention of using it to cause injury. [Counsel] reminded us that offensive weapons which are dealt with in section 1(1) fall into three classes, namely those made for use for causing personal injury, those adapted for such use and those not so made or adapted but intended by the accused for such use. In the present case, the Crown accepted that before the Crown could succeed, they would require to show that this was a weapon in the third category, that is to say, that it was intended by the appellant for use for causing personal injury. Whether or not it was, of course, depends upon the facts and circumstances established by the evidence. The sheriff in his note tells us that the Crown in this connection relied upon the nature of the knife, the lack of a sheath, the position of the knife in the car, the absence of hunting or fishing equipment, the time of night, the locus, which was a residential area, and the fact that the two men ran for the house after the police indicated that they wished to search them, and the Crown maintained that these were all factors which, taken together, justified the inference of guilt.

The sheriff in his note tells us that he regarded the evidence as very thin, but that none the less he came to the conclusion that the Crown had established that this weapon was indeed a class 3 weapon. [Counsel] emphasised that the men had not been in a public place in the sense of being in the street at the time, but they were in a motor vehicle and he maintained that there was insufficient material to justify the conclusion at which the sheriff had arrived.

"The advocate-depute, on the other hand, relied strongly upon the factors to which we have already made reference and he stressed what had been found in relation to the movements of the appellant in the car. He maintained that when regard was had to the fact that the appellant had clearly been attempting to dissociate himself from the knife, which was the inference which the sheriff expressed in finding 14, that was a very material consideration when considering whether it had been established that this was an offensive weapon. We agree that this was a thin case on the evidence, but we have come to the conclusion that the sheriff was entitled to draw the inferences which he did and that he was entitled in particular to conclude that this was an offensive weapon. Reference was made to *Lopez v Macnab*. In that case, the Lord Justice-General emphasised that whether or not a weapon was a class 3 weapon depended upon the facts and circumstances. Not only that, but the Lord Justice-General observed as follows:

> 'We have no doubt that it was open to the sheriff on these findings to conclude as he did. The question of the statutory intention is one which may be drawn as an inference from the facts and circumstances. Unless we can say there was no material on which that inference can be drawn, the finding of the sheriff cannot be disturbed.'

"In the present case we are satisfied that there was material upon which the sheriff was entitled to draw the inferences which he did. We are certainly quite unable to say that there was no material from which such an inference could be drawn and, that being so, we would not be justified in interfering with the inferences the sheriff has drawn. We are accordingly satisfied that the sheriff was well founded in repelling the submission of no case to answer. We are likewise satisfied that he was entitled to make findings 13 and 14 and that accordingly he was entitled to convict the appellant of the charge. We shall accordingly answer question 1 in the case in the negative and questions 2, 3 and 4 in the affirmative."

Appeal against conviction refused.

3.4.12 (xi) **Cummings v. Friel**

High Court of Justiciary, April 26, 1995

C. was charged with having with him offensive weapons, namely a machete and a meat cleaver. At trial a submission of no case to answer was repelled. C. was convicted and he appealed his conviction on the ground that the sheriff erred in law in repelling that submission. The appeal was refused.

The sheriff found the following facts and admitted as proved:

1. On the evening of 19 July 1993 the appellant was driving his Ford Fiesta motor car in Barrhead Road, Glasgow. Barrhead Road is a public place.
2. While the appellant's vehicle was being driven as aforesaid with a police vehicle behind it the occupants of the appellant's car displayed anxiety about the presence of the police vehicle by continually turning round.
3. The appellant's vehicle was stopped by a police patrol car at said locus at approximately 7.20 p.m. The police officer found a machete with a ten-inch blade (sheathed) and a small meat cleaver (unsheathed) below the driver's seat.
4. The appellant was in possession of said weapons at the time he was stopped.
5. When questioned by the police no-one in the appellant's vehicle admitted ownership of the items. When cautioned and charged with a contravention of s.1 of the Prevention of Crime Act 1953 the appellant replied, "They werenae mine".
6. The appellant had no lawful authority or reasonable excuse for his possession of the machete and meat cleaver.
7. The appellant's purpose in having the said items in his possession at the material time was to use them for causing personal injury to others.

Lord Justice-General (Hope)

"The narrative of the evidence with which we have been provided is based upon what was said by two police officers who were on mobile patrol in a marked police vehicle. At about 7.20 p.m. on 19 July 1993 they came upon a blue Fiesta motor vehicle in Glasgow Road, Barrhead. They did so by accident, but during the course of their journey the five youths who were in that car constantly looked behind them in the direction of the police vehicle. This had the effect of arousing the officers' suspicions and they stopped the vehicle. The appellant was the driver. The youths were asked to leave the car, which they did. There was then a cursory examination of the interior. The police found a large knife or machete in a sheath and a small meat cleaver which was unsheathed below the driver's seat. Evidence was given about the dimensions of these articles. The occupants were asked whether they admitted ownership and no one spoke up. The appellant gave no explanation when he was asked if the items were his.

"The sheriff took the view, so far as the question of possession was concerned, that the evidence from the police officers as to where the articles were found was sufficient for that purpose. He noted that they had said that the articles were found below the driver's seat. His opinion was that, on the evidence, they were readily accessible only to the appellant who was the driver of the vehicle and consequently were in his possession. So far as the question of the intention to use the articles was concerned, he had regard to the behaviour of the occupants of the motor car including the appellant, to what he describes as the time of night, as this was 7.30 p.m. on a summer's evening, and the conduct of the passengers and the appellant in the vehicle.

"[Counsel for the appellant] reminded us that in the definition which is set out in subs. (4) of s.1 of the 1953 Act the definition of an offensive weapon refers to 'any article made or adapted for use for causing injury to the person or intended by the person having it with him for such use by him.' He submitted that the question was not so much as to whether the accused had the article in his possession, it was a question as to whether he had the article with him for the purposes of that subsection and whether it was with him for the purpose of such use by him, that is use for causing personal injury.

"Against the background of the wording of that subsection he submitted that there was insufficient evidence to entitle the sheriff to infer that the appellant had these articles with him when he was the driver of his motor car. He pointed out that there were five people in that car and that, although there was evidence that the articles had been found below the driver's seat, it could not be said that these articles were not accessible to others in the same motor car. So far as use was concerned, he submitted that the evidence about the occupants of the car looking around and behind them during the course of the journey was not enough for that purpose, having regard to the fact that this was during the hours of daylight. In any event, it was necessary for the Crown to attribute the intention of use to the appellant himself, and that was not something which the sheriff was entitled to find in the Crown evidence.

"In our opinion the place within the motor car where these articles were found was of importance in considering what inferences the sheriff would be entitled to draw when he came to consider the whole evidence. In this respect the case is similar to *Murdoch* v. *Carmichael* 1993 S.C.C.R. 444. In that case the appellant was a passenger in a car which was stopped by the police. A large knife was found lying unsheathed with its handle in the passenger footwell, and the conclusion was drawn that the sheriff was entitled to infer from that evidence that it was the appellant as the passenger who was in possession of the article for the purposes of the statute. In the opinion of the Court at page 447G the Lord Justice-Clerk drew attention to the fact that the knife was found with its handle in the passenger footwell and to the description of the appellant's movements when he was in the front passenger seat before he left the car. Although there were two persons in the car, it was these factors which entitled the sheriff to reach the view which he did.

"In the present case, there is nothing in the evidence about movements of the appellant which would entitle any inference to be drawn. But in our opinion the fact that these two articles were found together under the driver's seat of the car, which belonged to the appellant and being driven by him, was sufficient at the stage of the no case to answer submission to justify the sheriff in holding that there was enough in the Crown case to entitle him to repel that submission.

"So far as the intention of use by the appellant is concerned, in our opinion the position in which these two articles were found, and their nature, form part of the whole evidence in the case to which the sheriff was entitled to look. And for the time of day, the behaviour of the appellant and his companions is relevant also. No doubt this was during the hours of daylight in July, but the way in which the appellant and his companions were behaving was such as to arouse suspicion. When that is taken together with the position and nature of the articles, we considered that the sheriff was entitled to hold at the stage of the no case to answer submission that there was enough in the Crown case to entitle him to repel the submission which was made to him to that effect.

"The evidence in the case may be described as thin as [counsel for the appellant] indeed did describe it, but that is a feature which this case shares with others of this kind. What matters is whether there was sufficient evidence for the sheriff to be entitled to repel the submission, and for the reasons which we have given we are not persuaded that he erred in law in the decision which he took."

Appeal refused.

NOTE
This appeal is reported briefly at 1995 G.W.D. 20–1126.

Section 1(1) of the 1953 Act: "in any public place"   **3.5.1**

(i) Woods v. Lindsay   **3.5.2**

(1910) 6 Adam 294

A complaint charged a contravention of s.3 of the Prevention of Gaming (Scotland) Act 1869 by being in a railway station "being a public place", in possession of articles for the purpose of card-sharping.

Held, that a railway station was a public place within the meaning of the statute.

Lord Justice-General (Dunedin) (at p. 298)
"There are certain things which are neither *mal in se*, nor even, in the full sense of the word, *mala prohibita*, but are only *mala prohibita* if done in certain places. Betting is a familiar example. It follows that the considerations in these cases will not equally apply to others of a different class."

(ii) R. v. Theodoulou   **3.5.3**

[1963] Crim.L.R.573

T. was convicted of carrying an offensive weapon in a public place. He was arrested in a "coffee club" and had an open razor in his pocket. His defence was that the club was not a public place. The judge directed "well, it is perhaps for you to decide, as it is a matter or question of fact, but people do not cease to be members of the public just because they go into a club. The idea of the Act is to protect people wherever they may be, in the highway or a club, whatever it may be, from offensive weapons ... and to stop people carrying these things in public. Therefore it is for you to decide; but there cannot be the slightest doubt that it (the club) is a public place."

Held, that it might well be that the club was a public place in that anybody could go into it and there were no formalities to be observed. However, there was in fact no evidence one way or the other as to the nature of the club and the judge was wrong in withdrawing the issue from the jury by ruling that whatever the nature of the club it was a public place.

Appeal allowed.

3.5.4 **(iii) R. v. Mehmed**

[1963] Crim. L.R. 780

M. was convicted of having with him in a public place an offensive weapon, *viz.* a pistol, and sentenced to six months' imprisonment. He was acquitted of attempting to discharge the pistol with intent to do grievous bodily harm and possessing it with intent to endanger life.

In the course of a family quarrel at a private dwelling-house to which he had gone, M. produced the pistol, cocked it and pointed it at R. who promptly kicked him in the stomach. The pistol went off, the bullet lodging in the floor. M.'s defence was that he was never in possession of the pistol which was an invention on the part of the prosecution witnesses. He appealed against conviction on the grounds, *inter alia*, that the verdicts were inconsistent, that there was no evidence he had the pistol in a public place, and that the judge failed to direct that it had to be proved that he had the pistol knowingly (relying on *R. v. Cugullere* [1961] Crim.L.R. 410) and did not sum up the defence adequately.

Held, (1) the verdicts were logically explicable on the basis that the jury were satisfied that M. had the pistol but not that he intended to use it against anyone; (2) having regard to M.'s defence, if the jury were satisfied that he had the pistol they were entitled to infer that he brought it to or took it away from the house through public streets; (3) since M. was not saying that the pistol was in his possession without his knowledge the question of whether he had it knowingly did not arise; (4) the summing-up was very brief but it contained all the proper ingredients, *i.e.* a proper direction on the onus and standard of proof and the nature of the charges, the case for the prosecution and the essence of the defence.

Appeal dismissed.

3.5.5 **(iv) Cawley v. Frost**

[1976] 1 W.L.R. 1207

C. was a spectator at a football match. The football pitch was surrounded by a speedway track about seven yards wide, where the public were not allowed. The spectators were separated from the track and the pitch by a fence. At the conclusion of the match the rival spectators climbed over the fence and surged on to the pitch, running across the track, shouting abuse at each other. C. was arrested on the speedway track and was charged with using threatening behaviour in a public place contrary to s.5 of the Public Order Act 1936. He was convicted before the juvenile court. His appeal to the Crown Court was allowed on the ground that although he was guilty of threatening behaviour the speedway track was not a public place.

On appeal by the prosecutor on the ground that the whole of the football ground was a "public place" within the definition in s.9(1) of the 1936 Act.

Held, allowing the appeal, that where the public had access to premises, those premises should be considered in their entirety and the fact that the public were denied access to certain areas of the premises did not exclude those areas from being part of "a public place" within the meaning of s.9 of the 1936 Act; that the football ground, including all its appurtenances, formed a public place and, accordingly, the defendant had committed an offence contrary to s.5 of the Act.

Milford Stevenson, J. (at p. 1211)
"Speaking for myself, and looking at the facts which emerge from this case stated, I cannot escape from the view that the Shay ground including all its appurtenances together formed a public place for the purposes of the Act of 1936, and that the defendant in running onto it in the circumstances I have described on the findings of the court below did commit the offence with which he was originally charged before the Halifax justices.

"I fully appreciate that, where you are dealing with what may be generally described as a stadium or area which is designed for various forms of public entertainment, such an area may well include parts to which the public are not expected to go, and indeed steps may be taken to exclude them from it. A fairly obvious example is a kitchen or restaurant on a race course. It may be some part of the stabling which is normally part of a race course complex. It is an easy but I think not a useful expenditure of time to multiply examples of that kind.

"Every such case must depend on its own facts, but I am left in no doubt on the description of the Shay at Halifax which is set out in the case we are now dealing with that this speedway track was part of a public place. The fact that there was a fence obviously designed to discourage, if not prevent, members of the public from jumping over it and onto the pitch is fairly obvious. But in my view that makes no difference whatever for the purpose of deciding whether this offence was committed in the kind of public place which this statute contemplates.

"I would therefore allow this appeal. I do not find it necessary to refer to a large number of authorities which have been cited because I do not think any of them help. This is a question of fact in every case, and I think the facts here should be determined in the way I have indicated. I would therefore allow this appeal and send the matter back to the Crown Court with a direction to continue the hearing."

Caulfield, J. (at p. 1212)

"I agree. To support the decision of the Crown Court in this case means that those who are disposed to be hooligans in Halifax during a football match can delight themselves by insulting each other to the annoyance of the public provided they restrict their arguments and their insulting words to the speedway that surrounds the football pitch.

"I am of course, in relating the facts in this way, showing or trying to show the absurdity of such a situation from the point of view of common sense, but I approach my decision on the interpretation of 'public place' as contained in the Act of 1936. The words to which I pay particular attention are the words 'premises or place'. In any particular case, whether it be the Ascot Race Course, Old Trafford Football Ground or Cricket Ground, or the Shay at Halifax, I think the proper approach is to identify the premises to which the public have access and then to decide whether or not there has been an offence committed in those premises.

"It is plain in my judgment from the facts here that the speedway track surrounding the football pitch was part of the premises. In those circumstances the finding of the Crown Court in my judgment is wrong. I would therefore follow the course that this case should be remitted to continue the hearing."

Lord Widgery, C.J. (at p. 1212)

"I agree with both judgments and with the order proposed. It must be remembered, I think, that the Public Order Act 1936 was designed to promote good order in places to which the public have access. That was the purpose of the Act itself. That may have an influence on its proper interpretation.

"In my judgment where you have an establishment which is set up to provide for the public, such as the Halifax Town Football Club or Wembley Stadium, one ought to approach it on the basis that this is a public place in its entirety. I do not think that one ought to be in any way influenced against that conclusion by the fact that for the convenience of organising the crowds, or otherwise for administrative purposes, certain areas within the stadium have been roped off and are denied to the public by the intervention of the police. The fact that areas of that kind are not in fact to be enjoyed by the public on a given occasion does not justify the apportionment of the total establishment into a number of separate parts and the application of a separate judgment to each part. Prima facie you look at the whole establishment and you are not, as I say, deterred from doing that merely by finding that certain portions of the establishment have been denied to the public for one reason or another.

"The case therefore will go back for the Bradford Crown Court to continue the hearing."

Appeal allowed.

(v) Mok Chi-ho v. The Queen 3.5.6

(1979) H.K.L.R. 118

At 2.05 a.m. two police detectives saw a private car with five persons in it being driven along a road. At 2.50 a.m. they saw the same private car parked on another road and sitting in the car were the driver and the appellant. Under the appellant's seat were found three knives and when questioned the appellant stated that the knives were for self-defence.

The appellant was charged with and convicted of two charges, namely (1) being in possession of offensive weapons in a public place under s.33(1) of the Public Order Ordinance and (2) loitering at night and being unable to give an account of himself under s.26(a) of the Summary Offences Ordinance.

On appeal against conviction the court had to decide *inter alia* whether a private car on a public road was a public place for the purposes of s.33(1) of the Public Order Ordinance.

Held, that a private car on a public road is a public place for the purposes of s.33(1) of the Public Order Ordinance.

Yang, J. (at p. 119)

"The Canadian authority of *Rex* v. *McLeod* (1950) 97 Can.Crim.Cas. 366 is in point. There the question was whether a person found consuming liquor inside a motor vehicle parked in a public parking area was rightly convicted of drinking in a public place contrary to section 38 of the Government Liquor Act R.S.B.C. 1948 C. 192. O'Halloran J.A. noted that the defendant was not charged with drinking in a motor vehicle as in itself a 'public place' but was charged with drinking in a public place. The learned judge concluded that since the motor vehicle was in a public place, then if drinking took place therein, there was most certainly evidence up to that point to justify a finding that drinking occurred in a public place. He also referred to the sort of circumstances which a court should consider in determining whether or not a car is a public place. He said (at p. 368):

> 'It is not disclosed whether the motor vehicle was being used for private or public purposes; it might have been a passenger bus or it might have been a motorcycle. We do not know how many people were in or around the vehicle at the time; whether the car was an open jeep, a truck, or enclosed family car; whether the drinking took place publicly in open view; whether the respondent was one of a party in several motor cars who had gathered at respondent's car for a drink, or other relevant circumstances in the absence of which a Court of review is unable to determine if the law has been correctly applied to the facts in the particular case.'"

Appeal refused.

3.5.7   **(vi) R. v. Heffey**

[1981] Crim.L.R. 111

H. was prosecuted under s.1(1) of the Prevention of Crime Act 1953 following an altercation which took place on the third-floor landing of a block of council flats in which he was alleged to have wielded a carving knife at three police officers. At the close of the prosecution case defence counsel submitted that the landing was not a "public place" within the meaning of the definition laid down in the Prevention of Crime Act 1953. After argument in which a number of cases were referred to, principally *R. v. Edwards and Roberts* [1978] Crim.L.R. 564, the judge held that it was offensive to a common sense interpretation of the English language to say that the landing in question was a "public place" within the meaning of the Act, and therefore upheld the defence submission.

The only evidence in relation to the landing was that it was the top landing of the block of flats, and that it was shared between two flats, the defendant's and another.

Found not guilty.

NOTE
This was a decision of a judge at first instance in Liverpool Crown Court.

(vii) Knox v. Anderton 3.5.8

(1983) Cr.App.R. 156

K. was seen by a policeman to be standing on the landing of a building. That landing gave access to flats there. K. and another man were shouting abuse at one another. The policeman got himself between K. and the other man. K. had raised a hammer in an aggressive manner and he attempted to hit the other man. K. was arrested and charged with having with him in a public place an offensive weapon, namely a hammer, contrary to s.1(1) of the 1953 Act. At trial the only issue was whether the landing was a "public place" within the meaning of the 1953 Act. K. was convicted and appealed against that conviction.

Webster, J. (at p. 159)
"This is a defendant's appeal by way of case stated by Justices for the County of Greater Manchester sitting at Salford in respect of their adjudication on November 13, 1981, whereby they convicted the appellant of having, on July 27, 1981, without lawful authority or reasonable excuse with him in a public place called Langworthy Estate an offensive weapon, namely, a claw hammer, contrary to section 1 of the Prevention of Crime Act 1953.

"It was not disputed before the justices that on that date the defendant, when standing on the upper landing of a block of flats on the Langworthy Estate in Salford, had a claw hammer in his hand, and that this was an offensive weapon. The only issue raised before the justices, which was raised at the close of the prosecution evidence, was whether that landing was a public place within the meaning of that expression in the Prevention of Crime Act 1953. The justices rejected the submission made on behalf of the defendant that it was not a public place, whereupon the defendant, who had previously pleaded not guilty to the charge, changed his plea and pleaded guilty. The question for the opinion of this court is whether the justices' findings that the landings to the Langworthy Estate flats in Salford are a public place was wrong in law.

"Before considering the facts, it is convenient to note the definition of the expression 'public place' in section 1(4) of the Prevention of Crime Act 1953, which is that: 'In this section "public place" includes any highway and any other premises or place to which at the material time the public have or are permitted to have access, whether on payment or otherwise ...' This definition of 'public place' for the purposes of section 1 of the Prevention of Crime Act 1953 is in precisely the same terms as its definition for the purposes of the Public Order Act 1936, as amended by section 33 of the Criminal Justice Act 1972; although for the purposes of the Public Order Act 1936 there is also a definition of the expression 'private premises.'

"The facts found by the justices, so far as material, are as follows. The Langworthy Estate is the property of the local authority. There are in the region of 420 flats on the estate housing approximately 1,500 people. Plans of the estate produced to the justices showed that the flats are all of a uniform construction, there being four floors in all in each particular block with, in each block, numerous stairways giving access to each level so that people are able to move freely from one floor to the next. At ground floor level there is a walkway or pavement serving all ground floor flats which is repeated at each of the upper levels, the only difference between the upper and the ground floor levels being that there is a balustrade on the upper levels to prevent persons falling over the edge. Until the demolition of a nearby bridge shortly before the hearing before the justices, many people, not being residents on the estate, used to walk through the estate in order to reach a shopping precinct on the other side of the bridge from the estate, and no attempt had been made to stop them doing so. There is a community centre within the estate used both by residents of the estate and by non-residents. There is nothing to prevent a member of the public from entering the stairways of the blocks of flats, there is no barrier to prevent members of the public walking along the landings which give access to the individual flats, and there are no doors to the stairways or landings, which are open to the atmosphere. There are no notices to suggest that there is any restriction of access to the landings and stairways or to the whole estate except that there are notices on some of the buildings at the entrance to the estate which read 'Parking of vehicles above 10cwt. on the estate is Prohibited, Access is restricted to tenants and their visitors only.'

"[Counsel's] submission on behalf of the defendant amounted to a challenge of the justices' decision that the landing was a public place on two grounds, the first that the justices expressly misdirected themselves and the second that their decision was perverse, that is to say a decision which no reasonable justices, properly directing themselves, could reach upon the facts found by them.

"[Counsel] submitted that the justices expressly misdirected themselves in expressing the opinion 'that the Estate had had to be considered as a whole, with the exception of the actual dwellings.' We do not regard that as a misdirection. In CAWLEY v. FROST (1976) 64 Cr.App.R. 20; [1976] 1 W.L.R. 1207, where the question was whether a particular part of a football ground was a public place for the purposes of sections 5 and 9(1) of the Public Order Act 1936, Lord Widgery C.J. at pp. 24 and 1212 respectively said: 'Prima facie you look at the whole establishment and you are not ... deterred from doing that merely by finding that certain portions of the establishment have been denied to the public for one reason or another.' [Counsel] also, as we understand him, submitted that the justices misdirected themselves when expressing the opinion that they were entitled to have regard to the mischief at which section 1 of the Prevention of Crime Act 1953 is directed; but there is abundant authority to support that direction. We cannot, therefore, conclude that the justices expressly misdirected themselves.

"The question remains whether their decision was perverse.

"In support of his contention that it was, [counsel for the appellant] relied, primarily, on two points. He submitted that there is no evidence from which the justices could have inferred that members of the public had an implied licence to go on to the landings, and he relied upon a passage in the judgment of Bridge L.J. (as he then was) in LLEWELLYN EDWARDS AND ERIC ROBERTS (1978) 67 Cr.App.R. 228, 231, where Bridge L.J. said: ' ... it seems to this Court that it is quite impossible to hold that the expression "public place" can be construed as extending to the front gardens of private premises simply on the footing on which the learned judge relied that members of the public have an implied licence to pass through those private gardens in order to obtain access to the front doors of private premises if they have some lawful occasion for so doing. It is not *qua* members of the public that they thus enjoy access, it is *qua* lawful visitors.'

"As to this contention, however, it is to be remembered that the definition of a public place contains two distinctive alternative elements, namely, premises or a place to which at the material time 'the public have ... access,' and premises or a place to which at the material time 'the public ... are permitted to have access.' For reasons which will later become apparent in this judgment, it is clear to us that the justices in the present case decided that the landings were a public place for the first, not the second, of those two reasons, namely, because they were premises or a place to which at the material time 'the public have ... access.' They made and purported to make no finding that the public had any implied licence or permission to go on to the landings and they made no reverence to any such licence or permission in the reasons given for their decision. We, therefore, reject the first of [counsel's] points in support of his contention that their decision was perverse.

"His second point was a more broad one, namely, that it defied common sense to regard the landings as a public place; and in support of that contention he relied upon the decision in LLEWELLYN EDWARDS AND ERIC ROBERTS (*supra*) and upon a decision of Judge Nance in HEFFEY [1981] Crim.L.R. 111. The landings, he submitted, must be just as much a private place as were the front gardens in *Edwards and Roberts*; but as to that submission it has often been said that each case has to be decided upon its own particular facts, and in that case there was a gate which presumably separated the garden from the public road or pavement; see Bridge L.J. quoting the trial judge: "'Persons, members of the public, are by implication permitted by the owner/occupier of the dwellinghouse to approach that dwellinghouse via the garden and gate, the steps, and up to the front door... .'" It is true that in HEFFEY (*supra*) Judge Nance upheld a defence submission that the third floor landing of a block of council flats was not a public place; but there is no indication whatsoever in the short report of that decision as to the particular facts in that case.

"We do not, therefore, think that either of those two decisions enable [counsel] to show that the decision of the justices in this case, on the facts before them, was one which no reasonable bench of justices properly directing themselves could have reached. It seems clear that the first stage in the reasoning or fact-finding process which led to that decision was their 'opinion' (which is really a finding) that 'there was no restriction on members of the general public entering the Langworthy Estate.' That finding was, in our view, wholly consistent with the evidence as to the use of the estate by persons not residing there and as to such notices as there were purporting to restrict access to it. Had the question arisen, therefore, the justices would have been perfectly entitled, in our view, to have decided that the estate itself was a public place as, by inference, they have done. At what point, short of the front door of the individual flats, can it be said as a matter of inevitable inference from the facts found to have ceased to have been a public place? And in particular can it be said, as a matter of inevitable inference from those facts, to have ceased to have become a public place before the landings are reached? In our view there is no inevitable inference that it ceased to become a public place at any point before the landings are reached, in view of the justices' findings that there was nothing to stop members of the public from entering the stairways of the blocks, that there was no barrier to prevent members of the public walking along the landings which gave access to the individual flats, that there were no doors to the stairways or landings which were open to the atmosphere and that there were no notices to suggest that there was any restriction of access to the landings and stairways or indeed to the whole estate except the notices posted on some of the buildings at the entrance to the estate to which we have already referred.

"For all these reasons we would, slightly rewording the question for the opinion of this court, answer it by saying that the justices have not been shown to have made any error of law in finding that the landings were a public place and we, therefore, dismiss this appeal."

Appeal dismissed.

NOTE
In *Williams* v. *D.P.P.* [1992] Crim.L.R. 502, *Knox* v. *Anderton* was distinguished on the facts and it was held that the intercom and security locks on the entrance to a block of flats made the landing area outside those flats a private space.

(viii) Bates v. D.P.P.   3.5.9

The Times, March 8, 1993

B. appealed by way of case stated against his conviction by Thames Magistrates Court that on December 4, 1991 at the Blackwall Tunnel Northern Approach Northbound he had in his possession an unmuzzled pit bull terrier contrary to ss.1(2) and 7(1) of the Dangerous Dogs Act 1991.

A dangerous dog, as defined by s.1 of the 1991 Act, in a private car which was on a public highway was in a public place, within the meaning of s.10(2) of the Act and was therefore required to be muzzled and on a lead as prescribed by s.1(2)(d) of the Act.

Lord Justice Rose said that the wording of s.10(4) of the 1991 Act, except for a reference to a building with common parts, was in no way different from s.57(4) of the Firearms Act 1968 or s.1 of the Prevention of Crime Act 1953 and that the existing case law applied.

Appeal refused.

(ix) D.P.P. v. Fellowes   3.5.10

[1993] Crim.L.R. 523

F., the appellant, walked down the path from the door of his maisonette to accept a newspaper from a delivery boy, who had previously delivered there. As the boy handed the paper over the appellant's Rottweiler bit him on the thigh. The appellant was charged with being the owner of a dog which was dangerously out of control in a public place contrary to s.3(1) of the Dangerous Dogs Act 1991. Section 10(2) provided that "public place" meant any street, road or other place (whether or not enclosed) to which the public had or were permitted to have access for payment or otherwise and included the common parts of a building containing two or more separate dwellings. The justices concluded that as the boy had an implied and unrevoked licence to enter, having regard to the general purpose of the Act the garden of the property was a public place in that the public were permitted access to it. On appeal following conviction it was contended that the garden path was not a public place because those who entered did so not as a member of the public but as a visitor to the appellant's home (*Edwards* (1978) 67 Cr.App.R.228; *Williams* v. *D.P.P.* [1992] Crim.L.R. 502). The Crown argued that while the path was private property, it was also a public place within the special meaning of the statute.

Held, allowing the appeal, that there was considerable force in the Crown's argument if one simply read the statutory wording. Turning to the cases, *Edwards* concerned the Public Order Act 1936 which contained a definition both of private premises and of "public place". *Williams* v. *D.P.P.* concerned the issue of whether the tenth-floor landing of a block of flats was a "public place" for the purposes of the Criminal Justice Act 1967, s.91(4) which defined it as "any highway and other premises or place to which … the public have access, whether on payment or otherwise." It contained no definition of private premises, and the definition of "public place" in that statute and the one under consideration were almost identical, save that "public place" in the 1967 Act was said to include the various places referred to, whereas in the 1991 Act "public place" was said to mean any of the places it referred to. The difference in meaning was not material in this case, although, if anything, the 1991 Act definition was narrower. The other difference was that s.10(2) of the 1991 Act included the common parts of a building containing two or more separate dwellings, presumably as a result of the decision in *Knox* v. *Anderton* (1983) 76 Cr.App.R. 156.

In the light of the meaning given to "public place" in the Public Order Act 1936, and particularly in the Criminal Justice Act 1967, the path leading to the appellant's front door was not a public place within the meaning of the Dangerous Dogs Act 1991, s.10(2). The paper boy had visited it *qua* visitor and not *qua* member of the public. It was not possible to reach any different conclusion by a consideration of the purposes of the Dangerous Dogs Act 1991 alone. The only circumstances in which that Act provided for an offence in a private place was in s.3(2), which was a very narrow provision. Parliament had, for whatever reason, expressed this offence in narrow terms, and that was not wide enough to include events which occurred in places to which people were invited to attend as visitors, whether by express or implied licence.

Appeal allowed.

(x) Normand v. Donnelly 3.5.11

1993 S.C.C.R. 639

D., the respondent, was charged with a contravention of the 1953 Act by having an offensive weapon with him at the casualty department of an infirmary. The department was constructed on an open-plan principle, with a reception desk, a waiting area and cubicles with curtains for privacy. The evidence related to the finding of the weapon in the respondent's pocket while he was in a treatment cubicle. When asked about his possession of the weapon, the respondent replied, "It's for self-defence, to get me out the house." A police officer gave evidence that the cubicle was "a private place" and that anyone who walked into it would be asked to leave.

The sheriff acquitted the respondent on a submission of no case to answer on the grounds that the place where he had the weapon was not a public place and that there was insufficient evidence to infer that he had earlier had the weapon in a public area. The prosecutor appealed to the High Court by stated case.

Held, (1) that the privacy in which the doctor treats the patient can only be achieved if members of the public as such are excluded and that, on the evidence led, the sheriff was well founded in concluding that the cubicle was not a public place; but

(2) that there was sufficient evidence to allow an inference to be drawn that the respondent had passed through a public area before entering the cubicle and that an inference could be drawn from his reply that he had had the weapon with him then; and appeal allowed and case remitted to the sheriff to proceed with the trial.

Following acquittal the procurator fiscal appealed to the High Court by stated case, the matters desired to bring under review being:

"1. The sheriff erred in law in holding that a treatment cubicle within the casualty department of Glasgow Royal Infirmary was not a 'public place' for the purposes of the Prevention of Crime Act 1953, section 1.

2. The sheriff erred in law in holding that evidence of the respondent's possession of a knife within a treatment cubicle in the casualty department of Glasgow Royal Infirmary was not evidence of his possession of that knife in the waiting and reception areas of said department, when evidence had been led that the respondent had passed through the waiting and reception areas on his way to the cubicle and under caution had said, in respect of his possession of the knife, 'It's for self-defence, to get me out of the house.'"

In the stated case the sheriff (Duncan) stated, *inter alia*:

"The evidence of the police was to the effect that in the early hours of 23rd February 1992 they were carrying out their duties elsewhere in Glasgow Royal Infirmary when they were called to the casualty department and made aware of circumstances regarding the respondent. They approached a treatment cubicle within the accident and emergency department, which was partitioned off. The respondent was in the process of receiving treatment for a cut on his arm and was sitting on a treatment trolley, with his legs over the side. He was sitting side on. The police saw what appeared to be the handle of a cleaver-type knife protruding from his back pocket. Constable Love removed the cleaver from his back pocket. He was not taken into custody. In response to being cautioned at common law concerning his possession, he stated, 'It's for self-defence, to get me out the house.' When cautioned and charged with a contravention of section 1 of the Prevention of Crimes Act 1953 he replied, 'It was a panic attack.' ...

"There was evidence in cross-examination about the layout of the casualty department. No evidence was led in chief or in re-examination by the fiscal about the layout of the casualty department. General evidence was given by Constable Love that the patients initially report to reception and are asked to wait in a waiting area until they are called for treatment by the doctor. In submissions the Crown could not point to any evidence to show that the respondent had gone through that procedure or that he must have had possession of the cleaver in the waiting or reception areas of the casualty department.

"There was evidence that there was a reception desk, a waiting area and treatment cubicles. It was open plan. The cubicles had curtains for privacy. In cross-examination, Sergeant Gold said that it is not normal procedure for anyone to walk into a cubicle. If a person attempts to do so, he would be asked to leave. The doctor treated the patient in private. Sergeant Gold gave evidence that the cubicle was 'a private place'. There was very little evidence indeed taken from the police as to how the cubicle was formed, or whether it was a makeshift or permanent structure.

"At the conclusion of the Crown case it was submitted on behalf of the respondent that the Crown had failed to prove that the [respondent] had possession of an offensive weapon in 'a public place'. The respondent's solicitor pointed to the words used by Sergeant Gold. He also cited the case of *Coull v Guild*, 1986 S.L.T. 184, which involved the possession of an offensive weapon in the hospital grounds of the Victoria Hospital, Kirkcaldy, and also in a public street in Kirkcaldy. However, in that case the question of whether the hospital grounds were a 'public place' was not decided.

"The respondent's solicitor drew an analogy with a doctor's surgery, whereby a patient visits reception and is asked to have a seat in the waiting area until he is called for his consultation with the doctor in the doctor's room. He argued that the doctor's room could not be considered a public place within the terms of the Act, as the patient is there by invitation. He also drew comparisons with, e.g., insurance offices, where there is a public counter behind which there may be open-plan offices with typists at work. The public would have no right of access to the open-plan office and would be there only by invitation. Such an area, he submitted, would not be 'a public place'. In this case, he argued, the cubicle in which the respondent was receiving treatment, albeit within the general area of the casualty department, was not 'a public place'.

"For the Crown it was submitted that a hospital by its very nature is a public place. The staff, although qualified, are still members of the public. If a person was found in an operating theatre with an offensive weapon, that could be a public place and an offence would be committed under the 1953 Act. It was argued for the Crown that the public were permitted access to a hospital. The procurator fiscal depute agreed that the public had unlimited access to the casualty department of a hospital and to go through the system. That had not been taken in evidence and in some circumstances I would have to doubt the accuracy of the proposition. It was also argued that the pulling of two screens did not stop a place being a 'public place'. Unfortunately, again, there was no specific evidence as to how the cubicle had been formed.

"Section 1(4) of the Prevention of Crime Act 1953 states:

> 'In this section "public place" includes any highway and any other premises or place to which at the material time the public have or are permitted to have access, whether on payment or otherwise.'

"It appeared to me that the 'material time' related to the point at which the cleaver was proved to be in the possession of the respondent. At the material time he was in the treatment cubicle. The bare evidence was that the police only saw him in the cubicle. There was no evidence as to where he had been or come from. Further, given the evidence of the police and in particular of Sergeant Gold that he considered the cubicle to be a 'private place', I came to the conclusion that the Crown had failed to prove that the treatment cubicle was a 'public place' in terms of the Act. Accordingly the submission in terms of section 345A of the Criminal Procedure (Scotland) Act 1975, as amended, made on behalf of the respondent, was sustained.

"I reached this decision with some regret, considering the difficulties faced by hospital doctors and nurses, but looking to the wording of the Act and the evidence, which did not disclose where the respondent had been before entering the cubicle, it appeared the Crown had failed to prove its case. I was not prepared to draw the inference that the respondent must have, for at least some time, been in possession of the cleaver in the waiting or reception areas, each of which are public places. I did not consider that there was sufficient evidence before me to allow me to draw that inference."

The questions for the opinion of the High Court were:

"1.   Was I entitled to hold that the Crown failed to prove that the treatment cubicle in the casualty department of Glasgow Royal Infirmary was a public place?
2.   Was I correct in holding that there was insufficient evidence before me to allow me to draw the inference that the respondent must have been in possession of the cleaver in the waiting or reception area?
3.   Was I entitled to sustain the respondent's submission in terms of section 345A of the Criminal Procedure (Scotland) Act 1975, as amended?"

Lord Justice-Clerk (Ross) (at p. 642)
"In presenting the appeal the advocate-depute reminded us that the charge libelled a contravention of section 1(1) of the Prevention of Crime Act 1953 and he drew attention to the fact that section 1(4) of the Act defines 'public place'. In that subsection it is stated *inter alia*:

'In this section "public place" includes any highway and any other premises or place to which at the material time the public have or are permitted to have access, whether on payment or otherwise.'

"The advocate-depute drew attention to what the sheriff stated in her note regarding the evidence which had been led before her and he maintained that she had erred in holding that the treatment cubicle where the respondent was when the police found him was a public place. The evidence led before the sheriff disclosed that in the early hours of 23rd February 1992 police officers were called to the casualty department at Glasgow Royal Infirmary. They approached a treatment cubicle within the accident and emergency department, which was partitioned off. The respondent was in the process of receiving treatment for a cut on his arm and was sitting on a treatment trolley with his legs over the side. He was sitting side on. The police saw what appeared to be the handle of a cleaver-type knife protruding from his back pocket. One of the police officers removed the cleaver from that pocket. In response to being cautioned at common law concerning his possession of that article, the respondent replied 'It's for self-defence, to get me out the house.' He was then cautioned and charged. The sheriff goes on to describe the cleaver and she also says that there was evidence in cross-examination about the layout of the casualty department and she describes the procedure which was followed with patients. She goes on to say that there were a reception desk, a waiting area and treatment cubicles. It was open plan. The cubicles had curtains for privacy. In cross-examination Sergeant Gold stated that it is not normal procedure for anyone to walk into a cubicle and that, if a person attempts to do so, he would be asked to leave. The doctor treated the patient in private. Sergeant Gold gave evidence that the cubicle was 'a private place'.

"The advocate depute maintained that what the evidence revealed was that members of the public were treated in cubicles, but while there they remained members of the public. The advocate-depute accepted that within premises such as the casualty department of a hospital there would be areas from which the public were excluded, such as staff quarters or rooms which bore notices saying that they were private, but he maintained that the treatment cubicle was not such a place and that it was a public place within the meaning of the statute.

"On behalf of the respondent [counsel for the appellant] disputed that the treatment cubicle be regarded as a public place. He maintained that whether any particular area was a public place was a question of fact and degree. He referred to *R. v Waters* [(1963) 47 Cr.App.R. 149]. That was a case under the Road Traffic Act and although he relied upon the case for the approach which ought to be made to questions of this kind, we have not derived much assistance from the case. He did, however, stress that when considering whether a particular place was a public place or a private place, it was proper to consider whether steps were taken to confine admission to the particular place to a restricted class of persons only and he contended that if that was so, the place should be regarded as a private place.

"Having regard to what the sheriff says in the case regarding the evidence which was before her, we have come to the conclusion that the treatment cubicle in which the police officers found the respondent was not a public place within the meaning of the Act of 1953. It was not in our judgment a place to which the public were permitted to have access at the material time. The evidence indeed is to the contrary. As we have already observed, the evidence of the police sergeant was that it was not normal procedure for anyone to walk into a cubicle and, indeed, that if a person attempted to do so, he would be asked to leave. The doctor treats the patient in private and privacy in our view can only be achieved if members of the public as such are excluded. Accordingly on the basis of the evidence led before the sheriff we are satisfied that she was well founded in concluding that the treatment cubicle was not a public place but was a place from which the public as such were excluded. It follows that question 1 in the case will be answered in the affirmative.

"The advocate-depute, however, raised a second point in the appeal. He maintained that the sheriff had erred in declining to draw the inference that the respondent must have been in possession of the cleaver in the waiting and reception areas, each of which were public places. She stated in the case that she did not consider that there was sufficient evidence before her to allow her to draw that inference, whereas the advocate-depute maintained that at the stage of the no case to answer submission she ought to have appreciated that there was sufficient evidence before her which would allow her to draw that inference. He maintained that, having regard to the description which the police officers gave of the layout of the casualty department, it was really an inevitable inference that the respondent must have been in the reception waiting area before he reached the treatment cubicle.

"In the case the sheriff tells us that the general evidence was given by Constable Love that patients initially report to reception and are asked to wait in a waiting area until they are called for treatment by the doctor. The sheriff remarked that the Crown could not point to any evidence to show that the respondent had gone through that procedure or that he must have had possession of the cleaver in the waiting or reception area of the casualty department. We appreciate that there was no direct evidence to that effect but we have come to the conclusion that there was sufficient evidence to allow such an inference to be drawn. Having regard to the description of the area, we are satisfied that the sheriff would have been entitled to draw the inference that before he reached the treatment cubicle the respondent must have reported to reception and either proceeded straight from reception to the treatment cubicle or waited in the waiting area until he was called for treatment. It might then be a question as to whether the respondent must necessarily have had possession of the cleaver while he was in the waiting or reception area of the casualty department. In that connection his reply to caution is of significance because he stated, as has already been noted, 'It's for self-defence, to get me out the house', and it could accordingly reasonably be inferred from that evidence that the cleaver had been with him since he left his own house and accordingly that it must have been in his possession while he was in the casualty department prior to being taken into the treatment cubicle.

"Accordingly we are satisfied that in that connection the sheriff erred and shall accordingly answer question 2 in the negative. It follows that the third question must also be answered in the negative and having answered the questions as we have indicated we shall then remit the case to the sheriff to proceed with the trial."

[Appeal allowed.]

(xi) McGeachy v. Normand   3.5.12

1994 S.L.T. 429

McG. was charged on summary complaint with having charge of a dog which was dangerously out of control in a public place, contrary to s.3(1) of the Dangerous Dogs Act 1991. The sheriff found that an 11-year-old boy was bitten by the accused's dog when the boy was taking a short cut through the garden area of a block of houses which was bounded by a 7-foot-high fence. There were no findings to indicate that the garden area was a place to which the public had or were permitted to have access or that it was part of the common parts of the building to which it was attached. The sheriff found that it was a public place within the meaning of the 1991 Act and convicted the accused, who appealed by stated case.

Held (of consent of the Crown), that the facts fell short of what was needed to establish that the garden area was a public place within s.10(2) of the 1991 Act; and appeal *allowed* and conviction *quashed.*

Opinion reserved, on whether the common parts of a building could include parts of the solum of the property lying outwith the building.

Lord Justice-General (Hope) (at p. 430)

"The appellant is James McGeachy who went to trial in the sheriff court at Glasgow on a charge under s3(1) of the Dangerous Dogs Act 1991. The charge was to the effect that on 18 October 1992 in a public place, namely in Frankfield Road, Cardowan, Stepps, a German shepherd dog was dangerously out of control in respect that it attacked and injured an 11 year old boy. The charge went on to state that the appellant was the owner of, and was in charge of, the dog and that he was guilty of an aggravated offence in terms of the subsection.

"A motion was made at the end of the Crown case that there was no case to answer on the ground that the place where the incident occurred was not a public place within the meaning of the Act. This motion was repelled, and the appellant did not give evidence. At the end of the trial he was found guilty of the offence. The dog had already been destroyed by the time when the appellant was convicted. The sheriff confined his disposal of the case to the making of a fine and a compensation order.

"The findings of fact tell us that the complainer was making a short cut on his way home from a place where he had been playing football to his own house. The short cut took him through what is described in the findings as the garden area of a block of houses. This was next to the block of houses in which the appellant lived. The boy climbed the fence to the rear of this garden area which is said to have been some seven feet in height. When he was in the garden area the appellant's dog broke free from the appellant's control outside his door in the next block. It bounded over two fences and into the area where the boy was, where it attacked and bit him. The sheriff has found as finding 6 in the case that the garden area where the dog attacked and savaged the complainer was a public place within the meaning of the Dangerous Dogs Act 1991.

"There is no doubt that for the Crown to establish that an offence in terms of subs (1) of s3 has been committed it must prove that the dog was dangerously out of control in a public place. Subsection (3) of that section deals with a different situation where the incident takes place in a place which is not a public place. That is an indication, if further indication is needed, that it is essential for the Crown to prove, if the charge is brought under subs (1), that the offence was committed in a public place. Section 10(2) of the Act provides the definition of that expression in these terms, that 'public place' means any street, road or other place (whether or not enclosed) to which the public have or are permitted to have access whether for payment or otherwise, and includes the common parts of a building containing two or more separate dwellings.

"The findings of fact in this case are not at all clear as to the precise nature of the garden area in which the incident occurred. Counsel who appeared for the appellant submitted that all one could gather from the findings was that this was a garden area which had some kind of boundary round it. It was sufficient for the purposes of her argument that the findings did not indicate that this was an area to which the public had access, nor was there any indication that the public were permitted to have access to it. Furthermore, there was nothing in the findings to show that this garden area was part of the common parts of the building to which . it was attached. Basing her submission on the point that the onus was on the Crown to show that the garden area was a public place as defined in s10(2) of the Act, she submitted that the sheriff was in error in the decision which he reached on this point.

"The Lord Advocate informed us that he had decided that he could not support this conviction. He accepted that the stated case was not clear as to the precise nature of the garden area, and he considered that one could not be satisfied, on the findings, that the incident occurred in a public place. That may well have been due to the nature of the evidence which was led, which has been summarised for us briefly by the sheriff. He tells us that there was no evidence from any of the occupants of the garden area of the relevant block, and in particular that there was no evidence that the garden area was exclusive to any one or more apartments in it.

"The Lord Advocate went on to make reference to English authority to support the position which he has adopted in this case. Reference was made to *R v Edwards; R v Roberts* (1978) 67 CrAppR at p 231 where Bridge LJ said this about the meaning of the expression 'public place' in s5 of the Public Order Act 1936: 'it seems to this Court that it is quite impossible to hold that the expression "public place" can be construed as extending to the front gardens of private premises simply on the footing on which the learned judge relied that members of the public have an implied licence to pass through those private gardens in order to obtain access to the front doors of private premises if they have some lawful occasion for so doing.'

"Our attention was also drawn to *DPP v Fellowes* which was a case under the Dangerous Dogs Act 1991. In that case the appellant walked down the path from the door of his maisonette to accept a newspaper from a paper boy who had previously delivered there. As the boy handed the paper over, the appellant's rottweiler bit him on the thigh. The appellant was charged with being the owner of a dog which was dangerously out of control in a public place contrary to s3(1) of the Act. His conviction under that subsection was quashed on appeal, having regard in particular to the definition of public place in s10(2) of the 1991 Act.

"As the Lord Advocate pointed out, the circumstances of these cases indicate clearly that the facts of the present case, so far as elucidated by the findings, are insufficient to demonstrate that the garden area was a place to which the public had access or could be regarded as a public place within the ordinary meaning of those words. Indeed, there is no suggestion that the boy had an implied licence to be where he was when he was attacked. He was not on any of the paths leading to the front doors of the houses in the block, and in any event he had no intention of visiting any of the houses. So far as the extended meaning given to the phrase by the latter part of s10(2) of the Act is concerned, the Lord Advocate pointed out that the English authorities were to the effect that it was designed to bring into the definition common parts within the structure of a building, such as landings or staircases. Plainly that is not the situation with which we are concerned in the present case, as the boy was not within the structure of the building when he was attacked. It is not necessary for us to decide, in this case, whether the common parts of a building for the purposes of s10(2) can include parts of the solum of the property lying outwith the building such as its garden area, since the findings are insufficient to establish that the garden area where the boy was attacked was common to the block to which it was attached.

"We have summarised the Lord Advocate's arguments in order to indicate the basis upon which he decided that he could not support this conviction. So far as the facts are concerned, it appears to us that they fall short of what would be needed in order to establish that the place where this incident occurred was a public place within the definition in the Act. For these reasons we shall answer the first question in the case in the negative. We find it unnecessary to answer the other question and we shall of consent allow the appeal."

Appeal allowed.

3.5.13   **(xii) Rodger v. Normand**

1994 S.C.C.R. 861

R., the appellant, who was aged 21, was charged with driving dangerously "on a road or other public place", contrary to s.2 of the Road Traffic Act 1988. The locus of the offence was a school playground. Although it was the policy of the local authority who owned the school that the public should not be permitted in the school grounds after hours, there was no sign denying access, and it was well known that pupils played in the grounds after hours and that other children also went there to play. The playground was also used by other persons and it was said to be used like a leisure park. The appellant was convicted of careless driving, contrary to s.3 of the 1988 Act, and appealed to the High Court on the ground that the locus was not a road or public place. It was conceded in the appeal that it was not a road.

Held, that the test was whether the place in question was one on which members of the public might be found and over which they might be expected to be passing or were in use to have access, that in this case the persons who might be expected to be found in the grounds were not confined to pupils and teachers and others who had business there, that the children and others who went there did so without objection and their use of the grounds was tolerated by the proprietor, so that they were not trespassers, and that they went there because the grounds were open to the public or the public were permitted to have access to them, and accordingly they were a public place; and appeal refused.

R. was convicted ... and appealed to the High Court by stated case. The sheriff made, *inter alia,* the following findings in fact.

"1. On 1st October 1992 Brian Spear was riding a Yamaha motorcycle in the playing field area of St Augustine's School, Liddesdale Road, Glasgow. It was a trail motorcycle constructed for off-road purposes. The appellant was also present. The appellant had been told by the police to stay off the roads and to ride the motorcycle in fields or the playground.

2. The appellant asked for, and was given, the motorcycle to ride ...

3. At about 5.30 p.m. the complainer was playing in the school grounds with his friends ... He had a skateboard. They had seen the appellant and Brian Spear with the motorcycle in the playing fields. They went into the school grounds on a daily basis and got in through open gates which were kept open. Other children went there to play as well. Some children played on skateboards. It was common to find young boys there. They had nowhere else to play. It was popular with children as well as older persons. Youngsters from age five played there on tricycles. Football and golf were played. It was used like a leisure park. Brian Spear and other friends of the appellant used the school grounds. The appellant had ridden there on many occasions. There was also a club on Tuesday and Thursday nights. The policy of Strathclyde Regional Council, as the owners of the school, was that people should not be permitted into the school grounds after hours unless they had business there.

The gates were left open to allow such people in and out after hours."

In his note the sheriff stated, *inter alia*:

"On behalf of the appellant it was said that the interpretation involved a pragmatic and commonsense approach. The school grounds were surrounded by a fence and the public were not allowed to park vehicles within the school precincts. It was said that the fact that the gates were left open was irrelevant as no one would regard the school as a place to which they would normally go as members of the general public. It was also said that the regional policy was to allow the janitor a discretion as to whether or not he allowed children in and the public generally were excluded. Only a class of person, viz., children, were allowed entry, following the granting of permission ...

"[The Crown] contended that the park was 'a road or other public place' because children frequently played there and the appellant and his friends resorted there also.

"In all the circumstances I favoured the Crown's argument. The appellant himself said that children used the area like a leisure centre and that older people used the playground. He had often used the school grounds and ridden his motorcycle there frequently over a two-year period. It was used by his friends (who were not 'children') and was popular with older people. 'Older people' was used in a context which gave rise to the inference that it meant used by them for enjoyment. There was no physical obstruction to entry. No sign prohibited entry. Although the regional official said that only children were allowed in, that conflicted with the evidence of others, including the accused. In any event, the region did not appear to enforce such a policy. Moreover, it appeared to me that children are not a class of person when the term encompasses ages from four onwards and included children who were not pupils at that school. For these reasons I was of the view that the path which formed the locus was 'a road or other public place' in terms of the statute."

The questions for the opinion of the High Court were:

"1.   On the facts found to have been admitted or proved, was I entitled to hold that the locus was a road or other public place?

2.   On the facts found to have been admitted or proved, was I entitled to convict the appellant?"

Lord Justice-General (Hope) (at p. 863)

"The appellant went to trial in the sheriff court at Glasgow charged with the reset of a motorcycle, with driving the motorcycle dangerously in the grounds of St Augustine's Secondary School, Liddesdale Road, Glasgow, at excessive speed, whereby the motorcycle collided with a six-year-old boy, and losing control of the motorcycle, whereby it was damaged and the boy was injured, contrary to section 2 of the Road Traffic Act 1988, as amended, and with driving or riding the motorcycle without wearing protective headgear, contrary to regulation 4(1) of the Motor Cycles (Protective Helmets) Regulations 1980. The charge of reset was withdrawn by the Crown at the end of the Crown case. The appellant was found guilty of a contravention of section 3 of the Road Traffic Act 1988, as an alternative to the charge of dangerous driving, and he was found guilty as libelled in regard to the charge about not wearing protective headgear.

"A motion had been made that there was no case to answer in respect of these two charges. It was contended that there was insufficient evidence to show that the locus was a road or other public place for the purposes of the Road Traffic Act 1988. The ground on which the appellant now seeks to challenge his conviction is that the sheriff erred in law in repelling that motion and holding that there was sufficient evidence to show that the locus was a road or other public place in terms of the statute.

"Section 2 of the Road Traffic Act 1988, as amended, provides that a person who drives a mechanically propelled vehicle dangerously 'on a road or other public place' is guilty of an offence. Section 3, which provides for the alternative offence of careless and inconsiderate driving, refers also to the driving of the vehicle 'on a road or other public place'. Regulation 4(1) of the 1980 Regulations provides:

> 'Save as provided in paragraph (2) below, every person driving or riding (otherwise than in a sidecar) on a motor bicycle when on a road shall wear protective headgear.'

"Section 192(1) of the Road Traffic Act 1988, as amended by paragraph 78 of Schedule 4 to the Road Traffic Act 1991, provides that the word 'road' in relation to Scotland

> 'means any road within the meaning of the Roads (Scotland) Act 1984 and any other way to which the public has access, and includes bridges over which a road passes.'

"Section 151 of the 1984 Act defines the expression 'road' as meaning inter alia 'any way (other than a waterway) over which there is a public right of passage'. The learned advocate-depute conceded that the place where the appellant was riding the motorcycle was not a 'road' for the purposes of the Act, so it is not necessary for us to consider the application of the definition of that word to the facts of this case. The question is whether the place where he was riding his motorcycle was within the expression 'or other public place'. Strictly speaking, the advocate-depute's concession has the result that the appellant ought not to have been convicted of a breach of the 1980 Regulations, as they apply only to a person driving or riding a motorcycle on a 'road'. But no separate argument was directed to that charge, on which the appellant was admonished and dismissed by the sheriff, and we do not need to take up further time with it.

"The facts of the case are that the appellant was riding the motorcycle in the grounds of a school. Access to the grounds could be obtained by means of four entrances. There were three entrances on Liddesdale Road and another entrance leading from the playing-field area. The gates to all these entrances were left open, although the janitorial staff had instructions to lock them at 6.30 p.m. There was a car park in the school grounds where teachers and workmen with business at the school parked their cars. But the public could not park there and there was no through-road through the school grounds. Nevertheless it was well known that school pupils played in the school grounds after school hours and that other children also went there to play. Although it was the policy of Strathclyde Regional Council, as owners of the school, that people should not be permitted into the school grounds after hours unless they had business there, there was no sign at the entrances or elsewhere which denied access to the premises. The gates were left open to allow people in and out after hours. It was common to find young boys in the school grounds, as they had nowhere else to play. The grounds were used both by children and by other persons like a leisure park. Some children played on skateboards, and football and golf were played there also. The appellant, who was aged twenty-one, had been told by the police to stay off the roads and to ride the motorcycle in fields or in the playgrounds.

"The accident took place on a pathway at the rear of the secondary school building. The appellant was riding his motorcycle down the path, up and down which he had ridden several times previously, when he was confronted by the complainer, who was on a skateboard. It is not now disputed that the appellant, who was going too fast to avoid the complainer, was riding the motorcycle carelessly and that, if he was riding it in a 'public place', he was guilty of a contravention of section 3 of the 1988 Act.

"[Counsel for the appellant] submitted that, on the facts of this case, the place where the appellant was riding the motorcycle was not a public place. There was no through-road and the public could not park there. The grounds were used by children and some other people but not by the public in general. It was the policy not to admit people to the school grounds after school hours and there was no express or implied invitation to the public to enter them. In effect both the appellant and the complainer were trespassers and they could have been asked to leave the school grounds at any time by the janitor. The learned advocate-depute did not seek to argue that there was a public right of access. But he said that there was sufficient material in the sheriff's findings to show that the school grounds were used by the public. That was enough for them to be a public place. The sheriff had found that the school grounds were used like a leisure park by children and others who went there to play. While the reference to a public place meant a place used by the public generally, the test was whether its use was restricted to those members of the public who had business in the school or whether it was available to any member of the public who wished to go there for his or her own purposes.

"Although we are concerned in this case with the meaning of the phrase 'or other public place' and not with the meaning of the word 'road' as defined by the Act, there is common to both expressions the requirement that the place is one to which the public has access. The definition of 'road' in section 196(1) of the Road Traffic Act 1972, as in the equivalent provisions of the Road Traffic Acts 1930 and 1960, was that it means 'any highway and any other road to which the public has access.' The meaning of the phrase 'to which the public has access' was considered in *Harrison* v *Hill* 1931 S.L.T. 598 in regard to the definition of 'road' in section 121(1) of the 1930 Act and in *Cheyne* v *Macneill* 1973 S.L.T. 27 in regard to the definition of 'road' in section 257(1) of the 1960 Act.

"In *Paterson* v *Ogilvy* 1957 S.L.T. 354 the question was whether a private field used for the time being as parking ground for visitors to the Royal Highland Show at Inverness was a 'public place' within the meaning of section 15(1) of the 1930 Act, which rendered a person driving or in charge of a motor-car on a road or other public place when under the influence of drink liable to a penalty. It was held that it was, because it was a place which was used by the public and to which they had access. In *Thomson* v *MacPhail* 1993 S.L.T. 225 it was conceded that a private road leading to a reservoir was not a road within the definition of that expression for the purposes of the 1988 Act as it then stood. But it was held that the road was nevertheless used by the public and that it was a public place within the meaning of the statute. The test which was applied was that mentioned by Lord Justice-General Emslie in *Brown* v *Braid* 1995 S.L.T. 37, namely whether the place was one on which members of the public might be expected to be found and over which they might be expected to be passing or over which they were in use to have access. Those words were taken from the opinion of the court in *Cheyne* v *Macneill* at p. 30, where the point was made that the question was not one as to the measure or extent of the legal right of access or passage which members of the public could enforce or enjoy but as to the use which was made of the place by the public. As we see it the purpose of the statute, whether one is dealing with a road or other place, is to secure the safety of the public in places where the public may be expected to be or to have access.

"In the present case the findings show that the persons who might be expected to be found in the school grounds were not confined to the pupils and teachers of the school and others who had business there. They were used by children, and by older persons also, as a leisure park when the gates were open and they could have access to them out of school hours. [Counsel] said that this did not amount to use by the public generally and that, in any event, as they had no permission to be there, the persons who played in the grounds were trespassers. But in our opinion the findings show that the children and others who went there were in the school grounds without objection. Their use of the school grounds was not barred by any obstruction or otherwise prohibited. In practice they were allowed to enter the school grounds at will and their use of them as a playground was acquiesced in or tolerated by the proprietor. In *Cheyne* v *Macneill* it was said that 'access' as used in the definition of 'road' covers access by permission express or implied from, or acquiescence or tolerance by, the person or persons with legal right to control its use. In that sense the children and others in this case had access to the school grounds and they were not trespassers. In *Harrison* v *Hill* at p. 600 Lord Justice-General Clyde said that, when the statute speaks of 'the public', what is meant is the public generally and not the special class of members of the public who had occasion to go to the premises for business or social purposes. The distinction, then, is between persons who are there in response to an invitation, permission or request not issued to the public generally, and those members of the public who choose to go to the place because it is open to the public or because the public are permitted to have access to it. It was in the latter sense, as members of the public, that the children and others were in the school grounds when they went there to play.

"The sheriff held that the school grounds were a road or other public place, and the first question in the case is whether he was entitled to make that finding. On the approach which was taken by the advocate-depute, and in the light of the findings in this case, what the sheriff should have done was to hold that, although not a road, the school grounds were a public place within the meaning of the statute. We shall decline therefore to answer the first question. The second question asks whether, on the facts found to have been admitted or proved, the sheriff was entitled to convict the appellant. We shall answer that question in the affirmative and refuse the appeal."

Appeal refused.

NOTE
This decision is of importance in relation to a general definition of "public place" or, indeed, one in the context of the statutory provision relating to offensive weapons. In *Hand* v. *Lees,* 1993 G.W.D. 2–100 the appellant had an appeal against sentence refused where he had been asked by a teacher to leave the playground of his former school and produced a knife. It does not seem to have been put in issue that the locus was a public place. It may, of course, be arguable that the presence of the appellant made the school playground a public place.

Section 1(3) of the 1953 Act: power of arrest **3.6.1**

(i) R. v. Forbes **3.6.2**

[1984] Crim.L.R. 482

F. pointed a knife at a policeman and said "It's going to cut you." One hour later that policeman saw F. pointing the same knife at two other policemen. The first officer told F. that he was being arrested for being in possession of an offensive weapon. In the course of a struggle the officer was injured slightly.

F. was acquitted of possessing an offensive weapon. He was convicted of assault with intent to resist arrest. F. appealed on the ground that the trial judge had failed to direct the jury on the limitations on the powers of arrest for the offence of possession of an offensive weapon in terms of s.1(3) of the 1953 Act.

Held, that s.1(3) of the 1953 Act plainly connoted a future situation and accordingly what had occurred in the past was no more than of evidential value in the context of the purported arrest.

The jury had not been directed on the limitations imposed by s.1(3) in the circumstances of this case and that amounted to a misdirection. The provision had come as a surprise to many people, including their Lordships.

Police should ensure that they complied with the provisions of the 1953 Act at the time of arrest, and the prosecution should ensure that at the time of trial there was sufficient evidence to justify the case being put within the limits of s.1(3).

Appeal allowed.

3.6.3   (ii) Houghton v. Chief Constable of Greater Manchester

(1987) 84 Cr.App.R. 319

For the facts of this case, see para. 3.2.9 above.

May, L.J. (at p. 322)
"... under [section 1] subsection (3) the power of arrest only arises
where both parts of the subsection are satisfied, that is to say, where
a constable has reasonable cause to believe that a person is
committing an offence under [section 1] subsection (1) *and* the
constable is not satisfied as to that person's identity or place of
residence, or the other requirement of that subsection but which is
not relevant in the circumstances of the present case. The offence
created by section 1(1) is not an arrestable offence under section 2
of the Criminal Law Act 1967."

(At p. 324)
"[The] mere fact that a person has an offensive weapon on him, albeit
a weapon offensive *per se*, does not of itself, as section 1(3) of the 1953
Act makes clear, give a police officer the right to arrest. It is necessary
to be satisfied about the other requirements in that subsection."

And (at p. 325)
"Where the subsection [*i.e.* section 1(3)] speaks of 'that person's
identity or place of residence,' in my judgment all it means is that
person's name and address. As this is not an arrestable offence, where
an officer is satisfied of a person's name and address, then it will be
possible to proceed by way of summary process in respect of an alleged
offence under subsection (1) without difficulty. On the other hand, if
the officer is not satisfied about a person's name and address, then, if
he is not arrested then and there, the officer may lose him and not be
able to identify him for the purpose of proceedings thereafter."

                                        Appeal allowed
                                        (on another issue).

3.7.1   *Section 1(4) of the 1953 Act: definition of offensive weapon*

3.7.2   (i) Woodward v. Koessler

[1958] 3 All E.R. 557

K. tried to break into a cinema by forcing open the door with a
sheath knife and the elderly caretaker appeared. K. went up to the

man, holding the knife in a threatening attitude as if to strike with it, and said "Can you see this?"

K. was charged with a contravention of s.1(1) of the 1953 Act. At his trial the magistrates found him not guilty and the prosecutor appealed.

Lord Goddard, C.J. (at p.558)

"The justices came to the conclusion that the accused was not carrying an offensive weapon. Their reason apparently was that the words of the definition are rather obscure. By s.1(4) of the Prevention of Crime Act 1953:

> '"offensive weapon" means any article made or adapted for use for causing injury to the person, or intended by the person having it with him for such use by him.'

"It could be said that the sheath knife was not made for the purpose of causing injury, though I do not know what other use these sheath knives or flick knives have; but assuming that it is like a razor, made primarily for the purpose of shaving and not for the purpose of causing injury, where I think that the justices have gone wrong is in holding that, when the accused said that he did not intend to cause injury, that statement was conclusive. The justices have taken much too narrow a view of the words 'causes injury', because the accused obviously did intend to cause injury; frightening or intimidating a person is causing injury. If we were to hold that this young man with this shocking weapon was not in possession of an offensive weapon for causing injury, when he went up to an elderly man and said 'Can you see this?', it would be driving a coach and four through this useful Act. It would hardly ever be possible to get a conviction. We know well why it is rather an obscure definition, viz., because one of the weapons that these young hooligans like to use is a bicycle chain. The bicycle chain is not made for injury, but if a boy is swinging a bicycle chain saying 'Look out', that is using an offensive weapon."

Donovan, J. (at p. 558)

"I agree. Counsel for the accused founds himself on the words 'having it with him', and says that the accused must be found to have taken the weapon out with him with the intention of causing injury. Counsel says that in this case the accused took it for the purpose of breaking into the cinema. I do not agree with that narrow interpretation of the words 'having it with him'. All that one has to do for the purpose of ascertaining what the intention is is to look and see what use was in fact made of it. If it is found that the accused did in fact make use of it for the purpose of causing injury he had it with him for that purpose. I think that the evidence shows that the accused in this case did have it with him for the purpose of causing injury. I may add that after he was taken into custody he handed the knife, unseen, to one of his companions, so that when he was searched it would not be found on him. One wonders why, if he knew it was not for causing injury, he threatened the caretaker with it saying—'Can you see this?'"

Appeal allowed.

NOTE

The definition of "offensive weapon" is set out in s.1(4) of the 1953 Act. There is no classification of weapons within that statutory definition. Thus the phrase means any article made or adapted for use for causing injury to the person, or intended by the person having it with him for such use by him. It is now recognised generally, it is submitted, there are three types of offensive weapons arising from that definition. There is no authority for referring to offensive weapons as "Class One", "Class Two" or "Class Three."

Such a classification, in Scotland perhaps influenced by Sheriff Gordon's explanation of the law in *Criminal Law in Scotland* (2nd ed. 1978 at para. 30–44), is objectionable in that it implies that Class Three is less serious than the other two and Class Two is not so serious as Class One. That may not be so on the facts of individual cases.

3.7.3 **(ii) Farrell v. Rennicks**

(1959) 75 Sh.Ct.Rep. 113

R. and C. were charged with attempted housebreaking and also housebreaking. They pleaded guilty. R. was charged further with having on the same date and at the same place as the housebreaking having with him in a public place a sheath knife contrary to s.1(1) of the 1953 Act.

R. went to trial on the last matter and the circumstances of the case fully appear from the appended note issued by the sheriff along with his judgment.

"David Rennicks, you and John Crawford pleaded guilty to two charges (a) of attempting to break into 125, and (b) breaking into 123 Graham Street, Airdrie, on 5th May, 1959. For that you were both sentenced and have served your sentence. Both of you had previous convictions for theft. In the same complaint you, David Rennicks, were also charged that in Graham Street, aforesaid on the same date without lawful authority or reasonable excuse you had with you in a public place an offensive weapon, namely, a sheath knife, contrary to the Prevention of Crime Act, 1953, sec. 1(1). To that you plead not guilty. You and Crawford met on the afternoon of the 5th of May, 1959, went into a shop in Airdrie and each bought a sheath knife which is described in the carton which you have produced as a camping knife. It is also called an Eight-in-One, the reason being that the tool has a hardened steel blade, a can opener, a saw, a screwdriver, a bottle opener, a two-fold file, a corkscrew and a leather punch. The blade is fixed to a handle and stuck into the leather sheath and there is a loop round the handle which can attach the tool to a belt. In the handle are the other seven parts I have mentioned. You produced a receipt which, although it was obtained after you were charged, I accept as confirming that you and Crawford did in fact each buy one of these tools at that shop. It certainly could be used as an offensive weapon, particularly that part consisting of the steel blade (or knife). I shall refer to the whole tool now as a knife. In your evidence you said that you bought this knife for the purpose of using it as a tool for committing burglary. Crawford, on the other hand, says he bought it for camping purposes. You went from the shop to Sanderson's Bar in Airdrie and there remained until closing time. According to you, you discussed in the bar a burglarious intent, and you and Crawford left there and proceeded on your unlawful errand of breaking into the premises of the Chapelhall Co-operative Society Ltd., at 123–125 Graham Street, Airdrie. There you were ultimately both found by the police and arrested. The police evidence is that they found two jackets on the roof. In a jacket which belonged to you there was found this knife in its sheath and on your person there was found the loop of the leather sheath of the knife looped around a belt which you had round your waist. There is no evidence that at that time Crawford had any such knife either in his possession or in the other jacket which belonged to him. Your story is that you did not have this knife in your possession but had only the sheath of the knife in your jacket pocket and that Crawford had the knife part in his jacket pocket from which the police recovered it. The police evidence, on the other hand, consists of three constables, two of whom say that the knife in its sheath was found in the inside pocket of your jacket. The other constable said that only the sheath was found. I prefer the evidence of the first two constables. I am satisfied that you had both knife and sheath in your possession on the roof; I do not accept the story which you tell that you both went on the roof and that Crawford had his knife and sheath on him, you having given your knife and sheath to your brother Alexander in Sanderson's Bar prior to going to the Co-operative premises. Crawford's story is that in the bar you gave your knife to your younger brother Charles and that he (Crawford) having been asked by his father to give over his knife to him, refused to do so, whereupon you asked for Crawford's knife and he handed the knife in its sheath to you and while you were both on the roof Crawford asked you for the knife and you gave him the knifepart, retaining the sheath. I find your story, Crawford's story and your brother Alexander's story contradictory and unbelievable and in my view a tissue of lies in relation to what happened to the two knives in the bar and after. As I say, I am quite satisfied that you had the knife in your possession on the roof and were thus in possession of a sheath knife. That brings me to the next question—was this sheath knife an offensive weapon within the meaning of sub-sec. (4) of sec. 1 of the Prevention of Crime Act, 1953? To succeed the Crown must prove one of three things, either that the knife was 'an article made or adapted for use for causing injury to the person' or 'intended by the person having it with him for such use by him.' The fiscal, quite rightly in my view, did not seek to suggest that this knife came within either of the first two categories, but he has argued that it comes within the third category, that it was intended by you for such use. According to your story you bought the knife for the purpose of assisting you in committing burglary. According to Crawford's story you bought it for using when camping. My own view is that probably Crawford does not wish to disclose as you have frankly done that the knives were bought for the purpose of use in committing burglary. At any rate, I am going to give you the benefit of the doubt which is in my mind that you intended to use this knife for offensive purposes against the person. I think it quite possible that the reason why you bought this knife so eminently suited for the purpose was, as you say, to use it as a burglar's tool for offence against property and not for the purpose of causing injury to the person. So far as I know there have been only two cases on this charge mentioned in Law Reports and there were convictions in both. One is *Woodward* v. *Koessler* [1958] 3 All E.R. 557, where the facts are rather similar to this except for one vital difference, namely, that the youth accused on being discovered by the watchman went up to him holding the knife in a threatening attitude as if to strike with it and said to him: 'Can you see this?' The other case is the skean-dhu case in Aberdeen Sheriff Court. A skean-dhu is normally used on the person as part of Highland dress, but apparently in that case it was drawn from its usual ornamental position on the body and brandished in a manner which indicated the accused intended to use it to injure two policemen. The only mention I have seen of this case is in 1954 S.L.T. (News) at p. 67. In your case there is no evidence of threat. On the contrary, when challenged by the police from outside the premises into which you had entered, you opened the door to them and did not then have the knife on you."

Found Not proven.

(iii) R. v. McMahon 3.7.4

[1961] Crim.L.R. 622

M. was separately indicted for the offences of rape and possessing an offensive weapon and convicted in both cases. In the first case the jury were directed on the question of consent that: "for a woman to consent in the proper sense of the word it must be a voluntary exercise of her will. If she is deprived by persistence, by some degree of force, or persuasion, then it cannot be said that she is consenting." In the second case the jury were directed on the question of what constituted an offensive weapon by reference to s.1(1) and (4) of the Prevention of Crime Act 1953, and as follows: "If the intention was to cause injury to this woman then that knife, which might very well be an innocent object and implement in the ordinary way, might easily be an offensive weapon." Reference was then made to "physical injury." Section 1(1) of the Act of 1953 provides: "Any person who without lawful authority or reasonable excuse, the proof whereof shall lie on him, has with him in any public place any offensive weapon shall be guilty of an offence." Section 1(4) provides: "'offensive weapon' means any article made or adapted for use for causing injury to the person, or intended by the person having it with him for such use by him." On appeals to the Court of Criminal Appeal in each case: *Held*, that the direction to the jury on the question of consent in the first case was so plainly wrong that this court had no alternative but to set aside the conviction for rape. In the second case, the alleged offensive weapon was an ordinary penknife, *i.e.* a knife fitted with a single blade which was normally enclosed within a handle. The issue here was whether the words "for causing injury to the person" in s.1(4) of the Act of 1953 necessarily involved the infliction of physical injury or the intention to inflict such injury on a person. The matter had been raised in *Woodward v. Koessler* [1958] 3 All E.R. 557, in which it had been held that frightening or intimidating a person was "causing injury." In the present case the direction set a standard which was more favourable to the accused. In those circumstances, the appeal against the second conviction would be dismissed.

Appeal dismissed.

(iv) R. v. Edmonds 3.7.5

[1963] 2 Q.B. 142

E. and others were charged on an indictment containing three charges; first, conspiracy to rob, secondly, being suspected persons loitering with intent to commit a felony having in their possession a shotgun and starting pistol, and thirdly, being in possession of offensive weapons in a public place contrary to s.1 of the 1953 Act. The accused were acquitted by a jury on the first charge and the judge withdrew the second charge from the jury. The accused were convicted on the third charge and they appealed in regard to various misdirections said to have been given by the judge.

Winn. J. (at p. 150)

"The court does not wish to part from the case without saying that notice has been taken of the fact that in this summing up the judge, as earlier summings up which have come before the court, coupled with intent to injure as equivalent and as an adequate and sufficient alternative, intent to frighten. There is no foundation for that alternative in the statute. The relevant words are to be found in section 1(4) of the Prevention of Crime Act, 1953. It is the definition of offensive weapon: first of all, 'an article made or adapted for use for causing injury.' That is the category of articles which counsel for the appellants accurately described as weapons offensive per se; this case was not concerned with any article falling into that category. The second category is: 'any article intended by the person having it with him for such use by him,' and 'such use' plainly means use for causing injury to the person.

"The justification, the court assumes, which the judge had in mind for the adoption of his own phraseology including reference to intent to frighten is to be found in a decision of the Divisional Court reported in the name of *Woodward* v. *Koessler* [[1958] 1 W.L.R. 1225]. That was a case where upon the facts it was plain that a sheath knife had been so brandished with such accompanying threatening behaviour that injury might very well be conclusively assumed to have been done as a result of the shock thereby caused. Whether or not that case must stand upon its own facts, it seems to the court that it is, to put it at its lowest, unsafe and undesirable that directions to juries based upon subsection (4) of section 1 of the Prevention of Crime Act 1953 should include any references to intent to frighten unless it be made clear in the passage in which such reference is made that the frightening must be of a kind for which the term 'intimidation' is far more appropriate and of a sort which is capable of producing injury through the operation of shock; in the absence, at any rate, of such limitation of definition, it is far preferable that the matter be left upon the term of the statute itself."

Appeals allowed.

(v) Lopez v. MacNab 3.7.6

1978 J.C. 41

L. was seen in a public house with a kitchen knife and a customer there was alarmed. The knife was a sharp, pointed knife manifestly capable of inflicting serious injury. The public house manager took the knife from L. who left before the police arrived.

L. was charged with having with him in a public place an offensive weapon contrary to s.1 of the 1953 Act. He was convicted and he appealed.

At the appeal it was argued by counsel that the conviction should be quashed on the ground that as the knife was neither "made or adapted" for use for causing "injury to the person", if the Crown wished to prove that the knife fell into the category of being "one intended for use for causing injury" evidence of such intention would have to be led.

Lord Justice-General (Emslie) (at p.42)

"[L.] was charged on summary complaint with a contravention of the Prevention of Crime Act 1953, section 1(1), that is to say he was charged with having with him in a public place an offensive weapon. After trial he was convicted and the conviction is challenged on the question: 'On the facts set forth was I entitled to find the appellant guilty as libelled?' Now the particular question which was argued by [counsel for the appellant] was whether the Sheriff was entitled on the facts found to hold that the article which the appellant was undoubtedly carrying was an offensive weapon within the meaning of the section. The proposition was that the Sheriff was not so entitled. In order to understand how the point arises what section 1(1) does is to provide an offence in these terms: 'Any person who without lawful authority or reasonable excuse, the proof whereof shall lie on him, has with him in a public place any offensive weapon shall be guilty of an offence.' Now the first thing, plainly, which has to be done is to establish that an article which the Crown libelled as an offensive weapon is an offensive weapon within the meaning of the subsection. When that is done it is open to the appellant if he chooses to take advantage of the escape clause by showing lawful authority or reasonable excuse. An offensive weapon is one of three kinds. The first is a weapon proper, that is to say an article made as a weapon for use as a weapon. The second is an article which is converted in order to be a weapon. The third category of article which falls within the definition is one which is carried and which is intended by the person having it with him for use as a weapon. This appears clearly from section 1(4) which contains the definition. To return then to the proposition for the appellant it was that there was no material in the findings in fact in this case on which the Sheriff was entitled to hold that the article found in his possession was an offensive weapon. The article was 'a sharp, pointed kitchen knife' and so did not fall within the first two categories of offensive weapons with which the section is concerned. Was the Sheriff entitled to hold that it fell into the third of the defined categories? Initially the proposition was that it would have to be shown that the article described as a kitchen knife was being carried with the overt intention in some way displayed that it would be used as a weapon. From that extreme the appellant's counsel departed and we have to ask ourselves simply whether there was material in the findings on which the Sheriff was entitled to conclude as he did. The knife in question was a sharp, pointed kitchen knife manifestly capable of inflicting serious injuries. That is the knife. It was found in the appellant's possession in a public house. A customer reported his state of alarm in seeing a man in the bar with a knife. The manager approached the appellant from behind and seized the knife from the inside pocket of the appellant. He then told the appellant to clear off. The appellant did. The manager telephoned the police. The police arrived, searched the neighbourhood, could not find the appellant and did not face him up with the charge until he happened to be in the police station on another matter some 15 to 16 days later. We have no doubt it was open to the Sheriff on these findings to conclude as he did. The question of the statutory intention is one which may be drawn as an inference from the facts and circumstances. Unless we can say there was no material on which that inference can be drawn the finding of the Sheriff cannot be disturbed. We are unable to say that he was not entitled to conclude as he did. We shall accordingly answer the question in the case in the affirmative and refuse the appeal."

Appeal refused.

NOTE
   "Adapted for use": this expression is ambiguous inasmuch as it may either have the meaning of changed or altered or transformed for use or that of fit or apt or suitable for use; see *Davidson* v. *Birmingham Industrial Co-operative Society* (1920) 90 L.J.K.B. 206, and *Herrmann* v. *Metropolitan Leather Co. Ltd.* [1942] 1 All E.R. 294. It seems, however, from the context that the expression is to be given here the first-mentioned meaning.
   It was said by the appeal court in *Hutchison* v. *Friel*, 1993 G.W.D. 27–1671 that the case was similar to *Lopez* v. *MacNab*, *supra*, but in the former case the appellant had a "butcher's knife" which he dropped when he saw policemen and ran off and later offered no explanation for such possession.

(vi) R. v. Rapier

(1980) 70 Cr.App.R. 17

R. was charged with having with him in a public place an offensive weapon, namely, a carving knife. The judge directed the jury that, in accordance with s.1(4) of the 1953 Act, an intention to cause injury to the person may include an intention to intimidate. R. was convicted and sentenced to 12 months' imprisonment. He appealed against conviction.

Park, J. (at p. 18)

"In this case the prosecution evidence can be summarised in this way: In the early hours of July 25, 1978, the appellant demanded admission to a night club at Bath. Mr. Thorpe, one of the two doormen at the club, refused and there was a heated argument. The appellant asked if Thorpe wanted to fight and Thorpe told him that if he did not leave he would be removed by force. The appellant went to his car and returned with a long, thin object, described by Thorpe as like a silvery bar, held under his jacket. However, the other doorman, Mr. Henley, identified that object as a knife. He used some such words as, 'My God, he's got a knife.' Thorpe quickly closed the door of the club against the appellant and the police were called. Shortly afterwards the appellant returned and Thorpe identified him to the police as the person who had threatened him with a knife; by which time, of course, Thorpe had been told by Henley that the object which he had seen was a knife.

"When questioned by the police officers the appellant denied having a knife and refused to be searched until he was first arrested. He also denied having a car. The appellant was thereupon arrested on suspicion and searched, and on him were found car keys one of which opened a nearby car and fitted the ignition. In the car were a carving knife, a table knife and a kitchen knife. Later on that day the appellant denied approaching the club with a knife. He accused the doormen of lying and made certain allegations against the police.

"In evidence the appellant gave an innocent explanation of the presence of the knives in his car. He said that he went to the club by arrangement to collect two friends and parked on double yellow lines. Thorpe unreasonably refused him entry to the club and there was a heated argument, as Thorpe had said, but there was no offer to fight. He moved his car further away and waited for his friends. When they did not appear he returned to the club and found the police there. He had not previously returned to the club nor had he ever had the knife on his person. He admitted having told the police that they were not impartial, but that was because they did not interview some other coloured persons who were present and who might have helped him. There were these two conflicting accounts, the truth of which the jury had to determine.

"Section 1(1) of the Prevention of Crime Act 1953 provides as follows:

'Any person who without lawful authority or reasonable excuse, the proof whereof shall lie on him, has with him in any public place any offensive weapon shall be guilty of an offence...'

"Subsection (4) provides:

'... "offensive weapon" means any article made or adapted for use for causing injury to the person, or intended by the person having it with him for such use by him.'

"On this disputed evidence, therefore, the jury had to be told that the prosecution had to satisfy them, first of all, that the appellant had in his possession in the highway outside the night club at the time in question the carving knife which was said to be an offensive weapon. That was a question of fact for the jury, and the learned judge in his summing-up fairly and squarely left that question of fact to the jury. In returning a verdict of guilty they plainly rejected the appellant's account of what had happened and accepted substantially the evidence of the two doormen.

"Secondly, the jury had to be told that they must be satisfied that the carving knife was an offensive weapon, as it was not an article made or adapted for use for causing injury to the person. The jury, therefore, had to be told that the prosecution had to prove that the appellant intended to use it for causing injury to the person. On that matter the learned judge directed the jury in this way: 'The next matter the prosecution would have to prove is that in fact in the circumstances this carving knife was an offensive weapon, because you see, as has already been pointed out to you, a carving knife is not of itself an offensive weapon. It is made for the perfectly ordinary and legitimate use of carving food. It only becomes an offensive weapon if it is an article intended by the defendant at the time in question—that is in the street as he is approaching the club—for use for causing injury to any person, and that injury intended may be either physical injury (actually stabbing or cutting); or the intention may not actually go that far, it may be an intention to intimidate with the use of the knife. Unless the prosecution have proved one of those matters, the article is not an offensive weapon.'

"The main ground of appeal against the conviction in this case is the use by the learned judge of the words, 'it may be an intention to intimidate with the use of the knife'. The submission is that by using those words the learned judge did not properly direct the jury as to the meaning of the word 'intimidate.' Reliance is placed on EDMONDS (1963) 47 Cr.App.R. 114; [1963] 2 Q.B. 142. In that case the three appellants had been convicted of the offence of possession of offensive weapons. In the course of his summing-up at the Central Criminal Court the learned commissioner had said that the jury, in relation to the articles found on the three appellants, had to be satisfied that they had them in order to at least injure and frighten people, if not to hit them. The words used by the learned commissioner to the jury, at p. 120 and p. 148 of the respective reports, were these: 'So my final word to you is this, that if they have got those things on their person, about their person, and you are satisfied that they were in possession of these three not for some innocent purpose at all, but with the intention of injuring, frightening or alarming somebody, you follow, doing something quite unlawful, then they would be guilty on the third count.'

"The judgment of the Court in that case was delivered by Winn J. (as he then was). Towards the end of the judgment, at p. 121 and pp. 150, 151 ..., he said: 'The justification, the court assumes, which the learned commissioner had in mind for the adoption of his own phraseology including reference to intent to frighten is to be found in a decision of the Divisional Court reported in the name of WOODWARD v. KOESSLER [1958] 3 All E.R. 557; [1958] 1 W.L.R. 1255. That was a case where upon the facts it was plain that a sheath knife had been so brandished with such accompanying threatening behaviour that injury might very well be conclusively assumed to have been done as a result of the shock thereby caused. Whether that case must stand upon its own facts, it seems to the court that it is, to put it at its lowest, unsafe and undesirable that directions to juries based upon section 1(4) of the Act should include any reference to intent to frighten unless it be made clear in the passage in which such reference is made that the frightening must be of a kind for which the term 'intimidation' is far more appropriate and of a sort which is capable of producing injury through the operation of shock ...'

"This Court in the instant case wishes to emphasise that passage in the judgment of Winn J. In our view, in directing a jury in respect of an offence under this section the use of the word 'intimidate' should be avoided unless the evidence discloses that the intention of the person having with him the article alleged to be an offensive weapon was to cause injury by shock and hence injury to the person; it would seem that circumstances giving rise to that situation must be exceedingly rare.

"The question therefore arises in this appeal whether on a proper direction the jury in the present case would have convicted the appellant of this offence. The evidence disclosed that the appellant had a furious argument with the doorman and there was talk of a fight. At the end of that talk the appellant went back to his car, picked up a carving knife and walked back towards the club, trying to conceal the carving knife from the two doormen. The carving knife was noticed by one of them and the door of the club was promptly barred against the appellant.

"It seems to this Court that there is very much to be said for the view that the learned judge need not have introduced into his summing-up the word 'intimidate,' because on those facts it would seem that the only intention which the appellant could possibly have had would be to cause injury to one or other or both of them by the use of the knife. Nevertheless the word 'intimidate' was introduced into the summing-up. We have carefully considered whether this is an appropriate case for the application of the proviso. In the end we think it is possible that some members of the jury may have come to the conclusion that proof of intimidation without any further explanation of the meaning of that word would be sufficient to justify convicting the appellant of this serious offence. This Court is not satisfied that the jury would have convicted him on a proper direction.

"Accordingly the appeal will be allowed and the conviction quashed.

"Other grounds have been urged in support of the appeal against conviction but there is no substance in any of them. On this ground, however, the Court has reached the decision which has been stated."

Appeal allowed.

3.7.8   **(vii) R. v. Flynn**

(1986) 82 Cr.App.R. 319

F. was found to have with him in a public place an offensive weapon, namely a knife. He was charged with a contravention of s.1(1) of the 1953 Act. At his trial the jury were directed that they should approach the case in stages; first considering the article in question and then, if not satisfied that it was an offensive weapon *per se*, to consider whether or not F. had the necessary intent. F. was convicted and appealed on the ground that a failure properly to direct the jury that they must be unanimous in concluding either that the article was by its nature an offensive weapon or that F. had the necessary intent rendered the verdict unsafe and unsatisfactory.

Saville, J. (at p. 320)

"In summary, the facts of the case were as follows. According to the prosecution, on September 4, 1984, an unknown person complained to the police about something he had seen in the street and led them to a spot in Liverpool Road. There the officers saw a man and the appellant. According to the police, the appellant was shouting and waving a knife in the air which he threw down as they approached. The other man ran off. It was said that at first the appellant denied having seen the knife but later stated that he always carried one and that, 'If someone attacks me they'd better watch out'.

"When interviewed at the police station he made offensive replies (mainly of the two word variety) and gave no explanation as to his possession of the knife.

"In his evidence the appellant said he was in the Liverpool Road when he saw a group of youths one of whom had a knife which he was waving about. The appellant grabbed him and took the knife. The appellant remained in the area and a Mr. Kennedy came towards him. The appellant showed Mr. Kennedy the knife and explained how he got it. When the police arrived the appellant threw the knife in the gutter because he did not want to get involved. He denied that there had been any conversation between himself and the officers, and as to the interview he said he refused to give any explanations to the police because he was so angry at being arrested.

"The point of law the subject of this appeal arises in the following way. Section 1(4) of the Prevention of Crime Act 1953 defines an 'offensive weapon' as meaning, 'any article made or adapted for use for causing injury to the person, or intended by the person having it with him for such use by him.' Thus whether or not any particular article is an offensive weapon depends on one of two factors: namely, either the nature of the article itself, or the intent of the person having it with him. If one or other of these factors is established by the prosecution, together with possession in a public place, then the charge under section 1(1) is made out, unless the defendant can establish, on the balance of probabilities, that there was lawful justification or reasonable excuse for the possession of the offensive weapon.

"In the present case no criticism is made of the learned judge in relation to her summing-up on the definition of an offensive weapon, or on the burden and standard of proof required of the prosecution, or in relation to the question of lawful justification or reasonable excuse for the possession. What is said, however, is that the learned judge failed to direct the jury that (subject to a majority direction) it was necessary for them to be unanimous either in concluding that the article was an offensive weapon *per se*, or alternatively that the appellant had the necessary intent. Thus, it is said, some of the jury could have been led to convict the appellant on the grounds that the article was an offensive weapon *per se* (without either considering the question of intent or being unconvinced that such intent existed) while others might not have been persuaded that the article was of such a nature, but were satisfied that the appellant had the necessary intent. In such circumstances, it is submitted, the appellant could have been convicted without unanimity on either the nature of the article or the intent of the appellant, so that there was no overall unanimity on an essential ingredient of the offence.

"In support of this proposition reference was made to BROWN (KEVIN) (1984) 79 Cr.App.R. 115, where there were four counts of fraudulently inducing the investment of money and one of attempting to do so, contrary to section 13(1)(*a*) of the Prevention of Fraud (Investments) Act 1958. Each of the counts contained a list of different statements relied upon by the prosecution as constituting the inducement. In reply to questions from the jury the judge directed them, in effect, that on any particular count they did not have to be unanimous on any particular statement, so long as they were all satisfied one or other of the statements amounted to fraudulent inducement. This was held to be a misdirection. Eveleigh L.J. (at p. 119 of the report) in this Court said:

'In a case such as that with which we are now dealing, the following principles apply: 1. Each ingredient of the offence must be proved to the satisfaction of each and every member of the jury (subject to the majority direction). 2. However, where a number of matters are specified in the charge as together constituting one ingredient in the offence, and any one of them is capable of doing so, then it is enough to establish the ingredient that any one of them is proved; but (because of the first principle above) any such matter must be proved to the satisfaction of the whole jury. The jury should be directed accordingly, and it should be made clear to them as well that they should all be satisfied that the statement upon which they are agreed was an inducement as alleged.'

"On the basis of this authority and on the general principle that a jury must be unanimous in reaching a verdict (subject to the majority direction) it is submitted by the appellant that a failure properly to direct the jury that they must be unanimous in concluding either that the article was by its nature an offensive weapon or that the appellant had the necessary intent rendered the verdict unsafe and unsatisfactory.

"The prosecution made two main answers to this submission. First, it was said that even upon the assumption that it was necessary for there to be unanimity as to which type of offensive weapon was involved, a fair reading of the summing-up made this quite clear to the jury. Second, it was submitted that the true analysis of the position showed that for the purposes of this offence it was not necessary for the jury to be unanimous in concluding either that the article was an offensive weapon *per se* or alternatively that the appellant had the necessary intent, provided that all were agreed that the article was one which, for the one reason or the other, was an offensive weapon within the statutory definition. It was suggested that otherwise the logic of the appellant's argument would lead to the conclusion that the jury must also be directed that they must be unanimous, when considering the question of offensive weapons *per se*, either that the article was made or alternatively that it was adapted, for use for causing injury to the person.

"BROWN'S case, it was submitted, was distinguishable, for there (as was observed by Eveleigh L.J. at p. 117 of the report) the false statement was an essential ingredient of the offence, so that the jury had to be unanimous on at least one false statement. In the present case the jury must be unanimous that the appellant had an offensive weapon (*i.e.* the relevant essential ingredient)—and so they were, whether or not they all reached that conclusion by the same route.

"The present case, it was said, is much more in line with the decision on AGBIM [1979] Crim.L.R. 171, in which it was pointed out that it is not necessary for there to be unanimity among the members of the jury as to which items of evidence they accept or reject, provided they are unanimous on the necessary ingredients of the offence. Thus if, for example, there is evidence that the article was made for the stipulated use, evidence that it was adapted for the stipulated use, and evidence that the defendant had the necessary intent with regard to such use, it matters not which route any particular member of the jury uses to reach the conclusion that the article was an offensive weapon.

"There is a formidable argument persuasively presented by [Crown Counsel], but we do not find it necessary to express a concluded view on it, for we have come to the conclusion that his first submission is correct. It seems to us on reading the whole summing-up and it was made clear to the jury that they should approach the case in stages, first considering the nature of the article in question and then, if not satisfied that the article was an offensive weapon *per se* considering whether or not the appellant had the necessary intent. Thus, at p. 9C of the transcript, the learned judge said:

'The prosecution invite you to take the view, firstly, that it is a dagger and that a dagger is made with the initial purpose to cause injury to somebody else, to stab somebody with. Now, that is a thing you are going to have to think about. If you say, "Yes, we are sure that that is an offensive weapon by its very nature"—and nobody suggests that it has been adapted in any way, altered in any way. So you are being invited to say that that was made as a dagger in the first place and that daggers are there for causing injury to people, then that will have an effect on the burden of proof that I have told you about.' The learned judge then continued:

'If you say, "Yes, that is an offensive weapon by its very nature", then the burden of proof is as follows: it is for the prosecution to satisfy you so that you are sure that this defendant had it in his possession in a public place.' The learned judge then proceeded, in unexceptionable terms, to direct the jury as to the burden that then fell upon the appellant at this stage to establish lawful authority or reasonable excuse for the possession of this article in a public place. The learned judge concluded this part of the summing-up by saying: 'Now that is the position if you find that this is an offensive "weapon by its very nature."' The learned judge then continued: 'There is another type of offensive weapon', and proceeded to explain (again in unexceptionable terms) how otherwise innocent items or articles could become offensive weapons if the person having them had the necessary intent. Finally, the learned judge summarised what she had said on the whole question in the following terms at p. 16 of the transcript:

'So the first thing you have got to decide is whether you are satisfied so that you are sure that this is by way of being a dagger and an offensive weapon by its very nature. If you say, "Yes, it is", then the next thing you go on to consider is "Well, given that the defendant had it with him, has he satisfied us on the balance of probabilities that he had it in his possession having a reasonable excuse for so doing?" If you say, "Well I'm not sure that it is an offensive weapon by its very nature", then you say to yourselves, "Well in the circumstances in which he had it, did he have it with him to cause injury?", and you will again be considering—will you not—the reasonable excuse, because you cannot consider whether he had it with him to cause injury unless you consider the reason that he gives. But what you have got to remember is that if it is not an offensive weapon by its very nature, then the burden of proving that he had it with him to cause injury lies fairly and squarely upon the prosecution, and it will not lie in any way upon the defendant.'

"In the light of this summing-up we are satisfied that no reasonable jury could have been left with the impression that it was sufficient if some based their verdict on the nature of the article and some on the intent of the appellant. On the contrary, we consider that if the jury adopted the approach (the programme as it was put by [Crown Counsel]) of the summing-up, then clearly they must have reached their conclusion on the one basis or the other—and there is no indication whatever that they did not faithfully follow the approach of the learned judge.

"There was some suggestion in the argument that the use of the word 'I' (for example, at pp. 9 and 16 of the transcript) or even the use of the word 'you' in certain contexts, might have led members of the jury to believe that it was not necessary to reach a collective view but we are quite unpersuaded of this. Looked at as a whole, the summing-up was to our minds clearly being addressed to the jury as a whole and clearly indicated to them that they all had to be satisfied either that the article was an offensive weapon *per se* or that there was the necessary intent. It follows therefore in our judgment that even if such unanimity is required, the jury in this case were properly directed.

"It remains to mention that during an earlier stage of the trial it was suggested to the learned judge that the indictment should be amended so as to include two counts, one based on the *per se* basis, and the other on the intent of the appellant. In our view such a course is quite unnecessary; even upon the assumption that the jury should be unanimous on the one basis or the other, this in any event was made clear in the summing-up."

Appeal dismissed.

(viii) Goodwin v. Jessop   3.7.9

High Court of Justiciary, unreported, May 2, 1989

G. and another boy were seen by two policemen late one evening to be running away from the sound of a disturbance. Each boy was carrying a piece of timber. G. was seen to brandish or wave the piece of timber that he had. G. neither said nor shouted anything. The two boys were friendly towards each other.

The pieces of timber were produced at trial and, according to the findings of the stipendiary magistrate, gave the appearance of being joinery timber about three inches in diameter and some four to five feet in length. One piece of timber had nails protruding from it. The policemen giving evidence at trial could not say which boy had which piece of timber.

The stipendiary magistrate repelled a plea of no case to answer and after hearing defence evidence he convicted each boy. G. appealed against conviction. In the stated case the stipendiary magistrate noted that "in holding that the appellant had a case to answer, I am of course aware that the 'weapons' in question were not of a type which are *per se* offensive, and that it was accordingly necessary, for the Crown to prove that the wooden batons (sic) were being used for an offensive purpose or in an offensive manner."

Lord Justice General (Ross)

"Since pieces of timber are not offensive weapons *per se* within the meaning of the Act, and since there was no finding that they had been adapted in any way for use as offensive weapons, it was necessary, before the appellant could be convicted for the [Stipendiary Magistrate] to find that he possessed his particular baton intending it for use for causing injury to the person. These are the words which appear in s. 1(4) of the statute.

"The submission made by [counsel for the appellant] to us was that there was no sufficient material in the findings in fact for the inference of the necessary intent to be drawn by the [Stipendiary Magistrate]. In examining that proposition, we observe that the [Stipendiary Magistrate] did not apply the test relating to an offensive weapon which we have just mentioned. He indeed applied a wrong and higher test. He seemed to think it was necessary for the Crown to establish that the wooden batons which we have described were being used for an offensive purpose and in an offensive manner.

"We approach the question raised by this appeal by ignoring the wrong test which the [Stipendiary Magistrate] applied and by considering the matter under reference to the correct test which has to do with the intention of the carrier of the alleged offensive weapon. It comes to this: was there sufficient material in the findings in fact to support the inference that the appellant possessed the baton which he was carrying intending it for use for causing injury to the person?"

> After considering the
> findings in fact, the
> Court answered the question
> in the affirmative and
> appeal refused.

NOTE
This case is reported briefly at 1989 G.W.D. 20–837. Offensive weapons of the wooden plank variety are not thought of as lethal and are to be considered as of a different quality from knives and other lethal weapons: *Harrower* v. *Scott*, 1993 S.C.C.R. 114; *Beattie* v. *McGlennan*, 1990 G.W.D. 20–1125 and *Beveridge* v. *Annan*, 1990 G.W.D. 29–1668 also involve wooden implements but have varying mitigation. In *Doyle* v. *Wilson*, 1996 G.W.D. 12–694 the wooden implement was a 30-inch arm rest.

(ix) Ramsay v. Jessop   3.7.10

1991 G.W.D. 8–441

R. appealed his conviction of a contravention of s.1 of the 1953 Act on the ground that there had been insufficient evidence from which to infer an intention to cause personal injury.

Held, that where R had been seen loitering outside an hotel with his hand in his jacket pocket, which has found to contain a lock knife, and after being cautioned had replied "I'm fae Possil, I need it" there was sufficient evidence that he had intended to use the knife to cause personal injury.

Appeal refused.

(x) Duffy v. MacDougall   3.7.11

1993 G.W.D. 25–1543

D. was arrested in a house and put on his jacket, and was then searched by the police prior to entering the police vehicle at which point they found in the jacket a Stanley knife with a hooked blade in the open position, to which D. said "I was up in Fife and I carry it for protection". He was convicted of a contravention of s.1 of the 1953 Act and appealed.

Held, there was sufficient evidence of intent to cause personal injury in the present or future, having regard to the description of the knife, the place where it was found and the use of the present tense in the second part of D.'s reply (cf *Kane* v. *H.M. Advocate* 1988 S.C.C.R. 585). *R.* v. *Allamby* [1974] 3 All E.R. 126, relied on by D., could be distinguished.

Appeal refused.

3.7.12   **(xi) Lees v. Haig**

1993 S.L.T. (Sh.Ct.) 76

H., an accused person was charged with possession of an offensive weapon, namely a cleaver, in a public place in contravention of s.1(1) of the Prevention of Crime Act 1953. Evidence was led by the Crown that at about 10.30 p.m. the accused had dropped a rusty meat cleaver from the back of his jacket to the roadway. A submission of no case to answer was made.

Held, that the condition of the cleaver, its capacity to inflict serious injury, its possession in a public place at night and its being dropped on the roadway were sufficient evidence to support an inference of possession with intent to cause injury and submission repelled.

The accused pled not guilty and proceeded to trial on 25 November 1992. A submission of no case to answer was made. The sheriff repelled the submission. After evidence was led by the defence the accused was convicted of the charge. An appeal was taken to the High Court by stated case, in which the sheriff provided the following note:

The sheriff (at p. 76)

"The appellant appeared before me for trial on 25 November 1992 represented by his solicitor. The appellant was charged in the following terms: 'On 20 June 1992 in Pleasance, Edinburgh, being a public place, you did, without lawful authority or reasonable excuse, have with you an offensive weapon, namely a cleaver, contrary to the Prevention of Crime Act 1953, s1(1).'

"At the conclusion of the Crown evidence a submission in terms of s345A of the Criminal Procedure (Scotland) Act 1975 was made by the appellant's solicitor. The submission, which was opposed by the procurator fiscal depute, was in accord with the matter which the appellant now desires to bring under review and which is in the following terms:

> 'The sheriff wrongly rejected a submission by the defence agent that there was an insufficiency of evidence at the close of the Crown case. The item was not per se an offensive weapon. It had not been adapted for use as such. There was insufficient evidence arising from the facts and circumstances to entitle the court to conclude that it was intended to be used to injure another person.'

"The Crown evidence came from the witnesses, Police Constables Philip McCarthy and Robert Niven, both experienced police officers with respectively 14 and nine years' service.

"Constable McCarthy stated that on 20 June 1992 after receiving certain information from colleagues he went in a police vehicle with Constable Niven to the Pleasance, Edinburgh, arriving there about 10.30 pm. They parked the police vehicle and then approached a group of between 15 and 20 males who were all in the 35 to 40 age category. The composition of the group accorded with the information he had been given by colleagues. He spoke to the appellant, whom he identified in court, and asked him to leave the group and to accompany him to the police vehicle where the constable intended to search him to ascertain if he was in possession of an offensive weapon.

"As they left the group and walked towards the police vehicle which was parked nearby, a meat cleaver fell on to the roadway. It appeared to have come from under the appellant's jacket at the back. It was retrieved by Constable McCarthy and he identified a rusty meat cleaver (Crown label 1) produced in court as the one he had retrieved. The appellant was arrested and charged with a contravention of the Prevention of Crime Act 1953, s1(1), to which he made no reply. He was then taken to a police station.

"In cross examination the constable stated that some members of the group were related to the appellant. He claimed that his reason for approaching the appellant was because he fitted the description of a man given to him by his colleagues. In answer to further questioning he stated that although the appellant initially seemed willing to accompany him to the police vehicle, some of the group tried to persuade him not to go with the constable. Constable McCarthy also stated that they were about halfway to the van when he heard the sound of the meat cleaver dropping on to the roadway. He also stated that the meat cleaver had not been on the roadway as he approached the group.

"Constable Niven's evidence was to the effect that he and Constable McCarthy had driven to the Pleasance where they parked the police vehicle on receipt of information given to them by colleagues. He stated that they were looking for a particular male whose description they had been given and that it was their intention to search this male to ascertain if he was carrying an offensive weapon. He identified the appellant in court as the male whom they approached and spoke to. He was one of a group of males. As they were leaving the group the appellant dropped a meat cleaver on the roadway. It had dropped from behind the appellant's back. He identified the meat cleaver (Crown label 1) produced in court as the one dropped by the appellant. He stated that its rusty and pitted condition indicated that it could not have been used for its original purpose.

"In cross examination he admitted that initially he was not looking for a cleaver. On being further questioned, Constable Niven stated that although he did not actually see the appellant drop the cleaver he heard the sound of it striking the roadway. At this time they were on the periphery of the group heading towards the police vehicle. He further stated that if it had been dropped by anyone else in the group it would not have dropped on the roadway so close to the appellant's back. On being questioned as to whether or not it could have been thrown by someone else in the group he stated that if that had been the case it would have bounced on the roadway and it did not.

"In re-examination he claimed that the cleaver landed on the roadway within a foot of the appellant's back.

"As stated above, at the conclusion of the Crown evidence, the appellant's solicitor submitted that there was no case to answer.

"She submitted first that the meat cleaver was not per se an offensive weapon and referred me to the case of *Woods v Heywood*, 1988 SLT 849. Secondly, she submitted that the cleaver although rusty and pitted had not been adapted for use for causing injury. Thirdly, she submitted that since the cleaver was not per se an offensive weapon and had not been adapted for use for causing injury the Crown had to prove that the appellant had the cleaver with him with the intention of causing injury to some person. She further submitted that the Crown had not proved such an intention on the appellant's part. All that the Crown had proved was that about 10.30 at night he was one of a group of between 15 and 20 persons, some of whom were members of his own family and that there was nothing to indicate that the group's purpose was anything other than peaceable. She also submitted that there was no evidence to show that the appellant had been brandishing the cleaver which, taking the Crown case at its highest, fell to the roadway near to where the appellant was.

"In replying to the submission of no case to answer the procurator fiscal depute accepted that the cleaver was not per se an offensive weapon and that it had not been adapted for use for causing injury. She submitted, however, that there was evidence from which it could be inferred that the appellant's possession of the cleaver was intended by him for use for causing injury. She relied on what she described as three strands of evidence: first, the fact that the police officers having been given certain information were looking for a particular male with the intention of searching him to ascertain if he had an offensive weapon; secondly, that given the rusty and pitted state of the cleaver the appellant could not have had legitimate reason for having it in a public place; and thirdly that the cleaver fell from a place of concealment on the appellant's person on to the roadway.

"Although I was not referred to the case of *Lopez v MacNab*, 1978 J.C. 41, in reaching my decision on the submission of no case to answer, I had in mind that intention could be inferred from the facts and circumstances of possession of a weapon.

"In reaching my decision I considered that the following facts and circumstances were significant: (1) The condition of the cleaver was such that clearly it had not been used for the purpose for which it had been manufactured for some considerable time. (2) It was patently capable of inflicting the most serious injuries. (3) It was in the appellant's possession in a public place at a time when even if the cleaver had been in pristine condition one could not expect a person such as a butcher who might possibly have a reasonable excuse to have it with him, and (4) the appellant had it about his person before dropping it on to the roadway.

"The above facts and circumstances persuaded me that the Crown had led insufficient evidence to justify the appellant being convicted of the offence with which he was charged and accordingly, as already stated, I rejected the submission of no case to answer.

"The appellant then gave evidence as follows: He was unemployed. On the evening in question he was in the Pleasance in the company of members of his family and the group was on its way to a public house. He stated that the first time he saw the cleaver was at the police station. He also stated that he never saw any member of the group with the cleaver. In cross examination he denied that he had been in possession of the cleaver with intent of causing injury to some person.

"No other evidence was led by the defence.

"After considering further submissions from the procurator fiscal depute and the solicitor for the accused on the sufficiency of the evidence of possession I held that there was sufficient reliable and credible evidence on which I could convict the appellant, and I accordingly found him guilty of the offence charged."

Found guilty.

NOTE

The appeal to the High Court was subsequently abandoned.

(xii) Normand v. Matthews 3.7.13

1993 S.C.C.R. 856

M. the respondent was charged with a contravention of the 1953 Act in respect of a clasp knife. It was not suggested that the knife was made or adapted for use for causing personal injury and the only evidence that it was an offensive weapon came from a statement by the respondent, spoken to by two witnesses, that he had the knife for "protection". The sheriff upheld a submission of no case to answer on the ground that the reply was uncorroborated. The procurator fiscal appealed to the High Court.

Held, that where a person's intention is relevant to the commission of an offence, it must be established by evidence which requires to be corroborated, that that evidence may consist of his own words, his actings, or facts and circumstances, but that no further corroboration is required, because the clearest evidence of his intention is what he himself said about this, and accordingly evidence from two witnesses of a statement by the accused of his intention is sufficient evidence of that intention for any purpose for which it may be relevant; and appeal allowed and case remitted to the sheriff to proceed as accords.

In his note the sheriff stated:

"It was not in dispute in this case that the Crown bore the legal burden of proving (a) possession by the respondent and (b) that what he possessed was an offensive weapon within the meaning of section 1(4) of the Prevention of Crime Act 1953. It was not contended for the defence that there was insufficient evidence in law to establish the respondent's possession of the clasp knife. But it was submitted that there was insufficient evidence in law to entitle me to hold that the clasp knife was an offensive weapon. Section 1(4) of the 1953 Act defines an offensive weapon as any article made or adapted for use for causing personal injury or intended for such use by the person having it with him. It was accepted by both the prosecution and the defence that the clasp knife here in issue fell within the definition of an offensive weapon only if it were proved (the onus being on the Crown) that the respondent intended it for use for causing personal injury, but that the requisite intention could, in appropriate cases, be inferred from facts and circumstances spoken to in evidence (see, e.g., *Lopez v MacNab* 1978 J.C. 41; *Barr v MacKinnon* 1988 S.C.C.R. 561; *Miller v Douglas* 1988 S.C.C.R. 565; *Kane v H.M. Advocate* 1988 S.C.C.R. 585). In the present case the only issue in dispute between the parties was whether the evidence of facts and circumstances deponed to by the two police officers was sufficient in law to entitle me to make the necessary inference. The only evidence relied upon by the Crown was the accused's explanation, 'I need it for the open road for protection.' The prosecutor submitted that this explanation spoken to as it was by the two Crown witnesses, was per se sufficient. I did not accept this submission. I took the view that, albeit the respondent's statement was spoken to by a multiplicity of witnesses, it was no more than a single adminicle of evidence emanating from one source (the respondent himself) and that, in the absence of a further adminicle of evidence emanating from a separate source and pointing in the same direction, the Crown had led insufficient evidence in law to entitle me to draw an inference in their favour on the crucial issue of the respondent's intention. I formed the view that, as in the case where the Crown relies upon a confession by an accused person as evidence of his guilt, so in the case where it founds upon his statement as evidence of the intention wherewith he possessed a Class 3 weapon, there must be evidence from another source which confirms the truth of the statement and provides a sufficient independent check on the statement to corroborate it (see *Sinclair* v *Clark* 1962 S.L.T. 307; *Meredith* v *Lees* 1992 S.L.T. 802). In the instant case the Crown did not seek to argue before me that any of the facts and circumstances spoken to by the two police officers (other than the respondent's statement) supported an inference that he had the clasp knife with him for the purpose of causing personal injury. I accordingly took the view that there was no evidence other than the respondent's statement relevant to support such an inference and that there was insufficient evidence in law to entitle me to find that the clasp knife was an offensive weapon within the meaning of section 1(4) of the 1953 Act."

The questions for the opinion of the High Court were:

"1. Did I err in holding that there was insufficient evidence in law to entitle me to hold that the clasp knife was intended for use by the respondent for causing personal injury?
2. Did I err in sustaining the submission of no case to answer and acquitting the respondent?"

Lord Justice-General (Hope) (at p. 858)

"The respondent was charged in the sheriff court at Glasgow with having an offensive weapon with him in a public place, namely a knife, contrary to section 1(1) of the Prevention of Crime Act 1953. A motion was made at the end of the Crown case under section 345A of the Criminal Procedure (Scotland) Act 1975 that there was no case to answer. The sheriff sustained that motion, in respect that there was insufficient evidence to justify an inference that the respondent was in possession of the knife with the intention of using it to cause personal injury. Accordingly, he acquitted the respondent and it is against that decision that the prosecutor has now appealed.

"The sheriff has given a brief account of the evidence of the Crown witnesses, from which it appears that two police officers observed the respondent at about 7.30 p.m. in the city centre in Glasgow behaving in a suspicious manner outside a book shop. They reached the view that it would be appropriate to search him on suspicion of being in possession of stolen property. The respondent was given the full common law caution and in accordance with normal police practice he was then asked if he had any sharp instruments on his possession. According to one police officer, the respondent became somewhat agitated at this point, although the other police officer did not think that that was the position. He indicated towards a pocket in his jacket and drew out a clasp knife, the blade of which was in the closed position. The knife appeared to be very new and unused. After reminding the respondent that he was still under caution, he was asked by the police officers what his reason was for possessing the clasp knife. His reply was, 'I need it for the open road for protection.' He was then arrested and taken to the police office where he was cautioned and charged with possession of an offensive weapon, to which he made no reply.

"It should be observed at this stage that there is no doubt that there was corroborative evidence of the possession of the clasp knife by the respondent. There was also corroborated evidence that he gave the reply which we have mentioned when asked his reason for possessing the clasp knife. But the sheriff suggested in the course of the argument whether there was a case to answer that it might be contended that there was insufficient evidence in law to support an inference that the respondent possessed the knife with the intention of using it to cause personal injury. That indeed was the point which he later relied upon in reaching the decision which he took.

"In the note which is attached to the stated case the sheriff tells us that he did not accept the prosecutor's submission that the explanation given by the respondent was sufficient for a conviction on this charge. He took the view that this statement was no more than a single adminicle of evidence emanating from one source, namely the respondent himself. It was because there was an absence of any further adminicle of evidence from a separate source pointing in the same direction that he took the view that the Crown had led insufficient evidence in law to entitle him to draw an inference in their favour on the crucial issue of the respondent's intention. The sheriff adds that it was not contended for the Crown that any of the facts and circumstances spoken to by the police officers other than the respondent's statement supported an inference that he had the clasp knife with him for the purpose of causing personal injury.

"The learned advocate-depute submitted that the sheriff took the wrong decision in this case. He was wrong to look for what he described as corroboration of an inference. The best evidence of the respondent's intention was what the respondent himself had said. It had been established by sufficient evidence what he said and that he was in possession of the knife. That was quite sufficient to enable the sheriff to conclude that there was a case to answer. In reply [counsel for the respondent] submitted that it was essential for the Crown to lead evidence to corroborate the respondent's statement of his intention as to the use of the knife. He drew our attention to the discussion of this matter by the sheriff in his note and submitted that the sheriff adopted the correct approach in the light of the authorities to which he referred.

"With all due respect to the sheriff, we consider that he has misdirected himself on this short but important point. There is a difference between a confession by an accused that he has committed some act of a criminal nature and a statement by an accused as to his intention. It is well established by the various authorities to which the sheriff refers that in the case of a confession, evidence must be led from some other source to corroborate it. Where the question is what a person's intention was, as a fact relevant to the commission of an offence, this fact also must be established by evidence which requires to be corroborated. That evidence may consist of his own words, his actings, or facts and circumstances. But provided that the evidence about what he said or did, or as to the facts and circumstances, is corroborated, no further corroboration is required. This is because, where the question is what the intention was of the accused, the clearest evidence of his intention is what he himself said about this. And it is only from his own statement about his intention, or his own actings, or from facts and circumstances from which an inference can be drawn, that it can be discovered what was in his mind at the time. Accordingly, where there is evidence from two witnesses of a statement by the accused of his intention, that is sufficient evidence of his intention for any purpose for which his intention may be relevant.

"In this case what was required in order to make out the charge was evidence that the respondent intended to use the knife for causing personal injury. It is not contended that the reply which he gave was incapable of supporting the inference that that was his intention. So the evidence of this statement given by two witnesses was enough to prove what his intention was at the time. In our opinion that was sufficient, when taken with the other evidence, to entitle the sheriff to find that the clasp knife was an offensive weapon within the meaning of section 1(4) of the 1953 Act.

"For these reasons we propose to answer the two questions in the case in the affirmative. We shall remit the case to the sheriff to proceed as accords."

Appeal allowed.

NOTE

In *MacDonald* v. *Donnelly*, 1993 G.W.D. 38–2454, *Normand* v. *Matthews, supra,* was followed where M. was found in a public place with a screwdriver tucked into the waistband of his trousers under explanation that the screwdriver was for his protection: "There was a difference between a confession by the accused and a statement of his intention; evidence of two witnesses of a statement of his intention was sufficient to prove such intention."

In *Doyle* v. *Wilson*, 1996 G.W.D. 12–694 the appellant had replied to caution that he was not looking for trouble which the sheriff understood to mean that had trouble arisen then Doyle would have been willing to use his offensive weapon.

3.7.14   **(xiii) Houston v. Snape**

1993 S.C.C.R. 995

S. was charged with having a knife, contrary to the 1953 Act. The article, which was in a leather sheath in his inside jacket pocket, was described by two police witnesses as a dagger. It was over 11 inches long in all and its blade, which was seven inches long, came to a point and was sharp on one side only. The Crown case was that this was a 'category 1 weapon', i.e., that it was made for causing personal injury. The sheriff found himself in reasonable doubt as to whether the article was a dagger or sheath knife and acquitted the respondent. The prosecutor appealed to the High Court by stated case.

Held, that the fact that the weapon was in a sheath was in no way inconsistent with the conclusion that it was a dagger and that, taking together the evidence of the police and the examination by the court of the weapon, the court was satisfied that the sheriff was not entitled to have any reasonable doubt that the weapon was made for causing personal injury; and appeal allowed and case remitted to the sheriff to proceed as accords.

The procurator fiscal appealed to the High Court by stated case, the matters desired to bring under review being:

"(a) Whether the sheriff erred in finding that Label No. 1, a knife, was not per se an offensive weapon;

(b) whether the sheriff erred in finding the respondent not guilty."

The sheriff (Allan) made, *inter alia*, the following findings in fact.

"7. (a) The knife is 11 ¹/₄ inches or 286 mm long overall, the handle is 4 ¹/₄ inches or 108 mm long, the blade is 7 inches or 178 mm and is long, narrow and virtually symmetrical.

(b) The blade, which comes to a point, is sharp on one side only, the other side being like the back of the blade.

(c) The whole of the blade is completely contained within a leather sheath, which also extends up the back of the handle; the leather sheath contains two loops (one large and one small) through which a belt could pass."

In his note the sheriff stated, *inter alia*:

"In his address and submission to me, the appellant accepted that there was no question in this case of the weapon having been adapted in any way and that the second category did not therefore feature in this matter. He would submit to me that the weapon was in fact a category 1 weapon, and, as an alternative, that it was a category 3 weapon, with the intention being inferred from the circumstances.

"As regards the first category, the appellant submitted that this was a weapon made for use for causing personal injury and that it was properly described as a dagger. He accepted that, while the police officers had called it a dagger, they were not authoritative on the topic and that it was simply a description by the police officers based on their experience. The appellant indicated that he was not aware of any authority as to how a dagger was to be described. He submitted that a dictionary would be of no assistance and that a sheath knife was simply a knife in a sheath. In his submission, it was not conclusive as a description that the knife in this case was in a sheath since the sheath was simply protection.

"In the absence of any definition of a dagger, the appellant referred me to the case of *Farrell v Rennicks* (1959) 75 Sh.Ct.Rep. 113 (referred to at p. 105 of the book entitled *Offensive Weapons* by Dr Robert S. Shiels), which related to a sheath knife which had a number of other implements within the handle (described as 'an 8 in 1'). In that case, the knife had been held not to be a category 1 weapon and the court had held that there was no suggestion of it being carried with an intention to cause injury. The charge had accordingly been found not proven. It was accordingly submitted to me that there was no case law to help in this matter.

"The appellant accepted that there were logos on the sheath which could have been intended for wearing on a belt; but it was submitted that this was a neutral factor which was of no assistance. As regards the respondent's claim that the knife had come from Iraq, the appellant submitted that that might be more consistent with the weapon being a dagger than a sheath knife. The appellant accordingly submitted, first, that the knife was a dagger and was a category 1 weapon ...

"For the respondent, [solicitor] submitted that, on the evidence, I could not be satisfied that the knife was a category 1 weapon. For me to be so satisfied, he submitted that I would require to say, beyond reasonable doubt, that the knife was a dagger on the basis only of the evidence of the police officers. He drew attention to the fact that I had no other evidence of any kind nor from any source available to support the description of it as a dagger. In that situation, if this knife was a dagger, he questioned why it was so called. The characteristics which had been referred to by the police officers had been that the knife was long, pointed and had one sharp edge. [The solicitor] submitted, however, that these features were common to many knives, including kitchen knives. He therefore submitted that the description was not necessarily in any way consistent with the knife being a dagger. He submitted that sheath knives came in various forms and that, in the absence of any definition of a dagger, there was nothing in particular to lift this knife out of the category of a sheath knife and into the category of a dagger. For me to hold that the knife in question was a dagger, he submitted that I would have to exclude this knife from the description of a sheath knife and that I would require to do that without any evidence led by the Crown to support that, except a bald assertion by police officers without reference to any source, material or authority ...

"The primary question for my consideration was whether or not the knife in question could be described as a category 1 weapon, in this case a dagger. The evidence which was available to me from the police officers on this aspect was not really of great assistance, since there was little to distinguish the knife in this case from a sheath knife. In the absence of any statutory or other definition, the dictionary available to me described a dagger as a short, edged stabbing weapon. I am not aware that the length of a weapon lifts it out of the category of a sheath knife and into the category of a dagger. On a personal level, I would have expected a dagger to have sharp blades on both edges, whereas the knife in this case had only one edge sharpened. None of the cases to which I was referred offered assistance in the description of a dagger but I drew attention, in giving my decision, to the case of *Woods* v *Heywood* 1988 S.L.T. 489, which dealt with a machete. In that case, the definition in the dictionary allowed for it both as a tool and a weapon. In that situation, the court held that, where there were two purposes, one being for causing personal injury and the other for an innocent purpose, it could not properly be affirmed that the weapon in question was one which was made for use for causing personal injury. I find that judgment to be of assistance in the general approach to this matter and, since I was left in what I considered to be a reasonable doubt as to whether this was a dagger or a sheath knife, I felt that the benefit of that doubt should be given to the respondent and I was not therefore prepared to hold that it was a dagger. Since, in the terms of the decision in the case of *Coull* v *Guild* 1985 S.C.C.R. 421; 1986 J.C. 24; 1986 S.L.T. 184 (and particularly per the Lord Justice-Clerk at the foot of p. 423 and top of p. 424) it is clear that a sheath knife is not per se an offensive weapon, I could not hold this knife to be a category 1 weapon.

The questions for the opinion of the High Court were:

"1. On the facts stated, did I err in holding that the knife in question (Label No. 1) was not, per se, an offensive weapon?

2. On the facts stated, did I err in acquitting the respondent?"

Lord Justice-Clerk (Ross) (at p. 997)

"In presenting the appeal today, the Solicitor-General has pointed out that before the sheriff the Crown's position was that the knife in question was what is sometimes called a category 1 weapon, that is to say, that it was a weapon made for use for causing personal injury (Gordon's *Criminal Law* (2nd edn), para. 30–44). There was an alternative submission to the effect that if the knife was not a category 1 weapon then there was evidence to justify its inclusion in category 3, that is to say, that it was a weapon intended by the person having it with him for use for causing injury to the person. The Solicitor-General, however, explained that he was not presenting the alternative argument to this court and that the sole issue which he was raising was that the sheriff had erred in not holding that this was a category 1 weapon, that is, a weapon made for use for causing personal injury. He drew attention to the findings of the sheriff and to what the sheriff says regarding the evidence. It is unnecessary to rehearse the findings in any detail but it is plain that, when approached by the police, at their request the respondent removed from his inside jacket pocket this knife which was contained in a leather sheath. He told the police officers that his cousin had brought it back from Iraq and that he had received it as a present that evening. In finding 7 the sheriff gives a detailed description of the knife and its container. In his note the sheriff tells us that the evidence for the appellant consisted of evidence from two police officers, Constables Smart and Beaton. There was one production, namely Label No. 1, which was the knife concerned. He tells us that he found the police officers to be credible and reliable as witnesses apart from their description of the knife as a dagger. Subsequently he tells us that one police officer described the knife as being like a dagger, while the other police officer said in evidence that he would say it was a dagger. The Solicitor-General pointed out that, as well as having the evidence of these two police officers, the sheriff of course had before him Label No. 1, the knife itself, and that he was entitled to look at the knife.

"Before the sheriff it had been contended for the respondent that the proper view was that this knife was not a dagger but was a sheath knife and as such was a category 3 weapon. Of course, if it was a category 3 weapon, as we have pointed out, it would require to be established that it was intended by the respondent for use by him for causing personal injury. The Solicitor-General submitted that the sheriff had not been entitled to reach the view which he did regarding this weapon and he ought to have concluded that it was a dagger. [Counsel] for the respondent on the other hand, while accepting that the sheriff was entitled to look at the knife, maintained that the sheriff was entitled to arrive at the conclusion at which he did. [In his note], after referring to the case of *Woods* v *Heywood* 1988 S.L.T. 849, the sheriff says he found that judgment to be of assistance in his approach to the matter and states that since he was left in what he considered a reasonable doubt as to whether this was a dagger or a sheath knife, he felt that the benefit of the doubt should be given to the respondent and that he was not accordingly prepared to hold that it was a dagger.

"We have come to the conclusion that the sheriff did misdirect himself upon this matter. There was evidence before him from two police officers describing the weapon as a dagger and one would have thought that police officers were in a good position to form an opinion on an issue of that kind. The sheriff then had regard to the nature of the weapon which was before him. We are bound to say that, looking at the weapon ourselves, it appears to have many of the characteristics of a dagger and, having regard to the nature of the weapon and the evidence before him, we are not persuaded that the sheriff was entitled to entertain any reasonable doubt as to whether this was a dagger. He heard the evidence of two police officers, in addition to that he had the evidence of the knife itself. Both in the sheriff's note and in some of the submissions made by [counsel] significance appeared to be being attached to the fact that this weapon was kept in a sheath. It is the case that reference is often made to weapons which are described as sheath knives, but it is not the case that all weapons which are kept in sheaths are necessarily sheath knives. There is no reason why a dagger should not be kept in a sheath. Accordingly, the fact that this weapon was enclosed within a sheath is in no way inconsistent with the conclusion that it was a dagger. Having regard to the nature of the weapon, we are satisfied that when the evidence of the police officers and the examination of the weapon are taken together, the sheriff was not entitled to have any reasonable doubt that this was a weapon made for use for causing personal injury. Accordingly, we shall answer the first question in the case in the affirmative. It was agreed that the case would then have to be remitted to the sheriff in order that he could proceed as accords since he will still require to direct his attention to the question of whether the respondent had the weapon in his possession without lawful authority or reasonable excuse. We have concluded that it would be preferable at the present time not to answer the second question in the case. We shall accordingly answer the first question in the manner indicated and thereafter remit to the sheriff to proceed as accords."

Appeal allowed.

NOTE
In *Shepherd* v. *Friel*, 1994 G.W.D. 8–469 the focus of attention was a knife in a sheath. In the whole circumstances the sheriff was entitled to infer an intent to cause personal injury, in the words of the Appeal Court: "the fact that the knife was in a sheath not being conclusive against the Crown."

(xiv) O'Brien v. Fitzpatrick   3.7.15

High Court of Justiciary, March 31, 1994

The Crown appealed a sheriff's decision to find no case to answer against F. on a charge under s.1(1) of the 1953 Act. After F. had been detained on another matter, a search at the police station revealed a kitchen knife also in F.'s possession. He was not then asked to explain his possession of it but on being cautioned and charged shortly afterwards, explained that it was for his protection. The sheriff considered that the Crown should not be allowed to make up a stateable case by reference to something said only after caution and charge, and doubted whether the evidence was sufficient in any event.

Held, appeal allowed. No objection had been taken to the leading of the evidence, there appeared to be nothing wrong with the police charging F. when they did, and there was ample evidence to make a case to answer since the reply was sufficient evidence as to his intention.

Lord Justice General (Hope)
"The facts of the case are quite straightforward. The respondent was seen acting suspiciously with another youth at Troon Station by two police officers. He was cautioned and, on producing two books from under his jacket, explained that he had stolen them. He was then taken with his companion to Troon Police Station so that further enquiries could be carried out. While he was there he was searched by two police officers and a knife was found in the rear pocket of his jeans. This was a knife which had a blade about six inches long and could be described as a domestic cutting knife. At the time when the search was conducted the respondent was not asked for nor did he give any explanation with regard to his possession of the knife. But when shortly afterwards he was cautioned and charged, in terms of charge 3, he replied 'It's for my protection'.

"It was in the light of that evidence that the submission was made by the defence agent that there was insufficient evidence to justify the police charging the respondent with possession of an offensive weapon. It was said that mere possession of the knife was not sufficient in itself to justify the respondent being charged. It was pointed out that it was necessary for the Crown to be able to establish that the appellant had the knife with him for use as an offensive weapon without lawful authority or reasonable excuse. The submission was that no question was put to the respondent at the time when he was first cautioned which would enable that point to be dealt with in the evidence. The sheriff took the view that it was a narrow and difficult question whether the police were entitled to charge the respondent at the stage when they did. He recognised that normally a reply to caution and charge is admissible, but he felt that there was something wrong in allowing the Crown to make up what he described as a stateable case by reference to something which the accused said only after caution and charge. He also expressed some doubt as to whether there was sufficient evidence even if the statement was admissible.

"The Lord Advocate has asked us to answer the question of law in the negative on the ground that the sheriff erred in law in the decision which he took. He pointed out that the reply to caution and charge was led without any objection. It was, therefore, evidence in the case. It was a perfectly ordinary piece of evidence led in ordinary course, and the only question was whether what was said by the respondent in reply to caution and charge was sufficient to prove the charge when taken together with the other evidence. On the latter point, which is whether there was sufficient evidence if the reply was admissible, he drew our attention to

Normand v. *Matthews* 1993 S.C.C.R. 856 where a similar reply was given by the respondent when under caution but before being charged. It was not disputed that, if there was sufficient evidence that that was the reply, then the statement that he had the knife with him for his protection was enough to prove what his intention was and that this was to use the knife as an offensive weapon. [Counsel for the appellant] invited us to refuse the appeal, although he did not dispute the point that the police were entitled to charge the respondent when they did. He accepted that there was no rule that the police required to be in possession of sufficient evidence in law before charging the accused with an offence. Nevertheless he asked us to give effect to the sheriff's doubts and to take the view that he was entitled to hold that there was no case to answer.

"In our opinion however, the submissions of the Lord Advocate are well founded. It is significant that no objection was taken at the point when the relevant evidence was being led. Had objection been taken, no doubt the fairness of what was done could have been investigated, although we should add that we can see nothing wrong in the police charging the respondent in the light of the evidence which was available to them at the time. As to whether there was sufficient evidence, taking the matter at its highest as is appropriate at the stage when a no case to answer submission is being considered, there was in our opinion ample evidence here for there to be a case to be answered. The reply given was evidence in the case, and it was sufficient evidence as to the respondent's intention from which the inference could be drawn that he had the knife with him for use as an offensive weapon if the occasion required it, and that he had the knife with him without lawful authority or reasonable excuse.

"For these reasons we shall answer the question of law in the negative and we shall remit the case to the sheriff to proceed as accords."

Appeal allowed.

NOTE

This case is reported briefly at 1994 G.W.D. 18–110.

(xv) Cavanagh v. Carmichael 3.7.16

High Court of Justiciary, May 11, 1993

C. (Cavanagh) was convicted of a contravention of s.1 of the 1953 Act. Police officers had searched C. and they found that he had a three-bladed knife with him. The implement appeared home-made.

C. appealed against conviction and in essence complained that the sheriff had gone too far in interpreting the evidence.

Held, that the sheriff was entitled to reject an explanation of the appellant and to proceed as he did and to decide that the knife was an offensive weapon having been "adapted" within the meaning of s.1(4) of the 1953 Act.

Lord Justice-Clerk (Ross)
    "The Sheriff in the Findings has described what is referred to in the complaint as a three bladed knife. In Finding 6 he says,

> 'This implement consisted of three metal blades each of which was about two inches long and half an inch wide and tapered to a sharp point at both ends of the cutting edge of the blade. The blades were originally manufactured to be fitted into a Stanley knife or similar cutting tool. The group of three blades was bound firmly together at one and by several layers of black insulating tape. The effect of insulating tape was to create a handle with which the implement could be held at one end, but because of the flexibility of the tape, the blades could be pressured so as to open out into a fan shape.'

    "He goes on to say that when found the implement was situated inside a small sheath which appeared to be home made or improvised to fit the implement. The three blades of the knife could be fitted into the sheath with only the handle remaining outside. This object was found in the rear right hand pocket of the jeans worn by the appellant. When it was found the appellant was cautioned by the police officers. He was asked to explain his possession of the blades and he replied 'They're for doing the lino up the road.'

    "In his Note, the Sheriff describes the evidence of police officers. Constable Swan said he had never seen anything like it before. He accepted that he had never worked professionally as a carpet fitter or linoleum cutter but he stated that he did not think that this was a type of implement used normally in such trades. Both he and Constable Munro described the object as home made and Constable Munro said that he too had never seen anything like it before. The sheriff took the view that he was entitled to look at the implement and to take an ordinary or practical view of its nature and its size and shape. He tells us that he was careful not to go into areas where expert evidence might be required but he took the view that this three bladed knife would not be suitable to cut linoleum or similar substance because of the lack of leverage and the very small size of the handle in relation to the blades. He also made the point that a treble blade for cutting linoleum or other material did not seem to make sense and we appreciate the force of that. He also concluded that the way in which the blades could be made to fan out and also the way in which it was carried in a sheath in the appellant's pocket plus its size appear to him to make it suitable for the purpose of causing a slash or scar on anyone who might be attacked with the implement held in the hand. The sheriff stated that he did not wish to go very far along the route of interpreting the possible uses of such an implement, but he considered it legitimate to look at the implement and to consider it in the light of all the evidence and what was said about it.

"[Counsel for the appellant's] point was that the sheriff, he said, had gone too far along the route of interpreting the evidence and had really become a witness himself. We do not agree with that criticism of the sheriff's approach. [Counsel] accepted that if this case had been tried by a jury it would be open to the jury on the evidence to look at and consider the three bladed knife and then determine whether it fell within one of the three classes of offensive weapons defined in s. 1(4) of the Prevention of Crime Act 1953. If a jury was entitled to determine an issue of that kind, then in our judgment the sheriff under summary procedure was equally entitled to determine an issue of that kind.

"The only explanation which had been put forward for the appellant having this weapon was the explanation which he gave when cautioned. That was to the effect that he had it with him for the purpose of cutting linoleum. The sheriff rejected that explanation and having regard to the description which he gave of the knife, we are satisfied that he was entitled to reject the explanation. If that explanation was rejected then having regard to the description which the sheriff has given of the object we are satisfied that he was entitled to conclude that this was an offensive weapon within the second category defined in s.1(4), namely one adapted for use for causing personal injury. It was plain that the blades had been adapted in the manner described and in our judgment, having regard to the material before him, the sheriff was entitled to conclude that it had been adapted for use for causing personal injury."

Appeal refused.

NOTE
   This appeal is reported briefly at 1993 G.W.D. 25–1542 and in Crown Office Circular A24/93.

3.7.17   **(xvi) McGlennan v. Marshall**

Kilmarnock Sheriff Court, April 6, 1994

M. (Marshall) was charged with a contravention of s.1 of the 1953 Act. At the conclusion of the Crown evidence it was submitted for the defence that there was no case to answer. The basis of the submission was that the implements concerned were not *per se* offensive weapons and that there was not sufficient evidence from which the necessary intention could be inferred. In particular, it was submitted that the intention must relate to the "point of possession" and that evidence of similar objects being distributed from M.'s vehicle two days earlier was not relevant. The sheriff heard the Crown in reply and repelled the submission and proceeded to hear the defence evidence. M. was convicted and initially appealed against conviction but later abandoned that appeal before a hearing.

Held, the finding of various implements in a motor vehicle two days after a confrontation and real evidence of the condition of those implements allowed the inference to be drawn that they were intended for use as offensive weapons.

Stated Case

"Having heard the submissions of the parties, I found the following facts admitted or proved.

1. On 19 August 1993 a motor car registered number [...] was driven to a point at Jacks Road, Saltcoats where it was brought to rest.
2. At that place, a confrontation took place between three groups of youths.
3. The driver left the vehicle and distributed pick-axe handles, golf clubs and baseball bats to members of one of the groups of youths who took off in pursuit of members of the other group.
4. On 21 August 1993 the appellant was driving the same vehicle in Melbourne Terrace, Saltcoats when he was stopped by the police who informed him of their suspicion that he had with him offensive weapons.
5. The officers searched the vehicle. In the driver's door compartment they found a knife. In the rear seating compartment they found a golf club and in the boot they found the handle of a pick-axe.
6. The knife had a blade about four inches long. It was designed both for cutting and for stabbing. The tip of the knife had been broken off.

7. The shaft of the golf club was deformed, bent and twisted. It was no longer suitable for use as a golf club.
8. The socket of the pick-axe handle had been beaten and deformed and could not have been used for its designed purpose.
9. That pick-axe handle had been among the implements handed out from the vehicle on 19 August 1993.
10. The appellant was the driver of the vehicle on 19 August 1993.
11. Having been cautioned and charged with having these objects with him as offensive weapons the appellant said, 'They're all mine, Campbell's got nothing to do with it.' The Campbell concerned was a passenger in the vehicle.
12. The appellant gave no excuse or explanation for having with him the objects concerned.
13. The objects were intended by the appellant for use as offensive weapons."

Sheriff's Note

"At the stage of submission 1 I heard unchallenged evidence from the witness William Hunter. Briefly put, that witness's evidence was to the effect set out in what later became my first three findings in fact.

"The evidence of the finding of the objects within the car came from Constables Firth and Coles and the real evidence as to their condition from the productions.

"It appeared to me that the finding of the golf club and pick-axe shaft was capable of supporting the evidence of Hunter that such objects were distributed as weapons from the vehicle. From that evidence, the condition of the objects as I saw them and the finding of them together in the same vehicle two days later the inference was capable of being drawn that they were intended by the appellant for use as offensive weapons. That was the basis on which I rejected the submission.

"The appellant gave evidence. I accepted his evidence that he had indeed driven the vehicle to the general location on 19 August. I did not believe his evidence that the vehicle was brought to rest at a different nearby place, preferring the evidence of the appellant's brother that in fact it was brought to rest where the witness Hunter stated.

"The evidence of the appellant's brother was entirely consistent with Hunter's evidence that objects, including in particular the pick-axe handle, were removed from the vehicle because of a confrontation with a group of youths from Ardrossan.

"That witness's evidence was that he took the pick-axe shaft 'In case we got battered.' I did not believe the remaining evidence of the appellant, his brother or the witness Catherine Wallace as I found their evidence littered with inconsistencies.

"Finding 13 is an inference which I draw from the facts established including the events of 19 August 1993."

Found guilty.

NOTE
    It is clear that the sheriff had regard to the real evidence in this case and the condition of the productions was a material aspect of the case. However, judicial thoughts about productions must be disciplined for in *Darroch* v. *Carmichael*, 1994 G.W.D. 10–603 the sheriff admitted in a report to having allowed the sight of a knife with a 12-inch blade to influence him unduly.

3.7.18   **(xvii) Owens v. Crowe**

1994 S.C.C.R. 310

The appellant, O., was charged with having a "lock-knife" with him in a discothèque at 11.30 p.m., contrary to the 1953 Act. He did not give evidence at his trial. He was convicted and appealed in the High Court by stated case on the grounds that the sheriff had erred in rejecting a submission that there was no case to answer, there being no evidence that the appellant possessed the knife for the purpose of causing personal injury, and that he had also erred in holding that the knife had been adapted for causing personal injury. The appellant proposed adjustments to the stated case to indicate that the sheriff had held that the weapon was so adapted. The sheriff rejected these proposed adjustments, but gave no reasons for doing so. When the appeal first called in the High Court, the case was remitted to the sheriff to give his reasons for rejecting the adjustments. The sheriff explained that he had rejected them because he had not proceeded on the basis that the knife was adapted for causing personal injury, but on the basis that taking a knife of this nature into a discothèque was not consistent with innocent intentions and that the Crown had established a *prima facie* case.

    Held, that, having regard to the circumstances, the sheriff was entitled to draw the inference that the appellant had the weapon with the intention of causing personal injury; and appeal refused.

    O. appealed to the High Court by stated case, the matters desired to bring under review being:

        "(a) The sheriff erred in law by rejecting a submission in terms of section 345A of the Criminal Procedure (Scotland) Act 1975, as amended. This submission was made on the basis that the knife referred to was not an offensive weapon per se and there was no evidence adduced against the appellant from which it could be reasonably inferred that the appellant's possession of said knife was for the purpose of causing personal injury.

(b) The sheriff erred in holding that said knife fell into the category of a weapon that was adapted for causing personal injury. The only Crown witness to speak to the nature of said knife was a police officer who accepted that it was a lock-knife. This fact was demonstrated in court to the sheriff. The Crown conceded that a lock-knife was not an offensive weapon per se."

The sheriff (Ballance) made the following findings in fact.

"1. On the evening of 7th February 1993 the appellant attended the Lido Discothèque, Victoria Road, Kirkcaldy. The Lido Discothèque is a public place. There were between 500 and 600 people within the discothèque. There were four bands playing.

2. At about 11.30 p.m. he was ordered out of the premises due to a misunderstanding, but which followed on a minor disturbance in the said premises, after which several others were also ordered out. The appellant was unconnected with this disturbance.

3. While in the said discothèque, the appellant had in his possession a knife, which was produced as Crown Label No. 3.

4. The said knife was the clasp-knife type and the blade could be hinged back inside the handle. It could by means of a catch be locked in the open position. The blade was approximately four inches in length. The blade of the knife had a shape characteristic of a sheath knife.

5. The management prior to removing the appellant and others from the said discothèque had sent for the police.

6. When the appellant left the said discothèque he was detained by the police.

7. The appellant was then searched and the said knife was found in a pocket in his clothing. It was at that time in the closed position.

8. The appellant had no justifiable reason to have the said knife in his possession at the material time.

9. The appellant's purpose in having the said knife in his possession at the material time was to use it for causing injury to the person should he have become involved in threats or a fight."

In his note the sheriff stated, *inter alia*:

"In his submission of there being no case to answer, the solicitor for the appellant started from the proposition that a lock-knife is not a dangerous weapon per se and there were no circumstances from which it could be inferred that the appellant had the lock-knife for the purposes of causing personal violence. He referred to the cases of *Patterson* v *Block, The Times,* 21st June 1984, and *Jardine* v *Kelly* [1985] 6 N.I.J.B. 96. Neither of these reports were available as such, but both cases are narrated in Shiels, *Offensive Weapons*, pp. 177–178.

"In reply, the procurator fiscal depute maintained that it was always open to a court to determine whether any particular item was dangerous. In *Jardine* v *Kelly* the object in question resembled a common penknife. The knife found on the appellant obviously did not. The court was entitled in the circumstances to infer that it was being carried with intent to cause injury.

"It seemed to me that the appellant's submissions oversimplified the approach to the question. The expression 'lock-knife' is a descriptive term, not a legal classification, and whether or not it can or cannot be locked, while that may be a guide to its use or intended use, each case must be looked at in its own circumstances. Had the evidence shown that, for example, the knife was being carried during the day and the appellant had been making his way along a street, I would, despite the dangerous potential of the knife, have sustained the submission, failing any further criminative circumstances. Here the evidence showed that the appellant had entered the discothèque carrying a knife with a four-inch blade, which suggests prima facie a wrongful intent. No immediate justification for this or any immediately past or intended legal use of it suggested itself to me, or was suggested to me, and in this situation it seemed to me that it was for the appellant to give an explanation. For all I knew, there could have been a lawful purpose in having the knife at the discothèque, but only he could proffer this to the court. I accordingly repelled the defence submission.

"No evidence was led for any of the accused."

The questions for the opinion of the High Court were:

"1. On the evidence of the Crown, was I entitled to repel the appellant's submission under section 345A of the Criminal Procedure (Scotland) Act 1975?

2. On the evidence, was I entitled to make finding in fact 8?

3. On the evidence, was I entitled to make finding in fact 9?

4. On the facts as found, was I entitled to convict the appellant?"

On November 16, 1993 Lord Murray delivered the following opinion of the court.

Lord Murray (at p. 311)

"On 10th March 1993 the appellant was convicted in Kirkcaldy Sheriff Court of possessing a knife in a public place, contrary to the Prevention of Crime Act, section 1(1). At the conclusion of the court case the solicitor for the appellant made a motion in terms of section 345A of the Criminal Procedure (Scotland) Act 1975 that there was no case to answer. The sheriff repelled this plea. The appellant did not give evidence nor was evidence led on his behalf. The sheriff convicted the appellant.

"In giving his decision on the motion for no case to answer we were informed that the sheriff indicated that he had repelled that plea on the basis that the knife was not of such a nature that it was necessary for the Crown to prove in evidence that the appellant at the time intended to use the knife to cause injury to the person. In his findings in fact the sheriff states that the knife was a clasp knife whose blade could be hinged back inside the handle. Its blade could be locked in the open position by means of a catch. The blade was approximately four inches in length and it had a shape characteristic of a sheath knife. There are no other findings of fact bearing on the character of the knife. The last finding in fact is in the following terms:

> '9. The appellant's purpose in having the said knife in his possession at the material time was to use it for causing injury to the person should he have become involved in threats or a fight.'

"The matters which it was desired to bring under review on behalf of the appellant are stated in the stated case. Under head (a) it was sought to bring under review whether there was evidence in the case from which it could reasonably be inferred that the appellant's possession of the knife was for the purpose of causing personal injury. Under (b), in the light of the concession by the Crown in the case that the knife was not an offensive weapon per se, it was sought to bring under review whether the knife was a weapon adapted for causing personal injury. Adjustments for the appellant ... particularly (5) and (6), had been proposed to help to focus these issues. The sheriff had rejected these adjustments but had given no reason for so doing. In the foregoing circumstances the case should be remitted to the sheriff for him to explain the grounds of his decision having regard to the foregoing matters.

"The advocate-depute did not oppose the foregoing motion and pointed out that the sheriff was required by section 448(2D)(a) to give reasons for rejecting proposed amendments to a stated case.

"We agree that the case as presently stated does not deal satisfactorily with the issues which it is sought to bring under review. We shall therefore remit the case to the sheriff to explain on what evidence he concluded that an inference could reasonably be drawn that the knife was either adapted for use for causing injury to the person or was intended by the appellant for such use and to give his reasons as required by section 448(2D)(a) for rejecting adjustments proposed by the appellant directed to focusing the foregoing matters.

"In his report the sheriff stated, inter alia:

'I make these further observations following on the opinion of the court dated 16th November 1993.

'With the passage of time I find that I now have little actual recollection of the trial, except insofar as appears on my notes, and similarly I have little recollection of the hearing on proposed adjustments. I do remember that the solicitor appearing for the appellant was not the solicitor who conducted the trial and was not able to assist me greatly in relation to the significance and purpose of the adjustments. It had not been my intention to hold that the knife in question had been "adapted" for causing injury and for that reason I refused adjustments (5) and (6) as not being consistent with the opinion which I had formed of the nature of the knife.... .

'So far as concerns my reasons for inferring the intention of the appellant to use the knife if circumstances called for this in his view, it seemed to me that taking a knife of this nature into a discothèque was not consistent with innocent intentions and that the Crown had established a prima facie case.'"

On February 15, 1994 the Lord Justice-Clerk delivered the following opinion of the court.

Lord Justice-Clerk (Ross) (at p. 313)

"This is the appeal of Gary Owens, who went to trial in the sheriff court at Kirkcaldy along with some co-accused on a complaint containing a number of charges. The appellant was found guilty of charge (1), that is a charge of contravening section 1(1) of the Prevention of Crime Act 1953. He was also found guilty of consequential charge under the Bail Act but we are not concerned with that. He has appealed against conviction by means of stated case.

"At an earlier stage when this appeal called, a remit was made to the sheriff to provide a supplementary report so that he could explain on what evidence he had concluded that an inference could reasonably be drawn that the knife which was found in the possession of the appellant was an offensive weapon within the meaning of the Act and also so that he might give reasons for rejecting certain adjustments which the appellant had put forward. We now have a supplementary note from the sheriff.

"In presenting the appeal today [the solicitor advocate] for the appellant has pointed out that, as is plain from the case, two of the co-accused were acquitted at the no case to answer stage and in their case the knives which they had been carrying were described by the sheriff as 'kitchen knives with wooden handles of the potato-peeler variety but with straight blades three inches long or less'. The knife which the appellant had is described in the findings as being a clasp type with a blade which could be hinged back inside the handle. It could, by means of a catch, be locked in the open position. The blade was approximately four inches in length. The blade of the knife had a shape characteristic of a sheath knife.

"The first submission was that if the sheriff was satisfied that the kitchen knives carried by the co-accused were not offensive weapons, he ought, in the circumstances, to have reached the same conclusion in relation to the clasp knife carried by the appellant. We are not persuaded that that is a sound submission. It may well be that the co-accused were fortunate in being acquitted and that the sheriff ought to have taken a different view regarding the knives carried by them, but that is not at issue in this case. The sole issue in this case is whether the sheriff was entitled to convict the appellant and that in turn raises the question of whether he was entitled to conclude that the knife which the appellant had in his possession was an offensive weapon within the meaning of the Act.

"It is well established that whether an accused has an intention in relation to such a knife, that is an intention to use it for the purpose of causing injury, is something that a sheriff is entitled to infer from the facts and circumstances of the carrying of the knife in question. That was plainly recognised in *Lopez* v *MacNab* 1978 J.C. 41.

"It was contended by [the solicitor advocate] in the present case that the sheriff had made it clear when he convicted the appellant that he was doing so upon the view that the knife which he was carrying was one which had been adapted for use for causing personal injury, that is, the knife in question was what is commonly referred to as a category 2 weapon. The sheriff, however, in his additional note explains that this was not the position. In relation to that suggestion he says this:

> 'It had not been my intention to hold that the knife in question had been "adapted" for causing injury and for that reason I refused adjustments (5) and (6) as not being consistent with the opinion which I had formed of the nature of the knife.'

"He likewise explains that he refused further adjustments for the same reason.

"Accordingly, in his additional note, the sheriff has now given an explanation and a reason for refusing the adjustments and he has also made it plain that in this case the appellant was convicted because the sheriff was satisfied that the Crown had proved that the appellant had the weapon in question with him with the intention of using it to cause personal injury. In the final paragraph of his additional note the sheriff says:

> 'So far as concerns my reasons for inferring the intention of the appellant to use the knife if circumstances called for this in his view, it seemed to me that taking a knife of this nature into a discothèque was not consistent with innocent intentions and the Crown had established a prima facie case.'

"This is consistent with what the sheriff says in the note annexed to the stated case. The sheriff makes it plain in the case that what weighed with him was that the appellant had this knife in his possession. He also had regard to the nature of the knife. He had regard to the place where the appellant had the knife in his possession, namely a discothèque, which was a public place with between 500 and 600 people inside. He had regard also to the time at which he had the knife in his possession, namely 11.30 p.m. Having regard to these circumstances, we are satisfied that the sheriff was entitled to draw the inference that the appellant had the weapon with him with the intention of using it to cause personal injury. The sheriff in the case also deals with the question of whether the appellant had any reasonable excuse for having it in his possession and concluded that he did not.

"In these circumstances we are satisfied that the sheriff was entitled to repel the appellant's submission of no case to answer and that he was entitled to convict the appellant.

"In the case there are also questions asking whether the sheriff was entitled to make findings 8 and 9, but having regard to the description which he gives of the material before him we are satisfied that he was indeed entitled to make these findings. We shall accordingly answer the four questions in the case in the affirmative and it follows that the appeal is refused."

Appeal refused.

NOTE

Qureslic v. *Normand*, 1993 G.W.D. 10–673 is also an example of an offensive weapon being found in "a place of entertainment." The locus of the offence can be important: in *McLaughlin* v. *Scott*, 1996 G.W.D. 22–1268 the appellant was found within the precincts of the court with a knife.

Section 1(4) of the 1953 Act: "the person" **3.8.1**

R. v. Fleming **3.8.2**

[1989] Crim.L.R. 71

F. was charged with possessing an offensive weapon, a large domestic carving knife. He was aged 37 and had a history of psychiatric illness including symptoms of self mutilation. After he had made a telephone call to the operator at about 2 p.m. threatening to shoot somebody, armed police surrounded his house. He came out of the house carrying the knife which he dropped when challenged by police. His wife gave evidence for the Crown saying she feared only that her husband might harm himself and that she did not think he would harm others. The defence made a submission of no case to answer on the following grounds: (1) there was no evidence of intention to injure a third party; (2) on construction of s.1(4) of the 1953 Act an intention to harm oneself was insufficient. The prosecution admitted that s.1(4) was wide enough to sustain the argument that an intention to injure oneself is within the Act.

Held, allowing the submission of no case to answer, that there was no evidence from which a jury might possibly infer that the defendant intended to hurt anyone else, but that there was evidence upon which the jury might infer he intended to harm himself. However, even although s.1(4) of the 1953 Act speaks of an article intended for use for causing injury to "the person" and it does not say "another person," the whole point of that subsection in defining offensive weapon is that it must be offensive, in other words, aggressive to others. The intention to harm oneself cannot sensibly be held to be offensive, therefore it would not be proper to leave the case to the jury on the basis of an intention by the defendant to injure himself.

Acquitted.

NOTE
This was a decision of a court of first instance, Beverley Crown Court.

Part Two: 1959 Act Cases **3.9**

(i) Fisher v. Bell **3.9.1**

[1960] 3 All E.R. 731

A shopkeeper displayed in his shop window a knife with a price ticket behind it. He was charged with offering for sale a flick knife contrary to s.1(1) of the 1959 Act. The magistrates acquitted him and the prosecutor appeal.

Lord Parker, C.J. (at p. 732)

"Section 1(1) of the Act provides:

'Any person who manufactures, sells or hires or offers for sale or hire, or lends or gives to any other person—(a) any knife which has a blade which opens automatically by hand pressure applied to a button, spring or other device in or attached to the handle of the knife, sometimes known as a "flick knife" ... shall be guilty of an offence ...'

"The justices, without deciding whether the knife in question was a knife of the kind described in the statute, decided that the information must be dismissed on the ground that there had not been an offer for sale.

"The short facts are these. The respondent keeps a retail shop in Bristol and, in October, 1959, a police constable, walking past the shop, saw in the window, amongst other articles, one of these knives. Behind the knife in the window was a ticket with the words 'Ejector knife—4 [shillings].' The police officer went in and informed the respondent that he would be reported for offering for sale such knife, and the respondent replied: 'Fair enough'.

"The sole question is whether the exhibition of that knife in the window with the ticket constituted an offer for sale within the statute. I think that most lay people would be inclined to the view (as, indeed, I was myself when I first read these papers), that if a knife were displayed in a window like that with a price attached to it, it was nonsense to say that that was not offering it for sale. The knife is there inviting people to buy it, and in ordinary language it is for sale; but any statute must be looked at in the light of the general law of the country, for Parliament must be taken to know the general law. It is clear that, according to the ordinary law of contract, the display of an article with a price on it in a shop window is merely an invitation to treat. It is in no sense an offer for sale the acceptance of which constitutes a contract. That is clearly the general law of the country. Not only is that so, but it is to be observed that, in many statutes and orders which prohibit selling and offering for sale of goods, it is very common, when it is so desired, to insert the words 'offering or exposing for sale,' 'exposing for sale' being clearly words which would cover the display of goods in a shop window. Not only that, but it appears that under several statutes—we have been referred in particular to the Prices of Goods Act, 1939, and the Goods and Services (Price Control) Act, 1941—Parliament, when it desires to enlarge the ordinary meaning of those words, has a definition section enlarging the ordinary meaning of 'offer for sale' to cover other matters including, be it observed, exposure of goods for sale with the price attached. [S.20(4)(a) of the Goods and Services (Price Control) Act 1941.]

"In those circumstances I, for my part, though I confess reluctantly, am driven to the conclusion that no offence was here committed. At first sight it appears absurd that knives of this sort may not be manufactured, they may not be sold, they may not be hired, they may not be lent, they may not be given, but apparently they may be displayed in shop windows; but even if this is a casus omissus—and I am by no means saying that it is—it is not for this court to supply the omission. I am mindful of the strong words of LORD SIMONDS in *Magor & St. Mellons Rural District Council* v. *Newport Corporation* [[1951] 2 All E.R. 839]. In that case one of the lords justices in the Court of Appeal had, in effect, said [[1950] 2 All E.R. at p. 1236] that the court, having discovered the supposed intention of Parliament, must proceed to fill in the gaps—what the legislature has not written, the court must write—and in answer to that contention Lord Simonds in his speech said [[1951] 2 All E.R. at p. 841]:

'It appears to me to be a naked usurpation of the legislative function under the thin disguise of interpretation ...'

"For my part, approaching this matter apart from authority, I find it quite impossible to say that an exhibition of goods in a shop window is itself an offer for sale. We were, however, referred to several cases, one of which is *Keating* v. *Horwood* [[1926] All E.R. Rep. 88], a decision of this court. There, a baker's van was being driven on its rounds. There was bread in it that had been ordered and bread in it that was for sale, and it was found that that bread was under weight, contrary to the Sale of Food Order, 1921. That order was an order of the sort to which I have referred already and which prohibited the offering or exposing for sale. In giving his judgment, LORD HEWART, C.J., said [at p. 89]:

'The question is whether, on the facts, there were (i) an offering, and (ii) an exposure, for sale. In my opinion, there were both.'

"AVORY, J. agreed. SHEARMAN, J., however, said [at p. 90]:

'I am of the same opinion. I am quite clear that this bread was exposed for sale, but have had some doubt whether it can be said to have been offered for sale until a particular loaf was tendered to a particular customer.'

"There are three matters to observe on that case. The first is that the order plainly contained the words 'exposes for sale', and, on any view, there was in that case an exposing for sale. Therefore, the question whether there was an offer for sale was unnecessary for decision. Secondly, the principles of general contract law were never referred to; and thirdly, albeit part of the second ground, the respondents were not represented and there was, in fact, no argument. For my part, I cannot take that as an authority for the proposition that the display here in a shop window was an offer for sale.

"The other case to which I should refer is *Wiles* v. *Maddison* [[1943] 1 All E.R. 315]. I find it unnecessary to go through the facts of that case, which was a very different case and where all that was proved was an intention to commit an offence the next day, but, in the course of his judgment, VISCOUNT CALDECOTE, C.J., said [at p. 317]:

> 'A person might, for instance, be convicted of making an offer of an article of food at too high a price by putting it in his shop window to be sold at an excessive price, although there would be no evidence of anybody having passed the shop window or having seen the offer or the exposure of the article for sale at that price.'

"Again, be it observed, that was a case where, under the Meat (Maximum Retail Prices) Order, 1940, the words were: 'No person shall sell or offer or expose for sale or buy or offer to buy ...' Although Lord Caldecote, C.J., does refer to the making of an offer by putting an article in the shop window, before the sentence is closed he has, in fact, turned the phrase to one of exposing the article. I cannot get any assistance in favour of the appellant from that passage. Accordingly, I have come to the conclusion in this case that the justices were right, and this appeal must be dismissed."

Appeal dismissed.

NOTE

This case is more frequently cited as an example of statutory construction rather than for the actual decision; for a recent discussion see A. Ashworth, *Interpreting Criminal Statutes; a Crisis of Legality?* (1991) 107 L.Q.R. 419 at p. 429.

3.9.2   **(ii) M. Potter Ltd. v. Customs and Excuse Commissioners**

[1973] Crim.L.R. 116

Under the Restriction of Offensive Weapons Act 1959 forfeiture proceedings were taken against a company on a complaint that, contrary to s.1(1)(*b*), they had imported knives "each of which had a blade which is released from the handle by the force of gravity or the application of centrifugal force and which, when released, is locked in place by means of a button, spring, lever or other device, sometimes known as a 'gravity knife' ..." Each knife had a hinged blade which was clasped into the handle and could be opened by use of a thumbnail niche in the blade, in the same manner as an ordinary pocket knife; it differed from such a knife in size and also, *inter alia*, in having a locking device to prevent the blade from shutting itself into the handle. If the knife was held in the hand and a vigorous flicking movement was made with the lower arm which stopped sharply, the blade could be released from the handle and would be fully opened and locked in that position. People who could open the knife by such flicking succeeded only after considerable practice, and some people might never succeed. There was some evidence that such a knife was known as a "lock knife" and no evidence that it was ever known as a "gravity knife." Justices condemned the knives and an appeal to quarter sessions was dismissed on the basis that the blade was capable of being released by centrifugal force, which was the force predominantly used in the flicking movement. The company appealed by case stated to the Queen's Bench Divisional Court contending that the knife did not come within the prohibition of s.1(1)(*b*) in that the knife could not be described as one with a blade which "is released" by centrifugal force and in the absence of evidence that it was sometimes known as a "gravity knife."

Held, that following *Atkins & Son Ltd.* v. *Keyes* (unreported) February 5, 1971, D.C., "is released" in s.1(1)(*b*) meant "is capable of being released"; some element of fact and degree entered into assessment whether a particular knife was "capable" of having its blade released by such flicking, and quarter sessions were entitled to find as they had found. "Sometimes known as a 'gravity knife'" were words of description, and it was not necessary to show that a particular knife was sometimes so referred to if, in other respects, it came within the terms of s.1(1)(*b*).

Appeal dismissed.

Part Three: 1968 Act Cases   **3.10**

(i) R. v. Stones   **3.10.1**

The Times, November 29, 1988

S. was convicted after trial by judge and jury of aggravated burglary and sentenced to a period of imprisonment. He appealed against his conviction.

Glidewell, L.J.

"[T]he appellant admitted that he had taken part in the burglary of a dwelling house. He and another man were seen by an off-duty police officer loading stolen goods into a car.

"The police were called and the two men ran off, but the appellant was caught and arrested. When searched a household knife was found in his possession. When asked why he had it with him he said: 'For self-defence because some lads from Blythe are after me.'

"The prosecution submitted that if the appellant knowingly had the knife with him at the time of the burglary, with the intention of using it to cause injury to or to incapacitate the lads from Blythe if he met them, the offence was proved. It was not necessary to prove intention to use the knife during the course of the burglary.

"In the view of this Court that submission is correct. The mischief at which the section was aimed was clearly that if a burglar had a weapon with him which he intended to use to injure some person unconnected with the premises burgled, he might be tempted to use it if challenged during the course of the burglary.

"On a correct interpretation of the section there clearly was evidence which the jury accepted of intention to use the knife to injure or to incapacitate some person, therefore there was nothing unsafe or unsatisfactory in the conviction."

Appeal dismissed.

3.10.2   **(ii) R. v. O'Leary**

(1986) 82 Cr.App.R. 341

In the early hours of one morning, O. the appellant forced entry into a private house while unarmed. He searched the house, picking up a knife from the kitchen and proceeded upstairs where he was confronted by the occupants, husband and wife. A struggle ensued during which all three were injured. The appellant demanded and was given cash and a bracelet. The appellant was charged, *inter alia*, with aggravated burglary. At his trial a submission that he could not be guilty of aggravated burglary because he was not armed when he entered the house was rejected by the trial judge whereupon, on re-arraignment, he pleaded guilty. On appeal against the judge's ruling:

Held, that the time at which a defendant must be proved to have with him a weapon of offence to make him guilty of aggravated burglary contrary to s.10(1)(*b*) of the Theft Act 1968 was the time at which he actually stole; *i.e.*, in the instant case when he confronted the householders and demanded their cash and jewellery, which was the theft, when he still had the kitchen knife in his hand. The judge's ruling was, therefore, correct, and the appeal would be dismissed.

The Lord Chief Justice (Lord Lane) (at p. 342)

"On May 20, 1985 in the Crown Court at Inner London Sessions House before Judge Mason, the appellant, Michael O'Leary, pleaded not guilty to all counts on an indictment. At the instance of counsel the learned judge heard submissions on points of law. Following the ruling which the judge made upon these submissions, the indictment was put again to the appellant, and he then pleaded guilty to four counts of the indictment and was sentenced as follows: on count 1, burglary, four years' imprisonment; count 2, aggravated burglary, seven years' imprisonment concurrent; and on counts 5 and 6, both of which were s.20 wounding counts, three years' imprisonment on each also to run concurrently.

"The burglary in count 1 concerned another incident which took place at the very same house as the one with which we are concerned today, but on another occasion. Counts 5 and 6, the wounding counts, we need not bother with any further. It is count 2, the aggravated burglary, with which the submissions made to us by [counsel for the appellant] are concerned.

"The facts of the case, which are not in dispute, were these. In the early hours of January 31, 1985 the appellant entered a house in South East London, almost certainly in search of money and valuables, though such an intent, namely the intent at the time of entry to steal, was not alleged against him. At the time of that entry he was unarmed. He looked round the house downstairs. It seems he found nothing there which interested him, except a kitchen knife with which he armed himself.

"He then went upstairs. The occupants of the house, husband and wife, were disturbed. A struggle ensued in the course of which all three, husband, wife and the appellant, received injuries. The appellant demanded and was given, he at that point being armed still with the kitchen knife, some cash and bracelet.

"Counsel for the appellant submitted to the judge that in those circumstances, where the appellant at the time of entering the house, probably aiming to steal, was not equipped with a knife, he could not be guilty of aggravated burglary under section 10(1) of the Theft Act 1968. That submission was rejected by the learned judge. Hence the re-arraignment of the appellant and hence his plea of guilty as already indicated.

"In order to ascertain whether the learned judge was correct or not in the conclusion that he reached, it is necessary to read the relevant sections of the Theft Act 1968, which are sections 9 and 10.

"Section 9 provides:

'(1) A person is guilty of burglary if—(a) he enters any building or part of a building as a trespasser and with intent to commit any such offence as is mentioned in subs. (2) below; or (b) having entered any building or part of a building as a trespasser he steals or attempts to steal anything in the building or that part of it or inflicts or attempts to inflict on any person therein any grievous bodily harm.

'(2) The offences referred to in subsection (1)(a) above are offences of stealing anything in the building ...'

"Thus one turns to aggravated burglary. Section 10 provided:

'(1) A person is guilty of aggravated burglary if he commits any burglary and at the time has with him any firearm or imitation firearm, any weapon of offence, or any explosive ...'

"'Weapon of offence' for the purpose of that section means 'any article made or adapted for use by causing injury to or incapacitating a person, or intended by the person having it with him for such use.'

"In order to get this point out of the way, the appellant having pleaded guilty to this offence, quite plainly any question whether or not the knife was intended by him for use as a weapon of offence can be disposed of: he has admitted that it was.

"So we come to the question of whether this man, on the facts as indicated, was guilty of aggravated burglary.

"There are, as already indicated in section 9(1)(a) and (b) two means by which the prosecution can make out a charge of burglary: first of all by proving that the defendant entered as a trespasser with intent to steal, and secondly, by proving that the defendant having entered as a trespasser, actually stole. In order to discover whether aggravated burglary had been committed or not, it is necessary to determine which of those two limbs is the one which applies in the instant case.

"In order to find that out, one has to look at the indictment. Count 2 of the indictment reads as follows:

'Statement of Offence: Aggravated Burglary contrary to section 10(1) of the Theft Act 1968. Particulars of Offence: Michael O'Leary on the 31st day of January 1985 entered as a trespasser a building known as 104 Lyndhurst Grove, London, SE15, and stole therein a sum of money, a bracelet, a number of keys and a cash card belonging to John Marsh, and at the time of committing the said burglary had with him a weapon of offence, namely a knife.'

"If he had been charged under subsection (1)(a), the offence of burglary would be completed and committed when he entered and it would be at that point that one would have to consider whether or not he was armed. But in the case of subsection (1)(b), which is the one under which he was charged, the offence is complete when, and not until, the stealing is committed, provided again of course that he has trespassed in the first place. The prosecution did not have to prove an intent to steal at the time of entry as the charge is laid there. Indeed such an intent is irrelevant to the charge as laid.

"It follows that under this particular charge, the time at which the defendant must be proved to have had with him a weapon of offence to make him guilty of aggravated burglary was the time at which he actually stole. As already indicated, at that moment, when he confronted the householders and demanded their cash and jewellery, which was the theft, he still had the kitchen knife in his hand. No one alleged that he entered with the intent to steal, and that would not have been, had this matter proceeded to trial before a jury, a matter for the jury to consider at all. Indeed such evidence would, strictly speaking, be inadmissible and irrelevant.

"The judge ruled, as this court has indicated he should have ruled, namely that the material time in this charge for the possession of the weapon was the time when he confronted the householders and stole.

"... In short the learned judge was correct in the ruling that he gave in this case, and this appeal consequently is dismissed."

Appeal dismissed.

(iii) R. v. Kelly   **3.10.3**

(1993) 97 Cr.App.R. 245

K., the appellant, broke into a house in the early hours of the morning, using a screwdriver to effect entry. He was surprised by two young occupants while removing a video recorder from the living room. On leaving the house he was apprehended by the police. He was carrying the stolen goods and the screwdriver. He admitted burglary but was charged with aggravated burglary. It was the prosecution case that he turned off the light and jabbed one of the occupants with the screwdriver. It was the appellant's case that he had stolen the video before the occupants appeared, and had not produced the screwdriver. He was convicted of aggravated burglary and appealed on the ground that for aggravated burglary it was necessary to prove that he had the weapon with him with intent to cause injury before the occasion for the use of the weapon had arisen.

Held, dismissing the appeal, that since the relevant time for consideration of the appellant's intent to use the weapon for causing injury was the time he actually stole the goods, the use of the screwdriver at the time of the theft with the requisite intent, namely, the intent to injure if the need arose, had been established.

Potts, L.J. (at p. 246)

"On September 16, 1991, in the Central Criminal Court before Mr Recorder Crespi, Q.C., and a jury, the appellant was convicted by a majority of 10 to two of aggravated burglary. He had pleaded guilty to the offence of simple burglary.

"He now appeals against his conviction on a point of law.

"The prosecution's case was that on June 19, 1991, in the early hours of the morning, the appellant broke into a house in Brixton using a screwdriver to effect entry. He was surprised by the occupants of the house, a young couple, Mr Sheterline and Ms Matthews, while removing a video recorder from the living room. [Counsel] for the appellant today, and who appeared in the court below, has told us that the witness statement of Mr Sheterline, which we have, accurately reflects the evidence that Mr Sheterline gave before the learned recorder and the jury. The relevant part of that statement reads as follows:

> 'I went back into the living room and looked towards the bar and shouted, "Oi, what do you want?" On hearing this, a black man sprung up from behind the bar. He looked unshaven with short black hair and was wearing a black hooded anorak with the hood down. He said to me, "Where's the remote for the video?" I threw my knife over to the TV and video recorder which are in the far left hand corner of the room and handed both remote control units to him. Whilst I was there, he said, "Unplug the TV and video." He had already turned the light off and he had pulled the hood up over his head and I suddenly felt him push something into the left hand side of my rib cage. I could see it had a brown handle with a blunt metal end to it. It looked like a chisel. I said to the man, "Can I turn the light on because I can't see what I'm doing." He said, "No." I said, "Don't hurt us, just take the stuff and go, we won't say anything."'

"The appellant then attempted to leave the house with the video in one hand and the screwdriver in the other, but he was apprehended by the police who had attended in response to information received from a member of the public. When the appellant emerged from the house, a policeman saw him holding the screwdriver in his hand.

"The appellant gave evidence and said that he had stolen the video before the occupants appeared. He had not produced the screwdriver. It had been in his pocket throughout the incident. When he emerged from the house the screwdriver was still in the back pocket of his jeans, but it fell to the ground, because it ripped the cloth.

"By returning the verdict of guilty, the jury clearly accepted the account given by Mr Sheterline and rejected that of the appellant.

"At the end of the prosecution case, counsel for the appellant made a submission. It was to this effect: that in order to prove the offence of aggravated burglary, it was necessary for the Crown to prove that the defendant had the screwdriver with him in order to cause injury. The phrase 'had with him' should, it was submitted, be interpreted in the same way as under the Prevention of Crime Act 1953, and that in particular it was necessary to establish that the defendant had formed the necessary intent before the occasion to use violence had arisen.

"In this Court, that submission was enlarged upon. Counsel submitted that there must be some period of time, if only a few seconds, between the time when the offender armed himself with a weapon of offence and committed the burglary. Counsel for the appellant relied on *Ohlson* v. *Hylton* [1975] 1 W.L.R. 724, in which a carpenter, during the course of an altercation with a passenger in the underground, removed a hammer from his bag and struck his victim with it.

"It was submitted that in order to establish the offence of aggravated burglary, it was necessary to prove that the appellant had the weapon with him with intent to cause injury *before* the occasion to use the weapon had arisen, and that the mischief at which section 10 of the Theft Act was directed was the *premeditated* use of a weapon during the course of the burglary. A tool used to gain entry could not be converted into a 'weapon of offence' in the heat of the moment.

"It is necessary to refer to *Ohlson* v. *Hylton* in some detail. The headnote reads:

'The defendant, who was a carpenter, was on his way home from work carrying tools of his trade in a briefcase. At an underground station, where he was attempting to board a train, he and another man in the course of a dispute fell out of the train on to the platform. The defendant immediately took from his briefcase a hammer and deliberately struck the other man with it on the head so that he fell to the ground. The defendant was convicted of assault occasioning actual bodily harm and also a charge that without lawful authority or reasonable excuse, he had with him in a public place an offensive weapon, namely the hammer, contrary to section 1(1) of the Prevention of Crime Act 1953. On appeal to the Crown Court the conviction under section 1(1) of the Act of 1953 was quashed.

'On appeal by the prosecutor, on the question whether the intentional use of the hammer to cause injury established the offence of having an offensive weapon, although the original possession of the hammer was lawful:

'*Held*, dismissing the appeal that section 1(1) of the Act of 1953 was not contravened where a person seized a weapon for instant use on a victim; that the seizure and use of the hammer were part and parcel of the defendant's assault or attempted assault on the other man; and that to support a conviction under s.1(1), the prosecutor would have had to show that the defendant was carrying or otherwise equipped with the weapon and had intent to use it offensively before any occasion for its actual use had arisen.'

"Lord Widgery C.J. in the course of his judgment referred to section 1 of the Prevention of Crime Act 1953. That provides, so far as is material:

'(1) Any person who without lawful authority or reasonable excuse, the proof whereof shall lie on him, has with him in any public place any offensive weapon shall be guilty of an offence ...

'(4) In this section, "public place" includes any highway and any other premises or place to which at the material time the public have or are permitted to have access, whether on payment or otherwise; and "offensive weapon" means any article made or adapted for use for causing injury to the person, or intended by the person having it with him for such use by him.'

"It is to be noted that section 1(1) is not limited in time.

"The learned Lord Chief Justice summarised the arguments of the prosecutor and the appellant, and then, at p. 728C, said:

'This is a case in which the mischief at which the statute is aimed appears to me to be very clear. Immediately prior to the passing of the Act of 1953 the criminal law was adequate to deal with the actual use of weapons in the course of a criminal assault. Where it was lacking, however, was that the mere carrying of offensive weapons was not an offence. The long title of the Act reads as follows: "An Act to prohibit the carrying of offensive weapons in public places without lawful authority or reasonable excuse." Parliament is there recognising the need for preventive justice where, by preventing the carriage of offensive weapons in a public place, it reduced the opportunity for the use of such weapons. I have no doubt that this was a worthy objective, and that the Act is an extremely important one. If, however, the prosecutor is right, the scope of section 1 goes far beyond the mischief aimed at, and in every case where an assault is committed with a weapon and in a public place an offence under the Act of 1953 can be charged in addition to the charge of assault. In such a case the additional count does nothing except add to the complexity of the case and the possibility of confusion of the jury. This has in fact occurred.

'In the absence of authority I would hold that an offence under section 1 is not committed where a person arms himself with a weapon for *instant* attack on his victim. It seems to me that the section is concerned only with a man who, possessed of a weapon, forms the necessary intent before an occasion to use actual violence has arisen. In other words, it is not the actual use of the weapon with which the section is concerned, but the carrying of a weapon with intent to use it if occasion arises.'

"The learned Lord Chief Justice then went on to cite authority. He concluded his judgment with these words:

'Accordingly, no offence is committed under the Act of 1953 where an assailant seizes a weapon for instant use on his victim. Here the seizure and use of the weapon are all part and parcel of the assault or attempted assault. To support a conviction under the Act the prosecution must show that the defendant was carrying or otherwise equipped with the weapon, and had the intent to use it offensively before any occasion for its actual use had arisen.'

"Section 10 of the Theft Act provides:

'(1) A person is guilty of aggravated burglary if he commits any burglary and at the time has with him any firearm or imitation firearm, any weapon of offence, or any explosive; and for this purpose ... (b) "weapon of offence" means any article made or adapted for use for causing injury to or incapacitating a person, or intended by the person having it with him for such use ...'

"Section 10(1)(a) deals with firearms, section 10(1)(c) deals with explosives. The purpose of section 1 of the Prevention of Crime

Act 1953 and that of section 10 of the Theft Act 1968, in our judgment differ. The former is directed at the mischief identified by Lord Widgery C.J. in the passage quoted above. The latter is directed at the use of articles which aggravate the offence of simple burglary, so as to render the offender punishable with imprisonment for life. It is to be noted that section 10 identifies the time at which the burglary is aggravated.

"The decision of this Court in *O'Leary (Michael)* (1986) 82 Cr.App.R. 341 is relevant and binds this Court. The part of the headnote that is material reads as follows:

> 'In the early hours of one morning the appellant forced entry into a private house while unarmed. He searched the house, picking up a knife from the kitchen and proceeded upstairs where he was confronted by the occupants, husband and wife. A struggle ensued, during which all three were injured. The appellant demanded and was given cash and a bracelet. The appellant was charged, *inter alia*, with aggravated burglary. At his trial a submission he could be guilty of aggravated burglary because he was not armed when he entered the house was rejected by the trial judge whereupon on re-arraignment he pleaded guilty.'

"In giving the judgment of this Court on appeal against the judge's ruling, Lord Lane, C.J. said at p. 342:

> 'In order to ascertain whether the learned judge was correct or not in the conclusion that he reached, it is necessary to read the relevant sections of the Theft Act 1968, which are sections 9 and 10.
>
> 'Section 9 provides: "(1) A person is guilty of burglary if— (a) he enters any building or part of a building as a trespasser and with intent to commit any such offence as is mentioned in subsection (2) below; or (b) having entered any building or part of a building as trespasser he steals or attempts to steal anything in that building or that part of it or inflicts or attempts to inflict on any person therein any grievous bodily harm.'

"The learned Lord Chief Justice then read section 10, and went on:

> 'In order to get this point out of the way, the appellant having pleaded guilty to this offence, quite plainly any question whether or not the knife was intended by him for use as a weapon of offence can be disposed of: he has admitted that it was.
>
> 'So we come to the question of whether this man, on the facts as indicated, was guilty of aggravated burglary.

'There are, as already indicated in section 9(1)(a) and (b) two means by which the prosecution can make out a charge of burglary: first of all by proving that the defendant entered as a trespasser with intent to steal, and secondly, by proving that the defendant, having entered as a trespasser, actually stole. In order to discover whether aggravated burglary had been committed or not, it is necessary to determine which of those two limbs is the one which applies in the instant case.'

"The learned Chief Justice went on:

'In order to find that out, one has to look at the indictment. Count 2 of the indictment reads as follows: "Statement of Offence: Aggravated Burglary contrary to section 10(1) of the Theft Act 1968. Particulars of Offence: Michael O'Leary on the 31st day of January 1985 entered as a trespasser a building known as 104 Lyndhurst Grove, London, SE15, and stole therein a sum of money, a bracelet, a number of keys and a cash card belonging to John Marsh, and at the time of committing the said burglary, had with him a weapon of offence, namely a knife."'

"If he had been charged under subsection (1)(a), the offence of burglary would be completed and committed when he entered, and it would be at that point that one would have to consider whether or not he was armed. But in the case of subsection (1)(b), which is the one under which he was charged, the offence is complete when, and not until, the stealing is committed, provided again of course that he has trespassed in the first place. The prosecution did not have to prove an intent to steal at the time of entry, as the charge is laid here. Indeed such an intent is irrelevant to the charge as laid.

"It follows that under this particular charge, *the time at which the defendant must be proved to have with him a weapon of offence to make him guilty of aggravated burglary was the time at which he actually stole.* As already indicated, at that moment when he confronted the householders and demanded their cash and jewellery, which was the theft, he still had the kitchen knife in his hand. No one alleged that he entered with the intent to steal, and that would not have been, had this matter proceeded to trial before a jury, a matter for the jury to consider at all. Indeed such evidence would, strictly speaking, be inadmissible and irrelevant [our emphasis].

"In *O'Leary* the knife was a weapon of offence *per se*. In the present case it was not. In our judgment this does not affect the applicability to the present case of the principle expressed by Lord Lane in the above passage.

"The indictment faced by this appellant reads as follows:

> '*Statement of Offence*: Aggravated burglary contrary to section 10(1) of the Theft Act 1968.
>
> 'Particulars of Offence: Ronnie Kelly on the 19th day of June 1991, having entered as a trespasser a building, namely 56 Granville Road SW2, stole therein a video recorder and at the time of committing the said burglary had with him a weapon of offence namely a screwdriver.'

"Thus the charge derives from section 9(1)(b) of the Act and the time at which the appellant must be proved to have had with him a weapon of offence to make him guilty of aggravated burglary was the time he actually stole. The screwdriver would become a weapon of offence on proof that the appellant intended to use it for causing injury to, or incapacitating Mr Sheterline or Ms Matthews at the time of the theft, thereby aggravating the burglary: section 10(1)(b). This construction follows from the clear language of section 10 of the Theft Act, and is consistent with its purpose.

"In our judgment, the Prevention of Crime Act 1953 and the cases under it are directed at an entirely different mischief and do not assist in a true construction of section 10. In *Ohlson* v. *Hylton* the use of the hammer was, as Lord Widgery said, part and parcel of the assault. In the present case the use of the screwdriver with the requisite intent aggravated the burglary.

"That being the relevant law, did the learned recorder fall into error in the instant case?

"As to the appellant's first ground of appeal, to which reference has already been made, the learned recorder ruled as follows:

> 'In my view, in this kind of burglary, the burglary is committed when he steals the video. The essential question is whether he has the implement with him as a weapon of offence at the time that he steals the video. In my view, he steals the video, on the evidence, after he has produced the implement, because it is the production of the implement which the jury are entitled to find leads the householder, the girl, to unplug the video, or remove it all and take the video out.'

"He then ruled that there was a case to answer.

"As we have indicated, the appellant gave evidence and when the learned recorder came to sum up, he identified the issues of fact raised by that evidence when conflicts occurred between what was spoken to by the appellant and the witnesses called on behalf of the Crown.

"Today counsel for the appellant has submitted that the learned recorder thereafter compounded the error made in his ruling by misdirecting the jury as to the law relevant to section 10 of the Theft Act. We go on therefore to consider what the learned recorder said to the jury. At pp. 7 and 8 of the transcript the learned recorder directed the jury as follows:

'There is no doubt that he had the screwdriver with him at the time of the burglary. Did he have it with him as a weapon of offence? What is the time of the burglary? The time of the burglary on the form of the indictment is when he stole he video. When you look at your indictment—I will not trouble you to look at it now—you will see that the allegation is that, having entered as a trespasser, without any right to go in, he stole that video. So the burglary is effective when he stole the video. At that stage did he have the screwdriver with him as a weapon of offence?

'You may say to yourselves if the witnesses, the householder and the girl, are correct, he had it with him as a weapon of offence. He was using it to frighten them. Before you find that he did have it as a weapon of offence, you must find that he had it with him with the intention of injuring somebody. To frighten someone is not enough. You must be sure that he had it with him with the intention of injuring someone.

'A burglar does not usually begin burgling with the intention of injuring the householder. He hopes the householder will not appear on the scene. If the householder does appear on the scene and he produces a weapon of some kind, and the householder, to use a colloquialism "caves in" and does exactly what he is told, then he has no need to use it to injure … In my judgment an intention to injure means the intent to injure, if the need arises. In fact, no injury was done. The prodding—and I am using the word prod—is really a minor matter, even if it produced a bruise.

'The question which you have to decide, if you accept the prosecution witnesses on their broad picture, is whether he intended at the time that he stole the video—and that would mean at the time during the period when he was telling them to unplug it and so forth—did he intend then, if they resisted him in any way, to inflict injury upon them? That is a matter entirely for your judgment.'

"In our judgment, neither the ruling of the learned recorder, nor this direction can be faulted. Both accurately and succinctly stated the relevant principle of law. We accordingly reject the appellant's first ground of appeal.

"There is a second ground, which is: that the learned recorder erred in law in answering a question from the jury for further guidance on the question of intent. It is submitted that the recorder correctly directed the jury that an intention to threaten was insufficient and that it had to be proved that there was an intent to injure. He then proceeded, however, to illustrate the position by reference to an imitation firearm which was clearly not intended to cause injury on the one hand and a loaded pistol which was intended to cause injury on the other. It is said that the direction was capable of being seriously misleading as it tended to suggest that if the alleged weapon was one which was capable of causing injury, it must fall into the same category as the loaded gun and therefore have been intended to cause injury.

"The learned recorder answered the jury's question in these terms:

> 'Let me take it in stages. If you were not satisfied that the screwdriver left his pocket, then of course there would be no evidence that he intended to use the screwdriver as a weapon. Before you convict, the starting point must be that you are sure that the screwdriver was being held by him in his hand.'

"This direction, we interpose, clearly referred to the conflict in the evidence before the jury. The learned recorder went on:

> 'Secondly, to qualify as a weapon of offence within the meaning of the Act of Parliament, it is not sufficient if he has it in his hand simply to frighten, he must have it with the intention to injure.
>
> 'Over the last few moments, I have thought of a very simple illustration, although it could not really arise, because firearms are dealt with specifically in the Act. Supposing the burglar pointed a gun at the householder, does he intend to frighten or does he intend to injure? Supposing you discover it is an imitation gun. You might think that was a very strong reason to think that he did not intend to injure; he intended to frighten. To take the converse situation, supposing it was a loaded gun. You might think that there was little difficulty reaching the conclusion that he intended to injure, because otherwise why did he load it?
>
> 'Bearing in mind that when one is dealing with an intent to injure, you do not mean to injure in any event. If a man points a loaded gun at someone and says, "Do this or I will shoot you," and the man does what he is told to do, then there is no point in firing the gun.
>
> 'It must be the intent to injure if a certain event happens, if, for example, in this situation, the householder had tried to obstruct his escape from the house or had refused to help in

providing the video. I have taken two extreme cases and you may find the difficulty in this case arises because this is not an extreme case.

'You have to ask yourselves this question: "Are we sure that if the householder had not done what the burglar wanted him to do, the burglar would have injured him or the girl?"
'I cannot help you about what judgments you make of this ...'

"The learned recorder concluded:

'You convict if you are sure that there was an intent by the defendant if the householder and the girl had not done what he wanted, to injure them.'

"We are unable to accept the contention made on behalf of the appellant that the example given by the learned recorder, which related to the use of weapons, misled this jury. Taken as a whole and in context, we are satisfied that this passage accurately and fairly stated the law, and accurately and fairly dealt with the question raised by the jury and which the learned recorder had to answer. Therefore we reject this ground of appeal also.

"Accordingly, the appeal against conviction is dismissed."

Appeal dismissed.
Application refused.

Part Four: 1980 Act Cases **3.11**

(i) Burke v. MacKinnon **3.11.1**

1983 S.C.C.R. 23

B. was handed a razor by another person and he put it in his pocket. This was seen by a policeman who searched B. and found the razor in his pocket. B. had taken no steps to hide the razor from the policeman, other than to put it in his pocket. B. was charged with a contravention of section 4(2)(*b*) of the 1980 Act and convicted. He appealed.

In his stated case the sheriff made the following findings in fact, *viz.*:

"1. At about 1.45 p.m. on Saturday, November 28, 1981, acting on information received, Sergeant Forbes entered the booking office foyer at Gilmour Street Station, Paisley, where there was a large number of people some of whom were Glasgow Rangers supporters en route for a game at Hampden Park.

2. There he saw the appellant and another man (Hyndeman), both wearing Rangers scarves. Sergeant Forbes then saw Hyndeman remove a 'black-handled object' from his right-hand pocket and pass it across his body to the appellant who was standing on his left. The appellant then put the object in his right-hand trouser pocket.

3. Sergeant Forbes approached the appellant and informed him that he was going to search him in terms of the relevant section of the Act. The appellant made no objection. Sergeant Forbes then found a black-handled open razor in the appellant's right-hand pocket.

4. The appellant thereupon ran out of the station into County Square where he was caught by Sergeant Forbes and taken to Mill Street Police Station. There when cautioned and charged with the offence libelled, and in the presence of Inspector Shaw, the appellant replied, 'I got passed it.' Later, on the way to the cells, the appellant told Sergeant Forbes that Hyndeman had given him the razor."

In his note the sheriff stated:

"In my opinion (1) the reply to the caution and charge was sufficient corroboration of Sergeant Forbes's evidence that the razor was in the appellant's pocket when searched, (2) out of sight in the appellant's pocket is consistent with at least one of the dictionary definitions of concealment, and (3) whatever the specific definition of an offensive weapon may be in the Prevention of Crime Act 1953 an open razor in the pocket of a football fan en route to a football match undoubtedly calls for an explanation. The appellant elected not to give evidence."

The question for the opinion of the High Court was:

"On the facts stated, was I entitled to convict the appellant?"

Lord Justice-General (Emslie) (at p. 24)

"The appellant in this case is Brian Burke who was found guilty, after trial in the sheriff court, of an alleged contravention of section 4(2)(*b*) of the Criminal Justice (Scotland) Act 1980. The substance of the matter is that it was libelled against him that while a police constable, exercising the power of search conferred by section 4(1), was searching the clothing of the appellant, the appellant concealed from the searching officer a razor which was found in his pocket. The question in the case in which conviction is challenged is: 'On the facts stated, was I entitled to convict the appellant?' On the facts stated there is only one answer which can possibly be given, and that is 'No'. Findings 1 and 2 disclose what gave rise to the search in terms of section 4(1). The appellant in fact received a razor, an open razor, from a friend and put it in his pocket. The police officer who observed this transaction decided to use the powers contained in section 4(1). Finding 3 tells us what happened. Sergeant Forbes approached the appellant and informed him that he was going to search him in terms of the relevant section of the Act. The appellant made no objection. Sergeant Forbes then found a black-handled open razor in the appellant's right-hand pocket. Now there is no whisper there of the kind of concealment which is libelled in the charge because there was no active concealment from the searching officer. The razor remained where it had been put by the appellant and all the officer had to do to find it was to put his hand in the pocket where he knew that it probably was.

"The question is, however, whether the charge ought to have been libelled against the appellant under section 4(2)(*b*) in the circumstances disclosed in the stated case. We are of opinion that there was no room for a charge under section 4(2)(*b*) in those circumstances. Section 4(2) provides for new offences. One of them is where a person, who is being searched by a policeman acting under section 4(1), intentionally obstructs the searching officer. The second of the new offences is where a person who is being searched conceals from the searching officer an offensive weapon. So far as section 4(2)(*b*) is concerned there must, in order to support a relevant charge, be an active step of concealment to prevent discovery of the offensive weapon by the searching officer. In this case there would have been no difficulty at all, once the open razor had been found in the search, in charging the appellant with a contravention of section 1(1) of the Prevention of Crime Act 1953, but there was no basis in fact or in law for charging him with an alleged contravention of section 4(2)(*b*). In the result the appeal succeeds and the conviction will be quashed."

Appeal allowed.

(ii) Cardle v. Malcolm 3.11.2

Dumbarton Sheriff Court, December 16, 1993

M. was charged with a contravention of s.1 of the 1953 Act. At his trial the point at issue was whether the police officers had reasonable grounds for suspecting that M. was carrying an offensive weapon and thus entitled to search M. at the relevant time in terms of s.4(1) of the 1980 Act. A submission of no case to answer was founded on the evidence of M.'s agitation and dissociation from another man as being not amounting to reasonable grounds. The sheriff repelled the submission. M. did not give evidence and he was convicted and initially appealed that conviction, but abandoned his appeal before a hearing.

In the stated case the sheriff found the following facts proved:

"1. About 11.30 p.m. on March 11, 1993 Police Constable Alan Murray and Police Sergeant David Hall who were both in uniform were in Riverside Lane, Dumbarton.

2. Constable Murray and Sergeant Hall saw the appellant and another man standing in Riverside Lane, Dumbarton, at the rear of a public house. Both men were holding drinking glasses.

3. The police officers approached the two men with the intention of asking them to return their drinking glasses to the public house.

4. On coming closer to the two men the police officers noted that the appellant's companion had one end of a lanyard attached to his belt. The other end of the lanyard fetched up in his trouser pocket which was bulging.

5. The police officers thought that the appellant's companion was carrying an offensive weapon. Sergeant Hall decided to search him.

6. In the appellant's presence Sergeant Hall spoke to the appellant's companion and told him that he suspected he was carrying an offensive weapon and in accordance with the power given to him by s.4(1) of the Criminal Justice (Scotland) Act 1980 he told him that he intended to search him.

7. On hearing what was said to his companion by Sergeant Hall the appellant became agitated and moved a step back from his companion.

8. The search of the appellant's companion revealed that the bulge in the trouser pocket was caused by a bulky wallet.

9. The appellant's agitation and his movement away from his companion was seen by the police officers. As a result Sergeant Hall decided to search the appellant as he suspected him of carrying an offensive weapon.

10. Sergeant Hall told the appellant that he suspected that he was carrying an offensive weapon and that as authorised by s.4(1) of the Criminal Justice (Scotland) Act 1980 he was going to search him.

11. A folding knife which was in the closed position was found in one of the appellant's trouser pockets. The blade of the knife was about four inches in length.

12. The appellant was asked to explain his possession of the knife. He said 'I've read all the publicity about these stabbings and I decided to carry it for my own protection. I was drunk when I left the house.'

13. The appellant was then arrested and taken to the local police station where he was cautioned and charged with the possession of an offensive weapon to which he made no reply.
14. On March 11, 1993 the appellant without lawful authority or reasonable excuse had with him in a public place, namely, Riverside Lane, Dumbarton, an offensive weapon, namely, a knife, and thus contravened s.1(1) of the Prevention of Crime Act 1953."

The sheriff also made the following remarks in his note:
"Standing the fact that I believed the police officers it seemed to me as I have stated earlier that the appellant's apparent agitation and his movement away from his companion's side, which given the circumstances I inferred was an attempt to dissociate himself from his companion, could be held to be reasonable grounds for Sergeant Hall's suspicion that the appellant was carrying an offensive weapon. I held therefore that the search was in accordance with the provisions of s.4(1) of the Criminal Procedure (Scotland) Act 1980. In my view, given the circumstances, Sergeant Hall would have been failing in his duty if he had not searched the appellant."

Found guilty.

Part Five: 1988 Act Cases   **3.12**
It is the intention of s.139 of the Criminal Justice Act 1988 to prevent the carrying of fixed-blade knives in a public place. A folding knife which when fully opened automatically locks in the open position becomes in effect a fixed-blade knife. To be a folding pocket-knife the blade has to be readily and immediately foldable at all times simply by the folding process. A knife which on opening automatically locks and cannot be folded until a button has been pressed is not a folding pocket-knife within the meaning of s.139.

(i) Harris v. Director of Public Prosecutions   **3.12.1**

(1993) 96 Cr.App.R. 235

Case stated by North Westminster Metropolitan Stipendiary Magistrate sitting at Wells Street Magistrates' Court
"1. On December 31, 1990, information was preferred by the prosecutor against the defendant that he on November 3, 1990, at Prebend Street, Islington had with him without good reason or lawful authority an article which had a blade or was sharply pointed, namely a lock-knife, contrary to section 139(1), Criminal Justice Act 1988.

"2. The magistrate heard the information on February 15, 1991, and found the following facts:

(a) a police officer saw the defendant in a motor vehicle in Prebend Street at about 8.30 p.m. on November 3, 1990;
(b) the motor vehicle was stopped by the officer who asked to search the defendant and his car;
(c) the defendant then produced a silver-pointed lock knife, which was less than three inches long, from inside his jacket pocket.

"The statement of Police Constable Alan Earl was tendered in evidence under section 9, Criminal Justice Act 1967. His evidence was that on Saturday November 3, 1990, at about 8.50 p.m., he was on duty in full uniform with W.P.C. N. D. Vie driving an unmarked police car in Basire Street, London N1. He saw a grey VW Golf GTI motor car index [...] travelling south in front and indicated for the car to stop. When the vehicle stopped he observed that there were two occupants, the defendant who was the driver and a female passenger. He saw the defendant who appeared to be fiddling or concealing something near the handbrake area. Constable Earl spoke to the defendant, and advised him that he was going to search him and the car for anything he may unlawfully have hidden. He asked the defendant to empty his pockets, and the defendant produced a silver three-inch long-pointed knife from his inside jacket pocket. This knife was produced in the court as exhibit 1. The officer took the knife, opened it and saw that it had a pointed blade and that it locked in the fully open position. The defendant was cautioned and asked why he had the knife. The defendant said that he had it for cutting leaves in the garden.

"The defendant was dressed in a very smart blazer, shirt and trousers, and confirmed that he was going out for the evening. The officer invited him to explain why he had the knife with him, and said to him 'Well, I think it's for your own protection.' The defendant replied 'Yeah, if you want.' The defendant was arrested for possession of an offensive weapon, cautioned, and made no reply. He was then taken to Islington police station where he was charged and cautioned ...

"... The prosecutor made a formal admission under section 10, Criminal Justice Act 1967 that the weapon exhibited had a blade less than three inches long. The evidence adduced on behalf of the prosecutor was not disputed by the defendant.

"3. At the conclusion of the prosecution's case, the defendant submitted that there was no case to answer, on the basis that the knife was a folding pocket-knife and that the cutting edge of its blade was less than three inches in length, so that the knife did not fall within the provisions of section 139, Criminal Justice Act 1988.

"4. The magistrate was referred to the definitions of a pocket-knife and a pen-knife as set out in the *Shorter Oxford English Dictionary*, which are as follows:

> Pocket-knife: 'A knife with one or more blades which fold into the handle for carrying in the pocket.'
> Pen-knife: 'a small knife usually carried in the pocket, used originally for making and mending quill pens, (formerly provided with a sheath; now made with a jointed blade or blades which fit inside the handle when closed).'

"5. He was of the opinion that it could not be said that this lock-knife was a folding pocket-knife. Accordingly he rejected the submission advanced on behalf of the defendant.

"The defendant called no evidence, and the magistrate convicted him in relation to the information.

"The defendant appealed.

"The question for the opinion of the court was: Whether the magistrate was right in law to find that a folding-knife carried in the pocket having a pointed blade of less than three inches in length and capable of being secured in an open position by a locking device was not a folding pocket-knife within the meaning of section 139, Criminal Justice Act 1988."

(ii) Fehmi v. Director of Public Prosecutions   3.12.2

(1993) 96 Cr.App.R. 235

Case stated by Thames Justices of Inner London Area

"1. On November 2, 1990, an information was laid by an officer of the Metropolitan Police against the defendant Ahmet Fehmi, that he, on September 14, 1990, at Bethnal Green Road, E2 had with him in a public place without good reason or lawful authority an article with a blade or sharp point namely a knife, contrary to section 139 of the Criminal Justice Act 1988.

"2. The hearing of the information was adjourned for proper cause from time to time but was heard by the justices on October 3, 1991, when they were asked as a preliminary issue to examine the knife, the subject of the charge, and to rule whether they considered it an article the carrying of which in a public place was prohibited by the said section 139. The justices examined the said article and thus found as facts: (a) that the article was a knife with a blade the cutting edge of which was less than three inches; (b) that the blade was capable of being folded; (c) that when the blade was fully opened it automatically locked in that position;

(d) that to fold the blade back into the handle it was necessary to activate a button triggered mechanism; (e) that the knife was not a folding pocket-knife within the meaning of section 139(3); (f) that the knife was an article which had a blade or is sharply pointed within the meaning of section 139(2).

"3. It was contended by the prosecutor that the mechanism which locked the blade in the open position was such as to render the knife not one which the provisions of the said section permitted to be carried lawfully in a public place.

"4. It was contended by the defendant that the knife was one which could lawfully be carried in a public place notwithstanding the existence of the locking mechanism. If Parliament had intended otherwise, the statute would so state.

"5. The justices were not referred to any cases.

"6. They found as a fact that the knife was one the carrying of which in a public place was an offence under section 139 of the Act.

"The justices directed that the knife be retained by the prosecutor so that it would be available for any further proceedings.

"The justices went on to hear further evidence and argument not the subject of appeal and convicted the defendant.

"The defendant appealed.

"7. The question for the opinion of the court was whether in finding as the justices did that the knife was one the carrying of which in a public place is an offence was a correct determination or decision in law."

McCowan, L.J. (at p. 238)

"These are two appeals by way of case stated which have been heard together because they raise a single point."

[His Lordship then narrated the history of these two appeals.] ...

"... We were shown one of the knives in question, there being no difference between the two. What we observed was that when you first open it manually you cannot then fold it back. You have first to press a button on it in order to fold it back, so that when fully opened, the result is that it requires to be unlocked.

"I look next at section 139 and read it in so far as it is relevant:

'(1) Subject to subsections (4) and (5) below, any person who has an article to which this section applies with him in a public place shall be guilty of an offence.

(2) Subject to subs. (3) below, this section applies to any article which has a blade or is sharply pointed except a folding pocket-knife.

(3) This section applies to a folding pocket-knife if the cutting edge of its blade exceeds three inches.'

"Appearing for Mr Harris, [counsel] said that the only question in the case is whether the presence of the locking mechanism is sufficient to prevent it being a folding pocket-knife. He points out that this is a penal statute and, accordingly, he submits clear words are required. They are not, he says. There is nothing in the section which says that the presence or absence of a locking device affects the matter. The court asked him how far he took the argument. What, for example, of a knife which required a screwdriver to undo a screw before it could be unlocked and then folded back into the closed position? His answer was that it would be still a folding knife because it could be, albeit by a somewhat lengthy process, folded away. Again, the court asked him what he submitted was the thinking behind the statute. He accepted in this context that it does make a difference if the knife can be folded readily away. He accepted that it is obviously a more effective stabbing weapon if it is locked, for the very plain reason that without a lock there is a dangerous tendency, dangerous, that is to say, from the point of view of the wielder, to fold on the wielder's hand.

"[Counsel] also appeared for the other defendant, Mr Fehmi. His arguments were somewhat different. He stressed the other side of the coin. He submits that it is not more dangerous for being locked. He says that from the point of view of the user, it is much safer because it will not come back upon his hand. [Counsel] went so far as to describe it as a safety device. Again, he would not agree with [counsel] about the screw to which I referred a little while ago, because [counsel for the appellant Harris] says that the section covers manual folding, and if it is necessary to use a screwdriver in order to undo the locking device, then, this is a mechanical folding and not manual folding. There was some discussion about what is called a switch-blade. As I understand it, that means by pressing a button the blade will automatically fold outwards and, again, by pressing a button, it will automatically fold in again. Since this is a pivotal device and [counsel for the appellant Fehmi] was stressing the element of pivoting, I asked him why that would not cover the switch-blade. His answer is that it does not cover the switch-blade because the section is concerned to cover manual folding and not mechanical folding.

"For my part, I cannot accept his argument in this respect, because that would certainly involve importing a number of additional words into the section. His basic argument, as I have already indicated, is that to fold the blade it has to have a pivot. If it is pivoted, he asked rhetorically, how can it be said that because it has a locking device it is no longer a folding pocket-knife? Two hands, he stresses, are required to open this type of knife. That sharply differentiates it from a flick-knife. The locking device, he submits, cannot change the nature of the animal. The question is whether it folds open and folds shut.

"For the defendant in each case, [counsel] answers the question from the Court as to the thinking behind the statute by saying this. When the knife is locked it becomes in effect a fixed-blade knife and the intention of the statute is to prevent the carrying of such a knife. I accept that point.

"In my judgment, the right approach to the matter is this. To be a folding pocket-knife the knife has to be readily and indeed immediately foldable at all times, simply by the folding process. A knife of the type with which these appeals are concerned is not in this category because, in the first place, there is a stage, namely, when it has been opened, when it is not immediately foldable simply by the folding process and, secondly, it requires that further process, namely, the pressing of the button.

"For these reasons, I would give the answer to the question in each case, that the tribunals were right to find as they did, and I would dismiss the appeals."

Appeals dismissed

3.12.3   **(iii) Director of Public Prosecutions v. Gregson**

(1993) 96 Cr.App.R. 240

The fact that a defendant has forgotten that he has with him an article having a blade or sharp point to which s.139 of the Criminal Justice Act 1988 applies cannot constitute a defence of good reason within s.139(4) of the Act.

While the defendant was being questioned by police officers a knife with a fixed blade four inches in length fell from his jeans. He offered no specific reason or excuse for having the knife with him. He was charged with having with him in a public place, without good reason or lawful excuse, an article with a blade or sharp point more than three inches long, contrary to s.139 of the Criminal Justice Act 1988. At his trial the defence case was that he habitually used the knife at work for cutting cork floor tiles, and had left it in his jacket when he last used it six days previously. On the occasion in question he had forgotten that he had the knife with him. The justices dismissed the information being satisfied on the balance of probabilities that the defendant had good reason for having the knife with him. On appeal by the D.P.P. by way of case stated:

Held, allowing the appeal, that having a knife for a good reason, namely for the purposes of work, six days earlier could not amount to a good reason six days later when the defendant was not at work. Further, forgetfulness could not constitute a good reason within s.139(4) of the Criminal Justice Act 1988.

Case stated by Inner London (Thames) Justices
"1. On October 7, 1991, an information was laid by the Crown Prosecution Service in court on behalf of the prosecutor against the defendant that he on August 1, 1991, at Chrisp Street E14, had with him in a public place without good reason or lawful authority an article with a blade or sharp point, namely, a blade with a cutting edge which exceeded three inches, contrary to section 139, Criminal Justice Act 1988.

"2. The justices heard the said information on October 14, 1991, and found the following facts:

(a) At 6.25 p.m. on the date specified which was a Thursday, police were called to the defendant's address and outside that address saw the respondent arguing with another person. After some discussion, police left the scene but returned later and again saw the defendant outside the address.

(b) On this later occasion police officers intended to search the defendant but before so doing a knife which had a fixed blade of some four inches in length fell from the defendant's clothing, that is his jeans.

(c) On this latter occasion the defendant offered no specific reason or excuse for having the knife with him.

(d) The defendant habitually used the knife for purposes of his work in cutting cork floor tiles and habitually carried the knife in the pocket of the jacket he was wearing at the time of the incident and which he wore for work.

(e) The defendant had last worked six days prior to the incident, namely on Friday July 26, 1991, and he had forgotten to remove the knife before entering the street on this occasion.

"3. It was contended by the defendant that he had a good reason for having the knife with him in a public place in that he used it for his work and had forgotten it was with him on this occasion.

"4. The prosecutor did not reply to this contention.

"5. The justices were not referred to any cases.

"6. The justices were of opinion that the defendant had satisfied them on a balance of probabilities that he had a good reason for having the knife with him. Accordingly, they dismissed the information.

"The prosecutor now appealed.

"7. The questions for the opinion of the court were:

(i) whether in order to establish a defence of good reason within section 139(4) of the Criminal Justice Act 1988 a defendant has to prove a specific reason for his having the article with him in a public place on the occasion alleged.

(ii) whether a defendant who has forgotten that he has with him an article to which section 139 of the Criminal Justice Act applies can rely upon that forgetfulness as constituting a defence of good reason within section 139(4) of the said Act.

(iii) whether on the facts the justices found they made a correct determination and decision in law."

McCowan, L.J. (at p. 242)

"[Counsel for the D.P.P.] drew to our attention the case of *McCalla* (1988) 87 Cr.App.R. 327, and in particular to a passage in the judgment of the court given by May, L.J. on p. 379. Section 1 of the Prevention of Crime Act 1953 was then under consideration, the words of that, in so far as relevant, being:

'Any person who without lawful authority or reasonable excuse ...'

"In the passage in question May, L.J. said:

'As to the second alleged misdirection, we are quite satisfied that to have forgotten that one has an offensive weapon in the car that one is driving is not in itself a reasonable excuse under the Act. But when such forgetfulness is coupled with particular circumstances relating to the original acquisition of the article the combination of the original acquisition and the subsequent forgetfulness of possessing it may, given sufficient facts, be a reasonable excuse for having the offensive weapon with one.'

"As [counsel] pointed out, the court there was concerned with the expression 'reasonable excuse.' We are concerned with a quite different expression used in the 1988 Act, namely, 'good reason.'

"In my judgment, [counsel] is right to say that it is important to concentrate on the time in respect of which the defendant is charged. Six days earlier, no doubt this man had the knife on him for a good reason, because the justices found that it was a knife that he used in his work and would have had with him at his work and might well have put into his pocket at work six days earlier. But did he have it with him for a good reason at the time of his arrest? Having it for work reasons six days earlier cannot, in my judgment, be a good reason for having it on him six days later when not at work. The question, therefore, it seems to me, boils down to whether forgetfulness at the relevant time was a good reason. It does appear that the justices found that he had forgotten that he had it on him. I am bound to say that I am surprised at this finding, having regard to their finding of fact that the knife fell not from his jacket pocket where the knife, he said, had been put by him at the time of his work, but from his jeans, and the further finding that when that happened he offered no specific reason or excuse for having it with him. However, they did in fact find, as I understand it, that they believed that he had forgotten that he had the knife with him. Was that a good reason?

"In my judgment, forgetfulness may be an explanation. It cannot be a good reason. I would therefore answer the second question, by saying that the fact that a defendant has forgotten that he has an article to which section 139 applies cannot constitute a defence of good reason within section 139(4) of the Act. I would therefore go on to answer question 3, that they did not make a correct determination and decision in law. As to question 1, which poses the question, whether in order to establish a defence of good reason a defendant has to prove a specific reason for having the article with him in a public place on the occasion alleged, I prefer to give no answer to that question. I would prefer to hear the point much more fully argued. It is unnecessary to answer it for the purposes of this appeal, which I would allow."

Appeal allowed.

(iv) Godwin v. Director of Public Prosecutions 3.12.4

(1993) 96 Cr.App.R. 244

At the time when G., the defendant, was attacked in a public street by an assailant known to him and known by the defendant to bear a grudge, the defendant was found by police officers to have with him a red-handled kitchen knife with a pointed blade and cutting edge exceeding three inches in length. When questioned he told the police that he required the knife for use at his home and invited them to search his flat to establish the lack of kitchen utensils there, including knives. At his trial that defence was not contradicted by any prosecution evidence. The justices, finding the defendant's explanation most improbable in the circumstances of the case, convicted him. On appeal by case stated:

Held, dismissing the appeal, that once the Crown had discharged the burden of proving the ingredients of the offence against s.139(1) of the Criminal Justice Act 1988, the defendant was guilty unless he could discharge the burden imposed by s.139(4) of the Act. The justices were fully entitled to disbelieve the defendant's evidence without any evidence relating to it from the prosecution.

Case stated by Ealing justices sitting at Acton
"1. On November 7, 1990, an information was preferred by the prosecutor against the defendant that he on Wednesday October 24, 1990, at Hartington Road, W13, had with him in a public place an article which was sharply pointed and which had a cutting edge which exceeded three inches, namely a red-handled knife, contrary to section 139 of the Criminal Justice Act 1988.

"2. The justices heard the said information on March 14, 1991, and found the following facts:

(i) On October 24, 1990, at approximately 9.00 a.m. the defendant was attacked, outside the Unemployment Benefit Office in Hartington Road, W13. The assailant was known to the defendant who knew that the assailant was aggrieved by the defendant's association with a relative of the assailant.

(ii) The defendant had with him a red-handled kitchen knife, which had a pointed blade, and a cutting edge which exceeded three inches.

(iii) When interviewed by the police the defendant stated that he required the knife for use at his home. He invited search of his flat to establish lack of kitchen utensils including knives.

"The following is a short statement of the evidence:

(a) Steven Giffard on oath said he was queuing outside the Unemployment Benefit Office in Hartington Road, W13 at 9.00 a.m. on October 24, 1990 and saw a fight break out at the head of the queue. As he approached he saw that one of the men fighting the defendant (accepted by defence) had a knife. He asked the defendant to drop the knife—the defendant asked that the police be called. He repeated his request for the knife a few times and each time the defendant replied that he would give up the knife when the police arrived. The defendant wasn't doing anything with the knife—just holding it steady in his right hand about six inches from the other man's chest. He seemed very reluctant to use the knife and exercised great restraint as the other man was holding him by the hair and banging his head on the wall and issuing threats. The defendant was warding off the other man.

(b) Police Constable John McCreadie on oath said that he was on duty in full uniform on Wednesday, October 24, 1990, when called with Police Constable Freeman, to the D.S.S. Office in Hartington Road, W13 where he saw a white youth and a half-caste youth grappling by the doorway to the office. He approached and saw that the white youth had a small knife in his right hand. Asked to put it down and the knife was dropped. He took possession of the knife (produced Exhibit 1) and the two youths were separated. The defendant said to him, 'He started it, he followed me here. It was just for my protection.' The defendant also told the officer 'I was here to sign on and he turned up and started on me, so I pulled the knife. I know I shouldn't have done.'

The defendant was arrested and cautioned at 9.10 a.m. Between 1.50 p.m. and 1.59 p.m. in the interview room at Ealing police station the defendant was interviewed. During the interview he explained that at 8.30 a.m. on October 24, 1990, he had left his girlfriend's mother's home at 40 Cuckoo Avenue, West Ealing, taking the knife with him. On the way home to his new home he had to sign on at the D.S.S. Office in Hartington Road, and it was there that he was attacked. He stated he pulled the knife out of his pocket not intending to use it—just to scare off his attacker. During the interview the defendant invited police to visit his address to verify that there were no kitchen utensils there. No such check was carried out. At Ealing police station at 2.37 p.m. the defendant was charged, the charge read over and cautioned to which he made no reply.

(c) Constable Freeman gave evidence which was corroborative of Constable McCreadie.

(d) The defendant gave evidence on oath that on the night of October 23, 1990, he had stayed at his girlfriend's mother's address at 40 Cuckoo Avenue, West Ealing. His girlfriend was in hospital. The defendant was in the process of moving into a new home and intended staying there on the night of October 24, 1990. He had no kitchen utensils and asked his girlfriend's mother if he could borrow a kitchen knife so that he could prepare a meal that evening.

On leaving 40 Cuckoo Avenue he intended to go to his new address, via the D.S.S. Office to sign on, and the hospital to visit his girlfriend. He was aware of being followed by his attacker, a man he knew—a relative of his girlfriend—who disapproved of their relationship and had caused trouble in the past. While waiting in the queue at the D.S.S. Office he was attacked by this man and pulled the knife from his pocket to defend himself. The defendant agreed with the evidence given by the witness Giffard and stated he was only defending himself.

The defendant stated he had the knife with him to take it to the new home—he intended to use it that evening to prepare himself a steak and kidney pie; that he had utensils and cutlery with which to eat but no knife with which to cut the meat. He further stated that take-away meals disagreed with him. He was working at the time.

"3. It was contended on behalf of the defendant that he had a defence to the charge under section 139, Criminal Justice Act 1988 in that he had a good reason for having the knife with him in a public place—section 139(4).

"4. It was contended on behalf of the prosecutor that the defendant had the knife with him in a public place an article to which section 139, Criminal Justice Act 1988 applied.

"5. The justices were not referred to any cases.

"6. The justices were of the opinion that: The reason put forward by the defendant for having the knife, namely for food preparation later that evening was most improbable having regard to the circumstances of the case.

"Accordingly, they convicted the defendant and imposed a fine of £75.00. The justices made no order as to costs and no order for forfeiture of the knife.

"The defendant now appealed.

"7. The question for the opinion of the court was (i) whether there was any evidence before the court entitling us to disbelieve the defendant on the balance of probabilities; (ii) whether it is right in principle where a defendant has given an explanation which is not contradicted by any evidence and is not inherently unlikely and which could have been checked by the prosecution at a time when such a check would have been conclusive either way, and the prosecution declined to make such checks, that the prosecution should then invite the court to disbelieve the defendant's explanation, and whether it is right in such circumstances for the court to disbelieve such explanation."

McCowan, L.J. (at p. 246)

"[Counsel's] argument for the defendant in a nutshell was this. The justices, having received no evidence rebutting the explanation given by the defendant which, according to [counsel], was not an inherently incredible explanation, the presumption of innocence is resurrected.

"For my part, I entirely reject this suggestion. Once the Crown had discharged the burden upon them under section 139, the defendant is guilty of the offence unless he can discharge the burden put upon him by subsection (4). In this case, it is obvious that he failed, in the view of the justices, to discharge that burden. They were fully entitled to reach that conclusion, and having reached it, they would be bound to convict him.

"So far as the questions are concerned, for what they are worth, I would answer them by saying that they were entitled to disbelieve the defendant. In my judgment, this is an unarguable appeal and I would dismiss it."

Appeal dismissed.

Part Six: 1993 Act Cases   **3.13**

(i) Normand v. Walker   **3.13.1**

1995 S.L.T. 94

W., an accused person, was tried on a summary complaint for, *inter alia*, a contravention of s.1(1) of the Carrying of Knives etc. (Scotland) Act 1993. Evidence was given by two Crown witnesses that the accused was found in possession of a folding pocket knife. The blade of the knife, when measured in court by means of a ruler, was found by one of the witnesses to be $3\,^1/_4$ inches in length and by the other witness to be $3\,^1/_2$ inches long. At the close of the Crown case it was submitted that there was no case for the accused to answer because there was no evidence establishing the accuracy of the ruler used to measure the blade. The sheriff sustained the submission and acquitted the accused. The Crown appealed by stated case and argued principally that the length of the blade was an exception which in terms of s.312(v) of the Criminal Procedure (Scotland) Act 1975 it was not for the Crown to negative, although no notice of such argument had been given in the application for a stated case.

Held, (1) that as the appellant had not shown cause why he should be allowed to found his appeal on a ground not contained in his application for the stated case, the principal submission would not be entertained; (2) that where use was made of an everyday object such as a ruler such evidence was admissible without further evidence that the ruler had been in some way certified as accurate; (3) that the question at the close of the Crown case was not whether there was evidence which satisfied the sheriff but whether there was evidence which would establish, if accepted, that the blade exceeded 3 inches in length, and as there was such evidence the sheriff was not justified in sustaining the submission; and Crown appeal *allowed* and case remitted to sheriff to proceed as accords.

The sheriff appended the following note to the stated case:

"The solicitor for the accused submitted that there had been insufficient evidence led by the appellant to establish the length of the cutting edge of label 1. Timeous objection had been taken during the course of the trial to what these witnesses had said on the matter. Both witnesses had tried their best with the plastic object but there was no evidence of its accuracy and any such evidence should be disregarded. Without it, the appellant had failed to prove his case and I should sustain his submission of no case to answer. The depute fiscal submitted that the plastic object was obviously a ruler and the witnesses had been able to gauge the length of the cutting edge by means of its use in evidence. I should repel the submission.

"[The opinion] was a fairly short and crisp one, but in my opinion admits of only one answer. Where such a knife has a cutting edge that is visually round about 3 inches, then the Crown must prove the length of its cutting edge either by production of a certificate from the local weights and measures authority certifying the exact length or lodge a ruler or other means of measurement that is not simply an unmarked one of unknown provenance but bears on it to be certified as accurate by the relevant Government department. When P.C. Prince used the plastic object, which he believed, he said, to be a ruler, he said in evidence that the cutting edge was 3 $1/4$ inches. Police Inspector Kirkpatrick said much the same thing, that the object appeared to be a ruler and by using it he made the cutting edge to be about 3 $1/2$ inches. The discrepancy between the two may have been on the right side for the appellant, but the fact remains that without any evidence to show the standing of the plastic object, all such evidence would be worthless."

The sheriff posed the following question for the opinion of the High Court:

> "Ought I to have sustained the defence submission of no case to answer on the ground that there was no exact proof of the length of the cutting blade of label 1?"

Lord Justice-Clerk (Ross) (at p. 96)
"This is a Crown appeal in which the appellant is the procurator fiscal, Glasgow, and the respondent is George Walker. The

respondent was charged on a summary complaint libelling two charges. The first charge was a charge of breach of the peace and the second charge libelled a contravention of s1(1) of the Prevention of Crime Act 1953 or alternatively a contravention of s1(1) of the Carrying of Knives etc (Scotland) Act 1993. The case went to trial before the sheriff at Glasgow on 6 May 1994 when the respondent confirmed his pleas of not guilty to both charges. At the close of the prosecution case, the appellant's depute intimated that she was conceding that there was no case to answer in respect of the first alternative to charge 2, and after hearing parties, the sheriff sustained that submission. The respondent then intimated that he now wished to plead guilty to charge 1, and the court acquitted the respondent on charge 2. It is against the sheriff's decision to sustain the submission of no case to answer in respect of the second alternative to charge 2 that the appellant has now appealed.

"Evidence for the appellant consisted of evidence given by a police constable and a police inspector. There was one labelled article, namely, a folding pocket-knife, and an unlabelled plastic object which the sheriff states looked like a ruler, and which the sheriff later ascertained had been borrowed by the appellant's depute from the clerk of court. The effect of the evidence adduced by the appellant was that at the locus, the respondent threw label 1 away as he was approached by the two police officers who had previously been flagged down in their car by an unknown female civilian who pointed the respondent out to them for his behaviour towards his cohabitee and their child; label 1 is a folding pocket-knife that has a cutting edge to its blade of around 3 inches.

"… The submission made to the sheriff on behalf of the respondent was that there had been insufficient evidence led by the appellant to establish the length of the cutting edge of label 1. Objection had been taken during the course of the trial to what the witnesses had said upon that matter. It was contended that the witnesses had tried their best with the plastic object, but there was no evidence of its accuracy and any such evidence should be disregarded. Without such evidence, the appellant had failed to prove his case, and for that reason the sheriff was moved to sustain the submission of no case to answer.

"The appellant's depute submitted that the plastic object was obviously a ruler, and that the witnesses had been able to gauge the length of the cutting edge by means of its use while giving evidence. She accordingly invited the sheriff to repel the submission.

"The sheriff expresses the view that the issue was a fairly short and crisp one, and that in his opinion it admitted of only one answer. The sheriff in his note goes on to say:

'Where such a knife has a cutting edge that visually is round about three inches, then the Crown must prove the length of its cutting edge either by production of a certificate from the local weights and measures authority certifying the exact length or lodge a ruler or other means of measurement that is not simply an unmarked one of unknown provenance but bears on it to be certified as accurate by the relevant Government department.'

"The sheriff goes on to explain that the constable using the plastic object stated that the cutting edge was 3 $1/4$ inches whereas the police inspector making use of the same object stated that he made the cutting edge to be about 3 $1/2$ inches. The sheriff concluded that in the absence of evidence to show the standing of the plastic object, the evidence as to measurement of these witnesses was worthless.

"In presenting the appeal the learned advocate depute submitted that the format of s1 was such that the offence created by it was the carrying of a knife in a public place, and that the length as defined in s1(3) arose as an exception. The advocate depute drew attention to the terms of s312(v) of the Criminal Procedure (Scotland) Act 1975 and contended that effect must be given to the provisions of that subsection. The offence was having in a public place an article which has a blade or is sharply pointed (s1(1) and (2)). He submitted that s1(3) raised an exception, and that it was for the defence, namely the respondent, to prove such exception.

"... In support of his submission the advocate depute referred to a large number of cases. In reply counsel for the respondent submitted that the submission made by the advocate should not be entertained by the court since the appellant had not given proper notice of his contentions when applying for a stated case. When the appellant craved the court to state a case, it was stated on his behalf that the matter which was desired to be brought under review was:

'The sheriff erred in law in holding that there was insufficient evidence that label no 1, knife was not a knife within the terms of s1(1) of the Carrying of Knives etc. (Scotland) Act 1993.'

"In support of this submission, counsel sought to rely upon the terms of the High Court of Justiciary practice note dated 29 March 1985. It is clear, however, that this practice note relates to appeals in solemn procedure and appeals against sentence in summary procedure, and accordingly has no application to the present case.

The matter is however dealt with in the Criminal Procedure (Scotland) Act 1975 ...

"The appellant's application for a stated case contains no hint that the appellant is intending to contend that the matter is covered by s312(v) and in particular that s1(3) of the Carrying of Knives etc. (Scotland) Act 1993 contains an exception or qualification which the respondent must prove. That being so, we are satisfied that it is not competent in this case for the appellant to found upon such a ground of appeal.

"In an appendix to the case the sheriff tells us that he refused to allow certain adjustments for the appellant. The adjustments sought were:

'On p. 3 of the draft stated case add the following questions of law: (a) Was I correct to require evidence from the Crown of the length of the knife? (b) Esto I was correct to require such evidence, was I correct to find that the evidence tendered was insufficient?'

"The sheriff explains that he refused to allow such adjustments because he did not 'require' evidence from the Crown about the length of the cutting edge of the knife. The Crown volunteered that evidence and the sole question in the case appeared to relate to the sufficiency of the evidence led. The sheriff accordingly failed to see the point of the proposed additional questions of law and declined to add them to the case.

"In terms of s452(4)(f) it is open to this court to take account of any matter proposed in any adjustment rejected by the trial judge and the reasons for such rejection. However, although our attention was drawn to these proposed adjustments which had been rejected by the sheriff, the advocate depute at no time sought to show cause as to why the appellant should be allowed to found upon an aspect of the appeal which was not contained in his application for the stated case.

"There are many cases where this court has refused to entertain a ground of appeal which is not contained in the application under s444(1) of the Act of 1975 (*Stein v Lowe* [1993 S.L.T. 541]; *Fulton v Lees* [1991 S.C.C.R. 692]). In the present case the principal submission put forward by the advocate depute plainly took the respondent by surprise, and we are satisfied that there is no good reason why the appellant should be entitled to found his appeal upon this matter which was contained in the application for a stated case. The appellant has not shown cause why he should be allowed to do so, and it follows that the principal submission made by the appellant is not one which this court is prepared to entertain in this appeal. We are confirmed in this conclusion when we bear in mind that the advocate depute in his submission referred to a large number of reported cases, and explained that some of the decisions were inconsistent with other decisions. One case referred to was *Earnshaw v HM Advocate* [1982 S.L.T. 179] and, as counsel for the respondent observed, in view of the difficulty of reconciling all these decisions, it might be necessary if the issue were to be examined, for a full bench to do so.

"The advocate depute did however make further submissions to the court which did not fall within the grounds of which notice was given in the application for a stated case. He submitted that the evidence led was sufficient to prove that the blade of the knife label 1 exceeded 3 inches. He emphasised that the question arose at the stage of a submission of no case to answer. Accordingly the question was not whether the evidence satisfied the sheriff but whether there was evidence which would establish that the blade exceeded 3 inches in length if the sheriff decided to accept that evidence. The advocate depute reminded us that in the note annexed to the stated case, the sheriff recorded that one police officer stated that the cutting edge was 3 $^1/_4$ inches and the other police officer made the cutting edge 3 $^1/_2$ inches. There was accordingly before the sheriff evidence from two witnesses, if he accepted it, to the effect that the cutting edge exceeded 3 inches. Accordingly so far as sufficiency was concerned, there was a sufficiency of evidence.

"Although counsel did not concede that this was so, we are satisfied that at the stage of a submission of no case to answer there was sufficient evidence that the cutting edge of the blade exceeded 3 inches. That being so, the sheriff was not justified in sustaining the submission of no case to answer.

"We recognise that if no further evidence is led when the sheriff comes to determine whether or not the cutting edge of the blade exceeds 3 inches, he may not regard the evidence led as sufficiently convincing. However, we are satisfied that at the stage of no case to answer he was not well founded in holding that there was an insufficiency of evidence and therefore no case to answer.

"In the note the sheriff has expressed views to the effect that instruments of measurement require to be endorsed with some certificate to the effect that they are accurate. He cites no authority for such a proposition, which appears to us to go too far. In both civil and criminal cases, evidence is frequently given of measurements which have been taken by measuring instruments which are in common use, and it has never been stated that such measuring instruments require to be certified. For example in traffic accidents, evidence is frequently given of measurements from the point of impact or measurement of skid marks, and it is not the practice for evidence to be given that the instruments used to measure these distances have been certified. Where use is made of an everyday object such as a ruler, such evidence is in our judgment admissible without further evidence that the ruler has been in some way certified as accurate. Of course, if it is not plain that a witness has been using an object such as a ruler or measuring tape, we see no reason why such evidence should not be admissible and why it should not be acceptable evidence of the length or distance measured without further evidence to the effect that someone has certified the measuring instrument as accurate.

"Since the sheriff erred in holding that there was no case to answer, we shall answer the question in the case in the negative, and we shall remit the case to the sheriff to proceed as accords."

Appeal allowed.

NOTE
The length of a blade seems also to be of importance in regard to sentence: e.g. see *Christie* v. *McGlennan*, 1991 G.W.D. 26–1502 and *Logue* v. *Lees*, 1995 G.W.D. 1–33.

(ii) Lister v. Lees 3.13.2

1994 S.L.T. 1328

An accused person was tried on summary complaint with a contravention of s.1(1) of the 1993 Act. The accused, who had been found in a railway carriage and had been inhaling glue fumes, was arrested and searched. He had a spike in the lining of his jacket and explained that he had found it in the railway station and had used it to open his glue tin but had forgotten to discard it. The sheriff held that the accused's reason was not "good reason" because it did not commend itself as a proper and necessary exception to the general prohibition in the 1993 Act and, in any event, the reason was no longer valid when the accused was arrested. The accused was convicted and appealed by stated case.

Held, that the question was whether at the time of his arrest in the public place the accused had good reason for having the spike with him, and the accused's explanation did not constitute a good reason at that time (p. 1332J) and appeal refused.

Observed, that in determining whether there was "good reason" each case depended on its own facts and circumstances and the court should have regard to the general purpose of the Act and whether the reason appeared to constitute a justifiable exception to the general prohibitions contained in the legislation, but that the court should not make any moral judgment.

The accused appealed by way of stated case to the High Court against the decision of the sheriff. The sheriff appended the following note to the findings in fact:

"In giving evidence, the appellant stated that he had found the spike lying with other rubbish at the side of the railway track more than half an hour before [a railway employee] appeared on the scene. He said that he had used it only to open the one tin found in his possession. He said that he had used a sharp stone to 'bash in' the seals of the two empty tins later found in the railway carriage and had then pulled the seals out with his finger. He claimed that he had intended to throw the spike back onto the track where he found it, but that he had forgotten to do so in the stress of his hurried exit from the railway carriage.

"In his final submissions, the solicitor for the appellant relied solely on the statutory defence provided by s1(4) of the Act. He argued that the evidence supported the conclusion that the appellant had had 'good reason' for having the article with him in the public place. He drew a parallel with 'reasonable excuse' in s1 of the Prevention of Crime Act 1953, but contended that 'good reason' was a lesser test. This was because all the appellant had to prove was an explanation appropriate to his possession of the article at the particular time. In this case, the appellant's explanation was that he had, in effect, been using the article as a tool. Whilst his ultimate purpose (ie to inhale fumes from the contents) may not have been socially acceptable, neither was it unlawful. In all the circumstances, his reason for having the spike was a "good reason" in terms of the statutory provision.

"On two counts I rejected this argument.

"First, I did not consider the reason given to be a 'good reason'. There is no general definition of 'good reason' in the statute, nor, as yet, does there appear to be any reported authority on the meaning of these words. Nevertheless, the juxtaposing in subs (4) of 'good reason' with 'lawful authority' as co-equal statutory defences and the nature of the three sets of circumstances excluded for the purview of the statute by subs (5) indicated strongly to me that 'good reason' must mean something more than 'any' reason or even innocent reason. It should be a reason which commends itself to the court as a proper and necessary exception to the general prohibition. In the absence of any more specific guidance, it seemed to me the correct approach was to apply the same general principles as have held to be appropriate in deciding what constitutes 'reasonable excuse' for purposes of s1 of the Prevention of Crime Act 1953. In particular, I noted the observation of Lord Justice Clerk

Grant in *Grieve v Macleod* 1967 SLT p 71: 'that the only general proposition which can be laid down in regard to "reasonable excuse" is that each individual case must be judged on its own particular facts and circumstances.' Adopting that broad approach, I concluded that the appellant's stated reason for having the article with him in the public place, namely to open a tin of glue in order to inhale fumes from its contents, was not a 'good reason' for purposes of subs (4).

"Secondly, even if I were wrong in this conclusion, and the reason given by the appellant for having the article was in law good reason, it seemed to me that that reason was no longer valid at the critical time, namely at the time of his arrest in the public place. This was because, by then, he had already used the spike to open the tin of Evo-stick found on him, and there had been no evidence that he required it to open other tins. Indeed, his own evidence was to the contrary effect, viz that he had used the spike only to open the one tin, and would have thrown it back onto the railway track whence it came had he not forgotten to do so in the heat of the moment. At the critical time, therefore, he had no good reason for having the spike. In fact, he had no reason at all, merely an explanation of how he still came to have it.

"For these reasons I considered that the statutory defence had not been made out."

The sheriff posed the following questions for the opinion of the High Court:

"(1) was the appellant's stated reason for having this metal spike, namely to open a tin of glue for the purpose of inhaling its contents a 'good reason' in terms of s1(4) of the Carrying of Knives etc. (Scotland) Act 1993?

(2) If the answer to question 1 is 'Yes', did this remain a valid reason at the time of the appellant's arrest?

(3) On the facts found as admitted or proved, was I entitled to convict the appellant?"

Lord Justice-Clerk (Ross) (at p. 1331)

"Before the sheriff the solicitor for the appellant sought to rely upon the statutory defence contained in s1(4) of the Act of 1993. He maintained that on the evidence the appellant had had 'good reason' for having the spike with him in the public place. He contended that all that the appellant required to do was to have an explanation appropriate to his possession of the article at the particular time. The appellant had given an explanation to the effect that he had been using the article as a tool. Although his ultimate purpose, namely, to inhale fumes from glue, may not have been socially acceptable, neither was it unlawful. He accordingly maintained that the appellant's reason for having the spike was 'good reason', and that accordingly he had a good defence to the charge.

"The sheriff explains that he rejected the appellant's submission upon two grounds. In the first place the sheriff did not consider that the reason put forward on behalf of the appellant was a 'good reason'. He considered that 'good reason' must mean something more than 'any reason' or even 'innocent reason'. The sheriff concluded that 'good reason' in terms of s1(4) should be a reason which commends itself to the court as a proper and necessary exception to the general prohibition. The sheriff also drew an analogy from s1(1) of the Prevention of Crime Act 1953 which makes it an offence for any person to have with him in any public place any offensive weapon 'without lawful authority or reasonable excuse'. In this connection the sheriff referred to *Grieve v Macleod*. In the circumstances the sheriff concluded that the appellant's stated reason for having the spike with him in a public place, namely, to open a tin of glue in order to inhale fumes from its contents, was not a 'good reason' for the purposes of s1(4) of the Act of 1953.

"The sheriff went on to hold that even if he were wrong in this conclusion it appeared to him that the reason put forward by the appellant was no longer valid at the critical time, namely at the time of his arrest in the public place. By that time he had already used the spike to open the tin of glue, and had forgotten to throw the spike away in the heat of the moment. Accordingly at that stage, the sheriff held that the appellant had no good reason for having the spike. As the sheriff put it he had no reason at all, but merely an explanation of how he still came to have it with him.

"Counsel for the appellant maintained that the sheriff had erred in holding that something more than an innocent reason was required. He contended that the existence of an innocent reason would suffice to satisfy the test laid down in s1(4). The court should not pass moral judgments, and it was not a question of whether it was socially acceptable or not for someone to be engaged in sniffing glue. He accordingly contended that the sheriff was not well founded in his first conclusion. As regards his second conclusion, he maintained that at the time of his arrest the appellant had good reason for having the article with him in the public place because he had simply forgotten to dispose of it at an earlier stage.

"The advocate depute concentrated first upon the sheriff's second ground of decision. He submitted that the sheriff was well founded in concluding that at the time of his arrest, the appellant had already used the spike to open a tin, and that accordingly he had no good reason for retaining it. His own evidence was that he had forgotten to throw it away, and that could not be a good reason for having the spike with him.

"In support of his submission the advocate depute drew attention to *DPP v Gregson* (1993) 96 CrAppR 240. That case concerned a prosecution for a contravention of s.139 of the Criminal Justice Act 1988 which is in similar terms to s.1 of the Carrying of Knives etc. (Scotland) Act 1993. Section 139(4) is in the following terms:

> 'It shall be a defence for a person charged under this section to prove that he had good reason or lawful authority for having the article with him in a public place.'

"The language used in that subsection is identical to that used in s1(4) of the Act of 1993.

"In *DPP v Gregson* the court observed that the expression 'good reason' in the Act of 1988 was a quite different expression from 'reasonable excuse' used in s.1 of the Prevention of Crime Act 1953. We agree.

"In *DPP v Gregson* the accused maintained that he habitually used the knife which he had with him at work and that he had left it in his jacket when he had last used it six days previously and had forgotten that he had it with him. In dealing with that defence McCowan LJ said (at p 243):

> 'In my judgment, [counsel for the prosecutor] is right to say that it is important to concentrate on the time in respect of which the defendant is charged. Six days earlier, no doubt this man had the knife on him for a good reason, because the justices found that it was a knife that he used in his work and would have had with him at his work and might well have put into his pocket six days earlier. But did he have it with him for a good reason at the time of his arrest? Having it for work reasons six days earlier cannot, in my judgment, be a good reason for having it on him six days later when not at work. The question, therefore, it seems to me, boils down to whether forgetfulness at the relevant time was a good reason. It does appear that the justices found that he had forgotten that he had it on him. I am bound to say that I am surprised at this finding, having regard to their finding of fact that the knife fell not from his jacket pocket where the knife, he said, had been put by him at the time of his work, but from his jeans, and the further finding that when that happened he

offered no specific reason or excuse for having it with him. However, they did in fact find, as I understand it, that they believed that he had forgotten that he had the knife with him. Was that a good reason? 'In my judgment, forgetfulness may be an explanation. It cannot be a good reason.'

"We respectfully agree with the approach of McCowan LJ The question must be whether at the time of his arrest in the public place the appellant had good reason for having the spike with him. The appellant's explanation for having the spike with him was that he had forgotten to throw it away after he had used it. We agree with the sheriff that that may be an explanation but it does not constitute a good reason for having the spike with him at the material time.

"Since the sheriff was well founded in the second ground of his decision, that is sufficient for the disposal of this appeal. However, we were also addressed on the subject of the first ground of decision, and this raises the question of what is meant by the expression 'good reason' in the statute. We agree with the advocate depute that in construing that expression it is important to bear in mind the purpose of the legislation. The legislation contains a general prohibition against carrying in a public place an article with a blade or point, and the purpose of the legislation must be to protect the public from persons who may use such articles to cause injury or to threaten others. In these circumstances before a reason put forward can be regarded as 'good reason' it must be a reason which would justify an exception to the general prohibition contained in the statute. In the sheriff's note there appears to be some suggestion that the court should apply moral judgments and should determine whether the reason put forward is an innocent or non-innocent reason. We are satisfied that in determining whether any reason put forward amounts to 'good reason' the court should not be making any moral judgment. When considering the expression 'reasonable excuse' in s1 of the Prevention of Crime Act 1953, Lord Justice Clerk Grant in *Grieve v Macleod* 1967 SLT p 71, observed:

'that the only general proposition which can be laid down in regard to "reasonable excuse" is that each individual case must be judged on its own particular facts and circumstances.'

"Although 'good reason' is a different expression from 'reasonable excuse', in our opinion the same approach falls to be adopted when the court is considering whether what has been put forward on behalf of an accused amounts to 'good reason'. Each case must depend on its own facts and circumstances, and in determining the issue the court should have regard to the general purpose of the legislation, and where the legislation contains a general prohibition, the court must determine whether the reason advanced appears to constitute a justifiable exception to the general prohibition contained in the legislation. However, since each case depends upon its facts and circumstances, we do not find it possible to give any greater guidance than this as to what is meant by 'good reason' in the statute.

"For the foregoing reasons we are satisfied that the sheriff was well founded in this case in holding that the statutory defence had not been made out. We do not find it necessary to answer all the questions in the case, and we shall confine ourselves to answering question 3 in the affirmative, and it follows that the appeal is refused."

Appeal refused.

(iii) Stewart v. Friel   3.13.3

1996 S.L.T. 272

S. was tried on summary complaint with a contravention of s.1(1) of the 1993 Act. The accused, who was found in a public place, had in his pocket a knife with a roughly sharpened blade and a sharp point. The blade was capable of being folded into the handle but it locked automatically when in the open position and could not be moved from that position until a catch on the side of the handle was moved back. The sheriff repelled a submission that there was no case to answer and convicted the accused, who appealed contending that the knife was a folding pocket-knife.

Held, that a knife was not a "folding pocket-knife" in terms of s.1(3) unless the blade was always and immediately foldable, and since the article had a device which was designed, until it had been overcome, to prevent the blade being folded, it was a lock knife and not covered by subs. (3); and appeal refused.

Lord Justice-General (Hope) (at p. 272)
"The appellant went to trial in the sheriff court at Paisley on two charges which had been brought against him on summary complaint. The first was that he had with him in a public place, namely Gilmour Street railway station, Paisley, an article to which s1 of the Carrying of Knives etc (Scotland) Act 1993 applies, namely a lockable knife. The second was a contravention of s41(1)(a) of the Police (Scotland) Act 1967 in that he struggled violently with

two police officers then in uniform. At the conclusion of the Crown case a submission was made that there was no case to answer which the sheriff repelled. The appellant then gave evidence. At the end of the trial he was found guilty on the first charge and he was found not guilty on the second charge. An application was then made for a stated case to challenge his conviction on the first charge on the ground that the sheriff erred in law in repelling the submission of no case to answer, in respect that the Crown had not established that the knife was one to which s1 of the 1993 Act applies.

"Subsection (1) of the 1993 Act provides that, subject to subss (4) and (5), any person who has an article to which that section applies with him in a public place shall be guilty of an offence. Subsections (2) and (3) are in these terms:"

[His Lordship quoted the terms of subss (2) and (3) and continued:]

"... Subsections (4) and (5) each provide a person charged with an offence under subs (1) with a defence, but neither of these subsections was relied upon by the appellant in this case. The argument was directed to the provisions of subss (2) and (3), and in particular to the question whether the article which the appellant had with him was a folding pocket-knife the blade of which had a cutting edge which did not exceed three inches.

"The evidence for the Crown was that the appellant had been found by two police officers lying unconscious halfway up a staircase leading to one of the platforms in the railway station. They tried to revive him by speaking to him and shaking him without result. They then proceeded to search him to ascertain whether he was a diabetic or had some other illness. In the course of this search the found a knife in the top left outside pocket of his jacket. It had a roughly sharpened blade and a sharp point. The blade was capable of being folded into the handle of the knife, but it was locked automatically when in the open position. It was in the open position when it was found in the pocket of the appellant's jacket. Shortly after this discovery the appellant started to come round, and the events then occurred which led to his being charged with the offence under s41(1)(a) of the 1967 Act. Although no evidence was led about the length of the blade, the knife was produced and the sheriff was satisfied from his examination of it that its blade was slightly less than three inches long. The nature of the locking device was not described in the evidence, and the sheriff has said nothing about this in the stated case. In our opinion nothing turns on this point, but for completeness it should be added that the knife, which was shown to us, had a catch on the size of its handle which requires to be moved back from the locked position before the blade can be folded into the handle.

"The arguments which were presented to the sheriff were briefly to this effect. For the appellant it was submitted that there was no evidence that this was anything other than a folding pocket-knife, and as there was no evidence that its blade exceeded three inches he was entitled to the benefit of the exception described in subs. (3) of the Act. For the Crown it was submitted that it could be seen that this was not a pocket-knife as that expression is ordinarily understood, and that in any event the appellant had failed to discharge the onus of proof which rested on him that the article was a knife of the kind described in the subsection. The sheriff was of the opinion that the arguments about the onus of proof were misconceived, as the physical characteristics of the knife were the subject of evidence and it was then for the court to decide what description to apply to it in the light of that evidence. He was satisfied that, as it had a blade with a rough sharpened edge and a sharp point which could be locked in the open position, it was an article to which s1 of the Act applied.

"Counsel for the appellant did not seek to challenge the sheriff's view that arguments about the onus of proof were irrelevant in this case. In our opinion he was right not to do so, as there was ample evidence about the physical characteristics of the knife, which was produced in court and was available for examination to supplement and explain the witness's evidence. Nor did he dispute that this was an article which had a blade which was sharply pointed within the meaning of subs (2). The question to which he addressed his argument was whether this was a folding pocket-knife within the meaning of subs (3), there being no dispute that its blade did not exceed three inches.

"He submitted that, as the expression 'folding pocket-knife' was not defined in the Act, it fell to be given its ordinary meaning. He referred to the definition of 'pocket-knife' in the *Oxford English Dictionary*, which is that this expression means 'A knife with one or more blades which fold into the handle, for carrying in the pocket.' He said that all these elements were satisfied in this case, as the blade of this knife was capable of being folded into the handle for carrying in the pocket, and there was nothing in this definition which suggested that the presence or absence of a locking device made any difference to the question whether, applying ordinary common sense, it could be described as a pocket-knife. He then drew our attention to *Harris v DPP* [1993] 1 WLR 82 in which it was held that, for the purposes of s.139 of the Criminal Justice Act 1988, a 'folding pocket-knife' is a knife which is readily and immediately foldable at all times simply by the folding process, and that lock knives were not folding pocket-knives within the meaning of that section. He invited us to hold that that case was wrongly decided, on the ground that there was no reason to think that a knife was dangerous simply because the blade could be locked in the open position. He said that the blade might be safer to use if it was locked, and the locking device was simply there as a matter of convenience for the user.

"The learned advocate depute's response to this argument was that it was clear, as a matter of common sense, that a knife was not a folding pocket-knife if it had a mechanical device to prevent the blade from being folded unless that device was operated. He submitted that in any event Parliament must be presumed to have intended, having used the expression 'folding pocket-knife' in s1(3) of the 1993 Act, that this phrase should receive the same interpretation as had been placed upon it in *Harris v DPP*, as that was a recent decision relating to analogous legislation which Parliament would have had in contemplation when the 1993 Act was being framed. On this view it was not necessary to consider whether the decision in that case was correct, but it was a decision about the meaning of the phrase which made good sense. It was at least not so obviously unsound that we should not follow it for the purpose of placing a reasonable interpretation upon the same phrase in the 1993 Act.

"In our opinion a knife which has a blade which can be fixed in the open position by a locking device is not a folding pocket-knife within the meaning of s1(3) of the 1993 Act. The exception which is described in that subsection is contained in the two words 'folding pocket-knife'. It is not enough that the knife can be placed in the pocket, or that the blade can be folded to enable it to be placed there. It must be a folding pocket-knife. It cannot be described as a knife of that kind if it has a device which is designed, until it has been overcome, to prevent the blade from being folded. That device provides the knife with an additional feature which is not mentioned in the subsection. The description which it would be natural to give to a knife of that kind is that it is a lock knife or a locking knife, to distinguish it from a knife whose blade is always and immediately foldable.

"The interpretation of the expression 'folding pocket-knife' is consistent with what was decided in *Harris v DPP* The Court of Appeal was dealing in that case with the provisions of s139 of the Criminal Justice Act 1988 which, so far as relevant, is in these terms: [His Lordship quoted the terms of s139(1)–(3) and continued:]

"The article in question in that case was a knife whose blade, when fully opened, was immediately locked in that position. In order to fold it back into the handle it was necessary to activate a button triggered mechanism. The nature of the locking device was not decisive in that case. It was sufficient that the blade could be locked so that, when locked, it became in effect a fixed blade knife. McCowan LJ said at [1993] 1 WLR, p 87E–F:

> 'In my judgment, the right approach to the matter is this: To be a folding pocket-knife the knife has to be readily and indeed immediately foldable at all times, simply by the folding process. A knife of the type with which these appeals are concerned is not in this category because, in the first place, there is a stage, namely, when it has been opened, when it is not immediately foldable simply by the folding process and, secondly, it requires that further process, namely, the presenting of the button.'

"We respectfully agree with this approach. Had there been any doubt on the matter there would have been much to be said for the view that, in this case, as the wording of s1 of the 1993 Act is so close to that of s139 of the 1988 Act, Parliament must be taken to have had in view the decision in *Harris v DPP* in deciding to repeat the phrase 'folding pocket-knife', especially as that decision was reported only a few months before the Carrying of Knives etc (Scotland) Bill was first introduced: see *Barras v Aberdeen Steam Trawling and Fishing Co* 1933 SC (HL) 21. While that doctrine must be applied with caution, as was emphasised in *Haigh v Charles W Ireland Ltd* by Lord Diplock at 1974 SLT, p 42, and Lord Kilbrandon at p 43, the present case is one where one could be reasonably confident that it was appropriate. But we do not find it necessary to rely on this point, as it appears to us to be clear that a knife whose blade is equipped with a locking device cannot be said to be a folding pocket-knife within the ordinary meaning of these words.

"For these reasons we shall answer the question of law in the affirmative and refuse the appeal."

Appeal refused.

Part Seven: General Matters	**3.14**
A. INTENTION	**3.14.1**

(i)R. v. Dayle	**3.14.2**

[1973] 3 All E.R. 1151

D. was charged with an assault and with having with him in a public place an offensive weapon, namely, a car jack and wheel brace. He was convicted and appealed. The facts and the convoluted procedural history are set out in the judgment.

Kilner Brown, J. (at p. 1152)

"On 31st May 1972 the appellant was tried at Inner London Crown Court on an indictment alleging in count 1 an assault occasioning actual bodily harm and in count 2 having with him an offensive weapon without lawful authority or reasonable excuse, namely a car jack and wheel brace. In the event this second count was misconceived, quite unnecessary and led to all the difficulty which ensued.

"The prosecution case which was put to the jury by the trial judge was clear and simple. It was alleged that an injury to the complainant was caused by the appellant throwing the car jack or wheel brace which he took from the boot of his car in the course of a fight. The jury were invited to approach the matter on the basis that they should decide first whether it was proved that he threw the jack and brace and thereby assaulted the complainant and if so, automatically convict also on count 2. This approach made it difficult for the jury to return verdicts of guilty of assault and not guilty of carrying an offensive weapon. This might well have been the common sense answer, since it was an inoffensive article taken in the heat of the moment. The ultimate result indicates the difficulty which the jury felt, for they acquitted on the offensive weapon count and disagreed on the assault count.

"The reason why the matter was put to the jury in that way is, it seems, the matter in which the law is set out in Archbold's *Criminal Pleading, Evidence and Practice* [38th ed. (1973), p. 904, para. 2382]. Relying on *R v Powell* [[1963] Crim.L.R. 511], following *Woodward v Koessler* [[1958] 3 All E.R. 557], in the Divisional Court, it is stated that the use of an article to cause injury establishes that the defendant had it with intent to cause injury; the text rightly points to the difficulty of reconciling these decisions with that in *R v Jura* [[1954] 1 All E.R. 696].

"The jury having disagreed on count 1 a retrial was ordered on that count. Counsel for the Crown has most helpfully and frankly conceded that in view of the way the case had been put to the jury they should have been directed there and then to return a verdict of not guilty on count 1 once they had found the appellant not guilty of count 2.

"The retrial came before another judge at the Crown Court, St James's Square, a few days later. Counsel for the appellant, who has argued the case with ability and cogency, moved to quash the indictment. He submitted then, as he has to this court, that the acquittal on count 2 led to an inconsistent result by the first jury, who were at least not sure that the appellant had thrown the alleged weapon and who on the way the case was left to them, should have acquitted on count 1, or alternatively raised an issue estoppel. The trial judge felt himself bound by the authority of *R v Jura* and rejected the submission. He held that it was open to a jury to find that there was no possession of an offensive weapon when an inoffensive article lawfully carried was offensively used. He felt unable to rule that the first jury had produced an inconsistent result. The trial proceeded, the Crown case again being that the injury was caused by the appellant throwing the jack or brace. The second jury convicted the appellant of assault occasioning actual bodily harm. He was sentenced to nine month's imprisonment suspended for two years and fined £35. Now, by leave of the single judge, he appeals against this conviction.

"As will appear later we agree with the approach of the judge at the second trial to the law relating to the carrying of offensive weapons. This and the lack of a transcript of the summing-up at the first trial understandably led to his decision to allow a second trial on count 1. But the matter cannot rest there.

"As has already been indicated the prosecution's case at the first trial was that the two charges were linked to the extent that each was sustained by evidence that the appellant threw the jack or the wheel brace. Indeed the judge directed the jury that they were not to consider count 2 unless they were sure of guilt on count 1. This was consistent with his interpretation of the law relating to count 2.

"In the particular circumstances of this case therefore, the acquittal on count 2 must mean that the jury were not sure that the appellant threw either the wheel brace or the jack and, that being so, the inevitable result on count 1—having regard to the case the appellant was called on to meet and to the judge's direction—should have been not guilty. Had such a verdict been returned that would have been the end of the matter. There could not have been a second trial on count 1. In our judgment, justice demands that this result should now be achieved by allowing this appeal.

"We feel, however, that we should not leave this case without further reference to the decision of the Court of Criminal Appeal in *R v Powell*, a decision which is, in the opinion of this court, open to misinterpretation. Consideration of the full transcript of the judgment given by Winn J indicates that it was a case decided on the particular facts. The appellant had with him and had carried an imitation pistol the possession of which the court found could not be reasonably excused. He used it offensively. The

words in the judgment which have given rise to difficulty are
these:

> 'In accordance with the decision of the Divisional Court in
> *Woodward v Koessler*, it is clear that use producing injury
> establishes an intent when carrying it to use the article in order
> to cause injury with it.'

The statement was obiter to the decision on the facts of the case.

"The words 'use producing injury establishes an intent when
carrying [the weapon]', unqualified, are not in the view of this
court a statement of the law applicable to all circumstances.
Moreover, the words in *Woodward v Koessler* [at p. 558], 'All that
one has to do for the purpose of ascertaining what the intention is
is to look and see what use was in fact made of it' are too widely
expressed to be applicable in every case. In relation to those articles
which are not made or adapted for use as offensive weapons in
regard to which the onus remains on the Crown to establish the
intention in the accused to use the article to injure, the jury must
decide the issue of intent by reference to all the evidence, drawing
such inferences from the evidence as appear proper in all the
circumstances. The words used in the judgments in *Woodward v
Koessler* [at p. 557] and in *R v Powell* must be read in the light of the
provisions of s.8 of the Criminal Justice Act 1967. A more accurate
statement of the present law is that the use which is in fact made
of the article may, according to all the circumstances, be sufficient·
to establish the necessary intent. *R v Jura* was, as has been said,
decided on its special facts but this court considers itself bound by
the principle applied by Lord Goddard CJ when, having drawn
attention to the long title to the Prevention of Crime Act 1953 'An
Act to prohibit the carrying of offensive weapons in public places
without lawful authority or reasonable excuse' he said:

> 'The appellant was not carrying this rifle without lawful
> excuse because he was at a shooting gallery where for the
> payment of a few pence people could amuse themselves by firing
> at a target and was carrying the rifle for that purpose. He had an
> obvious excuse for carrying the rifle. He made use of the rifle in
> a way which was unlawful, for which he might have been
> convicted of a felony. If a person having a rifle in his hand for a
> lawful purpose suddenly uses the rifle for an unlawful purpose,
> the Offences against the Person Act, 1861, provides appropriate
> punishment for doing that, but the Act of 1953 is meant to deal
> with a person who, with no excuse whatever, goes out with an
> offensive weapon, it may be a "cosh", or a knife, or something
> else ...' [1954] 1 All E.R. at 697].

"The terms of s.1(1) of the Prevention of Crime Act 1953 are apt to cover the case of a person who goes out with an offensive weapon without lawful authority or reasonable excuse and also the person who deliberately selects an article, such as the stone in *Harrison v Thornton* [[1966] Crim.L.R. 388], with the intention of using it as a weapon without such authority or excuse. But, if an article (already possessed lawfully and for good reason) is used offensively to cause injury, such use does not necessarily prove the intent which the Crown must establish in respect of articles which are not offensive weapons per se. Each case must depend on its own facts.

"In the circumstances we do not find it necessary to consider the other matters raised in the grounds of appeal. For the reason given the appeal is allowed, the conviction quashed and the sentence set aside."

Appeal allowed.

NOTE

Section 8 of the Criminal Justice Act 1967 provides that "[a] court or jury, in determining whether a person has committed an offence—(*a*) shall not be bound in law to infer that he intended or foresaw a result of his actions by reason only of its being a natural and probable consequence of those actions; but (*b*) shall decide whether he did intend or foresee that result by reference to all the evidence, drawing such inferences from the evidence as appear proper in the circumstances." This authority for a "subjective" investigation applies in England and Wales but not in Scotland.

There are also very early English cases on a similar point. It has been held that a stick may be an offensive weapon, depending on the use to which it is to be put: *R. v. Johnson* (1822) Russ & Ry. 492 at p. 493; *R. v. Fry and Webb* (1837) 2 Mood & R. 42 at p. 43; and *R. v. Turner* (1849) 3 Cox C.C. 304 at p. 306.

(ii) R. v. Allamby and Medford   3.14.3

[1974] 3 All E.R. 126

A. and M. were convicted of a contravention of s.1(1) of the 1953 Act and they appealed against conviction. The facts are set out in the judgment.

James, L.J. (p. 127)

"On 29th November 1973 at the Crown Court at Winchester the appellants, Allamby and Medford, and one Griffiths were convicted of the offence of having with them in a public place an offensive weapon, contrary to s.1(1) of the Prevention of Crime Act 1953. Allamby was sentenced to six months' imprisonment, Medford to borstal training and Griffiths to six months' imprisonment which sentence was suspended for two years. Allamby and Medford appealed by leave of the single judge against conviction and sentence. Griffiths did not apply for leave to appeal. On 14th March we allowed the appeals against conviction and stated that we would put our reasons for doing so in writing.

"Section 1(1) of the 1953 Act provides:

> 'Any person who without lawful authority or reasonable excuse, the proof whereof shall lie on him, has with him in a public place any offensive weapon shall be guilty of an offence ...'

"'Offensive weapon' is defined by s.1(4):

> '... "offensive weapon" means any article made or adapted for use for causing injury to the person, or intended by the person having it with him for such use by him.'

"The particulars of the offence of which the appellants were convicted as set out on the indictment are that on 21st July 1973 they 'had with them in a public place namely the A303 at Winterbourne Stoke in the county of Wilts offensive weapons namely four knives'.

"The facts on which the prosecution relied were as follows. On 21st July 1973 at 6.15 p.m. a police officer stopped a motor car travelling on the A303 at Winterbourne Stoke, Wiltshire. Medford was the driver. Allamby and Griffiths were seated in the back seat. Another youth, Townsend, was in the front passenger seat. On a search of the car there was found, under the back seat, a flick-knife and two knives of the domestic carving-knife type. In the glove compartment was a fourth knife, of the kind used for cutting vegetables.

"When questioned by the police officer, the occupants of the car denied all knowledge of the presence of any of the knives. Subsequently Townsend made a statement. In the event he was not charged with any offence, but he gave evidence for the prosecution.

"Townsend's version was that on 20th July he and the three accused had travelled to Cornwall from Reading to visit a Miss Williamson, Medford's girl friend. The purpose was to persuade her to return to Medford and to frighten her then boy friend. Allamby had produced all four knives in the car and hid them under the seat. They were stopped in Wiltshire on their way back from seeing Miss Williamson. Miss Williamson confirmed this visit and gave evidence of Medford having said: 'We are prepared for violence to whoever is giving you the drugs.' All of them were playing with the knives and she cut her finger in trying to take one from Allamby. Townsend was clearly an accomplice. The recorder not only gave the jury an entirely proper direction on corroboration but invited them wholly to disregard his evidence as unreliable.

"The defence did not dispute the journey to Cornwall nor the purpose for which it was made. Allamby said he found the two carving type knives under the seat when looking for belongings which had fallen out of his pocket. All maintained that the flick-knife belonged to Townsend and that it was in his sole possession. He had passed it to those in the back of the car when the police officer approached. The vegetable knife was found in the glove compartment, because it had been replaced after they had played with the knives in Cornwall. The car, according to Medford, was owned by him in partnership with others. The jury were invited to draw the inference from that fact that those others were responsible for the presence of the knifes in the car.

"The flick-knife was an offensive weapon per se in that it was made for causing injury to the person. The other knives were not. If the jury found the fact to be that the defendants were jointly in possession of that knife there was no defence to the charge. Counsel for the defendants had in their final speeches sought to persuade the jury to find (i) that the defendants had nothing to do with the flick-knife and (ii) if the jury so found, that at the time of the alleged offence the other knives were not 'offensive weapons' because at that time none of the defendants intended to use them for causing injury to the person. In the summing-up the recorder invited the jury to disregard the flick-knife. It seems highly probable that they did so.

"The recorder in the summing-up directed in these terms:

> 'The second charge is the same time, the same date, the same place. It charges them that they had offensive weapons, namely four knives, and an offensive weapon for this purpose is an article which is intended by the person having it for use in causing injury to the person—a knife, by cutting or thrusting. So the question you have to decide, in the second count is, did each of these men have the knives with them with the intention of causing injury to the person?

> 'Now, let me break off there to deal with a point you heard argued by [counsel for Griffiths and Allamby], and which was also mentioned by [counsel for Medford]; and here you must take the law from me, and if I am wrong I shall be put right elsewhere. What is being sought to be said by the defence is this—that whatever evil intention may have attached to these knives in Cornwall did no longer attach when they were driving home from Cornwall to Reading, and were stopped. Members of the jury, that is in my judgment an unsound

contention, and I can perhaps illustrate its unsoundness in this way. If a man had a knife and he went out and stabbed someone with it, it would be idle for him to say if he was approached when walking home, "It has ceased to be an offensive weapon, it has now taken its place as an ordinary kitchen knife". It is an offence to have with you in a public place an offensive weapon, and an offensive weapon is one which, for this purpose, a particular person has because it is intended by him to be used for causing injury to the person. So you have got to look at his possession of the knife in the broad sense of the reason why he had it with him at that time, and it does not matter whether he was going out to stab the man or coming back.

'What is of course true is this—when you are dealing with something such as a kitchen knife, although you might be satisfied, and I am not in any sense saying you should be, although you might be satisfied on this occasion it was an offensive weapon because the man, the men, had it with them because they intended to use it offensively, it would not retain the state and character of that weapon for all time. Supposing on a completely different occasion they took the knife into the street because they wanted to make some repair to their motor car which was there, something of that sort. Then it would be absolutely absurd to say on that occasion it had the character of an offensive weapon, because a few days earlier it had been used, or had been intended to be used, offensively. You must look at the occasion in the broad sense of their going down and coming back from Cornwall and the question really boils down to this—why were they taking the knives to Cornwall?'

"The grounds of appeal of both appellants, so far as they were argued, are:

'1. The learned Recorder misdirected the jury by directing them to ignore the question of whether the defendant had any intention to use three kitchen knives so as to cause injury, at the time of his arrest, if they were satisfied that at some earlier occasion the defendant had such an intention notwithstanding that such intention had been expended at the time of his arrest.

'2. The learned Recorder wrongly interrupted Counsel for the defendant in his address to the jury and prevented him from submitting to the jury that at the time of the arrest the prosecution had failed to establish any intention on the part of the defendant to use the three kitchen knives so as to cause injury.'

"The effect of the recorder's direction was to tell the jury that they could convict in relation to the domestic knives if they were satisfied that the intent necessary to give those knives the character of 'offensive weapons' was present at any time during the period commencing when the defendants left Reading for Cornwall and ending at the time of their arrest, although that intention to use the knives for causing injury to the person was not proved to exist at the time and place of the offence charged.

"The Crown sought to support the conviction on the basis that the direction of the recorder was correct. Counsel argued that the Crown were not restricted by the particulars in the indictment in relation to 'time' and 'place' and could establish guilt by evidence relating to a different time and a different place, subject only to the limitation that such time and place were sufficiently proximate to the particulars of the offence charged. It was conceded, and the recorder directed the jury, that an article in relation to which there existed, at a particular time, the intention to use it for the purpose of causing personal injury would not necessarily retain for all time thereafter the character of an offensive weapon within the meaning of the statute.

"The question whether the accused had at the relevant time and place the intention necessary to bring the article in his possession within the definition of an offensive weapon is a question of fact for the jury. The recorder rightly left that question to the jury in the present case. But proof of that intention must be related to the time and place of the offence charged. The intention in relation to such an article may change from time to time. The place in which the accused has the article with him may be a 'public place' at one time but not at another. 'Reasonable excuse' for having the article may exist at one time but be absent at another. 'Time' and 'place' are material elements in the particulars of this offence, and the issue of guilt has to be decided by the jury in respect of the offence as charged. In the present case it was open to the prosecution to frame the charge in such a way as to cover a period of time when the defendants were in Cornwall. They did not do so. They proceeded on the narrow basis of the particulars in the indictment. This being so it was open to counsel for the defendants to invite the jury to find that the domestic knives were not offensive weapons at the time charged because any intent to use them for causing personal injury which may have existed at an earlier point of time had been abandoned. This was an issue which ought to have been left to the jury. How the jury would have resolved it we do not know. The direction of the recorder, already cited, characterised the defendants' arguments as 'unsound'. That was a misdirection. The jury could properly look at the occasion 'in the broad sense of [the defendants] going down and coming back from Cornwall' but could do so only for the purpose of deciding whether the articles in their possession were offensive weapons at the time and place charged. It was a misdirection to tell the jury, as the recorder did, that 'the question really boils down to this—why were they taking the knives to Cornwall?' By stating the issue in that way the recorder withdrew from the jury the issue of fact of the intention of the defendants at the time and place relevant to the charge, and the defendants were thereby deprived of the opportunity, to which they were entitled, of obtaining the decision of the jury on the question whether the domestic knives were at the relevant time and place offensive weapons within the meaning of the Act.

"It is for this reason that we felt obliged to allow the appeals."

Appeals allowed.

3.14.4 B. SELF-DEFENCE

3.14.5 (i) Ohlson v. Hylton

[1975] 2 All E.R. 490

The defendant was on his way home from work as a carpenter. He had with him a bag containing his tools of trade, including a hammer. At an underground station he tried to board a crowded train but he became involved in an altercation with a passenger on the train. As a result they both landed on the platform. The defendant took a hammer from his case and struck the other passenger on the head with it.

The defendant was charged with a contravention of s.1(1) of the 1953 Act and convicted by the magistrates. He appealed to the Crown Court where his appeal was allowed and the conviction quashed. The prosecutor then appealed to the Divisional Court.

Lord Widgery, C.J. (at p. 492)
"The relevant facts are as follows. At about 4.40 pm on 9th January 1974 the defendant was on the platform of Blackfriars underground station intending to board a train going east on his way home from work. It was an occasion when the trains were very crowded, and the defendant had difficulty in boarding the train. Already on the train was a Mr Malcolm, who was standing close to the doors waiting for them to be closed. The defendant attempted to board the train, notwithstanding the protests of Mr Malcolm, and the upshot of the difference between them was that Mr Malcolm either fell from or stepped

from the train and both he and the defendant finished up on the platform.

"The defendant was a carpenter and in his briefcase he had some of the tools of his trade, including a hammer. When he and Mr Malcolm fell out of the train on to the platform, the defendant immediately took the hammer from his briefcase and deliberately struck Mr Malcolm on the head so that he fell to the ground. It is evidence that on these facts the defendant was properly convicted of the first charge of assault, but his contention before the Crown Court was that he was not guilty of the second charge, namely a charge of having with him in a public place an offensive weapon.

"The relevant charge was brought under s.1(1) of the Prevention of Crime Act 1953 which, so far as material, reads as follows:

> 'Any person who without lawful authority or reasonable excuse, the proof whereof shall lie on him, has with him in any public place any offensive weapon shall be guilty of an offence ...'

"Section 1(4) provides:

> 'In this section "public place" includes any highway and any other premises or place to which at the material time the public have or are permitted to have access, whether on payment or otherwise; and "offensive weapon" means any article made or adapted for use for causing injury to the person, or intended by the person having it with him for such use by him.'

"The section thus divides offensive weapons into two categories. First, the type of weapon which is often described as offensive per se, namely an article made or adapted for causing injury to the person. The second category relates to articles not so made or adapted and which have a perfectly innocent and legitimate use but which nevertheless may come into the category of offensive weapons if the person having the weapon with him so has it with an intention to use it for causing injury to the person.

"It was argued by the prosecutor both here and in the court below that on a literal reading of the terms of the section this offence was proved. It is pointed out that at the moment when the defendant seized his hammer he had the intention of using it on the unfortunate Mr Malcolm. Accordingly it is said that there was at all events a short period of time in which the hammer, formerly in the innocent possession of the defendant, became a weapon which he had with him with the intention of using it on Mr Malcolm. Accordingly, counsel for the prosecutor submits, the offence is established.

"The defendant's argument, both in this court and in the court below, was that the section did not extend to the seizing and use of a weapon for the purpose of causing injury if the weapon was seized only at the moment when the intention to assault arose, and that the type of activity contemplated by the section is not the use of a weapon for offensive purposes but the premeditated carrying of a weapon for those purposes. On this approach it is argued that the weapon was never carried with the necessary intent, and that the fact that the intent must have been formed at a brief moment before the blow was struck is not enough to satisfy the terms of the Act.

"The Crown Court adopted the reasoning of the defendant and in its opinion used these words:

> 'The unlawful use of this hammer was covered by the charge of assault occasioning actual bodily harm. There was insufficient time between taking the hammer from the briefcase and the injury to Mr Malcolm for it properly to be said that the defendant was carrying the hammer as an offensive weapon. Accordingly the court allowed the appeal.'

"This is a case in which the mischief at which the statute is aimed appears to me to be very clear. Immediately prior to the passing of the 1953 Act the criminal law was adequate to deal with the actual use of weapons in the course of a criminal assault. Where it was lacking, however, was that the mere carrying of offensive weapons was not an offence. The long title of the Act reads as follows: 'An Act to prohibit the carrying of offensive weapons in public places without lawful authority or reasonable excuse.' Parliament is there recognising the need for preventive justice where, by preventing the carriage of offensive weapons in a public place, it reduced the opportunity for the use of such weapons. I have no doubt that this was a worthy objective, and that the Act is an extremely important one. If, however, the prosecutor is right, the scope of s.1 goes far beyond the mischief aimed at, and in every case where an assault is committed with a weapon and in a public place an offence under the 1953 Act can be charged in addition to the charge of assault. In such a case the additional count does nothing except add to the complexity of the case and the possibility of confusion of the jury. This has in fact occurred.

"In the absence of authority I would hold that an offence under s.1 is not committed where a person arms himself with a weapon for *instant* attack on his victim. It seems to me that the section is concerned only with a man who, possessed of a weapon, forms the necessary intent *before* an occasion to use actual violence has arisen. In other words, it is not the actual use of the weapon with which the section is concerned, but the carrying of a weapon with intent to use it if occasion arises.

"This seems to have been the view of Lord Goddard CJ in one of the earliest cases under the Act, namely *R v Jura* [[1954] 1 All E.R. 696]. In that case the defendant, lawfully shooting at a fairground rifle range, suddenly turned the rifle onto a woman and fired at her. It is not clear whether the court regarded the rifle as an offensive weapon per se, but if the prosecutor's argument is right a conviction was inevitable. Lord Goddard CJ said:

> '... the long title of the Prevention of Crime Act, 1953, is: "An Act to prohibit the carrying of offensive weapons in public places without lawful authority or reasonable excuse," ... The appellant was not carrying this rifle without lawful excuse because he was at a shooting gallery where for the payment of a few pence people could amuse themselves by firing at a target and was carrying the rifle for that purpose. He had an obvious excuse for carrying the rifle. He made use of the rifle in a way which was unlawful, for which he might have been convicted of a felony. If a person having a rifle in his hand for lawful purpose suddenly uses the rifle for an unlawful purpose, the Offences against the Person Act 1861, provides appropriate punishment for doing that, but the Act of 1953 is meant to deal with a person who, with no excuse whatever, goes out with an offensive weapon, it may be a "cosh" or a knife, or something else, without any reasonable excuse. If, with all respect to the learned judge, his direction were right in this case, it would mean that anybody who was found in possession of a shotgun going to a shooting party and used his gun for an unlawful purpose would be guilty of an offence under this Act. He would be guilty of an offence under the Offences against the Person Act 1861 but not under the Act of 1953. In my opinion, there is no evidence that this man was carrying the weapon without reasonable excuse, and, therefore, the learned judge ought to have directed the jury to acquit on that count.'

"Lord Goddard CJ's reference to a person 'going out' with a weapon might have been taken to mean that the matter had to be judged as at the moment when the defendant set out from home, but that point is dealt with in the next authority, namely *Woodward v Koessler* [[1958] 3 All E.R. 557]. In that case a boy had gone out armed with a sheath knife intending to use the knife to break into a cinema. Surprised by the approach of the caretaker, he then threatened the latter with the knife.

"Donovan J said:

'Counsel for the accused founds himself on the words "having it with him", and says that the accused must be found to have taken the weapon out with him with the intention of causing injury. Counsel says that in this case the accused took it for the purposes of breaking into the cinema. I do not agree with that narrow interpretation of the words "having it with him". All that one has to do for the purpose of ascertaining what the intention is, is to look and see, what use was in fact made of it. If it is found that the accused did in fact make use of it for the purpose of causing injury he had it with him for that purpose. I think that the evidence shows that the accused in this case did have it with him for the purpose of causing injury' [at p. 558].

"I accept that it is unnecessary for the prosecution to prove that the relevant intent was formed from the moment when the defendant set out on his expedition. An innocent carrying of, say, a hammer can be converted into an unlawful carrying when the defendant forms the guilty intent, provided, in my view, that the intent is formed before the actual occasion to use violence has arisen.

"Donovan J's words have however been widely accepted as supporting the argument of the appellant, namely, that if the weapon is used to cause injury, an offence under s.1 must have been committed. As will presently appear, the Court of Appeal has criticised this dictum of Donovan J, and counsel for the prosecutor himself accepts that it is too wide, but counsel must then face a formidable difficulty because I can see no distinction between the argument which he presents today and the words of Donovan J:

'If it is found that the person did, in fact, make use of it for the purpose of causing injury, he had it with him for that purpose, and I think that is good enough ...' [at p. 558].

"Donovan J's dictum was followed in *R v Powell* [[1963] Crim.L.R. 511] and is reflected in *Harrison v Thornton* [[1966] Crim.L.R. 388] where a defendant who picked up a stone and threw it at another was convicted of an offence under the section.

"These decisions have prompted an observation by the learned editors of Archbold [*Criminal Pleading, Evidence and Practice* (38th ed., para. 2382] that:

'The result is that an Act which, by its long title, is designed to prohibit the *carrying* of offensive weapons has been interpreted by the courts as prohibiting the *use* of such weapons. This in turn means that when a defendant has used a weapon offensively it will be impossible for him to establish the statutory defence of lawful authority or reasonable excuse, because his offensive use of the weapon establishes his unlawful intent ...'

"The last authority to which I wish to refer is the decision of the Court of Appeal in *R v Dayle* [[1973] 3 All E.R. 1151]. This case provides a striking example of the difficulties which can arise when a charge under the 1953 Act is added to a simple charge of assault. The prosecution case was that in the course of a fight the defendant had taken a car jack from the boot of his car and thrown it at his adversary. The jury disagreed on a count alleging assault, and acquitted on a count under the 1953 Act. On a retrial of the first count it was alleged that the acquittal on the second count would be inconsistent with a conviction on the first and raise an issue estoppel. The trial judge, following *R v Jura* [[1954] 1 All E.R. 696], held that there was no such inconsistency, and the jury convicted. The Court of Appeal quashed the conviction for reasons which need not concern us, but went on to make two important statements of principle.

"First, it was said that the words of Donovan J in *Woodward v Koessler* were 'too widely expressed to be applicable in every case', and that the necessary intent should be judged by reference to all the circumstances of the case. I had not regarded Donovan J's words as restricting the evidence on which intent could be judged, but rather as an answer to counsel's argument on the meaning of 'had with him'. The prosecutor relies on Donovan J for the proposition that if the weapon is used offensively, the defendant must 'have had it with him' with intent. If the judge's words are too wide, the mainstay of counsel for the prosecutor's argument is gone. The point is finally driven home by the second principle stated in *R v Dayle*, namely that the court should follow the approach laid down by Lord Goddard CJ in *R v Jura*.

"The Court of Appeal said in terms that the defendant's intent must be judged on the whole of the evidence, including, where appropriate, the fact that the weapon was used offensively. But I do not think that Donovan J ever meant to say anything other than this. The real question is whether the offensive use of the weapon is conclusive on the question of whether the defendant 'had it with him' within the meaning of the Act. Lord Goddard CJ thought that it was not and this must now be accepted as correct. Accordingly, no offence is committed under the 1953 Act where an assailant seizes a weapon for instant use on his victim. Here the seizure and use of the weapon are all part and parcel of the assault or attempted assault. To support a conviction under the Act the prosecution must show that the defendant was carrying or otherwise equipped with the weapon, and had the intent to use it offensively before any occasion for its actual use had arisen."

Appeal dismissed.

3.14.6   **(ii) R. v. Giles**

[1976] Crim.L.R. 253

G. went to the assistance of his brother-in-law who was involved in a fight in a club. One of the combatants turned round and hit him on the head with a bottle. G. picked up a glass in order to protect himself. After the participants in the fight and by-standers had been dispersed G. refused to put his glass down, maintaining that he intended to use it in his own defence against the man who had hit him. G. was charged with a contravention of s.1(1) of the 1953 Act.

To refute G.'s explanation the Crown relied upon circumstantial evidence and certain oral comments made by G. to the arresting officer.

Prior to making their final speeches counsel asked the court for directions as to who had to discharge the burden of proof.

The defence conceded that the glass fell within the second limb of an offensive weapon in s.1(4) of the 1953 Act and that if G. "had it with him" in the club, then the burden of providing "reasonable excuse" rested on the defendant—("any person who without lawful authority or reasonable excuse, the proof whereof shall lie on him, has with him ...").

However, on the authority of *Ohlson v. Hylton* [1975] 2 All E.R. 490 the defence argued that the "occasion" for using the glass had come, and the situation of "instant violence" applied. Therefore the issue to be decided by the jury was whether or not G. "had the glass with him" as defined in *Ohlson's* case. On this issue the burden of proof rested on the prosecution.

The Crown argued that this was not the issue to be left to the jury. Counsel for the prosecution urged that it was important not to confuse the two meanings of the word "occasion" and that when the judgment in *Ohlson's* care refers to "the occasion to use (the weapon)" within the context of that judgment the word "occasion" meant "moment" not "reason." The absence of continuity in "having" which in *Ohlson's* case provided the defence to the charge must be limited to the actual moment in time covering the delivery of the blow and the seconds immediately preceding and following it. On the facts relied upon by G. the moment of instant violence had come, but it had passed. The jury therefore had to consider the issue of "reasonable excuse," the burden of proving which lay on the accused.

The judge held that the prosecution's view was too narrow, and that a person who in a situation of specific threat picks up a weapon fearing that he may be attacked does not "have it with him" within the meaning of s.1(1) of the Act.

The jury were subsequently directed that they had to be satisfied by the prosecution that G.'s account was untrue, and that they did not have to consider the issue of reasonable excuse unless or until they were so satisfied.

Verdict not reported.

NOTE

This was a decision of a court of first instance, Nottingham Crown Court.

(iii) R. v. Humphreys   3.14.7

[1977] Crim.L.R. 225

Following a dance at a youth club a fight broke out during the course of which H., who had been attacked by O'D., stabbed O'D. in the back with a penknife which he had managed to extract from an inside jacket pocket while being assaulted by several youths. He was convicted of unlawful wounding and having an offensive weapon in a public place. His defence had been self-defence. He appealed against the conviction for having an offensive weapon on the ground of misdirection to the jury that if they found him guilty of the wounding it was difficult to see how he could not also be guilty on the second count. It was also submitted that he had had a defence on the second count which had thereby been withdrawn from the jury. He relied on *Dayle* [1973] 3 All E.R. 1151 and *Ohlson v. Hylton* [1975] 2 All E.R. 490. An application for leave to appeal against the conviction of wounding was not pursued.

Held, following *Ohlson v. Hylton*, if a person merely happened to have upon him an inoffensive weapon like a penknife and in desperation or in the heat of the moment drew that weapon *ad hoc*, and used it for injuring a person intending then and there to cause injury to another person, he was not guilty of the offence of having an offensive weapon in a public place, because he had not been carrying in a public place that weapon with the necessary intent to cause injury. His intention was formed, as it might be said, *ad hoc*. The jury should have been directed that if H. only formed the intent to use the knife defensively after the occasion had arisen he was entitled to be acquitted because his seizure and use of the weapon, taking it out of his pocket and using it, were part and parcel of the wounding of O'D. This was not a case where the court would consider the application of the proviso.

The case provided an illustration of the need for the prosecution to consider very carefully the question whether a count alleging an offence against s.1 of the 1953 Act should be added. It should be realised that on the interpretation which had been given to the section, the offence was a serious offence. The court emphasised that it was a serious offence and should only be included in an indictment when, in the opinion of the prosecution, justice really required that it should be.

Appeal allowed.

3.14.8 **(iv) Pittard v. Mahoney**

[1977] Crim.L.R. 169

The defendant, a youth, lived in an area in which serious incidents of physical violence had occurred involving the use of knives and bottles by unknown persons, and four of his acquaintances had been injured, the most recent incident having occurred some four weeks earlier. The defendant, who had no previous convictions for violence and was in genuine fear of being attacked by other youths with weapons, made up a metal ball and chain, intending to use it for his own defence against attack. He had it with him in a public place and was charged with an offence contrary to s.1 of the 1953 Act. The stipendiary magistrate, who was of opinion that the defendant, although having an offensive weapon with him in a public place, had discharged the burden of proving reasonable excuse for having it with him, and the information was dismissed. The prosecutor appealed by case stated to the Queen's Bench Divisional Court.

Held, that the principle in *Evans v. Hughes* [1972] 1 W.L.R. 1452 was to be applied. The defendant had not shown the kind of imminent danger which could possibly have justified the carrying of an offensive weapon. In deciding whether the carriage was justified, the nature of the weapon had to be taken into account. The defendant had not justified his conduct. The case would be remitted with a direction to convict.

Appeal allowed.

CHAPTER FOUR

Types of weapons   4.0

Introduction   4.1
Consideration is given in this Chapter to the various types of
implement that have fallen to be considered by the courts as
offensive weapons.

Air pistol   4.2

R. v. McGuire and Page   4.2.1

[1963] Crim.L.R. 572

M. and P. were convicted of possessing an imitation firearm at the
time of committing an offence of being suspected persons loitering
with intent to steal. They were seen trying the doorhandles of
unattended motor cars. They were stopped and it was alleged that
M. had an air pistol sticking out of his pocket. At the trial M. said
that the pistol had been planted on him by the police and P. said
that he knew nothing about the pistol until he got to the police
station. M. appealed on the ground that the judge told the jury
that the question of lawful object did not arise. P. appealed on the
ground of misdirection as to constructive possession: the judge
directed the jury to the effect that, if P. knew M. had the pistol and
acquiesced in him having it whilst they engaged in the offence, he
was guilty.

Held, (1) it was inconceivable that M., if he had the pistol,
was in possession of it for a lawful object and to have left the
issue to the jury would merely have been confusing; (2) the
judge in effect withdrew the issue from the jury by treating
as a question of law what was a matter of evidence and
inference.

Appeal by M. dismissed. Appeal by P. allowed.

4.3 *Baseball bat*

4.3.1 ## Egan v. McGlennan

1992 G.W.D. 40–2395

E. was charged with a contravention of s.1 of the 1953 Act in that he had a baseball bat with him. He was convicted and appealed.

Held, that before a baseball bat could be classified as an offensive weapon there had to be evidence that the person in possession of it intended to use it to inflict personal injury, and findings that E had concealed it under his jacket, had been acting suspiciously without specification as to the manner in which he had so acted, and had had it with him in a hotel and lounge bar, were insufficient to enable any such inference to be drawn, particularly when after the police had been called to the hotel the baseball bat had been found lying openly at his feet.

Appeal allowed.

NOTE
    Reid v. *Normand*, 1994 S.C.C.R. 475 is a good example of a prosecution in which a baseball bat was accepted to be an offensive weapon. The implement had been used to smash a window in a house. For an example of how seriously the English appeal judges take an assault involving a baseball bat, see *Attorney-General's Reference No. 8 of 1995* [1996] 1 Cr.App.R.(S.) 54.

4.4 *Bicycle chain*

4.4.1 ## Woodward v. Koessler

[1958] 3 All E.R. 557

For the facts see *supra*, at para. 3.7.2.

Lord Goddard, C.J. (at p. 558)
    "We know well why it [*i.e.* 'offensive weapon' in s.1(4) of the 1953 Act] is rather an obscure definition, viz., because one of the weapons that these young hooligans like to use is a bicycle chain. The bicycle chain is not made for injury, but if a boy is swinging a bicycle chain and saying 'Look out', that is using an offensive weapon."

Appeal by prosecutor allowed.

Bottle	**4.5**

(i) Broken bottle **4.5.1**

Bryan v. Mott **4.5.2**

(1976) 62 Cr.App.R. 71

B. was found to have with him in a public place a broken end of a milk bottle. He was charged with a contravention of s.1(1) of the 1953 Act. After sundry procedure he was convicted of that charge.

Found guilty.

NOTE

This case is considered *supra* at para. 3.2.8, in relation to the issue of reasonable excuse. The broken end of a milk bottle seems to have been accepted as an offensive weapon in the Magistrate's Court and in the Crown Court the view was taken that the item was an article adapted for use for causing injury to the person. The Lord Chief Justice, however, seems to regard the item as an offensive weapon *per se* (see p. 73).

(ii) Lemon juice bottle **4.5.3**

R. v. Hopkins **4.5.4**

[1996] 1 Cr.App.R.(S.) 18

H. pleaded guilty to having an offensive weapon, a lemon juice bottle containing hydrochloric acid. The appellant was a mini cab driver. He was found by a police officer to have the lemon juice bottle in the front of his cab. He had had trouble with some men a few years earlier. The lemon juice bottle contained a solution of 36 per cent hydrochloric acid which he explained he carried for protection. He was sentenced to six months' imprisonment and he appealed.

Held, that the offence was so serious that only a custodial sentence could be justified. The lemon juice bottle had not been used and the appellant had some general ground for fear as to his personal safety. Standing his personal circumstances, a sentence of three months' imprisonment would be substituted.

Holland, J. (at p. 19)

"The content of the bottle was tested and it was found to contain a 36 per cent concentration of hydrochloric acid—that is a concentration sufficiently strong to cause serious injury on contact:

indeed, any contact would require immediate first aid to avoid permanent damage ... The mixture was potentially hazardous in the extreme. The possession of it by the appellant threatened to cause really serious injury in the future."

Appeal allowed.

4.5.5 *(iii) Washing-up liquid bottle*

4.5.6 **R. v. Formosa and Upton**

[1990] 3 W.L.R. 1179

F. and U. were convicted of possession of a prohibited weapon contrary to s.5(1)(*b*) of the Firearms Act 1968. Each appealed against conviction on that charge. The facts are set out in the judgment of the court.

Lloyd, L.J. (at p. 1180)
"On October 25, 1989 in the Crown Court at Knightsbridge these two appellants were convicted of possessing a prohibited weapon contrary to section 5 of the Firearms Act 1968 and sentenced to three years' imprisonment. That was count 2 of the indictment. On count 3 they were convicted of having an offensive weapon, on which they were sentenced to 18 months' imprisonment concurrent. We need not trouble with the remaining counts of the indictment, save to observe that they were acquitted on count 1, conspiracy to rob. Their applications for leave to appeal against conviction were referred to the full court by the Registrar of Criminal Appeals since the question involved is a point of law. The appeal is confined to their conviction on count 2.

"The facts were that on 2 February 1989 police officers on mobile patrol noticed the appellants sitting in a red Ford Sierra motor car parked at the kerb of a West London street. In the view of the police officers they were behaving suspiciously. So the police officers reversed their vehicle alongside that of the appellants and went over to speak to them. Both appellants were wearing gloves and both had caps. Upton when asked said that the car was his. There was a machete lying on the floor beneath Formosa's feet. That was the subject of count 3 on which both appellants were convicted. Upton was discovered to have in his inside jacket pocket a Fairy Liquid washing-up bottle containing 400 millilitres of hydrochloric acid. That was the subject of count 2. The appellants were arrested and in due course the case came on for trial.

"It was submitted on behalf of the appellants that there was no evidence that the Fairy Liquid bottle was a weapon designed or adapted for the discharge of noxious liquid. The mere fact that the bottle had been filled with hydrochloric acid rather than washing-up liquid did not mean it had been designed or adapted to discharge the acid.

"The judge was not referred to any authority on the construction of section 5 of the Firearms Act 1968. He ruled that if the contents of the object were changed, then the object itself had been adapted and therefore he allowed the case to go before the jury.

"[Counsel] on behalf of both appellants argues that the judge's ruling was erroneous. He submits that an empty Fairy Liquid bottle is not a weapon in any sense of the word. There can be no dispute about the correctness of that submission. He goes on to submit that even if it becomes a weapon when filled with hydrochloric acid, it does not become a prohibited weapon within the meaning of section 5(1)(*b*) of the Act, since it cannot be said that the bottle has been 'designed or adapted' to discharge the hydrochloric acid. It was neither more nor less than a bottle containing hydrochloric acid. The appellants were therefore charged with the wrong offence. They should have been charged with an offence under section 1 of the Prevention of Crime Act 1953 with carrying an offensive weapon. For 'offensive weapon' is defined by section 1(4) as including any article intended by the person having it with him for use for causing injury to the person. There is no equivalent definition in section 5 of the Firearms Act 1968.

"In support of his submission [counsel for the appellants] referred us to three authorities; first, a ruling of Judge Price Q.C. in the Central Criminal Court in *Reg.* v. *Titus* [1971] Crim.L.R. 279; second, the decision of the Divisional Court presided over by Lord Parker of Waddington C.J. in *Maddox* v. *Storer* [1963] 1 Q.B. 451; finally, the decision of Mr. David Widdicombe Q.C. in *Backer* v. *Secretary of State for the Environment* [1983] 1 W.L.R. 1485. From these authorities there emerges this proposition, that the word 'adapted' takes its colour and meaning from the context in which it appears. Where it is used on its own, it may bear a wide meaning. Thus in *Maddox* v. *Storer* ... it was held that in Schedule 1 to the Road Traffic Act 1960 it meant simply apt or fit for the purpose in question. That meaning corresponds to the first of the two meanings in the *Oxford English Dictionary*. But where the word is used in conjunction with the word 'constructed' in the phrase 'constructed or adapted' it bears a narrower meaning. It imports then some physical alteration to the thing in question. This corresponds to the second of the two meanings in the *Oxford English Dictionary*. That was the meaning given to the word *French* v.

Champkin [1920] 1 K.B. 76 and in *Taylor* v. *Mead* [1961] 1 W.L.R. 435.
In the former case Lord Denning C.J. said, at p. 79:

> 'The justices seems to have treated the word "adapted" as if
> it were synonymous with "suitable" or "apt," whereas it must
> be construed as meaning altered so as to make the vehicle
> apt for the conveyance of goods.'

"Here the word 'adapted' is used in conjunction with the word
'designed'. On which side of the line does the present case come?
We have no doubt that it comes on the same side of the line as
French v. *Champkin*.

"It was argued by [counsel] on behalf of the Crown that
'designed' meant no more than 'intended,' and since the bottle
when filled with hydrochloric acid was clearly intended to be used
by the appellants for discharging the acid, it became a weapon
designed for that purpose.

"We cannot accept that argument. If the word 'designed' were
to bear that meaning it would fit most uneasily with the word
'adapted' in the composite phrase 'designed or adapted.' Moreover,
it must not be forgotten that the section is dealing with prohibited
weapons, the mere possession of which constitutes an offence. One
would expect, therefore, that the commission of the offence would
be capable of objective verification. The offence under section 5(1)(*a*)
clearly does not depend on the intention of the user. We would say
the same of the offence under section 5(1)(*b*).

"We conclude, therefore, that the word 'adapted' in section
5(1)(*b*) must bear the narrower of the two meanings; in other words,
it must mean that the object has been altered so as to make it fit for
the use in question.

"The case then comes down to this: was the empty bottle of
Fairy Liquid altered when it was filled with hydrochloric acid?
The answer in our view is clearly 'No.' There was no physical
alteration to the bottle. The bottle remained the same. It follows
that the bottle with the acid was not a weapon 'designed or
adapted' for the discharge of acid within the meaning of the section.

"The consequence of the alternative view would indeed be
alarming as was pointed out in the course of argument. It would
mean that a householder who filled a milk bottle with acid in order
to destroy a wasps' nest would be in possession of a weapon
adapted for the discharge of a noxious liquid and would therefore
be guilty of the offence of possessing a prohibited weapon; until,
of course, he had used the acid for the purpose in question when
the milk bottle would revert to its pristine innocence. That could
not be right. It shows that the possession of the Fairy Liquid bottle
by these two appellants was not the sort of case to which section 5

is directed. They could, and should, have been charged with an offence under section 1 of the Prevention of Crime Act 1953.

"It follows, in our view, that the ruling of Judge Price in *Reg.* v. *Titus* ..., which is the only case directly in point, was correct. In that case the judge held that a water pistol filled with ammonia was not a weapon designed or adapted for the discharge of any noxious liquid and was therefore capable of being an imitation firearm under section 57(4) of the Firearms Act 1968. We agree."

Appeal allowed.

Cosh   4.6

Grieve v. Macleod   4.6.1

1967 S.L.T. 70

G., a taxidriver in Edinburgh, had with him in his taxicab a piece of rubber hose about two feet long with a piece of metal inserted at one end. He was charged with and convicted of a contravention of s.1(1) of the 1953 Act. At trial and on appeal a defence of reasonable excuse was rejected.

Appeal refused.

NOTE
    For further discussion of this case see para. 3.2.4 *supra*. This particular item was never disputed as being an offensive weapon by the defence
    There are several instances of individuals going armed in the course of their employment. See *R.* v. *Spanner* [1973] Crim.L.R. 704; *R.* v. *Hopkins* [1996] 1 Cr.App.R.(S.) 18; and *Carlin* v. *Annan*, 1991 G.W.D. 38–2315. In the last case the appellant had five offensive weapons with him on his milk float.

Croquet mallet   4.7

A. v. B.   4.7.1

(1967) 31 J.C.L. 162

A policeman gave evidence in a trial in a juvenile court that he had seen a 16-year-old boy in a crowd at a football match wave a croquet mallet. Several of the spectators near the boy had to duck to get out of the way of the mallet. The policeman said that he had approached the boy and asked him why he had the mallet with him. The boy replied that he had it for "a bit of fun." The policeman had charged the boy with possession of an offensive weapon in a public place.

The boy gave evidence on his own behalf and he said that he had taken the mallet with him to the football match. It was part of his normal "football watching equipment." He said that he normally went to another ground and he took with him the mallet draped in the colours of the home team. At this match the mallet was undraped as he had not got material in the colours of either of the teams playing. The boy said that he had not threatened anyone and nor had he intended so to do.

The court held that the croquet mallet was not an offensive weapon *per se* and that it was not satisfied that the boy intended to use it to injure.

Found not guilty.

4.8   *C.S. gas canister*

4.8.1   **(i) R. v. Gachot**

The Times, October 16, 1991

G., a French grand prix racing driver, was involved in an altercation with a London taxidriver after a minor road traffic accident at Hyde Park Corner. During the argument G. produced the C.S. gas canister and sprayed the "paralyser" gas into the face of the taxidriver.

After trial G. was convicted of assault causing actual bodily harm and he pleaded guilty to possessing a prohibited weapon, namely the C.S. gas canister. He was sentenced to 18 months' imprisonment on the first charge and six months' imprisonment concurrent on the second charge.

Leave to appeal against conviction was refused. On appeal against sentence the sentence was varied to nine months' imprisonment of which six months were suspended. As G. had by then completed two months in jail the varied sentence allowed for his immediate release.

Appeal against sentence allowed.

NOTE

M. Gachot's case was reported extensively in the newspapers especially as the sentence passed by the trial judge produced public outrage in France. There, it seems, the CS gas canisters are available freely in the shops: *The Times*, August 31, 1991. One newspaper report informed readers that CS is a solid chemical which when dissolved in water and used in an aerosol stimulates the sensory nerves to produce a burning sensation. It is used elsewhere in Europe as a form of protection. It takes about 30 minutes to recover after being sprayed in the face with the gas.

Its effects are said to include: burning in the eyes and nose, uncontrolled tears, spasms of the eyelids, burning of the throat and in the chest, a sense of suffocation and panic, vomiting and coughing. Some people are allergic to the gas and for people with bad asthma it can be fatal: *The Independent*, August 17, 1991.

A C.S. gas canister is a weapon designed or adapted for the discharge of a noxious gas or other thing and consequently a prohibited weapon in terms of s.5(1)(*b*) of the Firearms Act 1968. However, given the nature and effects of the contents of the C.S. gas canister, it may be argued that such an item is an offensive weapon either *per se* or by reason of its intended use.

(ii) Donnelly v. H.M. Advocate 4.8.2

1988 S.C.C.R. 386

D, the appellant, a 16-year-old first offender, pleaded guilty to possession of a C.S. gas canister at a football match during which the canister was thrown into a group of rival supporters by someone else. The judge sentenced the appellant to eighteen months' detention in order to make it clear that such behaviour could not be tolerated, although he recognised that such a sentence was not justifiable as a reformative measure, or on the grounds of individual deterrence or retribution. The appellant appealed to the High Court against the sentence.

Held, that the sentence was inadequate; and sentence quashed and sentence of two years' detention substituted.

The appellant's note of appeal against sentence included the following ground:

"The sentence imposed was excessive having regard to the appellant's age, the fact that he had no previous convictions and had been remanded in custody for a substantial period of time pending the resolution of the case against him. The Crown accepted a plea of simple possession of the grenade and accepted a not guilty plea in respect of possessing the gas grenade with intent to endanger life. The appellant had never intended throwing the grenade or having it thrown by another person."

In his report the judge stated:

"On 28th November 1987 a C.S. gas grenade was thrown into a large body of spectators, then watching an association football match between Hibernian F.C. and Celtic F.C. at Easter Road stadium, Edinburgh. The spectator areas were filled to capacity; the start of the match had to be delayed because of the large number of spectators. There were some 7,000 spectators in the covered terracing on the east side of the ground. The spectators were packed in but were not squeezed together. That covered area was allocated to supporters of the home team (Hibernian F.C.). An adjacent uncovered area (to the south of the covered area) housed visiting supporters. In order to prevent spectators from invading the pitch, there was substantial fencing between the terracing and the pitch. Policemen and stewards lined the area in the vicinity of the fencing. At intervals in the fencing there were gates which could be opened at the discretion of the police. The gas grenade was thrown from the visitors' area, described above, into the covered area. The firing pin had previously been removed. The grenade fell, exploded and discharged its contents into the surrounding area. The contents were a fine powder which caused great irritation to the eyes, the breathing system and the skin of any person with whom it came into contact. As the powder drifted in the air it resembled smoke. I shall refer to it as 'gas'. When the grenade exploded and the gas spread, nearby spectators panicked and sought to leave the scene. At first, however, those controlling the gates did not realise the cause and nature of the disturbance and the gates were not immediately opened. There was considerable crushing before the gates were opened but thereafter the spectators spilled on to the field where they were able to escape the worst effects of the gas. Within minutes some 3,000 spectators spilled on to the pitch. Others found their way to parts of the terracing remote from the gas. In the course of the stampede from the scene, some spectators were trampled underfoot. The gas drifted on to the pitch and also in among the Celtic supporters in the uncovered area lying south of the covered terracing. Hundreds of spectators were directly affected by the C.S. gas. Eighty-one police officers were affected, some of them through going to the assistance of persons to whose hair or clothing the powder was adhering. Five spectators were thought to be seriously injured. Particularly affected were an asthmatic, an elderly infirm man and some boys. It was plain from the evidence that the incident could have ended in a major tragedy with many dead. Many people panicked, both through fear and through the sudden inexplicable suffering caused by the C.S. gas. Had the pressure not been relieved by the opening of the gates and by the success of some spectators in climbing over or under the fencing, serious crushing would have been inevitable. Some spectators were in fact crushed and rendered unconscious. Once the grenade exploded, the cloud of gas powder was blown about by the swirling wind and it could have directly affected anyone within a very large area.

"The grenade was thrown by Brian Gallagher. [He was sentenced to four years' detention on a charge of culpably and recklessly endangering lives.] He was one of a group of visiting supporters who had been demonstrating vociferously. He removed the pin and threw the grenade into the nearby Hibernian supporters' terracing during and towards the end of the second half of the match.

"The appellant, Joseph Robert Donnelly, pled guilty to certain charges at a preliminary diet on 4th March 1988. He was called as a Crown witness. He said that he had travelled alone to the match by bus and that he took the gas grenade with him. The grenade had 'C.S.' embossed on the pin. It was green and the size of a cricket ball. He stated that he had got it the night before from a person whose name and address he gave. He said he had got it to show off to people whom he would expect to meet when travelling in support of the Celtic football team; he had told some such people a couple of weeks earlier that he would show them it; at that time he said he knew of the grenade but did not possess it. He arrived at the match late and made his way into the Celtic corner halfway up the open terracing to the south of the covered terracing. According to his evidence he did not see anyone there he knew. He had a grenade in an inside jacket pocket. His evidence was that he was approached by John Mellon [a co-accused who was acquitted] and a number of others; at that time, he claimed, he did not know them. Mellon asked if he had a C.S. bomb and, on being told that he did indeed have it, Mellon asked to see it. At first Donnelly refused. Then somebody else asked for it so he took it out of his pocket. Various others questioned him about it. John Mellon then took it but Donnelly said he did not try to stop Mellon from taking it. Another member of the group took it from Mellon and the bomb was passed about. They all asked questions about it and kept passing it from one to another. As a result Donnelly lost track of it and each member of the group claimed that somebody else must have it. The group then started to move off and Donnelly followed them. He did not know who had the bomb. A short time thereafter the bomb was thrown from within a group of young 'casuals', supporters who were bouncing rhythmically up and down on the terracing. Donnelly said he did not know the identities of these supporters. The gas cloud drifted back and Donnelly and others ran on to the pitch. He was arrested about a fortnight later and while in custody met Gallagher who claimed responsibility for throwing the grenade. Gallagher was not previously known to him. In cross-examination Donnelly was asked if the person who gave him the grenade had told him that it was a dummy. He replied, 'He never told us it *was* a dummy; he said he thought it was a dummy.' After the conclusion of his evidence the Crown accepted certain pleas from the accused then on trial.

"No previous convictions were libelled against Donnelly. The social enquiry report disclosed that his family situation was stable and the family was supportive. It narrated that he was looking for 'approval' from his peers. He was a regular attender at home and away matches of the Celtic football club. Donnelly was in custody from the date of his arrest until 9th March 1988. In considering what was the appropriate method of disposal I had regard to the terms of section 207 of the Criminal Procedure (Scotland) Act 1975. I also considered the relevance to this particular case of the four principal general purposes that affect judicial sentencing, namely, reformation, prevention, deterrence and punishment/retribution. It did not appear to me that there was any likelihood that imposing a sentence of detention would contribute towards the reformation of Donnelly; that consideration did not, therefore, influence me in sentencing him to a period of detention. It did not appear to me that a period of detention would be necessary in order to prevent Donnelly from committing any such crime in the immediate future. In terms of actual punishment of Donnelly for what he admitted doing, I considered that no long period of detention would be necessary. Indeed, having regard to the period of time that he had spent in detention before trial it could well be that detention alone would be sufficient in terms of straightforward punishment for the offences admitted. The reason which I had for imposing the periods of detention which I did impose in respect of the admitted offences in the light of their surrounding circumstances was that I thought it proper by imposing such sentences to make it clear to the general public, or in any event to that section of it that attends football matches, that behaviour of the kind to which Donnelly pled guilty could not be tolerated. The danger to the public from the actual explosion of the gas grenade was very great indeed. Other incidents of various kinds at football grounds, both in Scotland and elsewhere, have illustrated that when large numbers of people panic at a football ground there may be many deaths. Accordingly the use of articles such as a C.S. grenade at a football match must be visited with severe punishments which will themselves amount to deterrents. Donnelly, of course, did not throw the gas grenade but he possessed it and deliberately took it to a football match which he must have known was likely to be very well attended. Without his action in taking the article there, having previously said that he would exhibit it to various people, the whole incident would not have happened. In that regard his culpability was, in my view, substantial. If the court were simply to impose upon a person who committed such offences in such circumstances a sentence which resulted in that person's immediate release the result would, in my view, be to send out the wrong message to others who might contemplate various forms of disruptive hooliganism at or in the vicinity of football grounds. The incident itself was given very wide publicity in Scotland and the trial itself was also attended by a good deal of publicity. It was, I consider, reasonable to suppose that persons who regularly attend football matches would be aware of the result of the trial.

"I do not consider that I left out of account any matter which is referred to in the grounds of appeal or took into account any matter other than those referred to above."

Lord Brand (at p. 389)

"The appellant was sentenced to sentences amounting in cumulo to eighteen months' detention in a young offenders institution. The charges for which he was sentenced were first, that he had in Glasgow the possession of a C.S. gas grenade; secondly, that he had possession of that gas grenade at a football match at a football ground in Edinburgh; and thirdly, that he was in breach of the provisions of the Bail etc. (Scotland) Act 1980. It is notorious that when trouble breaks out nowadays at soccer matches appalling injuries are liable to occur. It is said on behalf of the appellant that he did not play any part in the actual use of this grenade at the soccer match. That may be so, but without his possession of it and taking it through from Glasgow to Edinburgh, what occurred could not have occurred. In our opinion the sentences imposed by the learned trial judge were inadequate. In respect of the sentence of eighteen months' detention we are of opinion that that should be increased to two years' detention. The other sentences imposed will remain as they stand. All sentences will be concurrent. The appeal is refused."

[Appeal refused.]

NOTE

In *Ferguson* v. *H.M. Advocate*, 1991 G.W.D. 35–2128 it was held on appeal against sentence that 12 months' detention for carrying a canister of C.S. gas was not excessive where the appellant had intended to go to a football match. The court observed that "anyone carrying such a weapon in those circumstances could expect severe punishment." *Fallon* v. *H.M. Advocate*, 1990 G.W.D. 38–2204 is distinguishable on its particular facts.

(iii) R. v. Flanagan   4.8.3

(1994) 15 Cr.App.R.(S.) 300

F., the appellant, ran away from an incident. A police officer chased him, caught him and tried to detain him. F. produced a canister and sprayed the police officer in the face. F. was sentenced to $3^{1}/_{2}$ years' imprisonment for causing a noxious thing to be taken. He appealed that sentence which was reduced to two years.

Alliott J. (at p. 302)

"... the injuries sustained by the victim, whilst extremely unpleasant, were essentially transient and he was able to carry on with his duties, not least in recording his notes of the incident, after the interval of some two hours."

Appeal allowed.

NOTE
This appeal illustrates the nature of use to which the C.S. canister can be put and the serious approach to the item taken by the courts. Imprisonment was upheld in *Dickson* v. *Lees*, 1993 G.W.D. 30–1889 where tear gas was sprayed in the faces of two doormen at a disco, causing them "temporary blindness and breathing difficulties."

4.8.4   **(iv) R. v. Simmonds**

(1995) 16 Cr.App.R.(S.) 898

S. had a meal in a restaurant and attempted to pay for the meal with counterfeit notes. S. ran from the premises chased by the waiters and at a point in the incident he sprayed the faces of the waiters. He was sentenced to two years' imprisonment for possessing a prohibited weapon. He appealed and the sentence was reduced to nine months' imprisonment.

Scott Baker, J. (at p. 899)

"... the possession of a C.S. gas canister which was, in the event, as the Crown accepted, not used deliberately on the faces of the waiters, is necessarily an offence of considerable gravity."

Appeal allowed.

4.8.5   **(v) R. v. Payne**

(1995) 16 Cr.App.R.(S.) 782

P., the appellant, suffered from poor health but he was able, at the invitation of an unknown man for cash, to drive a van from France. At Dover customs officers found hidden in the bodywork of the van 1,796 canisters of C.S. gas. P. pleaded guilty to importing prohibited items contrary to s.5(1)(*g*) of the Firearms Act 1968 and he was sentenced to three years' imprisonment. On appeal the sentence was reduced to two years mainly because of the appellant's personal circumstances.

May, J. (at p. 784)

"The offence is not, in the view of this court, rendered less serious because there are other jurisdictions where possession for personal protection is not unlawful. Each case will depend on its own facts. It may be that in some cases it will be proved, or an inference can surely be drawn, that the canisters were intended for use in aid of serious crime and that the defendant knew this. In this case the judge accepted that it was not established that this appellant had such knowledge."

And later:

"This court considers that unlawfully importing C.S. gas canisters in anything other than a very modest quantity will normally be regarded as so serious that only a custodial sentence is justified. Depending on the circumstances, even small-scale importation may well cross the custody threshold."

Appeal allowed.

Electric stun device   4.9

Flack v. Baldry   4.9.1

[1988] 1 W.L.R. 393

F. was a registered firearms dealer. He was convicted in a magistrates' court for having in his possession, without the necessary authority, three weapons contrary to s.5(1) of the Firearms Act 1968. In respect of all three charges he was conditionally discharged for one year and ordered to pay £130 costs. He appealed by case stated in respect of his conviction in relation to one only of those weapons, called a "Lightning Strike."

Section 5(1)(*b*) of the Firearms Act 1968 provides that "(1) a person commits an offence if, without the authority of the Secretary of State for Defence he has in his possession ... (*b*) any weapon of whatever description designed or adapted for the discharge of any noxious liquid, gas or other thing ..."

Standing the facts, outlined below, and the terms of the statute, the Divisional Court of the Queen's Bench Division allowed the appeal. The case was remitted to the magistrates with a direction to acquit F. The prosecution then appealed to the House of Lords against the decision of the Divisional Court.

Lord Ackner (at p. 394)

"A 'Lightning Strike' is a hand-held electrical device designed to inflict pain and to cause temporary incapacitation. Such pain and incapacitation is caused by the flow of 46,000 volts of electricity between two electrodes on the Lightning Strike through a person's body. The advertisement for the device contains the following statements:

> 'Just a touch on the button of the device, and the subject receives an electrical *discharge* ... Then the subject loses his balance and will not be able to react in any way ... This *discharge* can get through more than one centimetre of clothes, causes confusion and disorientation leaving the subject dazed. The subject's immobilization shall be from 5 to 15 minutes depending on the intensity of the *discharge*' (my emphasis).

"In the case stated the justices most helpfully set out the *Oxford English Dictionary* definitions of discharge, which read as follows:

> '(i) Discharge (non-electrical)—to disburden; send out; send forth; to emit. (ii) Discharge (electrical)—to rid of an electrical charge; the emission or transference of electricity which takes place between two bodies.'

"The justices were of the opinion that whichever definition was applied, the flow of electricity between the two electrodes through the victim's body was a 'discharge.' In the case stated they raised two questions—(a) can an electricity charge created by the device be said to be discharged in its operation; (b) is 46,000 volts a noxious thing in itself?

"It was not disputed before your Lordships, nor before the Divisional Court that the 'Lightning Strike' is a weapon. Indeed, it is so described in its advertisement. Moreover, it was accepted in the Divisional Court and before your Lordships, that the electricity which is, to use a neutral word, released by the device is properly described, having regard to its effect upon the victim, as a 'noxious thing.' Thus, in essence, the sole issue for your Lordships' decision, is whether the Divisional Court was in error in deciding that there was no 'discharge' within the meaning of the subsection, when the device was operated.

"It was submitted to the Divisional Court on behalf of the respondent that the natural and ordinary meaning of 'discharge' denotes the physical ejection from the weapon of a physical object or substance which has been loaded into the weapon and which is contained within the weapon until it is ejected or released from it and electricity is not such an object. Accordingly, so it was submitted, although the word 'discharge' does have a particular meaning in relation to electricity, it must be interpreted in a way that is also appropriate in relation to liquids and gases, which are substances actually identified in the subsection. The word 'discharge' must therefore be limited to its wide general meaning noted by the justices. Kennedy J. accepted this submission and reluctantly concluded that applying the so-called wide general meaning, the weapon did not 'discharge' electricity. Parker L.J., with equal reluctance, concluded that the 'discharge' contemplated by the subsection involved the emission of something from the device, when the device was operated, and that this had not occurred.

"I do not share the difficulty experienced by the Divisional Court. If the so-called general, and non-technical meaning of the word 'discharge' is applied, to my mind it is quite clear that when the device is placed up against a human body or against the clothing of a human body and operated, electricity is then transferred from the device and passes through the human body. Electricity has thus been emitted from the device and it is this emission which has caused the victim to be stunned. In common parlance as the terms of the advertisement so clearly confirms the victim has received an electrical discharge, which discharge has resulted in his temporary immobilization.

"In the Divisional Court it appears that the appellant sought to support his contention that the word 'discharge' in section 5(1)(*b*) should be given its so-called technical meaning in relation to electricity, having regard to the terms of section 57(4). This provides:

> '"slaughtering instrument" means a firearm which is specially designed or adapted for the instantaneous slaughter of animals or for the instantaneous stunning of animals with a view to slaughtering them.'

"However, section 57(1) also defines the expression 'firearm' as meaning:

> 'a lethal barrelled weapon of any description from which any shot, bullet or other missile can be discharged and includes—
> (*a*) any prohibited weapon, whether it is such a lethal weapon as aforesaid or not; ...'

"This sends one back to section 5(1), because 'prohibited weapons' are those specified in that subsection. Thus it was said on behalf of the appellant that when defining 'slaughtering instrument' Parliament must have considered that some types of animal stunning devices to be weapons within the meaning of section 5(1)(*b*). However, if that be right, it produces a strange anomaly. Section 10(1), as amended by section 46 of, and paragraph 5 of Schedule 2 to, the Slaughterhouses Act 1974, provides that a person licensed under the Slaughterhouses Act 1974 may, without holding a certificate, have in his possession 'a slaughtering instrument.' Accordingly, if a stunning device used by a slaughterer comes within section 5(1)(*b*) then we have the surprising result that a slaughterer must obtain the authority of the Secretary of State to possess it, even though by virtue of section 10(1), he does not need to obtain a firearms certificate from the police. This seems hardly likely to have been the intention of Parliament and it may be thought desirable to take the opportunity provided by the Firearms (Amendment) Bill which is currently under consideration, to clarify this point. However, given that the word 'stunning' and the definition of 'slaughtering instrument' to be found in section 57 is of no assistance in the construction of the word 'discharge' in section 5(1)(*b*), this in no way, in my judgment, advances the respondent's case. I would accordingly answer the certified question as follows:

> 'A Lightning Strike hand-held electric stun device is capable of being a weapon designed to discharge a noxious thing contrary to section 5(1)(*b*) of the Firearms Act 1968.'

"Notwithstanding the existence of the Firearms (Amendment) Bill, your Lordships gave leave to appeal to your Lordships' House and expedited the hearing of this appeal, because of the great concern expressed by the appellant on behalf of the police authorities at the uncontrolled import and sale of these devices. If the decision at which I have arrived is acceptable to your Lordships, then there is no necessity for the proposed amendment to section 5(1)(*b*) of the Act stimulated by the observations of the Divisional Court and to be found in clause 1(3) of the Bill, viz. the addition of the following words at the end of section 5(1)(*b*) 'or for inflicting an electric shock.'

"For the reasons given I would allow the appeal, set aside the order of the Divisional Court, restore the adjudication of the justices and answer the questions which they raise and the certified question in the affirmative. I would further order that the costs of the appeal to the Divisional Court and to your Lordships' House be paid by the respondent to the appellant."

Appeal by prosecutor allowed.

NOTE

Quaere: Is the Lightning Strike an offensive weapon within the meaning of the 1953 Act? The point seems not to have been taken at all in the course of the appeal. In *Brown* v. *D.P.P., The Times*, March 27, 1992 it was held that the fact that due to some unknown fault an electric stun gun was not working did not change its character as a prohibited weapon.

Flail

4.10

(i) Glendinning v. Guild

4.10.1

1987 S.C.C.R. 304

G., [Glendinning], was in a public place with a flail which was formed with two pieces of lightweight wooden stick joined at one end by a chain. G. had the flail with him in a public place for he was on his way to a class in martial arts where he used the flail as part of his training. At his trial for possessing an offensive weapon in a public place it was not denied by G. that the item was an offensive weapon. G. was convicted and appealed.

Appeal allowed.

NOTE
The weapon was of a kind regarded as offensive *per se*: *Hemming* v. *Annan*, 1982 S.C.C.R. 432. The appeal in *Glendinning's* case is of more interest, however, in regard to the issue of reasonable excuse and the case is discussed *supra*, at para. 3.4.7.

(ii) Malnick v. D.P.P.

4.10.2

[1989] Crim.L.R. 451

M. was found in a public place to have with him a rice flail which was described as consisting of two pieces of wood joined by a chain. Such weapons were sometimes used in connection with martial arts in which M. had a long-standing interest and some expertise. At M.'s trial for possessing an offensive weapon in a public place it was conceded by the defence that rice flails were offensive weapons *per se*. M. was convicted and appealed.

Appeal dismissed.

NOTE
The live issue at M.'s trial was that of reasonable excuse and the case is discussed *supra*, at para. 3.2.12.

(iii) Copus v. D.P.P.

4.10.3

[1989] Crim.L.R. 577

The appellant was convicted of having an offensive weapon, contrary to s.1 of the 1953 Act. In protesting at the arrest of a friend he had deliberately provoked police officers to arrest him. In his boot was a rice flail—two pieces of wood, each about one foot long and approximately one inch thick, joined together by a chain six to eight inches long. In cross-examination a police officer gave evidence that such implements were used as weapons in martial arts. The appellant appealed to the Crown Court. The Crown Court dismissed his appeal, giving no reasons for its decision, but stated a case for the High Court. The Crown Court found (1) that the implement was an offensive weapon *per se* and (2) that the appellant had admitted to the police that he carried the implement for the purpose of causing injury to the person.

Held, dismissing the appeal, the conclusion that the weapon was offensive *per se* was legitimately reached on the evidence accepted by the recorder in conjunction with the nature of the article itself because the only evidence found acceptable was that such an implement is used as a weapon. No alternative use was put before the recorder and it was open to him to conclude that the implement was manufactured for the purpose for which it was customarily used. In the light of that conclusion, it was not necessary to decide upon the argument addressed to the Court on the admissibility of the alleged confession.

Per Watkins, L.J.: It would have been helpful of the recorder to have informed counsel at the end of the case, if not sooner, the conclusions which had been reached and the reasons therefore about the nature of the weapon and the admissibility of the confession. If that had been done, it need only have been done in a few sentences, it would have left no room for doubt as to the basis and no appeal would have been likely.

Appeal dismissed.

NOTE

Professor J. C. Smith has commented on this case: *ibid*., at p. 578. There he observes that in the present case the court did not take judicial notice of the fact that a rice flail is an offensive weapon but held only that there was evidence on which the trial court could find as a fact that this particular implement was made for causing injury to the person. The recorder had, as the Divisional Court found, rightly rejected a suggestion that he should take judicial notice that such implements are manufactured for use for flailing rice. It was therefore a question of fact; and the Divisional Court held that there was evidence on which he could properly find that the implement was an offensive weapon.

The onus of proving that the article is an offensive weapon is, of course, on the prosecution. The evidence before the trial court was that such implements are *used* as weapons and in connection with martial arts. But an article is not an offensive weapon by virtue of the fact that articles of that type are commonly used for causing injury to the person. Rolling-pins do not become offensive weapons *per se* because wives commonly use them for battering their husbands; rolling-pins are made for making pastry. The question is not what the article is used for, but what it is *made* for. Not surprisingly, there seems to have been no direct evidence of the purpose of the maker. Such evidence might be extremely difficult or impossible to obtain but that does not excuse the prosecution from proving the fact if it is, indeed, the fact in issue. If the article is properly called "a rice flail" one might reasonably expect that the maker manufactures it for the purpose of flailing rice. It was fairly observed in argument that the flailing of rice is not an activity practised in Woolwich (a matter of judicial notice?) but was the implement made in Woolwich, or anywhere in England? And, if it was made in England, was it for export to a rice-flailing country? If rice flails are manufactured in, and imported from, the East, it may well be that the purpose of the manufacturer is the flailing of rice and then it is, for the present purpose, immaterial that the purpose of the importer or the seller or buyer is that the implement shall be used for causing injury to the person. It may be that a better test would be "what is the article commonly used for?" The purpose of the maker seems to have little to do with the culpability of the carrier of the thing. But the law is plain that the article is an offensive weapon only if it was "made ... for use for causing injury" and that fact is not proved by evidence that it is commonly used for causing injury.

Hammer 4.11

Knox v. Anderton 4.11.1

(1983) 76 Cr.App.R. 156

K. was seen by a policeman to be standing on the landing of a building. The landing gave access to flats there. K. and another man were shouting abuse at one another. The policeman got himself between K. and the other man. K. had raised the hammer in an aggressive manner and he attempted to hit the other man. K. was arrested and charged with having with him in a public place an offensive weapon, namely a hammer, contrary to s.1(1) of the 1953 Act. At trial the only issue was whether the landing was a "public place" within the meaning of the 1953 Act. K. was convicted and appealed against that conviction.

Webster, J. (at p. 159)

"It was not disputed before the justices that on that date the defendant, when standing on an upper landing of a block of flats on the Langworthy Estate in Salford, had a claw hammer in his hand, and that this was an offensive weapon."

Appeal dismissed.

NOTE

For an example of a hammer as an offensive weapon see *Blair v. Friel*, 1993 G.W.D. 22–1364.

4.12   *Human head*

4.12.1   **R. v. Cockram**

The Times, June 8, 1992

C. appealed against sentence totalling 3¹/₂ years' imprisonment for offences of assault.

Boreham, J.
"The appellant head-butted a youth in the face ... as a result of which he lost three front teeth from the lower jaw and was permanently disfigured.

"As the Lord Chief Justice Taylor had stated during submissions on appeal, a head used violently against a face was a nasty weapon. The sentences were not open to criticism."

Appeal refused.

4.13   *Human teeth*

4.13.1   **R. v. Chadwick**

The Times, August 10, 1994

C. bit off another man's thumb through the distal phalanx and bit him on the nose and cheek.... . The recorder at Liverpool Crown Court ... accepted that the offence was serious but said that it was right to say that no weapon was used. C. was sentenced to two years' imprisonment. The Attorney-General sought leave on statutory authority to refer that sentence to the Court of Appeal as being in the circumstances unduly lenient. Leave was granted and the appeal was dealt with and C. sentenced to four years' imprisonment.

The Lord Chief Justice (Taylor)
"No previous relevant case gave assistance about the appropriate sentence to be imposed. The obvious reason was the rareness of the event. It seemed to be inhuman conduct. [The court disagreed with the view of the recorder.] The offender's use of his teeth as a pair of pincers to inflict disfiguring and permanent injury at point blank range was tantamount to using those teeth as a weapon."

Leave granted.

Knives 4.14

Butterfly knife 4.14.1

Grana v. Wilson 4.14.2

High Court of Justiciary, unreported, July 21, 1988

G. was in the back of a police car. A policeman saw G. pull an object from his trouser pocket and attempt to place it down behind the seat where he was sitting. The object was found to be a knife. G. was later charged with possessing an offensive weapon in a public place and after trial he was convicted. He was sentenced to three months' imprisonment and he appealed against sentence.

In his report the sheriff noted that there was no dispute that the knife was a "Class One" weapon in the same category as, for example, swords and flick knives. It was of a type used in martial arts and it was described by the policeman involved with the case as "more or less an unsprung flick knife."

The sheriff described the knife as being in two parts which were hinged to the blade at the end furthest away from the point. When the knife was closed, the two parts of the handle enfolded the blade, one on either side of it. To expose the blade, each part of the handle was folded back in an arc of 180 degrees so that the two parts joined together to form the handle proper. The blade itself was sharp and pointed. The hinges holding the two parts of the handle to the blade were very loose so that the knife could be opened, and the blade exposed, very quickly.

The sheriff cited *Smith v. Wilson*, 1987 S.C.C.R. 191, and his own dicta at p. 192 (cited *supra* at para. 5.7). Notwithstanding that the details of the present case differed somewhat from those in the case of *Smith v. Wilson*, it appeared to the sheriff that the reasoning expressed in the words cited applied in the present case just as it did in the earlier case.

Lord Grieve
"[Counsel for the appellant] submitted that what the sheriff had really done, was to look at the case of *Smith* (albeit he considered that it was not precisely on all fours with the present case) and reached the opinion that for offences of this nature, namely being found in possession of an offensive weapon in a car, the appropriate sentence, never mind the particular circumstances of the case, was a custodial one. It was said by the Lord Justice General, rightly in the case of *Smith*, that if the court was to alter the custodial sentence imposed in that case, it would simply be substituting its own opinion for that of the sheriff. That is not the function of the Court of Appeal.

"The sheriff has given his reasons, having regard to the particular facts in this case, for imposing the custodial sentence which he did. We cannot fault this approach and we consider he was fully entitled to take the course which he did."

Appeal refused.

NOTE

In *R.* v. *Higgins, The Times*, February 16, 1989, the appellant was a jewllery salesman who gave evidence that he used a butterfly knife found with him to cut into gold plate to show customers the depth of the plating. His appeal against conviction was set aside because of a procedural irregularity. Imprisonment was upheld in *Brown* v. *Friel*, 1995 G.W.D. 20–1132 where the appellant had with him a "particularly vicious" butterfly knife.

4.14.3   *Carving knife*

4.14.4   **R. v. Rapier**

(1980) 70 Cr.App.R. 17

R. became involved in an altercation outside a nightclub. The evidence indicated that he left and returned a short time later with a carving knife. He was charged with having with him in a public place an offensive weapon.

At trial the judge directed the jury *inter alia* that a carving knife was not of itself an offensive weapon; it was made for the perfectly ordinary and legitimate use of carving food. The prosecution required to show that the accused had the necessary intent at the relevant time. R. was convicted and appealed against conviction.

Appeal allowed.

NOTE

This case is discussed more extensively *supra* at para. 3.7.7 in relation to the definition of offensive weapons in terms of s.1(4) of the 1953 Act.

4.14.5   *Clasp knife*

4.14.6   **Bates v. Bulman**

[1979] 3 All E.R. 170

Bates [B.] assaulted A. in a street by slapping and punching him. B. then asked C. to hand him an unopened clasp knife which B. intended to use to injure A. That knife was given to B. who opened it and held it against A.'s head. The knife was not used, it seems, to cause any injury to A.

B. was charged with a contravention of s.1(1) of the 1953 Act. In convicting B. the magistrates found that the clasp knife was not made or adapted for use for causing injury to the person. B. appealed against conviction.

Appeal allowed.

NOTE

This case is discussed further *supra* at para. 3.4.4 in relation to s.1(1) of the 1953 Act.

Cut throat razor	**4.14.7**
R. v. Petrie	**4.14.8**

[1961] 1 All E.R. 466

For the facts see above at para. 3.3.2.

Salmon, J. (at p. 468)
"Counsel for the Crown has very fairly said that that [a direction to the jury at trial] cannot be supported because he cannot argue that a razor is an offensive weapon within the meaning of the Act, unless it is proved by the Crown that it was carried in a public place with the intention of injuring some person."

And later (at p. 469)
"It is clear that, as already indicated, there was abundant evidence that the appellant was carrying this razor with the intent necessary to make it an offensive weapon within the meaning of the Act. Indeed, if a man is found carrying a razor in a public place, there is at any rate some evidence on which a jury could say that he had the necessary intent. It would be entirely a matter for the jury."

Appeal allowed.

Double-edged knife	**4.14.9**
Mir v. Normand	**4.14.10**

1993 S.C.C.R. 654

M. was convicted of a breach of the peace and of having an offensive weapon contrary to the Prevention of Crime Act 1953.

He admitted a previous conviction for the latter offence, for which he had been fined £50 in 1992. The weapon in question was a double-edged knife with a blade seven and a half inches long, honed to "a quite remarkable sharpness." The sheriff sentenced the appellant to six months' imprisonment and recommended his deportation on the ground of the gravity of the offence. The appellant appealed to the High Court against the recommendation.

Held, that the question was whether or not the potential detriment to this country of the appellant remaining here was such as to justify the recommendation and that the sheriff had applied the correct test and was entitled to make the recommendation; and appeal refused.

In his report the sheriff (McKay) stated [at p. 655] *inter alia*:

"The weapon produced in this particular case was nothing short of murderous. The blade alone was seven and a half inches long, straight, double edged and sharply pointed. Each edge had been honed to a quite remarkable sharpness. Even when exercising considerable care in examining it, I nearly cut myself and I must warn your Lordships that I believe the blade to be bloodstained with what may be the appellant's own blood. The blade was also very thin. In these circumstances I concluded that a relatively modest blow would have driven it far into the body of any person whom it might strike."

4.14.11   *Flick knife*

4.14.12   **(i) R. v. Allamby and Medford**

[1974] 3 All E.R. 126

For the facts see *supra* at para. 3.14.3.

Roskill, L.J. (at p. 128)

"The flick knife was an offensive weapon per se in that it was made for use for causing injury to the person."

Appeal allowed (on other grounds).

4.14.13   **(ii) Tudhope v. O'Neill**

1982 S.C.C.R. 45

O'N. was arrested in a street following an incident outside a public house. He was searched and a flick knife was found in his jacket pocket. The knife had a decorative handle and it was closed at the time it was found.

O'N. was charged with having with him in a public place an offensive weapon, namely a flick knife. At trial the sheriff held that the flick knife was not made or adapted for causing personal injury. In the absence of any evidence of intention to use it for personal injury the charge was found not proven.

The Crown appealed against acquittal. In the stated case the sheriff made no findings about the nature of the knife, save to call it a flick knife.

Lord Justice-Clerk (Wheatley) (at p. 47)

"The respondent was charged with and acquitted of a contravention of section 1(1) of the Prevention of Crime Act 1953. The offensive weapon libelled in the charge was a flick knife, which was found in a pocket of a denim jacket which the respondent was wearing in a public place. All that is said about the flick knife itself in the findings in fact is that it had a decorative handle and was closed at the time. The submission of the Crown at the trial was that the automatic action of a flick knife and the fact that a flick knife was an illegal weapon in terms of the Restrictions of Offensive Weapons Act 1959 established that a flick knife was an offensive weapon made for causing injury to the person in terms of the definition in section 1(4) of the 1953 Act. The sheriff rejected that submission and acquitted the respondent, and it is against that decision that this appeal has been taken.

"The learned advocate-depute repeated that submission, and in our view did so effectively. He acknowledged that the Crown had to rely on the submission that a flick knife was per se an offensive weapon within the meaning of the Act, since in the circumstances neither of the other two definitions of an offensive weapon was applicable here. He maintained, however, that the nature of the weapon itself, by reason of its spring mechanism which allowed it to be used quickly in an emergency, clearly indicated that it was made for causing injury to the person. In contrast to such things as a skean-dhu or a kitchen knife or a penknife it had no other ostensible purpose. In further support of his submission he referred to the terms of the Restriction of Offensive Weapons Act 1959 and in particular the long title thereof, and two English cases. The long title of the 1959 Acts reads: 'An Act to amend the law in relation to the making and disposing and importation of flick knives and other dangerous weapons.' Section 1(1) makes it an offence inter alia to manufacture a flick knife, the mechanism of which is set out.

"The only argument put forward by counsel for the respondent was that although he personally recognised that a flick knife had the features ascribed to it by the advocate-depute, there was no finding in fact setting these out.

"We find the primary argument of the advocate-depute sufficient in itself to establish its soundness. It finds fortification in the 1959 Act and the two English cases to which we shall shortly refer. It does not seem difficult to accept that an article which Parliament has described and categorised as a dangerous weapon, illegal to make, is an offensive weapon per se within the meaning of section 1 of the 1953 Act. That was the view albeit obiter that Lord Goddard C.J. took in *Woodward* v *Koessler* [1958] 1 W.L.R. 1255 at p. 1256 and James L.J. per expressum took in *R.* v *Allamby* [1974] 1 W.L.R. 1494 at 1496–7. As Parliament has given it a statutory description in the 1959 Act we do not consider it necessary to have a finding in fact about the mechanism of a flick knife. We accordingly answer both questions of law in the negative and remit the case back to the sheriff to proceed as accords."

Appeal allowed.

4.14.14   **(iii) R. v. McCogg**

[1982] Crim.L.R. 685

M. was indicted for having with him in a public place an offensive weapon contrary to s.1 of the 1953 Act. The facts, which were not in dispute, were that he was searched by a police officer on suspicion of possessing cannabis; that in his pocket was found a flick knife; and that he had refused to answer any questions about it. On the morning of the trial defending counsel, who had taken over the case the evening before happened by chance to consult Brownlie's *Law Relating to Public Order* (1968) and found, at p. 17, a reference to the fact that spring-clip knives, to use the proper technical term, were employed extensively by fishermen, farmers, butchers and electricians. For this proposition Brownlie cited an article on flick knifes in [1959] Crim.L.R. 640, at p. 641, by Captain Athelstan Popkess, Chief Constable of Nottingham City Police. Accordingly, counsel sought an adjournment to inquire as to the possibility of obtaining expert evidence on the point but conceded the inquiry would be speculative. Alternatively, he invited the court to take judicial notice as to the proposition. Acknowledging the difficulty in which the defence were placed, the learned recorder nevertheless refused to grant either application, the first mainly on the grounds of further probably unmerited expense and the delay which had already elapsed since the original incident. No criticism attached to the defence for not alighting on the point until just before the trial; on the contrary, counsel was to be commended for his researches.

The defence was, therefore, run in this way. The question whether a particular article was an offensive weapon *per se* being exclusively a jury issue (*Williamson* (1977) 67 Cr.App.R. 35), counsel submitted to the jury that if they were satisfied that the flick knife had been "made ... for causing injury to the person" (s.1(4)), they should convict. If they were not so satisfied, then, in view of M.'s silence there being no evidence that he "intended ... having it with him for such use by him" (*ibid.*), they should acquit. In inviting the jury to consider whether they could be satisfied beyond reasonable doubt that the knife was made for causing injury defending counsel formulated his submissions more or less as follows: "From your knowledge and experience of matters you may think, Ladies and Gentlemen—particularly some of you gentlemen—that spring-clip knives have a long and respectable tradition of use in many honourable and lawful occupations and crafts. You may think that they have long been used by fishermen, farmers, butchers and electricians. Is this nothing more than a lazy man's clasp knife, essential where one hand is often by necessity occupied or where your nails have been worn down, for example by ropes?" Counsel also observed that although it was now unlawful to sell, hire or give away such knives, by virtue of legislation enacted following the bad press they had received in the late 1950s, it was still perfectly lawful to import them from countries where they might well be manufactured for non-violent purposes.

In a very short summing-up the learned recorder expressly adopted all defending counsel's submissions and after a fairly lengthy retirement the jury returned a verdict of not guilty.

Found not guilty.

(iv) Gibson v. Wales 4.14.15

[1983] 1 All E.R. 869

W. was charged with having with him in a public place an offensive weapon namely a flick knife. Magistrates acquitted W. on the basis that the prosecution had not proved that at the relevant time it was W.'s intention to use the flick knife to cause injury to the person. The prosecution appealed.

Griffiths, L.J. (at p. 870)

"The question before this court is posed as follows: whether a flick knife as defined in the Restriction of Offensive Weapons Act 1959 is an offensive weapon made or adapted for use for causing injury to the person, and therefore an offensive weapon per se contrary to s.1(1) of the Prevention of Crime Act 1953.

"The facts of this case, very shortly, are as follows. At 12.10 am on 14 October 1981 two police officers were on duty when they saw the respondent, who was in Curzon Street, a public place, take a knife from the back pocket of his trousers and operate it, showing it to two youths. He handed the knife to one of the youths who himself operated it, and then he put it back in his pocket. He was approached by the two policemen who asked him what he was doing there, and he answered that he was waiting for a girlfriend in order to give her a coat to keep her warm on the way home. He said that his only worry was that she would come out linked with some other bloke and there would be a riot. When asked what he meant, he said he would not start any trouble there but would wait until he got her back to Brierfield. He was questioned about the knife and he produced it. It was seen to be a flick knife. He was asked for an explanation. He replied by saying he had no explanation. He was not sure if he was allowed to have it. He was then arrested for having with him in a public place an offensive weapon.

"The magistrates, having heard argument, came to the conclusion that this flick knife was not what is commonly referred to as an offensive weapon per se, ie that within the meaning of s.1(4) of the Prevention of Crime Act 1953 it was not an article made or adapted for use for causing injury to the person. Having arrived at that conclusion they then went on to consider whether the prosecution had satisfied them that this young man had it on his person with the intention of using it for an offensive purpose, and they concluded that the prosecution had not discharged that burden of proof. Accordingly, they acquitted the young man of the offence.

"We have been told by this court that if we do answer the question in the affirmative and say that the magistrates should have found the flick knife to be an offensive weapon per se, nevertheless, the prosecution do not invite us to return the case to the magistrates. What the prosecution seek is guidance from this court on the very important question as to the category of offensive weapon into which the flick knife falls. Does it fall to be considered as an offensive weapon per se in that it is an article made or adapted for causing injury, or does it fall into the second category, namely a weapon which the prosecution have to prove in every case is being carried for an offensive purpose before a conviction can be secured?

"Anybody who has had the experience of travelling around the country trying serious crimes, as Her Majesty's judges have, will readily appreciate the dangerous nature of such a weapon and how frequently it is used to inflict fearful injuries. A flick knife is a singularly dangerous weapon because it can be held concealed in the hand in the course of a quarrel which may start with fisticuffs and suddenly be released and used before the other party engaged in the fight has any chance whatever to appreciate that he is to be attacked by a man with a knife.

"The attitude of Parliament to flick knives is revealed by the terms of a special statute designed to deal with flick knives. The Act is the Restriction of Offensive Weapons Act 1959. It is headed: 'An Act to amend the law in relation to the making and disposing and importation of flick knives and other dangerous weapons.' Section 1 reads as follows:

'(1) Any person who manufactures, sells or hires or offers for sale or hire, ... or lends or gives to any other person—(a) any knife which has a blade which opens automatically by hand pressure applied to a button, spring or other device in or attached to the handle of the knife, sometimes known as a "flick knife" or "flick gun" ... shall be guilty of an offence and shall be liable on summary conviction in the case of a first offence to imprisonment for a term not exceeding three months or to a fine not exceeding fifty pounds ...'

"It is interesting to observe that, stringent though that protection was, it was then further extended by Parliament by the Restriction of Offensive Weapons Act 1961. That Act provided that in addition to anybody who sold or offered for sale a flick knife, anybody who exposed or had in his possession for the purposes of sale or hire a flick knife was guilty of an offence.

"The effect of those two statutes was to absolutely outlaw flick knives, but it is interesting to note a significant omission. There is nothing in the statutes which makes it an offence to possess a flick knife. The only intelligible explanation for that is that Parliament must have considered that that position was adequately catered for by the provisions of the 1953 Act on the assumption that nobody could realistically consider that a flick knife was other than a dangerous weapon made for an offensive purpose. Accordingly, anybody who carried one on his person in a public place could be prosecuted under the 1953 Act. But the submission that attracted the magistrates in this case was founded on a decision of this court in *R* v. *Williamson* (1977) 67 Cr.App. 35. That was a case in which a judge had directed a jury that they should convict a man who had been found in possession of a sheath knife in a public place on the ground that a sheath knife was an offensive weapon per se. The court held that it was a question of fact for the jury in every case to decide into which class the weapon found on the accused fell. Was it to be considered an offensive weapon per se because it was made or adapted for this purpose, or did it fall into the latter category, namely a weapon that they were able to show was in his possession for an offensive purpose?

"The distinction is a very important one because, if the weapon is considered an offensive weapon per se, the burden falls on the accused to show that he has a lawful excuse for having it on him. But, if it is not an offensive weapon per se, then the burden is on the prosecution to prove that he had this particular weapon for an offensive purpose. The court there held that in the case of a sheath knife the matter must be left to the jury. This is, of course, readily understandable because almost every boy scout has a sheath knife, and indeed, many cubs and girl guides and one can readily appreciate that sheath knives are not made specifically for the purpose of being used as offensive weapons. In giving the judgment of the court Geoffrey Lane LJ said (at 38–39):

'It was for the jury to decide whether a weapon held by the defendant was an offensive weapon, bearing in mind the definition in the section which I have just read [s.1(4) of the Prevention of Crime Act 1953]. Consequently, whether the object in the possession of the defendant in any case can properly be described as an offensive weapon is a matter not for the judge but for the jury to decide. The jury must determine whether they feel sure that the object was made or adapted for use in causing injury to the person or was intended by the person having it with him for such use by him. There may be circumstances in which it is possible to say there is no evidence to the contrary in a particular case, but that is not the case here. If there is such a case, then in those circumstances the judge might, unobjectionably, direct the jury in those terms, but those cases must be rare. In normal cases of this sort, it remains a question for the jury, although the judge, after proper warnings to the jury, may add his own views in the subject.'

"It is also interesting to note that the views of Salmon J in an earlier case set out a number of objects which the judge clearly considered would obviously fall into the category of weapons which that judge clearly considered would that were offensive per se. In *R v Petrie* [1961] 1 All ER 466 at 468 ... Salmon J said:

'It is clear that the definition section of the Act [s.1(4) of the Prevention of Crime Act 1953] contemplates offensive weapons of, at any rate, two classes, namely,
  (a) an article which per se is an offensive weapon, that is to say, an article made or adapted for use for causing injury to the person; and
  (b) an article which, though it is not made or adapted for such use, is carried with the intent so to use it. A cosh, a knuckleduster, and a revolver are examples of articles in the first class. A sandbag and a razor are examples of articles in the second class.'

"If a cosh or a knuckleduster is an offensive weapon per se, then so too should a flick knife be considered.

"In my view, taking into account the views of the community as expressed by Parliament in the 1959 Act as amended by the 1961 Act, the time has now come when it must be appreciated that there is no reasonable alternative to the view that a flick knife is a dangerous weapon per se. It is made for the purpose of causing injury to the person. It may sometimes be used for wholly innocent purposes, even possessed for wholly innocent purposes, but there will be a very heavy burden on any person in possession of a flick knife to satisfy any court that he had it for such an innocent purpose. I would say that the magistrates here on the facts of this case fell into error and that a flick knife is now to be regarded as an offensive weapon per se for the purposes of s.1(1) of the Prevention of Crime Act 1953."

McCullough, J. (at p. 872)
"Whether a flick knife is an article made for use for causing injury to the person is a question of fact, but in my judgment it is a question which admits of one answer: it is.

"For the reasons given by Griffiths LJ I take this to have been the view held by Parliament in 1953 and 1961 and to be beyond argument. I too would allow this appeal."

Appeal allowed.

(v) R. v. Simpson 4.14.16

[1983] 3 All E.R. 789

S. was charged with having with him in a public place an offensive weapon, namely a flick knife. After trial by judge and jury he was convicted and he appealed against that conviction.

Lord Lane, C.J. (at p. 790)

"It was admitted at the trial that the appellant was in possession of the flick knife and in possession of it in a public place. In the event, after submissions made to the judge which we shall describe shortly, he raised as his defence reasonable excuse for the possession of that weapon, the flick knife, on the basis that he had it in his possession for nothing more sinister than the carrying out of electrical repairs to his motor car. This defence was, as is apparent, rejected by the jury.

"It was not contended before the jury by counsel for the defence that the weapon was other than one made for use for causing injury to the person. The reason for that matter was this. At the close of the prosecution case defending counsel sought an indication from the judge whether he, the judge, considered it to be open to the defendant to argue that the flick knife was not made for such use, or, as it is sometimes called, was not offensive per se. The judge held that on the authority of the decision of the Divisional Court in *Gibson v Wales* [1983] 1 All ER 869 ... that defence was not open to the defendant.

"The appellant now contends before us, through the arguments of his counsel, that the judge was in error in that conclusion and he submits that this court should not follow the decision of the Divisional Court in *Gibson v Wales*. That sets the scene for the appeal.

"It is necessary first of all to turn to the provisions of the Prevention of Crime Act 1953, on the interpretation of which, in the end, the decision of this court must be based. Section 1(1) reads:

> 'Any person who without lawful authority or reasonable excuse, the proof whereof shall lie on him, has with him in any public place any offensive weapon shall be guilty of an offence ...'

"Section 1(4) contains a definition of 'offensive weapon', and it is in these terms:

> '"offensive weapon" means any article made or adapted for use for causing injury to the person, or intended by the person having it with him for such use by him.'

"'If one analyses the words of the definition, there are three possible categories of offensive weapon. First of all the weapon made for use for causing injury to the person, that is a weapon offensive per se as it is called, for instance a bayonet, a stiletto or a handgun. The second category is the weapon which is adapted for such a purpose: the example usually given is the bottle deliberately broken in order that the jagged end may be inserted into the victim's face.

The third category is an object not so made or adapted, but one which the person carrying intends to use for the purpose of causing injury to the person.

"The question, simple to state but like most questions simple to state not so easy to answer, is whether the flick knife comes within the first category or not; and the subsidiary question is: if it does come within the category, in what terms should the judge direct the jury?

"The flick knife is an easily recognisable object. It has as a matter of fact been conveniently defined in s1(1)(*a*) of the Restriction of Offensive Weapons Act 1959 as—

> 'any knife which has a blade which opens automatically by hand pressure applied to a button, spring or other device in or attached to the handle of the knife, sometimes known as a "flick knife" or "flick gun" …'

"We observe in passing that the 1959 Act and its 1961 counterpart (which was passed in order to fill up a gap in the 1959 Act which was disclosed by *Fisher v Bell* [1960] 3 All ER 731 …) were designed to prohibit the importation, sale, display for sale and so on of flick knives in this country, the reason being that there had been a whole bevy of cases in which flick knives had been used often with lethal effect in affrays and brawls, and the public was, not unnaturally, alarmed. Parliament acted in order to allay such alarm. But the fact that Parliament and the public in general justifiably regarded this weapon and its use with that alarm does not necessarily mean that they are made for use for causing injury to the person.

"Griffiths LJ who delivered the leading judgment in *Gibson v Wales* … to which we have already referred, came to this conclusion:

> '… there is no alternative to the view that a flick knife is a dangerous weapon per se. It is made for the purpose of causing injury to the person. It may sometimes be used for wholly innocent purposes, even possessed for innocent purposes, but there will be a very heavy burden on any person in possession of a flick knife to satisfy any court that he had it for such an innocent purpose. I would say that the justices here on the facts of this case fell into error and that a flick knife is now to be regarded as an offensive weapon per se for the purpose of s1(1) of the Prevention of Crime Act 1953.'

"McCullough J, the other member of the court had this to say (at 872):

> 'Whether a flick knife is an article made for use for causing injury to the person is a question of fact, but in my judgment

it is a question which admits of only one answer: it is. For the reasons given by Griffiths LJ I take this to have been the view held by Parliament in 1953 and 1961 and to be beyond argument. I too would allow this appeal.'

"The opposing argument put forward is based on what was said by this court in *R v Williamson* (1977) 67 CrAppR 35. That was a case of a sheath knife, where obviously very different considerations apply from those which affect the position of a flick knife. It would plainly be impossible to classify all sheath knives as either offensive per se or not offensive per se, and in those circumstances the matter was plainly a question for the jury. But does a flick knife fall within the words used in *R v Williamson* (at 38):

'But what is sometimes lost sight of is this. It is for the jury to decide these matters. It is for the jury to decide whether a weapon held by the defendant was an offensive weapon, bearing in mind the definition in the section which I have just read. Consequently whether the object in the possession of the defendant in any case can properly be described as an offensive weapon is a matter not for the judge but for the jury to decide. The jury must determine whether they feel sure that the object was made or adapted for use in causing injury to the person or was intended by the person having it with him for such use by him. There may perhaps be circumstances in which it is possible to say that there is no evidence to the contrary in a particular case. But that is not the case here.'

"What has to be decided first of all is whether the flick knife falls within that exclusion which was put forward as possible in *R v Williamson*. It has first to be observed that the mere fact that a particular weapon can be, and perhaps often is, used for an innocent purpose does not necessarily take it out of the offensive per se category. That is the reason why we emphasise 'made' in the definition in the Prevention of Crime Act 1953, which I have read. For instance a bayonet may be used to poke the fire, a stiletto may be used as a letter knife, and indeed a hand-gun to shoot vermin. They remain nevertheless in the first category: they are 'made for use for causing injury to the person.'

"We have had our attention drawn to an article by Captain Athelstan Popkess CBE, Chief Constable of Nottingham City Police (1959) CrimLR 640). The passage to which our attention has been directed is in the following terms (at 641):

'As a matter of interest, flick knives are not manufactured in this country but are all imported. The German article is generally a useful knife. The Italian one, on the other hand, has no cutting edge but is exclusively a stiletto—it is only fair to say, however, that many of these are only meant to be used as paper-knives. Few chief constables are of the opinion that workers would be seriously handicapped if the sale of the knives were banned altogether. Fishermen, on the other hand, commonly use them; as do many miners and agricultural workers. But, in general, mining, farming and fishing areas report little or no use being made of these knives by tradesmen. One chief constable points out that if their use was really essential, British manufacturers would have been making them long since.'

"The second half of that passage seems to contradict the first. In any event it is the purpose for which they are made, not that for which they may be used, which is the question.

"The other volume to which counsel for the appellant drew out attention was Brownlie's *Law Relating to Public Order and National Security* (1968) p. 67. The passage to which our attention was drawn runs as follows:

'*What are offensive weapons?*—Section 1(4) [of the 1953 Act] defines "offensive weapon" to mean "any article made or adapted for use for causing injury to the person, or intended by the person have it with him for such use by him". The first class of articles are those *made* for the prime purpose of causing injury to the person. This includes bludgeons, clubs, bayonets, daggers, firearms (other than those commonly used for gaming), coshes, and knuckledusters. It is sometimes assumed that flick knives are within this class [He cites (1959) 123 JP Jo 370, and (1958) 121 JP Jo 733, to which we need not refer. He goes on:] In fact, knives of this type, more properly called spring clip knives, are used extensively by farmers, fishermen, butchers and electricians.'

"For that he cites as the second source the article by Captain Athelstan Popkess to which we have already referred and criticism of which we have already made.

"Our attention has also been drawn to a passage in the Third Supplement to Archbold's *Pleading, Evidence and Practice in Criminal Cases* (41st edn 1982) para. 19–250 which reads as follows:

'In *Gibson v. Wales* it was held that although the question whether a flick knife (as defined in section 1(1)(a) of the Restriction of Offensive Weapons Act 1959 ...) was made for use for causing injury to the person was a question of fact (see *R. v. Williamson* ...), it was a question to which there was only one answer—such a weapon was an offensive weapon *per se.* It is submitted that this decision, not binding on the Crown Court, is unlikely to be approved by the House of Lords. There are many situations where it may be a matter of life or death for a sailor to be able to cut a rope instantly. While a sheath knife will often suffice, there are occasions, for example when wearing wet weather gear and safety harness, when a flick knife in an outside pocket would be preferable. How the Court could say that either as a matter of law or as an irresistible inference of fact a tribunal must decide that a flick knife (perhaps constructed in a country where their sale is legal) was "made for use for causing injury to the person" is difficult to understand.'

"If that paragraph is correct, then doubtless a sailor who had a flick knife in his pocket would in any event be able to establish a good defence of reasonable excuse.

"It is interesting to note on the other side of the coin that the court in *R* v *Allanby* [1974] 3 All ER 126 ... assumed that the flick knife was an offensive weapon per se. It was a powerful court consisting of Roskill, James, LJJ and Caulfield J. James LJ delivered the judgment of the court, in the course of which he said (... at 128 ...):

'The flick knife was an offensive weapon per se in that it was made for use for causing injury to the person. The other knives were not. [There were other knives involved which were not flick knives.] If the jury found the fact to be that the defendants were jointly in possession of that knife, there was no defence to the charge.'

"It seems that in that case the contrary was not argued, but that passage shows what the immediate reaction of that particular court was to the proposition that we are now examining.

"There is a further decision in *R* v *Lawrence (Rodney)* (1971) 57 CrAppR 64 where a similar assumption seems to have been made by the court.

"This is one of the areas where there is great scope of unevenness in the administration of the law. If it is to be left in each case to a jury to decide whether or not a flick knife is an offensive weapon per se, the identical weapon may be the subject of different decisions by different juries.

"It is perhaps convenient to read a passage from *Cross on Evidence* (5th edn, 1979), p 160, which appears to be apposite to this consideration. It is under the heading, 'Judicial Notice' and under the sub-heading, 'Rationale'. It runs as follows:

'There are at least two reasons why we should have a doctrine of judicial notice. In the first place, it expedites the hearing of many cases. Much time would be wasted if every fact which was not admitted had to be the subject of evidence which would, in many instances, be costly and difficult to obtain. Secondly, the doctrine tends to produce uniformity of decision on matters of fact where a diversity of findings might sometimes be distinctly embarrassing.'

"It is never easy to say where the line should be drawn in this type of situation. This court has held that the category into which a sheath knife falls is a matter for the jury (see *R v Williamson*) because in effect it depends on the sort of knife which was in the sheath. We think that the flick knife falls on the other side of the line and that these knives do come into the category of weapons which are offensive per se, namely the first category which is raised by the definition in s1(4) of the 1953 Act. These weapons are plainly designed by the manufacturers to be carried conveniently in the hand or in the pocket and there concealed, to be brought into use with the minimum of delay to the assailant and the minimum of warning to the victim. There is no pause while the blade is pulled out from the handle against the spring or is removed from its sheath by hand. By their very design in this way they betray the purpose for which they were made.

"We are reinforced in that view by a Scottish decision to which we have been referred, *Tudhope v O'Neill* 1982 SLT 360 at 361. In the course of the judgment the judge, who is anonymous as is the rest of the court, said:

'The learned advocate-depute repeated that submission, and in our view did do effectively. He acknowledged that the Crown had to rely on the submission that a flick knife was per se an offensive weapon within the meaning of the [Prevention of Crime Act 1953], since in the circumstances neither of the other two definitions of an offensive weapon was applicable here. He maintained, however, that the nature of the weapon itself, by reason of its spring mechanism which allowed it to be used quickly in an emergency, clearly indicated that it was made for causing injury to the person. In contrast to such things as a sgian dhubh or a kitchen knife or a penknife it has no other ostensible purpose.'

"That submission was accepted by the High Court of Justiciary in Scotland.

"In a commentary on *Gibson v Wales* Professor J C Smith points out that it is of importance in the Crown Court, though for obvious reasons not in the magistrates' court, to decide whether this matter should be approached by the judge on the basis that judicial notice is taken of the fact that the flick knife is offensive per se, or whether on the other hand the nature of the knife itself constitutes overwhelming evidence that it should be held to be offensive per se (see [1983] CrimLR 113). The professor points out that in *Gibson v Wales* it seems that on this particular point Griffiths LJ took the view that it was a matter of judicial notice whereas McCullough J was of the contrary view.

"In the former case, if it is a matter of judicial notice, then of course the judge is entitled to direct the jury to find the weapon to be offensive per se. In the latter case, so argues Professor Smith in his commentary at any rate, on the authority of the majority speeches in the House of Lords in *DPP v Stonehouse* [1977] 2 All ER 909 ... the matter must be left to the jury to reach, if they so wish, what in the circumstances appears to be a perverse verdict.

"Once one reaches the conclusion, as we have done, that a knife proved to be a flick knife necessarily is one made for use for causing injury to the person, we take the view that this is a matter of which judicial notice can be taken and the jury can be directed accordingly. That is what we believe Griffiths LJ intended and we respectfully agree with his conclusion in all aspects of his judgment.

"This means that the passage which we have cited from the Third Supplement to Archbald is misleading. The editors might like to consider making the necessary amendments to that."

Appeal dismissed.

4.14.17   **(vi) Smith v. Wilson**

1987 S.C.C.R. 191

S. pleaded guilty to having with him in a public place an offensive weapon, namely a flick knife. He was sentenced to imprisonment and he appealed against the sentence as excessive.

Lord Justice-General (Emslie) (at p. 193)
"It has to be said that the offensive weapon in question was a flick knife in which the blade is retracted into the handle and springs out at the touch of a button ..."

Appeal refused.

NOTE
This case is discussed further *infra*, at para. 5.7 in relation to sentencing principles.

Gurkha or khukri knife 4.14.18

Jessop v. Murphy 4.14.19

Glasgow District Court, unreported, November 15, 1989

Late one evening M. was seen by a policeman to have a knife in the waistband of his trousers. The policeman approached M. who swore at him and ran away. M. was caught by the policeman and a colleague. They searched M. and found the knife after a struggle. That knife was a large "Gurkha" or "khukri" type knife, 22 inches long with a sharp curving blade some two inches wide.

M. was cautioned and charged with possessing an offensive weapon in a public place. He replied "I am sorry." After trial M. was convicted of that charge and fined £150.

M. appealed against conviction. In the note to the stated case the stipendiary magistrate held that the knife, being a Gurhka or khukri type knife, was *per se* an offensive weapon. Further, he held that if he was incorrect in that conclusion then on the facts M. did not have the knife with him for an innocent purpose but for causing personal injury.

Found guilty.

NOTE

Murphy appealed against conviction but when the appeal called in the High Court of Justiciary he failed to appear and the appeal fell "for want of insistence." The offensive weapon in the sentence appeal of *Falconer* v. *Lees*, 1993 G.W.D. 13–872 was a "kukri." The military theme was clear in *Ross* v. *Lowe*, 1991 G.W.D. 10–597 where the appellant received six months' imprisonment for having a bayonet.

Kitchen knife 4.14.20

(i) Macnab v. McDonald 4.14.21

(1972) S.C.C.R. Supp. 28

McD. was charged with a breach of the peace and having with him in a public place a knife contrary to s.1(1) of the 1953 Act. After trial he was convicted of charge one but charge two was found not proven. The Crown appealed by stated case.

The sheriff made the following findings in fact in the stated case, *viz.*:

"1. On Sunday, 31st October 1971, two police officers were on motor patrol duty when just after midnight they received instructions to investigate a gang of boys fighting in Wallace Square, Greenock. Their information was that weapons were being used.

2. At said Wallace Square the said police officers heard a man shouting who then went off westwards along Hamilton Street. The police officers followed and drove westwards along Hamilton Street.

3. Hamilton Street continues westwards till it reaches the junction with Westburn Street which runs roughly north and south. West of that junction the street becomes West Blackhall Street and continues westwards through the town.

4. At the corner of the junction of West Blackhall Street and Westburn Street, on the south side of the junction, the police officers observed a group of four boys standing. The said group of four boys were the respondents; all four respondents were together.

5. The said four respondents were all shouting at a group of boys and girls who were walking eastwards along the north side of West Blackhall Street.

6. All four respondents were heard shouting 'Young Strone rule' and 'F..k off you bastards' at this group of boys and girls across the street.

7. As the police officers drove westwards along Hamilton Street they were able to observe the fourth respondent, Edward Ferns McDonald, was waving a knife. The blade of the knife glinted in the headlights of the police motor-car. As the police officers drove up to the four respondents they observed the fourth respondent, the said Edward Ferns McDonald, drop said knife into the gutter.

8. The police officers drove up to where the said four respondents were standing and apprehended all of them.

9. The police officers then found said knife, which the respondent McDonald had been waving, lying in the gutter near to where the respondent McDonald had been standing. It was a vegetable knife; it was not touched or altered in any way. The said knife was not used or required to be used by the respondent in connection with any employment or task that he was undertaking that night.

10. The said four respondents were taken to the police station where they were cautioned and charged. The first, second and third respondents were charged with breach of the peace as libelled, to which charge each of said three respondents replied 'I never did nothing'.

11. The fourth respondent, the said Edward Ferns McDonald, was charged with breach of the peace as libelled, to which charge he made no reply. He was also charged with a contravention of section 1(1) of the Prevention of Crime Act 1953, to which charge he replied 'Not guilty'.
12. The said knife was lodged as a production and is marked Label 1. It was identified by the two police officers as the knife found in the gutter near to where the respondent was standing."

In his note the sheriff stated:

"All that the evidence established was that the respondent was seen waving a knife and that when he realised the police were approaching he dropped it in the gutter. At the time the respondent was one of a group of four shouting at another small group of boys and girls across the street. There was nothing in the evidence to show the respondent did anything beyond shouting and waving the knife.

"The knife in question clearly comes within the third category on the definition of offensive weapon as contained in the Prevention of Crime Act 1953, section 1(4). In that situation it was for the Crown to prove beyond reasonable doubt that the knife was intended by the respondent for use for causing injury to the person. In my view the Crown did not do so. While the circumstances certainly raised a suspicion, the evidence led did not, in my view, establish that intention on the part of the respondent."

The question for the opinion of the High Court was:

"On the facts stated, would I have been justified in inferring that the knife was intended for causing injury to the person?"

When the appeal was heard in the High Court no formal opinion was delivered, although their Lordships indicated that on the facts stated the sheriff should have inferred that the knife was intended for use for causing injury; and case remitted back to the sheriff to proceed as accords.

Appeal allowed.

(ii) Lopez v. MacNab 4.14.22

1978 J.C. 41

For the facts and circumstances in which a kitchen knife was in the possession of a person in a public place see *supra*, at para. 3.7.6.

Appeal refused.

4.14.23   *Lock knife*

4.14.24   **(i) Patterson v. Block**

The Times, June 21, 1984

P. was convicted of a contravention of s.1(1) of the 1953 Act by magistrates and he appealed against that conviction.

Held, that where a defendant had with him a lock knife, which was not an offensive weapon *per se*, and the only evidence against him was his statement to the police that he carried it for his self-defence, the Court could properly draw the inference that for the purposes of defending himself he would, if necessary, use the knife to cause injury to the person.

Appeal dismissed.

4.14.25   **(ii) Jardine v. Kelly**

[1985] 6 N.I.J.B. 96

K. was spoken to by a policeman in a part of Belfast where there had been trouble before. K. adopted a light-hearted attitude and he started to walk away from the policeman. K. was stopped and searched and a knife was found in his trouser pocket.

The knife so found was described by the policeman as a lock knife. It had one blade 7.7 cm long, with a cutting edge on one side and tapering from 1.1 cm to a point. When not in use the one blade folds back into the handle which was 7.5 cm long. On the non-cutting edge of the blade is a groove for a thumbnail to allow the blade to be opened. There were no springs or other devices to assist quick or easy opening. When the blade was opened there was a small catch to lock the blade in place to prevent the blade from bending back towards the handle in use.

The policeman showed the knife to K. and he was told by K. that it was to get him home in case he was jumped on "by the Prods." The knife was closed when found in K.'s pocket and it was not any form of a flick knife.

K. was charged with having with him an offensive weapon under the relevant delegated legislation for Northern Ireland. At the end of the Crown case, K.'s solicitor submitted that there was no case to answer for the knife was not in itself an offensive weapon—a matter of concession—and it had not been adapted in any way to make it an offensive weapon, and there was no evidence of K.'s intention to use the knife at the relevant time.

The Resident Magistrate agreed and dismissed the charge saying that in the opinion of the court the knife resembled a common penknife and it was not in itself an offensive weapon, and that there was insufficient evidence on which the Crown could rely of relevant intent on the part of K. to use the knife to render it an offensive weapon.

The Crown appealed and the question stated for the opinion of the Court of Criminal Appeal was whether the Resident Magistrate was correct in law in holding that the prosecution had not established a *prima facie* case that the knife in the possession of K. in the light of its declared intention was an offensive weapon as provided for in the delegated legislation.

O'Donnell, L.J. (at p. 99)

"The short answer to the question raised in the Case Stated is 'No.' A weapon which is not offensive in itself may become an offensive weapon depending on the intention of the user. In *Patterson* v. *Block* reported in *The Times* of June 21, 1984, the Court of Appeal in England held that a lock knife was not *per se* an offensive weapon, and the only evidence against the defendant being his statement to the police that he carried it for self defence the Justices could properly draw the inference that for the purpose of defending himself he would if necessary use the knife to cause injury to the person.

"In *R.* v. *Peacock* [1973] C.L.R. 639 the Court of Appeal in England also held that it must be very rare that someone not under immediate fear of attack could claim to be entitled to carry a weapon for self defence on the off-chance of being attacked. No currency should be given to the proposition that the law permitted people to arm themselves and fight it out if they encountered trouble.

"In the instant case the verbal statement made by the respondent to the police that the knife was to get him home 'in case he was jumped on by the Prods' is capable of at least two constructions. (1) That he would use the knife to defend himself if attacked, or (2) that he intended to produce the knife unopened simply to scare away the intending aggressor. The first interpretation makes the knife quite clearly an offensive weapon, the second does not.

"A further possible interpretation of the statement is that the defendant was in fact being facetious which might be borne out by the light-hearted attitude which apparently he adopted to the constable. In such case of course it would bear neither of the two possible constructions.

"Clearly therefore there is a *prima facie* case. A *prima facie* case must be distinguished from a case proved beyond reasonable doubt, and in *R.* v. *Wilson* [1975] N.I.J.B. Vol. 7 at pp. 7/8 Jones, L.J. set out clearly the distinction between the two.

"It may be, at the conclusion of the case, the Resident Magistrate will still have a reasonable doubt as to which purpose was intended, but clearly this does not mean that at the conclusion of the Crown case there was not a *prima facie* case.

"Accordingly we would answer the question raised in the Case Stated 'No' and return the case to the Resident Magistrate to decide in accordance with the law as above stated."

Appeal allowed.

4.14.26   *Modelling knife*

4.14.27   **Ralston v. Lockhart**

1986 S.C.C.R. 400

R. was charged *inter alia* with having an offensive weapon in a public place. At his trial the sheriff disbelieved R.'s explanation for his possession of the knife and held that the combination of the time of arrest, R.'s running off from the police and his failure to rebut the inference the sheriff drew from these two factors, justified a finding that R. intended to use the knife for causing personal injury, and convicted him of a contravention of the Act. R. appealed against conviction of that charge.

Lord Justice-Clerk (Ross) (at p. 401)

"[The appellant] has appealed by way of stated case but his appeal relates only to charge (5). Charge (5) libelled a contravention of section 1(1) of the Prevention of Crime Act 1953, that is that he did on the occasion specified in the police office in Chester Street, Glasgow, being a public place, have without reasonable excuse or lawful authority with him an offensive weapon, namely, a knife. The findings in fact are brief. It appears that two uniformed police officers on mobile patrol observed a car travelling towards them. It came to a sudden stop and the appellant left the driver's door and ran off. He was apprehended some seventy yards further on and was taken to Shettleston Police Station where he was searched. A modelling knife was found in and removed from his left-hand jacket pocket. The knife consisted of a slim handle of about six inches' length with a fixed blade at one end. There was no cover on the blade. The blade was sharp and had a pointed end. It was capable of inflicting serious injury. The sheriff had due regard to the provisions of section 1, subsection (1) of the Act of 1953. He accepted that the knife in question was not a weapon made for use for causing personal injury. He accepted also that it had not been adapted for use for causing personal injury. That being so he accepted that it was for the Crown to show under the section that the accused had the weapon with the intention of using it to cause personal injury. He referred to the case of *Lopez* v *MacNab* [1978 J.C. 41], and in his note the sheriff says that he based his entitlement to draw the inference that the appellant had the weapon with the intention of using it to cause personal injury from that decision.

"In support of this appeal [counsel for the appellant] has drawn attention to various differences between the facts in the case of *Lopez* and the facts in the present case. He has pointed out that the knife in question in the case of *Lopez* was different in character to the knife here. More importantly, he has pointed out that in the case of *Lopez* the findings showed that the accused in that case had the knife with him in a public bar and at some stage had produced the knife from his pocket so that it was seen by a member of the public who was in a state of alarm at what he saw. These facts are obviously quite different from the facts in the present case which I have already narrated. The sheriff undoubtedly applied the correct test in recognising that he required to be satisfied that the appellant had the weapon with the intention of using it to cause personal injury. In his note he drew that inference from what he describes as the combination of the time of apprehension at 2 a.m., the flight of the appellant on observing the police vehicle and his failure to rebut the inference of such intention in respect that he gave an explanation which the sheriff did not find acceptable. In our opinion the time of apprehension and the fact that he ran away when he observed the police are not facts from which the necessary intention under section 1(1) could be drawn. The other charges on the complaint involved theft of a motor-car and if the appellant was driving a stolen motor-car it is understandable that he should run away when he observed a police vehicle. Accordingly the fact that he ran away is not in our opinion a fact from which the intention to use the knife to cause personal injury could properly be drawn. No doubt the sheriff discounted the explanation given by the appellant for his possession of the knife, but the onus of establishing that the accused had the weapon with the intention of using it to cause personal injury rests upon the prosecution and the prosecution cannot discharge that onus by relying upon the fact that an explanation put forward by the accused is not acceptable. To do that would be to invert the onus. Having regard to the fairly meagre facts in this case and to the fact that the matters relied upon by the sheriff would not, in our opinion, justify his drawing the inference of intention which he did draw, we have come to the conclusion that the sheriff was not entitled to hold it proved by inference from the facts and circumstances established in the case that the knife was an offensive weapon in terms of section 1(1) of the Act."

Appeal allowed.

4.14.28   *Sheath knife*

4.14.29   **(i) Woodward v. Koessler**

[1958] 3 All E.R. 557

While K. was trying to break into a cinema by forcing open the door with a sheath knife, the caretaker came along. K. went up to the caretaker, holding the knife in a threatening attitude as if to strike with it, and said, "Can you see this?"

Held, K. was guilty of an offence by s.1(1) of the 1953 Act because he had with him a knife and at the time when he went up to the caretaker his conduct showed an intention to use the knife for causing injury to the person of the caretaker.

Appeal by prosecutor against acquittal allowed.

NOTE
This case is discussed further *supra* at para. 3.7.2.

4.14.30   **(ii) Farrell v. Rennicks**

(1959) 75 Sh.Ct.Rep. 113

One of two men convicted of housebreaking and attempted housebreaking was also charged in the same complaint with having with him in a public place, a sheath knife, contrary to s.1(1) of the 1953 Act.

Held, at trial, that the circumstances revealed that the knife had been intended to be used as a housebreaker's tool and not for the purpose of causing injury to the person.

Found not proven.

NOTE
This case is discussed further *supra* at para. 3.7.3.

(iii) R. v. Williamson 4.14.31

(1977) 67 Cr.App.R. 35

W. pleaded not guilty to having with him in a public place an offensive weapon, namely a sheath knife, contrary to s.1(1) of the 1953 Act. The trial judge ruled that the sheath knife was an offensive weapon *per se* and W. changed his plea to guilty. He appealed against conviction on the ground that the judge's ruling was incorrect.

Geoffrey Lane, L.J. (at p. 36)

"The circumstances of an appeal against conviction, when there has been a plea of guilty, requires a little explanation. We are told by counsel that what happened at the Court of trial was this. The learned judge asked counsel, both for the prosecution and for the defence, to come and see him and the question, as we understand it, both of the theft and of the possession of the offensive weapon, was discussed between the learned judge and the two counsel. As a result of what the learned judge said, it was clear to [counsel for the appellant], appearing as he does today on behalf of Williamson the appellant, that the learned judge had made up his mind that the weapon in this particular case was certainly *per se*, in the nature of things, made for causing personal injury. Accordingly the learned judge was going to direct the jury in that way, which meant [counsel for the appellant] thought, that any further continuance of the plea of not guilty by his client would be a waste of time.

"As a result of that all the parties went back into Court and [counsel for the appellant] then in open Court said this to the judge: 'I have given careful thought to the charge in count 2 of possessing an offensive weapon. As your Honour will be well aware, under the Prevention of Crime Act pursuant to which this offence is laid there are three types of offensive weapons; first, weapons which are substantially designed for causing injury. A service rifle or bayonet, a revolver, a cosh, knuckle-duster or dagger, fall into that category. Secondly, razor blades inserted into a potato or cap peak, a broken bottle, a chair leg, and the like. My understanding is, in relation to both those categories of offensive weapons, that the prosecution need do no more than prove that the defendant was in possession of such weapon. Unless he can prove reasonable excuse he is guilty of the offence. The third category of offensive weapons are articles which in themselves are encased but which only become offensive weapons when coupled with some offensive or aggressive intent. My argument would have been in relation to count 2 that this knife which we have seen is not in itself an offensive weapon but, to be turned into a third category one, is one of those about which the prosecution must prove some offensive or aggressive intent at the time when the defendant had it with him in his possession. If there was to be a trial on count 2 the Court would have to sum up whether or not this weapon fell into one or other of these three categories. I am not prepared to assume the responsibility upon myself of deciding into which category this sheath knife comes. I have taken my client's instructions, and if your Honour were to rule, as I anticipate you will do, that it is a weapon—that is to say, a weapon in relation to which the prosecution need do no more than prove possession to establish the offence—then my client is prepared to plead guilty; but that can only be pursuant to a ruling from your Honour.' The learned judge said 'It appears to be an offensive weapon *per se*, and I so rule.' Thereupon the indictment was put again and the defendant pleaded guilty.

"It is to be noted that learned counsel relied, for exercising his discretion in the way that he did, upon a passage in *Smith and Hogan on the Criminal Law* (3rd ed.), at p. 318, where various articles are categorised as being the sort of articles which are, *per se*, made for causing personal injury, where it is said: 'It is very important to distinguish the third category of articles which are neither made nor adapted for causing injury, but are carried for that purpose. This includes a sheath-knife ...,' and the reference there is WOODWARD v. KOESSLER [1958] 3 All E.R. 557. That was a decision of the Divisional Court, presided over by Lord Goddard C.J., where the accused was trying to break into a cinema by forcing open a door with a sheath knife, the caretaker came along; the accused went up to the caretaker, holding the knife in a threatening attitude as if to strike with it, and said 'Can you see this?' It was held that 'the accused was guilty of an offence against section 1(1) because he had with him a knife and at the time when he went up to the caretaker his conduct showed an intention to use the knife for causing injury to the person of the caretaker.'

"One passage at p. 558 in the judgment of Lord Goddard C.J. reads as follows: 'It could be said that the sheath knife was not made for the purpose of causing injury, though I do not know what other use these sheath knives or flick knives have; but assuming that it is like a razor, made primarily for the purpose of shaving and not for the purpose of causing injury, where I think that the justices have gone wrong is in holding that, when the accused said that he did not intend to cause injury, that statement was conclusive.'

"It seems to this Court that that passage, which is the material one in the report, is no ground for categorising a sheath knife as being of any particular nature.

"We have been referred to a number of other cases: FARRELL V. RENNICKS [1960] Crim.L.R. 133; 75 Sh. Ct. Rep. 113, a decision of the Sheriff's Court of Lanark held at Airdrie, in which a gaming knife, which was basically a scout's knife, having in its handle a number of other tools like screwdrivers, scissors and so on was used. The learned sheriff-substitute came to the conclusion that that could not be said to have been a knife which was made for the purpose of inflicting personal injury. In PETRIE (1961) 45 Cr.App.R. 72; [1961] 1 All E.R. 466, a cut-throat razor was said not to be, *per se*, an offensive weapon, because it is designed for shaving and not for personal injury.

"But it seems to us that in the end it is of no assistance to look at cases in order to try to determine the category into which any particular weapon can be put. One turns for guidance simply to the Act itself, to see what it says and section 1(1) of the Prevention of Crime Act 1953 reads as follows: 'Any person who without lawful authority or reasonable excuse, the proof whereof shall lie on him, has with him in any public place an offensive weapon shall be guilty of an offence ...,' and then the penalty is set out.

"In section 1(4) of the following words appear: '"offensive weapon" means any article made or adapted for use for causing injury to the person, or intended by the person having it with him for such use by him.'

"As has been pointed out in numerous cases, that provides three categories of weapons. The first category is the weapon which is made for causing injury to the person. The second type of weapon is one not made for the purpose but adapted for it, such as, as counsel pointed out in this case, a potato with a razor blade inserted into it. The third type of weapon is one neither made nor adapted but is one which is intended by the person having it with him for the purpose of causing personal injury to someone. That sort of thing could be any object that one can think of.

"But what is sometimes lost sight of is this. It is for the jury to decide these matters. It is for the jury to decide whether a weapon held by the defendant was an offensive weapon, bearing in mind the definition in the section which I have just read. Consequently whether the object in the possession of the defendant in any case can properly be described as an offensive weapon is a matter not for the judge but for the jury to decide. The jury must determine whether they feel sure that the object was made or adapted for use in causing injury to the person or was intended by the person having it with him for such use by him. There may perhaps be circumstances in which it is possible to say that there is no evidence to the contrary in a particular case. But that is not the case here. If there is such a case, then in those circumstances the judge might, unobjectionably, direct the jury in those terms, but such cases must be rare. In the normal case of this sort, it remains a question for the jury, although the judge, after proper warnings to the jury, may add his own view on the subject.

"In the present case this is well illustrated. Each side has submitted forcefully to the Court his own views about the sheath knife. The Crown have asked this Court to rule that in every case a sheath knife is an offensive weapon *per se*; by that it is meant that it is the kind of weapon made for causing personal injury. With equal force and not less eloquently, the appellant says this Court should decide as a matter of law that a sheath knife is not made for causing personal injury. And the fact that there is that divergence of opinion illustrates more clearly than anything else that it is not for the Court to decide this matter, it is for the jury. One only has to pause for a moment to consider what is meant by a sheath knife. It is not described as a weapon. It means a knife in a sheath. That is not what the jury are worried about or should be worried about. They should be concerned with the nature of the knife which is in the sheath. To suggest that this Court can determine in advance the nature of every knife which may be in a sheath demonstrates the absurdity of the situation in which this Court finds itself. We do not know what this knife was like and even if we did, it is not for us to usurp the functions of the jury and to decide into which category it falls under the Prevention of Crime Act 1953. In short the judge was wrong in ruling as he did. It was on the basis of that incorrect ruling that the plea was changed to one of guilty. It was an error of law that the ruling was made. Consequently this conviction must be quashed."

Appeal allowed.

4.14.32   **(iv) Coull v. Guild**

1985 S.C.C.R. 421

G. was seen late one night in the grounds of a hospital and in a street. He had with him a sheath knife. He was cautioned and charged with a contravention of s.1(1) of the 1953 Act and he replied "I was going to get rid of it." C. was convicted and he appealed against conviction.

Lord Justice-Clerk (Ross) (at p. 423)
"The next question is whether the sheriff was entitled to hold that the knife in question was an offensive weapon. Section 1(4) of

the Act of 1953, provides inter alia that: '"offensive weapon" means an article made or adapted for use for causing injury to the person, or intended by the person having it with him for such use by him.' In terms of the definition, there are thus three categories of offensive weapons: (1) any article made for use for causing injury; (2) any article adapted for use for causing injury; and (3) any article intended by the accused for such use by him.

"In the present case, it is found in fact that the appellant was carrying a sheath knife, and the sheriff in his note explains that it seemed to him 'that it was, per se, looking at it, an offensive weapon'. This means that the sheriff determined that the sheath knife was an offensive weapon in terms of the first of the three definitions quoted above, i.e., that it was an article made for use for causing injury to the person.

"Counsel for the appellant contended that a sheath knife did not fall under the first of the three definitions. He referred to Gordon's Criminal Law (2nd Edition) at page 862, and pointed out that the learned author there placed sheath knives in the third category, i.e., where the Crown required to show that the accused had the weapon with the intention of using it to cause injury.

"Counsel for the appellant also referred to *Woodward* v *Koessler* [1958] 1 W.L.R. 1255. In that case, Lord Goddard C.J. (with whom Donovan J. and Ashworth J. agreed) held that the sheath knife was an offensive weapon by virtue of the third definition (i.e., that it was intended by the accused to be used for causing injury). However, he stated, 'Perhaps it could be said that the sheath knife was not made for the purpose of causing injury, though I do not know what other use these sheath knives or flick knives have ...' (at p. 1256]. Lord Goddard there appears to be suggesting that sheath knives, as well as flick knives, fall under the first category, but, with all respect, we doubt whether that view, which was expressed obiter, can be applied as a general principle to findings in fact such as those in the present case.

"So far as flick knives are concerned, there is authority for the view that a flick knife is per se an offensive weapon within the meaning of the Act, i.e., that it falls under the first definition, but this is partly because a flick knife is a dangerous weapon which it is illegal to make under the Restriction of Offensive Weapons Act 1959 (see *Tudhope* v *O'Neill*, 1982 S.C.C.R. 45).

"In our opinion the present case is distinguishable on its facts from *Tudhope* v *O'Neill*. There is nothing in the findings to suggest that the sheath knife referred to therein was a knife of a type the manufacture of which is prohibited by law. Nor is there any finding that a sheath knife may not be manufactured or used for lawful purposes. Although the sheriff in his note observes that a sheath knife might be of value to a fisherman or a Boy Scout, there is no finding to that effect. In all the circumstances and in the light of the findings in the case, we do not see how the sheath knife could be said to be per se an offensive weapon. No doubt there are some weapons such as swordsticks, knuckle-dusters, coshes, bayonets and daggers (as suggested in Gordon) which may be said to be per se offensive weapons; they are made for use for causing injury to the person and all that the prosecution need prove is that an accused had one with him, and it will then be for him to show that he had it 'with lawful authority or reasonable excuse' under section 1(1) of the Act of 1953. In contrast, there is no finding in the present stated case either that sheath knives in general are made for causing injury to the person or that the particular sheath knife referred to therein was made for such use. In these circumstances the prosecutor would, in our opinion, have had to establish either that the sheath knife was adapted for use for causing injury to the person or that it was intended by the accused to be used by him for such a purpose.

"The advocate-depute submitted that the sheath knife was made for use for causing injury, and that it should be treated as similar to a dagger. For the reasons already given, we reject that submission. The advocate-depute was driven to say that every knife should be treated as being made for causing injury to the person, but that submission was plainly wrong. Many knives are clearly not made for use for causing injury. This was recognised in *Tudhope* v. *O'Neill* where the Lord Justice-Clerk contrasted a flick knife with such things as a skean-dhu or a kitchen knife or a penknife. Similarly in *Lopez* v. *MacNab*, 1978 J.C. 41 the sheriff was held entitled to conclude a sharp, pointed kitchen knife fell within the third category mentioned in the opinion of the court at p. 43.

"The advocate-depute's final submission was that finding 9 in the stated case showed that the accused had intended to use the sheath knife for causing injury, i.e., that it fell under the third definition. This was only very faintly argued, and there is no indication in the stated case that any such argument was presented to or considered by the learned sheriff. Moreover, there is no question in the stated case which raised this particular issue, and we are not satisfied that the findings in fact made by the sheriff were directed to the matter at all. In that situation we do not consider it appropriate to entertain on appeal a question which does not appear to have been raised at the trial. The point sought to be argued, which may be of some importance, can no doubt be considered in a future case where the findings in fact and questions of law are properly directed to it.

"The sheriff makes it quite plain that he convicted the appellant upon the narrow footing that the sheath knife was per se an offensive weapon within the meaning of the Act. For the reasons expressed above, we are of opinion that the learned sheriff erred on this matter."

Appeal allowed.

Skean-dhu **4.14.33**

Macleod v. Green **4.14.34**

Aberdeen Sheriff Court, unreported, March 1954

G. pleaded guilty, *inter alia*, to a charge of having with him in a public place an offensive weapon, namely a skean-dhu. He was fined £2 and forfeiture was not ordered.

Found guilty.

NOTE

It is relevant to add that the additional charges against George Green were assaulting two police constables by drawing the skean-dhu and pointing it at them in a threatening manner and committing a breach of the peace.

The following note appeared in a contemporary issue of the *Scots Law Times* (1954 S.L.T. (News) 67):

"The case has aroused much public interest and has reached the House of Lords where a question was asked in these terms: 'To ask Her Majesty's Government if they have noted the case where a man under the Prevention of Crime Act, after being punished for threatening to use a skean-dhu, was punished in addition for carrying it; and having regard to the fact that a skean-dhu is carried openly, and also to the assurances given by Her Majesty's Government when the second reading of the Bill was debated, whether they propose to take any step to assure the people of Scotland that a customary native dress is not to be proscribed, as in the years after 1745, with all the dismal consequences that ensued upon the proscription.'

"To this the Minister of State replied: '... this man was convicted of having an offensive weapon with him in a public place because he brandished his skean-dhu in a manner which indicated that he intended to use it to injure two policemen. My right honourable Friend, the Lord Advocate, is, however, taking steps to ensure that if a similar case arises again the statutory charge will not be included against the offender. I can assure the noble Lord that no departure from the assurances with regard to the wearing of a skean-dhu as part of Highland dress is intended.'

"With respect, this question and answer are surely ill-founded unless it is known how George Green was dressed—the point on which the record of the proceedings is silent. Was he in Highland dress or not? If he was, then the Lord Advocate was right in giving the assurance he did. But if a man is carrying a skean-dhu in the pocket of his 'drape' suit, then surely he could properly be charged with carrying an offensive weapon 'without lawful authority or reasonable excuse'—certainly 'without reasonable excuse'.

"There was much discussion about section 1 of the Act when the Bill was before Parliament but it seems clear enough that whether or not an individual can be charged with a contravention of that section depends entirely on the circumstances. This is well brought out in a recent English case (*R. v. Jura* [1954] 1 All E.R. 696). There a man was accompanied by a woman friend at a shooting gallery in a public park. His friend apparently irritated him and in a moment of anger he turned from his target and shot her—an action with which many might sympathise but which the law does not permit! Oliver, J., directed the jury to the effect that possession of the rifle became unlawful when it was turned deliberately on the woman and the accused was convicted of a charge under section 1. The Court of Appeal had no difficulty in quashing the conviction on that count because, as Goddard, L.J., very properly remarked, the accused 'had an obvious excuse for carrying the rifle'. So, too, would a man in Highland dress have an obvious excuse for carrying his skean-dhu. To inflict bodily injury with the rifle or skean-dhu in such circumstances is an offence, but not under section 1 of the Prevention of Crime Act, 1953."

4.14.35   *Stanley knife*

4.14.36   **(i) R. v. Webster**

(1985) 7 Cr.App.R.(S.) 359

For the facts, see *infra* at para. 5.4

Rose, J. (at p. 360)
"A Stanley knife is capable of inflicting a very serious injury indeed."

Appeal dismissed.

4.14.37   **(ii) Kane v. H.M. Advocate**

1988 S.C.C.R. 585

K. was charged on indictment with two matters; first, theft by housebreaking and, secondly, possession of an offensive weapon contrary to s.1(1) of the 1953 Act. K. was convicted of both and sentenced to periods of detention. He appealed *inter alia* against conviction of the offensive weapon charge.

Lord Justice-Clerk (Ross) (at p. 588)
"So far as the second charge is concerned the sheriff in his report tells us that the weapon involved, which was a Stanley knife, the blade of which was in a fixed position ready for use, had been found in the inside right pocket of the appellant's jacket when he

was searched by the police. The sheriff, correctly, directed the jury that the knife was what is sometimes called a class three offensive weapon, that is to say it is the sort of weapon where it is for the Crown to show that the accused had the weapon with the intention of using it to cause personal injury.

"The evidence upon which the Crown relied in that connection was that the Stanley knife had been found in the appellant's jacket with the blade fixed in the exposed position. The sheriff then left it to the jury as to whether, from that, they were prepared to draw the inference that the appellant had had the knife with him with the intention of using it to cause personal injury.

"In presenting the appeal [counsel for the appellant] has maintained that there was not sufficient evidence to entitle the jury to draw that inference and that the matter should not have gone to the jury. In replying to these submissions the advocate-depute has drawn attention to the case of *Ralston* v *Lockhart* [1986 S.C.C.R. 400]. That was a case where the appellant had been found to have a modelling knife in his left-hand jacket pocket. The knife consisted of a slim handle about six inches in length with a fixed blade at one end and there was no cover on the blade. In that case the court held that the Crown had not proved that the appellant had the necessary intention. The advocate-depute, however, maintained that, although admittedly the evidence in the present case was clearly thin, there was sufficient evidence to justify the conclusion that the appellant had the weapon with him with the intention of using it to cause personal injury. He relied upon the fact that the weapon consisting of this knife could have been dismantled and made safe but that instead of that it had been put in his pocket with the blade in a fixed position as we have already described. It need not have been in that condition because, as the sheriff reminds us in his report, the Stanley knife was of the nature that the blade could be placed inside the handle of the knife by unscrewing a bolt on the side of the handle and taking the blade out and thus putting it safely inside the handle.

"We have come to the conclusion that this case can be distinguished from the case of *Ralston* v *Lockhart* for the reasons which the Crown put forward. In *Ralston* v *Lockhart*, there was no suggestion that the weapon could have easily been dismantled and made safe. We are satisfied that the sheriff was fully justified in leaving the matter to the jury and leaving it to the jury to determine whether they could draw the inference of the necessary intention from these facts. We are satisfied that the jury were entitled to draw the inference of such an intention in this case. It follows, therefore, that the appeal against conviction is refused."

Appeal refused.

NOTE
Ralston v. Lockhart is discussed further at para. 4.14.27, *supra*. The seriousness of having an implement such as a Stanley knife is emphasised by the immediate imprisonment in *O'Connor v. Lees*, 1996 G.W.D. 24–1372.

4.14.38 Knife—position

4.14.39   **Miller v. Douglas**

                                    1988 S.C.C.R. 565

M. was charged with having with him in a public place a kitchen knife with a seven inch blade. He was convicted and he appealed on the grounds that the sheriff was not entitled on the facts to convict, and that M. had a reasonable excuse for carrying the weapon because he was under imminent threat of attack.

Lord Justice-Clerk (Ross) (at p. 570)
"Putting the matter shortly the appellant and a companion were walking along the road when they were assaulted by a number of youths, some of whom were armed with knives or batons. After initially seeking to defend himself the appellant ran on to the beach and to his home. As he was running he heard screams coming from his companion who had been seriously assaulted by these assailants. The appellant at his home made a 999 ambulance call and then proceeded to return in search of his companion. He took with him a kitchen knife with a blade seven to eight inches long which he apparently put in his pocket. As he returned to an area near the locus he encountered two individuals who had been passing by and had given assistance to the appellant's companion. The appellant, who had apparently been drinking, formed the view that these two individuals had been responsible for assaulting his companion, although this was not the case. They explained what their involvement in the matter had been, but the appellant didn't accept the explanation and an argument ensued. One of these two individuals came close to punching the appellant and had to be restrained by his companion. At this time the appellant had protruding from his jacket at chest height the handle of the knife. Finding 12 is in the following terms:

> 'At the moment at which the appellant was under threat by Paul McFarlane the appellant was pulling back from the confrontation and he made no attempt to handle the knife.'

"The findings then explain that the police came on the scene, that the appellant was apprehended and he made a statement to the police describing the situation.

"In presenting the appeal against conviction [counsel for the appellant] put forward two propositions. The first question which she posed was whether, when determining whether the appellant had intended to use the knife to cause personal injury, the sheriff was required to consider only the evidence regarding the few moments when he was observed by the police officers and when it was found as a fact that he had pulled back from the confrontation and made no attempt to use the knife, or whether the sheriff was entitled to make the broader approach and [consider] what the situation was when he was at the locus. This submission was made because the sheriff had correctly regarded this case as being one of those cases which fell into the third category of offensive weapons as defined in section 1(4) of the Act of 1953, and it was necessary for the Crown to show that the appellant had the weapon with him with the intention of using it to cause personal injury. The advocate-depute submitted that the sheriff was entitled to look at the broader picture and he reminded us that the terms of the complaint libelled that the offence had been committed on this particular public road. Therefore, the advocate-depute said, the sheriff was entitled to consider not just the last few minutes when the appellant was seen to be withdrawing from the confrontation but the situation as it existed on the public road when the confrontation was taking place between the appellant and these two men. In our opinion the advocate-depute is correct in making that submission. Looking at the matter upon that broad basis the sheriff says in his note that the only possible inference from the fact that the appellant had the knife readily at hand, protruding from his jacket, was that he intended to use it in the event of the assault by his earlier assailants on him being resumed. In our opinion the sheriff was justified in drawing that inference and indeed we did not understand [counsel for the appellant] to seek to dispute that, because her argument, as we understood it, was that the sheriff should have made the narrower approach and only considered the situation during the last few minutes before the police apprehended the appellant."

Appeal refused.

NOTE

In *McIntosh v. Docherty*, 1990 G.W.D. 13–672 the appellant had a sword concealed in his trouser leg. In *Mackin v. Friel*, 1992 G.W.D. 12–661 the appellant had an iron bar hidden beneath his jacket. In *Pelosi v. Normand*, 1993 S.C.C.R. 45 the appellant was seen to transfer a knife from his jacket pocket to the front of his trousers "presumably to evade an admission search" at a disco. In *Neill v. Normand*, 1993 G.W.D. 3–171 the appellant had a meat cleaver concealed in the rear waistband of his trousers. In *McPheators v. O'Brien*, 1994 G.W.D. 36–2125 the knife was hidden by the appellant in his waistband.

4.15   *Machete in scabbard and black widow catapult*

4.15.1   (i) Southwell v. Chadwick

(1987) 85 Cr.App.R. 235

S. was seen in a wooded area to be carrying under his belt a machete knife in a scabbard and a catapult. He ran off but was caught by two policemen. He was charged with a contravention of s.1(1) of the 1953 Act.

At his trial in the magistrates' court, S. said that he had the implements to kill grey squirrels which he required for food for wild birds. He kept these birds under licence.

The magistrates held that both weapons were made for use for causing injury to the person and therefore came within the first limb of the definition of an offensive weapon in s.1(4) of the 1953 Act.

They held further that the manner in which S. intended to use the weapons was irrelevant. Also, his excuse was not a reasonable one having regard to the frequency with which children used that woodland area.

S. appealed against conviction.

Stephen Brown, L.J. (at p. 239)

"In an argument, both succinct and relevant, [counsel for the appellant], points to the relevant findings of the justices. They are to be found in paragraph 2(9) of their findings of fact. It reads:

> 'That the appellant's ambition in "Daisy Dip" on the said afternoon was limited to killing grey squirrels (of which there were plenty) with missiles from his catapult and to chopping down tree branches upon which to carry any squirrels so killed with his unsheathed knife.'

"Then, in paragraph 2(7) they found 'that the said knife and catapult were both dangerous articles capable of causing grave personal injury.' He submits that the justices were in error in purporting to find on the evidence which they record and upon which they made those particular findings that either of these articles was made for use for causing injury to the person in the context of the reported decisions on this subsection, in other words, that they were articles which were dangerous *per se*. It was not suggested by the prosecution in this case that the second limb of subsection 4 of section 1 was relevant; that is to say that the appellant had with him these particular articles intending to use them for causing injury to the person. Quite plainly, their findings of fact show that his intention was not related to any person at all but was specifically directed to killing grey squirrels.

"[Counsel for the prosecution] in an equally succinct and brief argument has submitted that the role of this Court is to decide whether on the evidence before them the justices could reasonably have come to the conclusion that these two articles were dangerous *per se*. It is not suggested by the Crown that either of these articles was adapted for use in the language of the subsection for causing injury to the person. Plainly, they were not. The machete was in a scabbard or sheath and the catapult was manufactured as described. The question was not, therefore, whether there was evidence that they could be used but whether they were *made* for the use of causing injury to the person. In my judgment there was no such evidence. They were articles which had a legitimate use and, although it was a remarkable sight no doubt for police constables to come across a young man with these particular articles in this wood, nevertheless, the justices have to apply the strict words of the section. It does not in fact appear that this young man had any malicious intent directed to persons at all on their findings, so far as the use of these articles was concerned; that is to say, any use directed towards causing injury to any person. Whether or not there might be some other provision, perhaps a by-law, which could regulate his use of them for the purpose of killing squirrels is not a question here in point. In my judgment, the magistrates erred in coming to the conclusion that these two articles, or either of them, were dangerous *per se*. Accordingly, I would allow the appeal."

Appeal allowed.

(ii) Woods v. Heywood 4.15.2

1988 S.C.C.R. 434

W. was charged with having with him an offensive weapon, namely, a machete, in a public place. On conviction he appealed against the same. The matter desired to bring under review being:

"The learned sheriff erred in law in holding that a machete was an offensive weapon per se in terms of section 1(1) of the Prevention of Crime Act 1953. There was no evidence which could enable the sheriff to form a view that the accused was in possession of the machete for the purposes of causing personal injury. The Crown conceded at the trial that the accused did not have the machete for the purposes of causing personal injury. There was no evidence led by the Crown to rebut evidence on behalf of the accused that the machete was a tool."

In the stated case the sheriff made the following findings in fact:

"(1) On Sunday 15th February 1987, about 4.30 p.m., the appellant and Mark Balzanellie were walking along the east bank of the River Nairn near Bridge Street, Nairn. Where they were walking was a public place.

(2) The appellant and Mark Balzanellie had been messing about and pretending to fight with each other.

(3) The appellant, who is a baker to trade, was carrying, inside his unbuttoned jacket, a long-bladed sharp knife known as a machete.

(4) The appellant was asked to explain why he was carrying the machete and he explained that he was going to use it to cut wood for his mother's fire.

(5) The appellant had no permission to cut wood along the banks of the River Nairn; he had not cut wood there before; he had not previously used a machete to cut wood.

(6) The machete belonged to Mark Balzanellie. He had used it to cut shrub and whins when he had worked as a gamekeeper on a private estate near Crieff. He had given it to the appellant some two or three weeks previously.

(7) The appellant attended Nairn Police Station voluntarily where he was cautioned and charged as libelled. He made a reply. He replied: 'It was a silly mistake on my behalf. I should have known better.'

(8) *The Shorter Oxford English Dictionary* defines machete as follows: '**Matchet** also **machet(t)e** ... 1598. A broad and heavy knife or cutlass, used, esp. in Central America and the West Indies, both as a tool and a weapon.'

(9) The description 'a broad and heavy knife or cutlass' describes well the machete (Label 1) which was produced in evidence. Label 1 was attached to the machete taken from the appellant.

(10) The said machete is an article made for use for causing injury to the person.

(11) The appellant had the said machete with him in a public place.

(12) The appellant had the said machete with him without lawful authority or reasonable excuse."

In his note the sheriff stated, *inter alia*:
"The appellant was cautioned and charged and made the reply which I have found in finding 7. In his own evidence the appellant

sought to explain this reply, perhaps with some leading from his solicitor. The gloss he put on the reply was that he meant that he should have covered the machete and that he would have taken an axe but he had no cover for the axe. He said he had not used the machete for cutting wood before and that he had got it from his friend some two or three weeks earlier. His friend had already said how he had given the machete to the appellant and had explained the use to which he had put it as a gamekeeper—cutting of scrub and whins on a private estate near Crieff.

"I did not accept the appellant's explanation for having the machete with him. That it could be used to clear scrub and whins and brushwood, I could accept. The appellant's explanation of his reply was, to my mind, a not very credible attempt to bolster up his defence. His evidence, that he would have taken an axe if he had had a cover for it, did not ring true when it is seen that he took a machete for which there was also no cover. I simply did not believe the appellant. For these reasons I have made no findings which might support the appellant's evidence that he had the machete with reasonable excuse ...

"It is clear from the definition that offensive weapons fall into at least two classes (*R.* v *Petrie* [1961] 1 W.L.R. 358 ..., per Salmon J.), namely, 'class one', those made or adapted for use for causing injury to the person, and 'class two', those intended by the person having it with him for such use by him. The distinction is important: where the weapon is a 'class one' weapon, the prosecution need only prove that the accused had it with him 'without lawful authority or reasonable excuse'; where the weapon is a 'class two' weapon, the prosecution must prove that he had it with him with the intention of using it to cause personal injury. 'Class one' weapons are sometimes referred to as offensive weapons per se (*Tudhope* v *O'Neill*, 1982 S.C.C.R. 45 ... *Gibson* v *Wales* [1983] 1 W.L.R. 393 ...). I understand it to be a question of fact whether any article is an offensive weapon per se (*Gibson*), although I would have thought that it is probably within judicial knowledge that certain weapons (e.g. knuckledusters and coshes) are offensive weapons per se. I think it is probably the law that an article which is an offensive weapon per se is not necessarily taken out of that category merely because it could be, and often is, used for an innocent purpose (see *Gibson* and *R.* v *Simpson (Calvin)* [1983] 1 W.L.R. 1494 ...).

"The appellant's solicitor argued that the machete was a 'class two' weapon and that the respondent had not proved that the appellant had it with him intending to cause injury to the person. I agree that the Crown had not proved that the accused had it with him for the purpose of causing such injury and I have made no such finding. In any event, the respondent conceded that he could only seek a conviction on the basis that a machete was a 'class one' weapon and that the appellant had it with him without lawful authority or reasonable excuse. If your Lordships hold that the weapon has not been proved to be a 'class one' weapon, or that it is not a 'class one' weapon, then I would have thought the appeal succeeds.

"I consider that two questions arise in this appeal, both questions of fact: (1) is a machete an offensive weapon per se, and (2) if it is, has the appellant proved that he had it with him with reasonable excuse? On the second question I was prepared to accept that a machete is used as a tool, but I did not accept the evidence that the appellant had it with him for such a purpose.

"I turn to the first question. I have tried to approach the question from the point of view of common sense because the respondent led no evidence from any expert on weapons. I put aside my own acquired knowledge (*not* judicial knowledge) of the use to which a machete was put in the war in Burma and the Malay Peninsula and my personal knowledge of use to clear overgrown scrub and brushwood, and topping turnips. I consulted *The Shorter Oxford English Dictionary* as my starting-point. I believe this is permissible even though parties have not referred me to it (*Edinburgh Corporation* v. *Lord Advocate*, 1923 S.C. 112 ...). Under the word 'machete' I was referred to 'matchet' and finding 7 is what I found under that heading. From my examination of the machete I can well see why it should have a use as a weapon and a tool, and it appeared to me to be made for the purpose, *inter alia*, of causing injury to the person. In the case of *Gibson* v. *Wales*, Griffiths L.J. (as he then was) said [at p. 398 G–H]:

> 'In my view ... a flick knife ... is made for the purpose of causing injury to the person. It may sometimes be used for wholly innocent purposes, even possessed for innocent purposes, but there will be a very heavy burden on any person in possession of a flick knife to satisfy any court that he had it for such an innocent purpose.'

"McCullough J. said that it was a question of fact whether a flick knife was an offensive weapon per se and then said: 'it is.' There may be a distinction in that case that a flick knife is prohibited by the Restriction of Offensive Weapons Act 1959, as amended by the Restriction of Offensive Weapons Act 1961. The fact that an article is made for the purpose of a tool *and* for causing personal injury does not, I think, mean that it must necessarily be taken out of the category of a 'class one' weapon. In this case I did not consider that I was dealing with the 'wappenschaw' of the rustics who joined the fencibles in Thomas Hardy's novel *The Trumpet Major* to defend the country from Bonaparte's expected invasion. Their pitchforks and other agricultural tools were clearly 'class two' weapons. Dicta in *Gibson* and *R. v. Simpson (Calvin)* indicate that although an article has a known purpose as a tool, as well as a weapon for causing injury to persons, yet the article can still be a 'class one' weapon." The questions for the opinion of the High Court were:

"(1) Was I entitled to make finding 10?
(2) Was I entitled to make finding 12?
(3) On the facts stated, was I entitled to find the appellant guilty as charged?"

Lord Justice-Clerk (Ross) (at p. 437)

"In presenting the appeal today, [counsel for the appellant] has maintained that the sheriff was not justified in arriving at the conclusion which he did. The sheriff makes it plain that he formed the conclusion that this machete was an article made for use for causing injury to the person. In Gordon's *Criminal Law* (2nd edn), at p. 862, the learned author deals with this section of the Prevention of Crime Act 1953 and points out that offensive weapons fall into three classes. The first class is those made for use [for] causing personal injury. The second class is those adapted for such use and the third class is those not so made or adapted but intended by the accused for such use. The sheriff in the present case took the view that the machete was made for use for causing personal injury and in his note he makes it plain that that is the only basis upon which he proceeded. He accepts that if, contrary to his view, the machete should be regarded as falling under the third category, then on the material before him he would not have been entitled to convict. So the sharp question which arises is whether the sheriff was well founded in holding that the machete was an article made for use for causing injury to the person. In finding 8 the sheriff refers to the definition of machete in *The Shorter Oxford English Dictionary*. The definition proceeds as follows: 'A broad and heavy knife or cutlass, used, esp. in Central America and the West Indies, both as a tool and a weapon.'

"[Counsel for the appellant] maintained that since the machete had this dual purpose, it could not be said to fall under the first of the categories defined in section 1(4) of the Act of 1953. The advocate-depute, on the other hand, maintained that even though it had a twofold purpose, it could still be affirmed that it was a weapon made for use for causing personal injury, that being one of the purposes of the weapon. In our opinion the submission by [counsel for the appellant] is to be preferred. Where there are, as in

the present case, twofold purposes, namely one which is for causing
personal injury and the other for an innocent purpose, it cannot
properly be affirmed that the weapon in question was one which
was made for use for causing personal injury. It might have been
made for the innocuous purpose, i.e., as a tool. Accordingly, we
are satisfied that the sheriff in this case was not entitled to make
finding 10 in the case and it follows from that that he was not
entitled to convict the appellant as libelled. We shall accordingly
answer question 1 and question 3 in the negative, and it follows
that the conviction will be quashed."

                                                    Appeal allowed.

NOTE
This appeal decision caused some surprise in the legal profession.

4.16   *Metal bar*

4.16.1   **Evans v. Hughes**

                            [1972] 3 All E.R. 412

H. was seen in a public place to have with him a six inch long
metal bar. Policemen asked H. what the bar was for. After some
prevarication H. said that he carried it for protection. He said that
he knew that the metal bar was an offensive weapon. Later, in a
statement to the police, he said that a week earlier he had been
assaulted by three boys. He said he had carried the bar for self-
protection and if the boys had attacked him again he would have
used the bar on them.
    The magistrates acquitted H. on the ground that, first, the metal
bar being a defensive weapon was not an "offensive weapon"
within the meaning of s.1(4) of the 1953 Act. Secondly, that even if
the bar was an offensive weapon H. had a reasonable excuse for
having it with him. The prosecutor appealed.

Lord Widgery, C.J. (at p. 414)
    "The first task of the justices was to decide whether this bar was
an offensive weapon at all, because the question whether it was
carried with lawful authority or reasonable excuse does not arise
unless and until it is shown to be an offensive weapon.
    "It was obviously, and I turn to the definition, not an article
made or adapted for use for causing injury to the person. It was
a metal bar and not made or adapted for use as a weapon at all,
but on the respondent's own admission it was intended by him

to be used for self-defence if he was attacked, and therefore in my view it was intended by him for use for causing injury to the person and the justices when they concluded, as they did, that this was not an offensive weapon were in my judgment wrong."

Appeal dismissed on other grounds.

NOTE
This case is discussed *supra* at para. 3.2.5.

Metal tube **4.17**

(i) Brown v. Walkingshaw **4.17.1**

1992 G.W.D. 38–2249

B. was sentenced to three months' detention for a contravention of s.1 of the 1953 Act. The item that formed the basis of the charge was a length of chrome-coloured tubing about $2-2^1/_2$ feet long, which had been taped at both ends with insulating tape and filled with sand and small stones, "presumably to make it heavier." He appealed against sentence only.

Appeal refused.

(ii) Friel v. Dailly **4.17.2**

Paisley Sheriff Court, December 7, 1992

D. was charged with having with him in a public place an offensive weapon, namely a metal scaffolding tube. At the end of the Crown case it was submitted, *inter alia*, that the metal scaffolding tube was not an offensive weapon. The submission was repelled. D. did not give evidence. He was convicted and fined. D. appealed and in the stated case the sheriff described the implement thus: "It was a piece of scaffolding approximately two feet in length and clearly cut at both ends from a length of scaffolding tube. There was at one end a roughly fashioned handle, perhaps some six or so inches long, created by bandage or other material wrapped round the metal and then affixed to it by several windings of adhesive tape. This provided a very much better grip of the metal tubing than simply holding the bare metal. The only purpose in doing this would be to enable the metal tubing to be wielded. It had clearly been adapted and its adaption had no possible use other than as an offensive weapon."

Found guilty.

NOTE
Dailly did not appear for his appeal against conviction and his appeal was refused for want of insistence.

4.18 *Motor car*

4.18.1 **(i) R. v. Russell**

[1993] R.T.R. 249

R. was sentenced to imprisonment and to disqualification following conviction of reckless driving. His appeal was solely on a point relating to disqualification. The judgment of the court is set out for the interesting point of the use of a vehicle as an offensive weapon.

Ognall, J. (at p. 250)
"On 9 May 1990 in the Crown Court at Teeside the appellant, Ian Eric Russell, now twenty-five years of age, fell to be sentenced by the recorder for a number of offences on indictment T891595. By counts 1 and 2 of that indictment he was arraigned, and pleaded guilty to the offence of assault occasioning actual bodily harm, and also to count 3, an offence of reckless driving. In addition he was charged with driving with excess alcohol.

"On counts 1 to 3 of that indictment he was sentenced to two years' imprisonment on each count concurrent. In addition, for the offence of reckless driving he was ordered to be disqualified for holding or obtaining a licence for driving a motor vehicle for a period of seven years. He was also dealt with for a quite separate matter of attempted theft, for which he was sentenced to three months' imprisonment consecutive to the two years to which I have already made reference, thus making 27 months' imprisonment and seven years' disqualification.

"For the offence of driving with excess alcohol he was ordered to serve a concurrent sentence of six months' imprisonment and disqualified from driving for 12 months concurrent with the disqualification period of seven years. He now appeals against the length of disqualification by leave of the single judge.

"The facts of the matter disclose in the view of this court very serious misbehaviour by the appellant. On September 7 1989 he and his friend, Armstrong, were in a night-club on Redcar Esplanade. His friend Armstrong got into a dispute with some other young men inside the club which led to some minor brawl in which the appellant was not involved. But the trouble spilled out on to a pavement outside where the appellant was knocked to the ground by a man called Canfield.

"That having taken place, the appellant made his way to the old GPO van which he and Armstrong jointly owned. Thereafter he effectively used that van as a weapon by driving it, aiming at the man Canfield. As luck would have it, because he ran away, Canfield was only struck a glancing blow. Two other young pedestrians, a man and a woman, who were in the vicinity of the night-club, and standing fairly close to Canfield, were struck by the van. Fortunately neither of these persons suffered any serious injury, but the woman has thrown into the air and was for a time apparently rendered unconscious. Thus the offences of assault occasioning actual bodily harm.

"The appellant, as I have said, has a very bad record indeed, inter alia, for offences of violence going back to 1981: in 1981 he was dealt with for threatening behaviour, in 1983 for criminal damage, in August 1986 for grievous bodily harm, in July 1987 for assault occasioning actual bodily harm, in November 1987 for wounding, in September 1988 for assault occasioning actual bodily harm, and in April 1989 for assaulting a police constable.

"The recorder in passing sentence on the appellant had this to say about him:

> 'You did the worst thing one could do with a motor vehicle; you drove it at somebody, you used it as a weapon. In one sense it was worse than when the average case of causing death by reckless driving when the driver is over the alcoholic limit because a deliberate intention to hit pedestrians is obviously worse than hitting them by accident or recklessly.'

"He reviewed some of the features of the appellant's conduct. He said, as to the proposed period of disqualification which he was to order:

> 'It seems to me that it is out of the question for you to be lawfully driving a motor vehicle until you are substantially older and of a more responsible frame of mind.'

"In addressing the court [counsel] on the appellant's behalf, has of course properly acknowledged that the offences giving rise to the 24 months in custody were very serious indeed and that no proper complaint could be made against that length of custodial sentence. However he submits that, consonant with principle and authority as well as with the circumstances of this case, a disqualification of seven years is too long. He has reminded us of the principles spelt out by this court on a number of occasions with regard to periods of disqualification ordered to take effect upon relatively young offenders. In particular he has reminded the court of the observations to be found in, first, *Reg.* v. *Weston* (1982) 4 Cr.App.R.(S.) 51, and, latterly, in *Reg.* v. *Hansel* (Note) [1983] R.T.R. 445.

"In both those cases, [counsel] submits, the court dealt with the principles governing the making of an order of disqualification. It should have regard to the effect of such order and its length in two respects upon the defendant: first, in so far as it might enhance the likelihood on release from his custodial sentence to further transgression of the road traffic rules. Secondly, and most importantly, the adverse effect a lengthy period of disqualification would have upon the defendant's prospects of effective rehabilitation upon his release from custody.

"[Counsel's] submissions are two-fold. He submits first of all that the recorder was wrong in the circumstances of this case to equate the gravity of the appellant's conduct with that of the offence of causing death by reckless driving. He places more in the forefront of the submissions that in disqualifying the appellant for seven years the recorder failed to give any sufficient weight to the principle of rehabilitation to which I have made earlier reference.

"There is no doubt that this was very serious conduct indeed and we are not disposed to dissent from the way in which the recorder drew the analogy with the offence of causing death by reckless driving, but we are impressed with the latter submission. In our view the recorder failed, in ordering disqualification for a term of seven years, to give sufficient weight to the undoubtedly profound adverse effects that a disqualification for that period would have on the appellant upon his release from custody, which would in all probability be in the early part of 1991.

"We propose to give effect to that by quashing the seven years' disqualification and reducing it to a period of five years.

"Accordingly, and to that extent only, this appeal is allowed."

Appeal allowed.

NOTE
This appeal was reported three years after the appeal hearing.

(ii) R. v. Jones

4.18.2

(1991) 93 Cr.App.R. 169

J., aged forty, with no relevant previous convictions, pleaded guilty to recklessly driving and unlawful wounding. He had driven his car at the victim, with whom he had recently quarrelled. In attempting to jump clear, the victim received minor injury. The appellant then drove the car at him again, unsuccessfully. He was sentenced to nine months' and 18 months' imprisonment concurrent and disqualified from driving for three years. On appeal against sentence on the ground that it should be reduced to reflect the fact that the driving was over a short distance and a short period of time:

Held, that the case was as much a case of the misuse of a motor car as a weapon to terrify and cause injury, not once but twice, demonstrating a degree of determination by a man driving in a furious temper. The basic gravamen was the wounding charge, and it was in that context, rather than a simple case of reckless driving, that the sentence had to be considered. Any interference either with the term of imprisonment or with the disqualification would not be justified.

Judge, J. (at p. 169)

"The judge when passing sentence commented that what the appellant had done might well have landed him with a charge for an offence far more grave than of reckless driving and unlawful wounding, and said that anybody who drives a car on the roads of this country must realise that they are in charge of a potentially lethal weapon, and indicated that the evidence in the case had persuaded him that the appellant was as much a danger on the road as if he had a loaded rifle. The judge indicated that he took the view that this was a bad case not only of reckless driving but also of wounding.

"The argument before this Court is that the sentence passed on the appellant should either have been suspended in whole or in part or, alternatively, that a lower sentence was appropriate. Attention was focused on the age of the appellant, the fact that for effective purposes he was of good character and that he had made no attempt to evade his responsibility for what had happened by pleading not guilty. The argument was further advanced that as a case of reckless driving this driving happened over a very short distance and within a very short period of time and that therefore the sentence should be reduced to reflect that fact. In the judgment of the Court this is not a case which requires

attention as a case of reckless driving as much as a case involving
the misuse of a motor car as a weapon to terrify and indeed to
cause injury. This happened not once but twice, which
demonstrates a degree of determination. There is ample evidence
to suggest that the appellant was driving in a furious temper
intent on causing fear and possible injury. So the basic gravamen
of the wounding charge was the wounding charge, and it is in
that context, rather than in the context of a simple case of reckless
driving that the sentence has to be considered."

Appeal dismissed.

4.18.3   **(iii) R. v. Peapell**

Court of Appeal (Criminal Division), Unreported, July 7, 1992

P. had a record for violence and he was convicted of assault occasioning actual bodily harm and common assault and was sentenced
respectively to four years' and six months' imprisonment, concurrent. Concurrent suspended sentences of six months' imprisonment for affray were activated consecutively. The background to
the offences was that a relationship with T., by whom he had a
daughter, had broken up and T. had obtained an injunction preventing him from seeing her or the child. He was constantly in
breach of the injunction by confronting T. and her family and making various threats. He drove his car onto a wide pavement striking T.'s father and causing injuries, but missing T.

Held, that assault using a motor vehicle as a weapon was always
a very serious matter. The maximum sentence was five years. There
was no plea of guilty and no mitigation to speak of. The court bore
in mind that this was P.'s first custodial sentence and that his father
had died while he had been in custody, but a sentence near the
maximum had been justified.

Appeal dismissed.

4.18.4   **(iv) Barry v. Lees**

High Court of Justiciary, July 7, 1994

B. was found guilty of both reckless and careless driving arising
out of a prolonged incident of bad driving. His appeal was
restricted to sentence and in particular the period of disqualification
that had been imposed.

Lord Justice-Clerk (Ross)
"The terms of the charge of which he was convicted make it plain that the appellant's dangerous driving took place over a period of time and that he was using his motor vehicle in a dangerous manner almost as a weapon with which to harry the complainer. In these circumstances we are quite satisfied that the sheriff was entitled to take the view that a fairly lengthy period of disqualification was called for ...

"... In the note annexed to the case the sheriff says that he has no doubt that the appellant in this case deliberately went out to cause danger on the road. In these circumstances the sheriff says that he did not appear to him to be a suitable person to hold a driving licence for a long time. Having regard to the nature of this offence we are satisfied that the sheriff was fully justified in taking that view. When regard is had to the nature of the offence and to the fact that the appellant has previously been disqualified for careless driving we have come to the conclusion that six years' disqualification imposed by the sheriff cannot be regarded as excessive."

Appeal refused.

NOTE
The use of a motor vehicle as a weapon is well demonstrated in *Anderson* v. *H.M. Advocate*, 1988 G.W.D. 10–405; *McAulay* v. *H.M. Advocate*, 1990 G.W.D. 1–20; *Beatson* v. *H.M. Advocate*, 1990 G.W.D. 13–657; *Welsh* v. *H.M. Advocate*, 1990 G.W.D. 37–2116; and *Borowska* v. *Whitelaw*, 1991 G.W.D. 22–1280. These sentencing cases reveal motor cars being used in the course of assaults.

Nunchaca sticks	**4.19**
(i) Hemming v. Annan	**4.19.1**

1982 S.C.C.R. 432

H. was found in a public place shortly after 1 a.m. with a pair of nunchaca sticks which he said he used for karate training. He had not engaged in such training for 18 months. The sticks had been made by him at a relative's house the previous evening and at the relevant time he was taking the sticks home.

H. was convicted of a contravention of s.1(1) of the 1953 Act and appealed. In his note the sheriff observed that he took the view that the nunchaca sticks, although associated with karate training, are essentially a weapon made for causing personal injury.

The sheriff added that in the course of H.'s evidence he had referred to the nunchaca sticks as a "weapon," and said that he had seen them used against people in karate demonstrations. H. had given a demonstration of how he had used the nunchaca sticks and the sheriff noted that he was left in no doubt that the sticks could be used as a formidable weapon capable of inflicting considerable injury.

The sheriff had heard evidence from a policeman to the effect that, when learning karate, he was recommended by a professional karate instructor not to use the nunchaca sticks for ordinary karate training and this evidence was not disputed.

Lord Justice-General (Emslie) (at p. 434)

"An offensive weapon for the purposes of section 1 of the Act is defined in section 1(4) and means any article made or adapted for use for causing injury to the person or intended by the person having it with him for such use by him. Now the sheriff purports to have found that the nunchaca sticks in this case constituted an article made for causing injury to the person and the question which we have to resolve, following upon the submissions to which we listened, was whether the sheriff was entitled to find as he did. The question that the sheriff had to resolve was what were the sticks made for? Upon a consideration of the material in the stated case we have to reject the submission for the appellant that the sheriff was not entitled to hold that the nunchaca sticks constituted an offensive weapon as defined. There was material in our judgment upon which his finding can be justified. That material included the evidence of the appellant himself who referred to the sticks as a weapon and who apparently explained to the sheriff that he had seen them used 'against' people in karate demonstrations. Not only did the appellant himself give evidence about the use of nunchaca sticks, he gave, it appears, a demonstration of how he used them, leaving the sheriff in no doubt that these sticks could, as he puts it, be used as a formidable weapon capable of inflicting considerable injury."

Appeal dismissed.

NOTE

The sheriff asked in his stated case whether nunchaca sticks constituted an offensive weapon of the category made for use for causing personal injury and the High Court of Justiciary answered in the affirmative. Sheriff Gordon observes in his commentary in this case (*ibid* at p. 435) that although this case is a little unusual in that the sticks were made by the appellant himself, so that the specific question at issue was whether he had made them for use (by himself or others) for personal injury, "it will doubtless be regarded as authority for the proposition that nunchaca sticks are offensive weapons *per se.*"

(ii) Kincaid v. Tudhope 4.19.2

1983 S.C.C.R. 389

K. was seen to have with him in a public place a set of nunchaca sticks. He was at that time, 4 a.m., on his way home from a dance. He had earlier taken the sticks from a friend's car where he had left them by mistake, and taken them with him to the dance hall where he deposited them with the steward.

K. was convicted and he appealed against that conviction. In the stated case the magistrate found in fact that the nunchaca sticks "(otherwise known as Chinese fighting sticks)" consisted of two rounded wooden batons approximately three inches in diameter and about one foot in length. They were linked by a metal chain at their top ends. The chain was about nine inches in length.

Further, the sticks were offensive weapons and were designed for use against the person. The sticks were also used for the purpose of developing muscular strength and speed of reaction. They were swung around the user's body, rather as majorettes swing a baton.

Lord Justice-General (Emslie) (at p. 390)
"After trial the appellant was convicted and the only issue at the trial was whether the appellant had demonstrated that he had reasonable excuse for having what was conceded to be an offensive weapon in his possession at the described place. Now the time at which he had possession of this offensive weapon was four o'clock in the morning in a street named Walnut Street in Glasgow. For the reasons given in the note by the justice he was not satisfied that the appellant had discharged the onus upon him of demonstrating that he had a reasonable excuse for his possession in a public place of this offensive weapon at four o'clock in the morning and because he took that view he convicted.

"This appeal is brought to challenge conviction and is concerned simply with the issue of reasonable excuse. The first question in the case is this: 'Was I entitled to hold that the appellant had no reasonable excuse for his possession of the said sticks in the circumstances narrated?' That is not, perhaps, as well stated as the question should be. The question for us is, was there material in the case upon which the justice was entitled not to be satisfied that there was reasonable excuse for the possession of the offensive weapons at four o'clock in the morning in Walnut Street in Glasgow on the described date? [Counsel], for the appellant, has argued that the stated case is far from a model of clarity and furthermore that, in making up his mind on the critical question of reasonable excuse, the justice seems to have assumed, quite wrongly, that the appellant was responsible in the first place for taking the sticks from a private place, namely the garage near his house, into the city centre and thereafter, for having taken the sticks from the city centre through the streets of Glasgow to a dance hall where he handed the sticks in. It appears that at the conclusion of the dance, having picked up the sticks, the appellant set out homewards again through the streets of Glasgow until the time he was stopped by the police. Initially we thought that there was at least some substance in the submission but with some hesitation we have come to the view that upon the relevant material in the case we cannot affirm that the justice was not entitled to take the view which he did. The passage at the [end] of the stated case which contains the erroneous assumption falls to be read with the account of the circumstances given [earlier] and what it seems to come to is this: the justice, we think, understood perfectly well that the appellant, on the night in question, had picked up the sticks from the back of a friend's car where they had remained by mistake and thereafter instead of proceeding homewards with them straight away had decided to carry on with his evening's plan and had gone to the dance hall and had waited until the end before returning home. The case is a narrow one. Its circumstances are not very different from those in the case of *Hemming* v. *Annan* which is reported only in [1982 S.C.C.R. 432]. In all the circumstances, accordingly, we have come to be of the opinion that the appeal must be refused. We reached that conclusion with some hesitation because of the slight doubt which we first entertained about the factors which had influenced the mind of the justice at the time."

Appeal dismissed.

4.19.3   **(iii) Moncrieff v. Jessop**

1989 G.W.D. 25–1076

M. was convicted of a contravention of s.1 of the 1953 Act. He appealed against that conviction.

Held, that where unchallenged evidence was led that a najook was a Chinese fighting stick and the defence had withdrawn a submission that it was not *per se* offensive, that a magistrate was entitled to conclude that it was made for use for causing personal injury within s.1(1) of the 1953 Act.

NOTE
In *Magee* v. *McGlennan*, 1993 G.W.D. 12–810 the charge was one of assault by use of Chinese fighting sticks.

Pickaxe handle **4.20**

R. v. Cugullere 4.20.1

[1961] 1 W.L.R. 858

For the facts and circumstances in which three pickaxe handles bound with adhesive tape formed the basis of a charge of contravening s.1(1) of the 1953 Act see above at para. 3.4.2.

Appeal allowed.

NOTE
In *Knight v. Normand*, 1991 G.W.D. 34–2072, an appeal against sentence, the offensive weapon concerned was a pickaxe handle inscribed with, "This is for your head." The item had been found in the boot of the appellant's car.

Potato peeler **4.21**

McLaughlin v. Tudhope 4.21.1

1987 S.C.C.R. 456

M. was found in a public place by two policemen who searched him. They found that M. had a knife in the zipper pocket of his jerkin. He gave no reason or excuse for his possession of the knife. He was charged with possession of an offensive weapon and was convicted. He appealed and the stipendiary magistrate made findings in fact in his stated case.

In regard to the item it was found to have been some form of kitchen implement, one end being a knife and the other end a potato peeler. The potato peeling blade was missing and the sheath or cover for the knife was not there, leaving simply a fixed-blade knife with a handle. The knife was about seven inches in length, the blade being three inches long with a sharp point.

In his note the stipendiary magistrate indicated that the main point of contention at trial was whether the knife was an offensive weapon, and if so, into what classification it fell. He convicted M. because this domestic implement had been modified in at least two ways to allow its adaption to an offensive weapon and M. had no excuse for its possession at the relevant time.

Lord Justice-Clerk (Ross) (at p. 457)
"In presenting the appeal [counsel for the appellant] has maintained that on the findings the stipendiary magistrate was

not entitled to find that the knife in the appellant's possession was an offensive weapon in terms of the Prevention of Crime Act 1953. Section 1(4) of the Act of 1953 contains a definition of 'offensive weapon'. 'Offensive weapon' means 'any article made or adapted for use for causing injury to the person or intended by the person having it with him for such use by him.' It was agreed that in the present case if the knife in question was to be an offensive weapon within the meaning of the Act that could only be upon the basis that it had been adapted for use for causing injury to the person. [Counsel for the appellant] maintained that the findings did not justify the stipendiary in reaching such a conclusion.

"In his note the stipendiary magistrate states that he had little hesitation in concluding that there was here a domestic implement that had been modified in at least two ways to allow its adaptation to an offensive weapon. This matter must be determined on the basis of the findings which the stipendiary magistrate made. In his findings he records that the appellant's person was searched and the knife was found in the pocket of a jerkin which he was wearing. The knife is described in finding 7 in the following terms:

> 'That the knife appeared to have been some form of kitchen implement, one end being a knife and the other end a potato peeler, but in its present state the potato peeling blade was missing and the sheath or cover for the knife was not there, leaving simply a fixed-blade knife with a handle. The knife was about seven inches in length, the blade being three inches long with a sharp point.'

"In our opinion, having regard to that finding, the stipendiary magistrate was not justified in concluding that the knife had been adapted for use for causing injury to the person. All that he says regarding any change in relation to the condition of the knife is that the potato peeling blade was missing and the sheath or cover was not there. There is no suggestion that the appellant had anything to do with the removal of the potato peeling blade or the sheath or cover. There is nothing said as to who was responsible for these two parts being missing or being not there. There might be a perfectly innocent explanation for those two parts being missing, and there is nothing to justify the inference that the parts had been removed in the course of adapting the knife for use for causing injury. The advocate-depute pointed out that because there had been delay in prosecuting this appeal the knife had been destroyed, and he submitted that it was therefore not possible to reach any definite conclusion upon whether this particular knife was an offensive weapon as defined in section 1(4). With that proposition we do not agree. It is not necessary for this court to see the actual knife. The issue has to be determined upon the basis of the findings which the stipendiary magistrate has made.

"The advocate-depute also drew attention to reasons which the stipendiary magistrate gave for rejecting certain proposed adjustments. In these reasons it is recorded that a defence witness said that when he first saw the implement that night the potato peeler blade was still connected. That may well have been evidence that was led before the stipendiary magistrate but it has not been made the subject of a finding in fact. So far as we are concerned, we must determine the issue upon the basis of the findings. We are quite clear in this case that the findings in fact which give a description of the knife are not sufficient to justify the conclusion being drawn that this particular knife had been adapted for use for causing injury to the person."

Appeal allowed.

NOTE

In his commentary on this case Sheriff Gordon observes that the Act "does not require that the adaptation be carried out by the accused—what matters is whether the article has been adapted, not who adapted it. There appears to be no authority as to whether the test of adaptation is wholly objective or depends on the intention of the adapter. Whether or not the modification had been carried out by the accused would, however, be relevant to whether it was intended for use by him for causing personal injury."

Razor blades **4.22**

Barr v. MacKinnon **4.22.1**

1988 S.C.C.R. 561

B. was seen by policemen to be waving a stick. He was arrested for a breach of the peace. He was found to have two unwrapped razor blades in his pocket. B. used razor blades in his work but he had not been at work for four days and was not wearing his working clothes.

B. was charged with a breach of the peace and a contravention of s.1(1) of the 1953 Act. After trial he was acquitted of the former and convicted of the latter. He appealed that conviction on the ground that there was insufficient evidence of an intention to cause personal injury.

Lord Justice-Clerk (Ross) (at p. 563)

"[Counsel for the appellant] drew our attention to the terms of section 1(1) of the Prevention of Crime Act 1953 which makes it an offence for a person without lawful authority or reasonable excuse to have with him in any public place any offensive weapons. Offensive weapon is defined and it is now well recognised that offensive weapons fall into three classes. The first class is those made for use for causing personal injury; the second is those adapted for such use, and the third is those not so made or adapted but intended by the person having it with him for such use by him. The suggestion of the Crown in the present case was that razor blades fell into the third category to which we have referred, and that was the conclusion at which the sheriff arrived. [Counsel], on behalf of the appellant, maintained that the findings in the case did not justify the sheriff in arriving at that conclusion. The advocate-depute on the other hand maintained that the sheriff was justified in reaching that conclusion; in support of his submission he referred us to the case of *Lopez* v *MacNab* [1978 J.C. 41]. The facts in that case were somewhat different to the facts in the present case. In that case the court laid down that the question of the statutory intention was one which might be drawn as an inference from facts and circumstances. In the case of *Lopez* v *MacNab* they held that the sheriff was entitled to draw that inference. The weapon in question there was a sharp, pointed kitchen knife. It was found in the appellant's possession in a public house. A customer had reported being alarmed on seeing the man in the bar with a knife and the manager then approached the appellant from behind and seized the knife from his inside pocket. The police were then called. As we say, in that case, the court held that the sheriff was entitled to draw the inference of intention to use the weapon for the purpose of personal injury.

"Each case of course must be decided on its own facts. So far as the facts in the present case are concerned the advocate-depute maintained that the necessary inference of the statutory intention to use the blades to cause injury to the person could be drawn from the fact that there were two blades, not one, from the fact that they were in the trouser pocket unguarded and unprotected, the fact that he had not been at work for several days and that he was not wearing his working trousers. The sheriff, however, in this case had accepted that the appellant was employed by a double-glazing firm and that in the course of his employment he did use razor blades to scrape windows. There was thus an explanation for his having possession of razor blades. It is in our view significant [that] when the police came upon this disturbance there was no question of the appellant having done anything which would suggest an intention to make use of what was in his pocket. To the contrary, all that is found is that at the material time he had in his possession a stick which he was waving about in the air. That, in our opinion, does not support the suggestion that he had with him razor blades with the intention of using them to cause injury to the person. Having regard to the nature of the findings in this case we are satisfied that the sheriff was not entitled to draw the inference which he did and to which he gave expression in finding 11. There is nothing in the facts found proved here which in our opinion would justify the inference that the appellant had possession of these two razor blades in a public place with the intention of using them to cause personal injury."

Appeal allowed.

Serrated saw blade	**4.23**
Neilson v. Wilson	**4.23.1**

1996 G.W.D. 7–381

N. appealed against a sentence of three months' detention. He was found at a railway station with a home-made knife with a 12-inch serrated saw blade, the only purpose of which was to cause personal injury. Since the offence N. had successfully addressed his alcohol problem. The sentence was not excessive.

Appeal refused.

Shotgun	**4.24**
(i) R. v. Hodgson	**4.24.1**

[1954] Crim.L.R. 379

H. discharged a shotgun from his car when following another car. H. was charged with having with him in a public place an offensive weapon, namely the shotgun. Pearson, J. directed the jury that a shotgun is not an article made for causing injury to the person and therefore the Crown must establish an intention on the part of the accused at the time of firing the shotgun, to use it for causing injury to the person. The question whether the accused had such an intention is for the jury to decide.

Decision not reported.

NOTE
Hodgson's case is cited in the commentary to *R. v. Jura* [1954] Crim.L.R. 378, see *supra* at para. 3.2.2., to which in principle it is similar.

4.24.2   **(ii) R. v. Gipson**

[1963] Crim.L.R. 281

G. was convicted of carrying an offensive weapon contrary to the 1953 Act. He was very fond and very jealous of a girl, R. He discovered that R. had been out with another man. He drove to her house taking with him a shotgun which he said he had been using for shooting pigeons earlier in the day. He saw R. in the street in company with some young men. He loaded the gun and fired it in the air. He said that he did so not to frighten R. or her companions but "to make me feel bigger, to make her feel more of me." The trial judge having ruled that a shotgun was not an offensive weapon *per se* failed to make it clear to the jury that the burden was on the prosecution to prove that G. intended to use it for causing injury to the person, and appeared to hold the view that the burden had shifted to R.

Held, the court agreed that a shotgun was not an offensive weapon *per se.* It followed that the burden was on the prosecution of proving intent to cause injury: *R. v. Petrie* (1961) 45 Cr.App.R. 72. In the present case it was all the more essential that there should have been a clear intention to that effect since the gun was fired into the air and there were no accompanying words of intimidation (as in *Woodward v. Koessler* [1958] Crim.L.R. 754).

Appeal allowed.

4.24.3   **(iii) R. v. Sparks**

[1965] Crim.L.R. 113

S. was convicted of carrying an offensive weapon, namely, a shotgun. He brought it to a meeting at which the sale of stolen property was to be negotiated, saying: "You told me he had brought his minders and I thought I would back you up with this. We ain't going to lose all that gear for nothing." The judge directed that a shotgun was an offensive weapon and, as S. denied having it, no question of lawful authority or reasonable excuse arose.

Held, an ordinary shotgun not being an offensive weapon *per se* the direction was wrong, in that the judge did not leave to the jury the question of the intention for which it was carried. However, it was a clear case for the application of the proviso to section 4 of the Criminal Appeal Act 1907.

Appeal dismissed.

Shuriken **4.25**

McGlennan v. Clark **4.25.1**

1993 S.L.T. 1069

C, an accused person, was charged on summary complaint with a contravention of s.1(1) of the 1953 Act. The accused was searched by police officers who found a shuriken in his trouser pocket. It was a non-flexible metal plate with several sharp radiating points. The accused stated to the police that it was used for throwing. The sheriff sustained a submission that there was no case for the accused to answer on the ground that there was no evidence that the item was a weapon or offensive *per se*. He refused to take into account the declaration in para. 1(h) of the Schedule to the 1988 Order in determining whether the shuriken was an offensive weapon *per se*. The Crown appealed.

Held, (1) that the nature of the shuriken was such that the sheriff should have concluded that there was a prima facie case that it was an offensive weapon; (2) that where it was clearly stated in a statutory instrument that an article was to be regarded as an offensive weapon, it could be regarded as an offensive weapon *per se* for the purposes of the Prevention of Crime Act 1953, and there was accordingly a case to be answered; and appeal allowed and case remitted to the sheriff to proceed as accords.

The sheriff reported in the stated case in the following terms, *inter alia*:

"When the Crown case closed the solicitor for the respondent submitted that there was no case to answer. He said that the item was not an offensive weapon per se, ie a weapon made for use for causing personal injury, and there was nothing in the evidence we had heard to indicate that the respondent intended to use it as a weapon. The appellant's depute conceded that there was no evidence of any intention to use the item as a weapon. He maintained that it was an offensive weapon per se. I allowed him an adjournment to produce some authority for that proposition. Thereafter he was unable to produce any case to that effect. He put before me a copy of the Criminal Justice Act 1988 (Offensive Weapons) Order 1988. The Schedule thereto reads: [The sheriff quoted the terms of para 1 of the Schedule and continued:]

"He submitted that in terms of the statutory instrument the item could be held to be an offensive weapon per se. The solicitor for the accused submitted that the statutory instrument did not make the item an offensive weapon per se.

"I took the view that there was no case to answer. Section 141 of the Criminal Justice Act 1988 strikes at any person who manufactures, sells or hires or offers for sale or hire, exposes or has in his possession for the purpose of sale or hire or lends or gives to any other person a weapon to which that section applies. It does not refer as far as I know to the Prevention of Crime Act 1953 and it was not suggested to me that it did. I have been able to find no case brought under the Prevention of Crime Act in which a 'shuriken' has been found to be an offensive weapon per se. The only weapons, apart from those concerning which there is no doubt, about which there have been such a finding appear to be rice flails, sword sticks and flick knives. Whether an article is an offensive weapon for the purposes of s.1 of the Prevention of Crime Act 1953 is a question of fact: *R v Williamson* (1977) 67 CrAppR 35. The first witness simply said that the item was for throwing. Despite being given an opportunity to expand on that answer he merely repeated it. He did not characterise the item as a weapon at all. The second witness only identified the item and said that it was a throwing star. He was not asked and gave no opinion on what it was used for. As neither officer gave evidence that the item was a weapon, far less an offensive weapon per se, I upheld the submission and acquitted the respondent. It seemed to me when the appellant's depute referred to the statutory instrument that I was being asked in the absence of evidence to declare that the item mentioned in para 1(h) therein was an offensive weapon per se which as I apprehend it is beyond my power. I would like to observe that in this court such charges as this are regularly brought and in many of them the arresting police officers display the same coyness when asked to state what their evidence is about the items which they find. Deputes who mark and frame such charges do not seem to apply their minds to what they intend to try to prove, which seems to me to be important in view of the generally cautious nature of the evidence given by the police officers in such cases. As I see it, it is not for this court to supplement the actual evidence by declaring what is or is not an offensive weapon per se but to deal with the matter in the light of the evidence presented."

Lord Justice-General (Hope) (at p. 1071)
"The evidence for the Crown consisted of that of two police officers. They described a search which they carried out on the respondent who had been placed in a police vehicle after a disturbance. They found an item in his rear right hand trouser pocket which the first police officer said was known as a shuriken, a Chinese throwing star or a death star. When asked what its purpose was he replied it was used for throwing, and the article

when examined was described by the police officer as being a non-flexible metal plate with several sharp radiating points. The article itself was produced in court and was identified as label no. 1. The second police officer corroborated the first on the finding of this item in the possession of the respondent. He identified it as the throwing star which they found in his possession. It was on that evidence that it was submitted that there was no case to answer.

"Section 1(4) of the Prevention of Crime Act 1953 contains a definition of the expression 'offensive weapon' which is in these terms: '"Offensive weapon" means any article made or adapted for use for causing injury to the person, or intended by the person having it with him for such use by him.'

"There is no suggestion in this case of any adaption, and there was no evidence in the Crown case as to its intended use by the respondent. The article was simply found in the rear right hand trouser pocket. The essential question was whether the nature of the article was such that there was a case to be made against the respondent that it was made for use for causing personal injury.

"There are two chapters in the evidence which can be looked at for an answer to this question. Before we do that, however, we should mention that counsel who appeared for the respondent conceded that the nature of the article was such, on the evidence that had been led for the Crown, that the only purpose which it could be said to have was for causing injury to the person. He accepted that this could be seen readily from the nature of the article itself which has been produced at this trial, and he conceded that this appeal should be allowed and the case remitted to the sheriff to proceed as accords. The learned Solicitor General concurred in that motion, but he also drew our attention to some of the remarks made by the sheriff, particularly about an alleged coyness by arresting police officers as regards items which are said to constitute offensive weapons. He suggested that some comment was necessary to assist the sheriff as to how cases of this kind should be approached.

"Turning then to the chapters in the evidence which are of importance, the first is the nature of the article itself. What is plain from the narrative of the evidence, and was no doubt plain from an examination of the article, is that it consisted of a metal plate with several sharp radiating points. It was designed to be thrown. It was designed so that when it reached its target it would be likely to penetrate or at least cut it. Prima facie it was an article made for use as a weapon. This is not one of those cases where it could be suggested that the article had dual purpose, such as, for example, *Woods v Heywood*, 1988 SLT 849. There is no hint in the Crown evidence that this was something that could be used as a tool or an implement of some kind, nor is there any suggestion that it had any sporting or innocent recreational use. On the Crown evidence there was no innocent purpose for which a throwing star or death star might be used. Its nature was, therefore, such that the sheriff should have, without hesitation, concluded that there was a prima facie case to be made that this was an offensive weapon on the ground that it was made for use for causing injury to the person.

"The second point to be made relates to the provision in the Criminal Justice Act 1988 (Offensive Weapons) Order 1988. The Schedule to that order reads as follows: [His Lordship quoted the terms of the Schedule and continued:]

"One has only to compare the wording of para (h) of the Schedule with the narrative of the evidence to see that the article which is label 1 in the present case falls precisely within the description of an offensive weapon for the purposes of that Schedule. It was submitted to the sheriff that reference could be made to the statutory instrument in order to decide the question whether this was an offensive weapon per se. The sheriff rejected that argument, on the ground that that Schedule did not appear in an instrument made under the Prevention of Crime Act 1953. He considered the question before him to be a question of fact to be determined solely on the evidence. But in *Tudhope v O'Neill* 1982 SLT at p 361, Lord Justice Clerk Wheatley made the point that assistance can be derived from other statutory provisions, whether they be in primary legislation or in a statutory instrument, which describe what are to be regarded as offensive weapons. Where one finds in a statutory instrument, which must be taken to have been approved by Parliament, that is clearly stated that an article of the kind produced in the present case is to be regarded as an offensive weapon, with the result that in terms of s141 of the 1988 Act it is illegal to make, sell, hire or lend or give it to another person, then it seems to follow naturally that it can be regarded for the purposes of the Prevention of Crime Act as an offensive weapon per se which will found the basis for a prosecution under that Act if a person is found in possession of it without lawful authority or reasonable excuse in a public place.

"Accordingly this case seems to us to be one where on the Crown evidence there was a case to be answered. We do not accept the criticism the sheriff makes about coyness having been displayed by the police officers, since the article itself spoke so forcibly as to its nature and its use, and the question whether it was an offensive weapon was one for him, not the police officers, to decide. For these reasons we shall, as we were invited to do, answer the question in the case in the negative, and we shall remit to the sheriff with a direction that he should proceed as accords."

Appeal allowed.

Sock filled with sand   **4.26**

Ashbee v. Jayne   **4.26.1**

[1966] Crim.L.R. 49

Late one night the defendant took a car without the owner's consent, and filled a sock with wet sand and put it in the car. He then drove to a garage, and after some suspicious behaviour tampered with the cash register in the attendant's absence; during this time he had the sock in his pocket, but he never used it. The police were called. When asked about the sock, the defendant said, "As a matter of fact you need these things these days." He was charged with having an offensive weapon, contrary to s.1(1) of the 1953 Act.

The justices concluded that the sock was not made or adapted for use against a person except possibly for self-defence, and not made or adapted by the defendant for use to cause injury to the person; that at most the defendant might have used it in self-defence; and that the prosecutor had not proved that the defendant had intended to use the sock for causing injury.

The prosecutor appealed.

Held, that the justices had been rather muddled in their approach. They appeared to think that the "implement" was not made or adapted to cause injury because the defendant's motive might have been self-defence. That was a wrong approach: a revolver was no less an offensive implement because it was carried for the purpose of self-defence. Once possession of an offensive weapon was proved, if the article was made or adapted for use for causing injury to the person then the onus shifted to the defendant to prove, on a balance of probabilities, lawful authority or reasonable excuse; but if the article was not made or adapted for such use the onus remained on the prosecution throughout to show that the defendant carried it with the intention of using it to injure. The justices should have looked at the sock and then decided by looking at it whether it was made or adapted so as to cause injury. It would, however, be useless to send the case back because the exhibit would have long since been destroyed; so the appeal would be dismissed.

Appeal dismissed.

4.27 *Steel bar, cycle chain, metal clock weight and studded glove*

4.27.1 **Bradley v. Moss**

[1974] Crim.L.R. 430

The defendant was stopped by police officers on the evening of May 15, 1973 while he was running on a road. The officers found in his possession a length of polished steel ($10^1/2$ inches long), a two foot length of cycle chain, a metal clock weight and a studded glove. When questioned, he said that he had heard a lot of shouting from some youths and had changed his normal route to avoid a possible confrontation. He said that he had carried the weapons because he was expecting trouble from a gang of youths, that there had been trouble in the past, and that the weapons were for his protection as some lads had been after him. He appeared before a juvenile court on an information alleging that he on May 15, 1973, at Northwich, without lawful authority or reasonable excuse had with him in a public place a steel bar and the other articles, contrary to s.1 of the 1953 Act. At the hearing the justices found that the defendant was unpopular with older youths in the area, that on several previous occasions those youths had either chased him or threatened to assault him, that he had reported those incidents to the police and, that although he had not been assaulted before May 15, 1973, he had been attacked and beaten by a gang of youths on May 31, 1973. The justices found that the articles were offensive weapons but they were of the opinion that the defendant genuinely believed that there was an imminent threat which affected the circumstances in which the weapons were carried, a belief which was confirmed sixteen days later when he was attacked by a gang of youths as a result of which he received hospital treatment. They held that the defendant had lawful authority or reasonable excuse, within the meaning of s.1 of the 1953 Act, for carrying the weapons and on that basis they acquitted him. The prosecutor appealed by case stated to the Queen's Bench Divisional Court.

Held, that applying the principle in *Evans* v. *Hughes* [1972] 1 W.L.R. 1452, 1455 to the present case, there was no sort of lawful authority or reasonable excuse within the meaning of s.1 of the 1953 Act for carrying the weapons. The defendant did not need to carry all four weapons for protection. It was also necessary to reiterate that the carrying of weapons by a person for defence must be related to an imminent and immediate threat of danger at the time when he carried them, and the regular and routine carrying of weapons was not sanctioned. The justices clearly gave an unduly wide meaning to the phrase "lawful authority or reasonable excuse" in s.1. In the circumstances of the present case they were bound to say that there was no reasonable excuse. The case would be sent back to the justices with a direction to convict.

Appeal allowed.

Stone **4.28**

Harrison v. Thornton **4.28.1**

(1979) 68 Cr.App.R. 28

H. and T. were involved in a fight with two other men, B. and A., in a public street. During the fight the police arrived. B. was then holding T. on the ground and punching his face. H. then picked up a stone, threw it at B., but missed. H. was charged with a contravention of s.1(1) of the 1953 Act. He was convicted and appealed on the basis that the stone was not an offensive weapon within the meaning of the act.

Marshall, J. (at p. 31)

"The finding of the learned magistrate is set out in paragraph 5 [of the stated case]: 'The defendant had neither lawful authority nor reasonable excuse for his possession of the piece of stone, because (a) the law confers no authority on any person to throw a stone to try to disengage two combatants, and (b) as a matter of fact, the defendant had not reasonable excuse for arming himself with the stone because before he did so, the police had arrived and, in any event, if he wished to intervene to assist his companion [T.] he should have done so by attempting to pull the combatants apart. (ii)(a) The piece of stone was within the definition of an offensive weapon contained in section 1(4) of the Prevention of Crime Act 1953, since, when the defendant picked it up, he intended to use it for causing injury to the person of [B.], and, (b) It was immaterial that the defendant had armed himself with the stone at the scene of the fight and had not brought it with him. Accordingly I convicted the defendant.'

"The argument that has now been advanced in this Court is based upon the fact first of all that the defendant had not come on to a public place armed with a stone; secondly that in the context of this particular section a stone is not an offensive weapon. In my view the learned magistrate was perfectly right in holding that having taken up a stone to throw at one of two combatants that were continuing fighting, and putting forward as the excuse for that that he was doing that merely for the purpose of parting the combatants is one which the magistrate was in fact quite right in rejecting. As soon as he had armed himself with the stone and had in fact used it by throwing it, in my judgment in this particular case the stone became an offensive weapon within the definition as set out in subsection (4) of section 1 of the Act of 1953.

"The second argument as I understand it is an argument that in this case the offence that is now under appeal was allied to a second offence of which the defendant was acquitted by the magistrate, and having been so acquitted he ought not to be convicted of this particular offence. In my judgment an argument based upon that consideration is not a sound one. The two cases that have been quoted in support of the argument, the case of JURA (1954) 38 Cr.App.R. 53; [1954] 1 Q.B. 503 and DUFFY (1966) 50 Cr.App.R. 68; [1967] 1 Q.B. 63, one decided in 1954 and the other in 1966, are cases which are not really applicable to the facts of this case. On the findings of the learned magistrate I would in fact dismiss the appeal and say that in my judgment he was right in convicting the defendant of the offence that he did."

Lord Widgery, C.J. (at p. 32)

"I also agree, I would only add that [counsel for the appellant's] argument was really based on a passage and the headnote in *Jura's* case ... that the Prevention of Crime Act 1953 was intended to apply to persons who with no excuse whatever set out with an offensive weapon. In fact that was a very different case where a man was perfectly lawfully in possession of an air rifle which never became an offensive weapon at all until the moment when he decided to misuse it. This is a case where from the moment the stone was picked up it was an offensive weapon. I would also dismiss this appeal."

Appeal dismissed.

4.29   *Studded belt*

4.29.1   **McMahon and Another v. Dollard**

[1965] Crim.L.R. 238

D. 1 and D. 2 were among a group of 15 young persons marching along a footpath, taking up the whole width of the footway. They were dressed in black leather jackets and were chanting, "Down with the mods" and as people riding motorscooters passed they shouted "we will have you over." D. 1 and D. 2, together with the other youths, were charged with using threatening behaviour, contrary to s.5 of the Public Order Act 1936; in addition D. 2 was charged with possessing an offensive weapon, a studded belt, contrary to s.1 of the 1953 Act. They were convicted and appealed.

Held, (1) that the whole group had acted together and each member was guilty of threatening behaviour; but (2) that there was no evidence to show that D. 2's belt was intended for use for any other purpose than keeping up his trousers, or that it had been studded for any offensive purpose, so that his conviction of possessing an offensive weapon must be quashed.

Appeal allowed.

<table>
<tr><td>Sword stick</td><td>4.30</td></tr>
<tr><td>(i) Davis v. Alexander</td><td>4.30.1</td></tr>
</table>

(1970) 54 Cr.App.R. 398

Early one morning a policeman on duty saw two youths walking along the road, one of whom was waving in the air what appeared to be a walking stick. The policeman stopped, examined the walking stick and found that it was a sword stick.

The policeman charged the youth with having an offensive weapon with him in a public place and the youth replied, "I had an excuse, I had just picked it up from being mended and was just taking it home."

At trial the magistrates found three matters: (1) that the walking stick was an offensive weapon *per se*; and (2) that the appellant had no reasonable excuse for having it with him at the time, they having disbelieved his story that he was just taking it home from having it repaired. The third matter which they found was that the respondent had no intention of using the sword stick to cause injury to any person, and it was as a result of that finding and after consultation with their clerk that they acquitted the respondent. The prosecutor appealed.

Lord Widgery, C.J. (at p. 399)

"Section 1 of the Prevention of Crime Act 1953, which makes it an offence without lawful authority or reasonable excuse for a person to have with him in a public place any offensive weapon, defines 'offensive weapon' in subsection (4) as 'Any article made or adapted for use for causing injury to the person, or intended by the person having it with him for such use by him.' In other words offensive weapons may be of two classes; either an article which is an offensive weapon *per se* made or adapted for causing injury to the person, or an article which can have a purely innocent purpose which will only be an offensive weapon for the purposes of the Act if it is intended for use to cause injury to a person. The justices, in my judgment, came to an entirely correct conclusion in saying that the sword stick was an offensive weapon *per se*, being clearly made for the purpose of causing injury to the person. They seemed to think, however, that not only was it necessary to find that it was an offensive weapon *per se*, but also that the respondent had it with him with the intention of using it to cause injury to a person. That, of course, is a very vital ingredient if the offensive weapon is not an offensive weapon *per se* and only becomes one if it is carried with the intent to cause injury. But once they found that it was an offensive weapon *per se*, and I think they were clearly right in so finding, and found further that there was no lawful authority or reasonable excuse for the respondent having it with him then it automatically followed that he was guilty of an offence. I would send this case back to the justices with a direction to convict."

Appeal allowed.

4.30.2   **(ii) R. v. Butler**

[1988] Crim.L.R. 695

B. was convicted of carrying an offensive weapon. The weapon was a sword stick which he used to wound a youth who attacked him in a train carriage. In evidence B. said he had the stick because of difficulty in walking, he did not carry it as a weapon of offence or defence. He appealed against conviction.

Held, the judge accurately directed the jury as to what was a reasonable excuse. Furthermore, he left to the jury the question of whether or not this item was an offensive weapon *per se.* That was, if anything, over-generous to the defence.

The court drew attention to the decision of the Divisional Court in *Davis v. Alexander, supra,* where the Court regarded as entirely correct the conclusion that a sword stick was an offensive weapon *per se,* being clearly made for the purpose of causing injury to the person.

Appeal dismissed.

NOTE

Professor J. C. Smith, Q.C. has commented on this case: *ibid.* at p. 696. He wrote that when Mr Butler was attacked viciously, "he was entitled to use reasonable force in self-defence and the Lord Chief Justice stated that in the circumstances he used the swordstick 'perfectly properly in self-defence.' When a person is attacked he may use anything which he can lay his hands on to defend himself, so long as the force he uses is no more than is reasonable in the circumstances, as they appear to him. The defendant's possession of the sword stick was unlawful up to the moment when it became reasonable to use it in self-defence, whereupon it presumably became lawful; but that could not undo the offence already committed.

"The defendant argued that he had a reasonable excuse because he never considered that he had an article made or adapted for causing injury at all. It appears that it was left to the jury to consider whether this was a reasonable excuse and they were not satisfied that it was, the burden of proof being on the defendant. No doubt he would have had a reasonable excuse if he had thought the article was an ordinary walking stick and had not realised that it contained a sword. As he did know that it contained a sword, it might be asked, what did he suppose it was made for if not for injuring people? But a plausible answer might be that he thought it was made to be kept as a curio or 'collectors' item.' A sword seems at first sight to be obviously an offensive weapon within the meaning of the Act; but does the maker of swords for the Lifeguards today really make them with any expectation that they will be used for cutting or stabbing any person? Are they not in fact made for ceremonial purposes, not for causing injury to the person? But it would probably not be easy to dissuade a court from taking judicial notice that a sword is an offensive weapon, *per se,* and anyone who walked through the streets carrying one would be likely to find himself convicted of an offence, even though he was only 'showing off.'"

One may take issue with the phrase "*only* 'showing off.'" The purpose of the 1953 Act is to prevent injury and to show off a sword in a public place is to risk the occurrence of precisely what the 1953 Act is aimed at.

In practice it is sometimes said that it is unfair to an accused that he should have to answer both charges of contravening s.1(1) of the 1953 Act and an assault on an individual where the offensive weapon in the former is used in the latter. *R. v. Butler* makes it clear that where there is the passage of some time, both charges may be brought and required to be answered. For a Scots case in point see, *infra, Campbell* v. *H.M. Advocate* at para. 5.5.

Syringe 4.31

Taylor v. H.M. Advocate 4.31.1

1992 G.W.D. 11–601

On appeal against sentence, *held*, that nine months' imprisonment was not only not excessive but was lenient, although not backdated, where T., having persisted in talking to a young lady on a train, had threatened the guard, who had sought his particulars when he could not produce a valid ticket, with a syringe and claimed to be HIV positive, when he had a bad record, including 10 convictions for breach of the peace, and the offence had been committed three weeks after he had been released from prison.

Appeal refused.

NOTE

In Scotland, charges involving syringes tend to be either breach of the peace, such as in *Taylor* v. *H.M. Advocate, supra,* or culpable and reckless conduct, see *Gemmell* v. *H.M. Advocate,* 1990 G.W.D. 7–366 and *Kimmins* v. *Normand,* 1993 S.L.T. 1260. However, there appears to be no reason in law why a syringe must not be considered to be an offensive weapon in the appropriate facts and circumstances.

4.32 *Timber*

4.32.1 **Goodwin v. Jessop**

High Court of Justiciary, unreported, May 2, 1989

G. and another boy were seen by two policemen late one evening to be running away from the sound of a disturbance. Each boy was carrying a piece of timber. G. was seen to brandish or wave the piece of timber that he had. G. neither said nor shouted anything. The two boys were friendly towards each other.

The pieces of timber were about three inches in diameter and some four to five feet in length. One piece of timber had nails protruding from it. The policeman giving evidence at trial could not say which boy had which piece of timber.

The stipendiary magistrate recognised that the pieces of timber were not offensive *per se,* but in the whole circumstances held that the Crown had proved them to be so used and that the boys had the requisite intent. G. appealed.

Appeal refused.

NOTE

This case is discussed *supra* at para. 3.7.9. Similar circumstances arose in *McIntosh* v. *Jessop,* 1990 G.W.D. 1–17 and in *Smillie* v. *Wilson,* 1995 G.W.D. 10–542 but a more sophisticated weapon is to be found in *Fitzgerald* v. *Jessop,* 1990 G.W.D. 26–1468, viz. "a pole with a nail protruding".

4.33 *Toy pistol*

4.33.1 **(i) R. v. Powell**

[1963] Crim.L.R. 511

P. was convicted under the 1953 Act, s.1(1), of carrying an offensive weapon. He went to a hospital to visit a girl who had gone there for treatment. D., the girl's uncle, who was a porter at the hospital, tried to get P. to leave the grounds. It was alleged that P. drew a toy pistol from his pocket and pointed it at D. and then hit him with it. P. said he had the pistol with him because he was looking after it for someone and he denied taking it out of his pocket or striking D. with it. He appealed against conviction.

Held, the use of an article to cause injury establishes that the defendant had it with him with the intent to cause injury: *Woodward v. Koessler* [1958] Crim.L.R. 754; the toy pistol was therefore an offensive weapon. The place where the incident took place was public because visitors to the hospital and their friends were permitted to enter that part of the grounds. Where it is shown that the defendant had with him in a public place an offensive weapon the onus shifts to him to show that at that time—and not merely at an earlier time or when he left home or some other place—he had lawful authority or reasonable excuse. In the circumstances P. was properly convicted. The decision in *R. v. Jura* [1954] Crim.L.R. 378 depends on the special facts of the case.

Appeal dismissed.

(ii) R. v. Titus and Others   4.33.2

[1971] Crim.L.R. 279

T. and five others were charged on indictment with having with them imitation firearms with intent to commit an indictable offence, contrary to s.18 of the Firearms Act 1968. The weapons in question were water pistols filled with ammonia. Counsel for the defence submitted that the water pistols were weapons "designed or adapted for the discharge of any noxious liquid" within s.5(1)(*b*) of the Act, and so were not within the definition of imitation firearms contained in s.57(4) of the Act. Counsel for the prosecution submitted that "designed" meant "designed by the manufacturer of the weapon" and "adapted" required more than simply filling with a noxious liquid.

Held, by the trial judge that the water pistols were not weapons designed or adapted for the discharge of a noxious liquid and accordingly the water pistols were capable of being imitation firearms within the definition contained in s.57(4) of the act.

Found not guilty.

NOTE

An imitation firearm is defined as "any thing which has the appearance of being a firearm (other than such a weapon as is mentioned in s.5(1)(*b*) of this Act)." It follows that, if the water pistols were within the definition in s.5(1)(*b*) they could not be imitation firearms as the Crown alleged.

The report does not narrate the circumstances in which T. and the others came to have water pistols filled with ammonia with them. However, it is not difficult to envisage circumstances in which the water pistols filled with ammonia were offensive weapons within the meaning of s.1(4) of the 1953 Act. That is particularly so if the individual who has the pistol with him intends to commit a crime such as theft or assault or intends to resist arrest or to prevent the arrest of another; see s.18(1) of the Firearms Act 1968.

4.34   *Truncheon*

4.34.1   **(i) R. v. Spanner**

[1973] Crim.L.R. 704

S. and others were each convicted of carrying an offensive weapon. They were employed as security guards at dance halls and each carried a truncheon "as a deterrent" and "as part of the uniform." The trial judge directed the jury that they had no lawful authority to carry the truncheons and that as a matter of law in his view their reasons for carrying them did not amount to a reasonable excuse. S. appealed.

Held, accepting that the question was one for the jury, the judge's view was correct. Weapons must not be carried as a matter of routine or as part of a uniform.

Appeal dismissed.

NOTE

In the commentary to the above case it was asked what the position was of the "thousands of men said to be employed by private security forces and to be armed with batons or sticks. Are they all committing offences daily?" The answer is in the affirmative on this authority and since the 1973 decision private security forces are not, or rather ought not, to be "armed" as they had been.

4.34.2   **(ii) Houghton v. Chief Constable of Greater Manchester**

(1987) 84 Cr.App.R. 319

For the facts see above at para. 3.2.9.

May, L.J. (at p. 323)

"The first [point arising in this case] is whether a policeman's truncheon is an offensive weapon *per se* within the comments that I have just made in relation to section 1(3) of the [1953] Act. I for my part have no doubt that it is. One trusts, and fortunately it is the fact, that police officers rarely use their truncheons for the purpose of defence. But that is what they are for. It is not an article which, as I think, can be equated to a sandbag, or even to a razor. A razor is not intended to be used as an offensive weapon, although unfortunately it is so often put to that purpose. A razor is intended to enable a person to shave. A truncheon, in my judgment, cannot be said to possess *per se* any such innocent quality. It is intended, if it is going to be used at all, to be used for the purpose of offence, albeit that offence may be part of the defence on the part of the police officer concerned. Consequently I reach the conclusion without hesitation that a police officer's truncheon is an offensive weapon *per se*."

Appeal allowed in part.

(iii) McKee v. MacDonald   4.34.3

1995 S.L.T. 1342

McKee was charged on summary complaint with a contravention of s.1 of the Prevention of Crime Act 1953. He was found in possession of a light wooden baton which was in the shape of an old fashioned police truncheon on which was painted the words "View sun from Spain". The sheriff considered that the baton was made for causing personal injury and convicted the accused, who appealed on the grounds that it was not *per se* offensive and that in any event he had a reasonable excuse for possessing it because he had been given it as a present but had forgotten that it was in his motor car.

Held, that it could not be said beyond reasonable doubt that the baton was an offensive weapon *per se* as it was in the form of a souvenir, was comparatively light and did not contain the qualities which would equiparate it with a police truncheon and appeal allowed and conviction quashed.

Observed, that the court would be very hesitant at holding that the accused had a reasonable excuse simply because the accused had forgotten about the baton.

Lord Sutherland (at p. 1343)
"The appellant is David McKee who was convicted of possessing an offensive weapon, namely a wooden baton, in a public place without lawful authority or reasonable excuse.

"The piece of wood in question was found by two police constables in the back seat of the appellant's car when they were carrying out a routine check.

"The sheriff held that this weapon was a truncheon and therefore was an offensive weapon per se. We have had the benefit, as indeed did the sheriff, of seeing this particular weapon and it is a baton approximately 18 inches in length in the general shape of the old fashioned police baton. It has painted on it the legend 'View sun from Spain' and has a coloured cord threaded through the handle. What is perhaps more significant about it, although this is not a matter that the sheriff deals with in his findings or his note, is that it is extremely light in weight for the amount of wood which it contains.

"Counsel for the appellant submitted that just from its appearance and design it would not be described as an offensive weapon per se. The fact that it bore a resemblance in shape to a truncheon did not necessarily make it a truncheon.

"The sheriff had founded upon the case of *Houghton v Chief Constable of Greater Manchester* [(1987) 84 Cr.App.R. 319] and counsel maintained that that case if anything assisted him rather than assisting the Crown May LJ commented in that case that a truncheon cannot be said to possess per se any innocent quality. Even a razor may have an innocent quality because of course it is intended to enable a person to shave. A truncheon, on the other hand, is intended, if it is going to be used at all, to be used for the purpose of offence albeit that offence may be part of defence on the part of the police officer concerned. Consequently he reached the conclusion without hesitation that a police officer's truncheon is an offensive weapon per se. In that case, of course, what was being discussed was an actual police officer's truncheon.

"Counsel founded upon the observation by May LJ that a truncheon cannot be said to possess any innocent quality, whereas the piece of wood produced in the present case appears to be in the form of a souvenir and appears to be intended to be of a decorative nature and, what is more to the point, it lacks the essential quality of a truncheon, namely that it should be of a solid piece of material which could cause injury if used.

"The advocate depute maintained in reply that an offensive weapon does not cease to be an offensive weapon just because it can be used for another purpose. What has to be looked at is its intrinsic nature. A flick knife does not cease to be an offensive weapon per se because it has on it 'A present from Paris' and the advocate depute maintained that we were in the same situation in the present case.

"We would entirely agree with him insofar as his observation about a flick knife is concerned but we do not agree with him in relation to any suggestion that we are in the same situation here. If we look at the weapon concerned it does not appear to us to be designed for the purposes of offence and to have only that quality. It appears to us to be in the form of a souvenir, comparatively light for its nature and does not contain the qualities which would equiparate it with a police truncheon.

"On the whole matter we are not satisfied that it can be said beyond reasonable doubt that this was an offensive weapon per se and therefore we consider that the sheriff should have upheld the submission of no case to answer and should not have convicted the appellant. We shall therefore answer both questions in the negative. We should add that counsel also maintained that even if it was per se an offensive weapon the appellant had it in his possession with a reasonable excuse. The excuse was said to be that he had been given this weapon by a friend the day before, she having brought back a number of souvenirs from Spain and given him this one and he simply put it in the back of his car and forgot about it. We need say no more about this matter as we are proposing to quash the conviction anyway, but we should merely observe that we would be very hesitant about saying that there could be any question of a reasonable excuse where the suggestion was that it was there simply because the appellant had forgotten about it. However, it is not necessary to deal with that matter in any detail."

Appeal allowed.

Wire rope　　　　　　　　　　　　**4.35**

Smith v. Lees　　　　　　　　**4.35.1**

1993 G.W.D. 12–808

S. was convicted of a contravention of the 1953 Act and he appealed that conviction.

Held, that where a two foot length of steel wire rope wrapped in insulating tape had been found in S.'s car at 3.25 a.m., placed within easy reach of the driver, the sheriff had been entitled to conclude that it was an offensive weapon, namely a cosh, that it had been made or adapted for use for causing injury to the person and was intended for such use in terms of s.1(4) of the 1953 Act, and to reject S.'s explanation that it was used for controlling a rottweiler dog when there were no bite marks or dog hairs on the binding and no sign of a dog's presence in the car itself.

Appeal refused.

CHAPTER FIVE

5.0 Sentencing

5.1 Introduction

There are two aspects to the sentencing of individuals who have been convicted of contraventions of the 1953 Act. First, there are general sentencing principles or attitudes and secondly, there are principles or attitudes specific to offensive weapons. The literature on sentencing generally is substantial; what follows is a chronological reference to the cases relating to offensive weapons.

5.2 (i) Addison v. MacKinnon

1983 S.C.C.R. 52

A. was convicted of having an offensive weapon, namely a piece of wood. He appealed against conviction and sentence and the sheriff made in the stated case findings-in-fact that indicated that A. had been in a public street carrying a piece of wood, broken off at one end, coming to a jagged end. It was four feet long and was part of a clothes pole. A co-accused was carrying a clothes pole, broken off at one end and tapering to a sharp point. It was about seven feet long. Both weapons were capable of inflicting serious injury. A. and the co-accused were shouting gang slogans and swearing. A. was waving his piece of wood about.

After conviction the sheriff considered detention but, as A. was a first offender, he was obliged on statutory authority to obtain a social inquiry report. That report in due course revealed an impression in the social worker's mind that A.'s family appeared to be respectable people with a high regard for social norms and values, who said that they had never had any previous involvement with the authorities. The social worker indicated that A. impressed him or her as being a quiet, pleasant boy who had had no previous involvement in any delinquent activity until the present offence.

The sheriff recorded in a note to his stated case that on the question of sentence he sentenced A. to a term of detention because of the serious nature of the charge. There was clearly some serious gang activity in the particular housing scheme on the night in connection with weapons being carried not only by A. and his co-accused, of which activity A. was part. The impression which A. created in court was certainly not the impression which he managed to convey to the social worker.

Lord Justice-Clerk (Wheatley) (at p. 54)

"It is quite clear from the sheriff's note that the reason why he decided to send the appellant to a young offenders institution was the nature of the contravention of the Act of Parliament. Certainly the sheriff had the advantage of presiding at the trial which disclosed the background circumstances against which the offence was committed. He also had the advantage of seeing and hearing the appellant in court and forming his own impression of the type of person with whom he was dealing, and he mentions this point, presumably to counter a contrary impression which had been expressed by the social worker in the social enquiry report."

Later

"[I]n deciding as he [the sheriff] did that no other sentence was appropriate than the one which he imposed, namely detention, in view of the serious nature of the offence, he does not explain why he ignored the non-custodial alternatives. In particular he does not deal with the very important factor which in our opinion is always a serious one in cases of this or any other nature, namely that the offender has not previously offended. While we are normally reluctant to interfere with the disposal of the judge in the court below, we feel that in all the circumstances the sheriff here has not given sufficient consideration to the fact that this was a first offender."

> Appeal against sentence allowed
> and a fine of £100 imposed.

NOTE

Addison v. *MacKinnon, supra*, was distinguished in *Smith* v. *Wilson*, 1987 G.W.D. 13–452 and an appeal against sentence was refused because "the sheriff devoted the greatest care and attention to the question of disposal and gave full reasons for his decisions which were perfectly adequate."

(ii) O'Rourke v. Lockhart 5.3

1984 S.C.C.R. 322

O'R. was charged with possession of an offensive weapon and he pleaded guilty. Police had been summoned to a public house as there had been a disturbance there. They arrived and saw O'R. running in a nearby street, brandishing a knife at passers by. He was bleeding from a cut to his mouth. He was arrested and the knife was taken from him.

His explanation was that he had been assaulted by others. His recollection of events was not very clear. He had returned home after the assault, collected the knife referred to and took it back onto the streets. No-one had been injured by the accused.

O'R. admitted a record which included six previous convictions for breach of the peace and he had been imprisoned for a short time for an assault. He was sentenced to sixty days' imprisonment and he appealed against that sentence.

In a note in the stated case the sheriff observed that it seemed to him that the mitigating factors were exiguous. O'R. had disengaged himself from whatever trouble had occurred; returned home; selected the "very formidable knife"; and had returned with it apparently seeking revenge or at least intimidation.

Lord Justice-General (Emslie) (at p. 323)
"It is evident, we think, that the sheriff perhaps paid too little attention to the antecedents of the offence which were admitted and that, further, the sheriff attached too great importance to the significance of the appellant's record to relation to this particular offence with which we are dealing today."

Appeal against sentence allowed
and fine of £250 imposed.

NOTE
Sheriff Gordon in his commentary on this case, *ibid*, at p. 324, observes that it is noteworthy that the court appears to regard as mitigatory the fact that this offence followed an attack on the appellant who returned to the street after deliberately arming himself.

5.4   **(iii) R. v. Webster**

(1985) 7 Cr.App.R.(S.) 359

W. was seen by policemen to urinate on the wall of an underground station waiting room. He was arrested for that and then searched. He told the policemen that he had a Stanley knife in his coat pocket and he said that he used it at work and left it in his jeans. When he was changing to go out that evening he found the knife and transferred it to his coat "just in case." He added, "if you lived in Shepherds Bush with all the [black people] you'd carry a knife. If they attacked me I wouldn't recognise them but if I slash one of them on the face I'd be able to find him again."

W. was convicted of having an offensive weapon in a public place and he was sentenced to 12 months' imprisonment. He appealed against that sentence.

Rose, J. (at p. 359)

"It is quite correct to say, as [counsel for the appellant] reminds this court that the Stanley knife was an instrument which would be used by the appellant in the course of his employment whilst cutting fibre glass. Indeed it is also right to say that employees were encouraged to use their own tools, and take them home or lock them away each evening.

"The appellant is 27 years of age and a single man. He has worked in a variety of jobs. He has eleven previous convictions which include seven offences at different times in his career of assault occasioning actual bodily harm, two of using threatening or abusive words and two convictions, of which this is in the second, of possessing an offensive weapon. The previous conviction occurred in March 1983, when he was sentenced by the Bow Street Magistrates to a period of three months' imprisonment concurrently with a similar sentence for assault occasioning actual bodily harm.

"[Counsel for the appellant] urges upon us that as the maximum sentence for this offence is a period of two years' imprisonment, as the weapon was not a flick knife and in view of the appellant's personal circumstances, a sentence of 12 months' imprisonment is too much.

"This Court is not persuaded to take that view. A Stanley knife is capable of inflicting a very serious injury indeed. This is not a case in which it could be said on behalf of the appellant that he had shown remorse by pleading guilty. This is not a case in which his record could be relied upon when circumstances of mitigation were called in question."

Appeal dismissed.

NOTE

In the circumstances, the appellant in *Maciver v. H.M. Advocate*, 1991 G.W.D. 27–1579 was lucky to have community service substituted for detention, but in *Park v. H.M. Advocate*, 1996 G.W.D. 23–1327 the appellant received 18 months' imprisonment for having a Stanley blade fitted into a cardboard handle. Self-defence was also put forward in *Humble v. H.M. Advocate*, 1995 G.W.D. 26–1393.

5.5   **(iv) Campbell v. H.M. Advocate**

1986 S.C.C.R. 516

C. was charged on indictment with a simple assault that involved striking another on the body with a razor, and possession in a public place of that razor. He pleaded guilty and after a social inquiry report was obtained he was sentenced to one year's imprisonment on each charge, these sentences to be consecutive to each other. C. appealed by note of appeal against sentence on the ground that the sentences were in themselves excessive and also unreasonable in being consecutive.

In his report to the High Court of Justiciary the sheriff indicated that he viewed the charge as a very serious one. The reason C. gave for carrying the weapon was not accepted by the sheriff nor apparently by a social worker who had prepared a report prior to sentence being passed.

The sheriff regarded it as fortunate that no injury was sustained by the complainer: only damage to his clothing. C. had armed himself with a razor and when threatened by three youths, with no weapons, had produced it to defend himself. The sheriff emphasised C.'s previous convictions for violence and observed that the present offences had occurred just after he had been released from prison in England.

The sheriff felt that although no injuries were sustained by the complainer in the assault, twelve months' detention on that charge was necessary to show to C. that "society will not tolerate such behaviour when the violence is of a continuing nature." It seemed to the sheriff that C. must have been looking for or expecting trouble, otherwise why arm himself with a razor before going out?

The sheriff reported in regard to the second charge that the weapon was small and therefore readily concealed on the person. At the same time it was very sharp and it could have inflicted severe injuries.

Lord Justice-Clerk (Ross) (at p. 517)
"[Counsel for the appellant] has maintained that each period of detention for one year was excessive and that the sentences should not have been ordered to run consecutively. So far as the first charge is concerned he has stressed that there was no injury and of course no injury was libelled in that charge. None the less to assault a third party and strike him with a razor is a serious form of assault whether injury results or not. In many cases it may be a matter of chance as to whether or not injury results from the assault. [On charge] (1), being a charge of assault involving the use of a razor,

we are quite satisfied that a sentence of one year's detention … cannot be regarded as excessive. So far as the second charge is concerned it is also a serious offence for a person to have with him in a public place an offensive weapon such as a razor and in the circumstances here again we are not satisfied that the sentence of one year's detention in respect of that offence can be regarded as excessive."

"[Counsel for the appellant] argued strongly that these two offences were really one, that they could not be separated, and that therefore in the circumstances the sheriff ought not to have ordered that the sentences should run consecutively. We cannot accept that submission. So far as the statutory offence is concerned, it was committed as soon as the appellant placed a razor in his pocket or on his person and proceeded to a public place. That offence would have been committed whether or not the offence libelled in charge (1) had ever been committed."

Appeal refused.

NOTE
Having an offensive weapon in a public place and also using that weapon in an assault are separate offences; for the position in England see *supra, R. v. Butler* at para. 4.30.2.

(v) Mullen v. Wilson 5.6

High Court of Justiciary, December 16, 1986

M. was arrested by policemen for shouting in a public street and brandishing a sword. He had apparently been involved in an incident a short time earlier. He was injured as a result of that incident to the extent of having bruising about the face and several cuts on his head.

M. had found the sword on a grass verge near to where the incident had occurred. The sword had a sharp pointed blade about two feet long. It seemed that the sword could be used either as a conventional sword or as a bayonet fixed to the end of a rifle.

M. pleaded guilty. He had previous convictions but the last had been a trivial matter some eleven years earlier. It was submitted on behalf of M. that to be sent to prison would result in him losing his job in a local shipyard.

The sheriff sentenced M. to three months' imprisonment concurrent on each of two charges, namely possessing the offensive weapon in a public place and breach of peace. M. appealed against sentence.

Lord Justice-Clerk (Ross)

"In his Report, the learned sheriff explains why he took a serious view of the offence. What weighed with the sheriff apparently was that someone might have been seriously injured or indeed killed that evening, but of course nothing like that in fact happened. The sheriff took the view that it was important that he should demonstrate as emphatically as he could that behaviour of this kind could not be tolerated. He thus concluded that sentences of imprisonment were necessary.

"In our opinion the object which the sheriff apparently desired to achieve could just as well be attained by the imposition of a fine. In our opinion the learned sheriff has not given sufficient weight to the fact that the appellant only has a minor criminal record (all previous offences having been dealt with either by admonitions or moderate fines), nor has he given sufficient weight to the fact that the offences were on the whole fairly trivial ones. Likewise the sheriff has not attached sufficient weight to the fact that if this man is sent to prison he will lose his job. The appellant has kept out of trouble since 1975, there was no question of an assault, and therefore in our opinion there was no need for him to receive a custodial sentence."

> Appeal allowed and a fine of
> £25 imposed *quoad* charge one
> and an admonition given *quoad*
> charge two.

NOTE
This case is reported at 1987 G.W.D. 4–118.

5.7   **(vi) Smith v. Wilson**

1987 S.C.C.R. 191

S. was the front seat passenger in a car stopped by the police in the early hours of the morning. A search revealed that S. had a flick knife in his jacket pocket and also a small quantity of cannabis resin.

A policeman asked S. to account for possession of the flick knife and he replied: "It's not mine. I got a loan of it from my mate." He was asked if any one of the other occupants was who he had in mind and he replied: "No, none of them, another mate up in Glasgow but I suppose it's my rap."

S. pleaded guilty to possessing an offensive weapon and also cannabis resin. He had one previous conviction for a minor assault.

Social inquiry reports were favourable. Mitigation by his solicitor highlighted *inter alia* that S. had been found with the knife in his possession in a car in transit rather than in a public place. The sheriff sentenced S. to three months' imprisonment for possessing a flick knife and 14 days' imprisonment for possessing cannabis resin. S. appealed against the sentence as being excessive.

In his report to the High Court the sheriff outlined various options and observed that: "It is hardly necessary to remind your Lordships of the frequency with which assaults occur nowadays in which very serious, and sometimes fatal, injuries are caused as a result of the use of knives. Moreover, your Lordships have over the years given innumerable warnings about the very severe penalties which will be imposed upon those persons who are found guilty of such assaults. In these circumstances, it respectfully seems to me that it is the responsibility of this court to take such steps as it can to deter and punish those who carry, or are minded to carry, knives as offensive weapons and to demonstrate emphatically that the mere carrying of a knife as an offensive weapon in a public place cannot, and will not, be tolerated."

Lord Justice-General (Emslie) (at p. 193)

"The significant feature of *Addison's* case, however, where a custodial sentence was quashed on a first offender for a Prevention of Crime Act offence, was that in the sheriff's report he gave no reasons for discarding the non-custodial alternatives, and that is made abundantly clear in the opinion of the court. That circumstance permitted the court to look at the matter afresh and the case accordingly turns on the speciality that it had to do with a particular appeal in which the court was free to substitute its own opinion for that of the presiding sheriff. This, however, is not a case like *Addison* because, having read the sheriff's report, it is plain that he devoted the greatest care and attention to the question of disposal, and unlike the case of *Addison* he gives very full reasons for deciding to do what he did. We do not rehearse these reasons because they are set out at some length [in] his report, and notwithstanding that the appellant is a first offender and that a community service place was available, we are entirely persuaded that the sheriff's reasons are perfectly adequate and we are not in a position to substitute our own view for his, even if we had been inclined to think that another disposal would have been appropriate for this offence which the sheriff rightly regarded as a serious one, carrying potential danger."

Appeal refused.

NOTE
Imprisonment for having a flick knife was upheld in *Aitken* v. *MacDonald*, 1991
G.W.D. 13–780; *R.* v. *Smith* (1992) 13 Cr.App.R.(S.) 665; *Early* v. *Normand*, 1993 G.W.D.
7–477; *Steele* v. *Normand*, 1993 G.W.D. 29–1824; *R.* v. *Beveridge* (1993) 14 Cr.App.R.(S.)
211; and *Crossley* v. *Hamilton*, 1995 G.W.D. 27–1447.

5.8   **(vii) Brennan v. MacKinnon**

                                  1987 G.W.D. 14–507

Two policemen approached B. and two other men. B. had in his
hands a chair leg with a piece of lead taped to it. Of the other two
men, one had a baseball bat which he was swinging above his head
and the other had a pair of Japanese fighting sticks. The last man
recognised the policemen, dropped his weapon and ran, as did B.
and the other. They were arrested.

     B. pleaded guilty to possessing an offensive weapon. At the time
of sentencing B. was serving a sentence of 30 months' detention.
However the sheriff took the view that the weapon was a nasty
one being adapted for causing greater injury and B. had a poor
record. The circumstances in which B. had the weapon clearly
showed that its use was imminent. Accordingly, the sheriff decided
to impose a sentence of three months' detention to run consecutively from the end of his then sentence. B. appealed.

Lord Justice-Clerk (Ross)
     "The question of whether or not to make a sentence consecutive
or concurrent is very much a matter for the judge imposing the
sentence. If the sheriff had made this period of three months'
detention concurrent with the sentence presently being served the
result would be that the appellant was not really receiving any
punishment in respect of this offence. Having regard to the nature
of the offence we are of the opinion that the sheriff was clearly
justified in ordering that the three month period of detention should
commence at the expiry of the sentence of thirty months."

                                                    Appeal refused.

NOTE
This case is reported briefly at 1987 G.W.D. 14–507.

5.9   **(viii) Moore v. H.M. Advocate**

                     High Court of Justiciary, September 25, 1987

M. went to see his father in Saltcoats and while there M. was arrested in the course of a fracas involving M.'s brother and a taxi-driver. When the police arrived they saw M. throw away an object which was recovered and found to be a sheath knife with a tapered blade of some four and a half inches in length. M. was arrested and in the course of a struggle with the police he head-butted a constable, causing a bruising injury to his nose.

M. was charged *inter alia* with possessing an offensive weapon in a public place and assaulting a policeman. He pleaded guilty to these two charges which were on indictment. He was sentenced to 18 months' imprisonment and six months' imprisonment respectively and concurrently. He appealed against sentence. In his report the judge indicated that the sentences were determined by the circumstances of the offences and also by the accused's record of convictions. He emphasised that M. was only just out of prison when these two offences were committed.

Lord Justice-Clerk (Ross)
"The trial judge in his report tells us why he came to impose the sentence which he did. He says the two sentences imposed were determined by the circumstances of the offences and by the accused's record. He points out, and this is very important, that the appellant had seen fit to arm himself with a knife when he had been out of prison for only seven days. The appellant has a very formidable record of previous convictions and these include convictions for violence. In these circumstances for him to arm himself with a knife was undoubtedly a very serious contravention of the Prevention of Crime Act 1953, s.1."

Appeal refused.

NOTE
A brief report of this appeal is to be found at 1987 G.W.D. 34–1225.

(ix) R. Shorter   5.10

(1988) 10 Cr.App.R.(S.) 4

S. was seen by police officers to run away from an incident in which he was not involved apparently. In the back of a police vehicle S. was seen taking steps to try to get rid of something. It was found to be a domestic knife of the sort used on vegetables. When S. was asked what the knife was for, he replied: "It's for sticking in [people] like you, what do you think it's for?" He was then arrested and cautioned and replied: "I ain't saying [nothing]. I don't have to talk to you." S. was charged with possessing an offensive weapon in a public place and he was convicted. He was sentenced to six months' imprisonment and he appealed against that.

Woolf, L.J. (at p. 5)

"In considering [counsel for the appellant's] submission that the sentence of six months' immediate imprisonment was too long, one has to take into account the way the matter was dealt with at the trial by the appellant and the appellant's behaviour when he was initially arrested. It is also highly relevant that in 1981 (admittedly when he was only 17) there was an offence of possessing an offensive weapon (copper tubing) dealt with by the magistrates' court, when he was fined £50; and again in February 1983 there was an offence of possessing a flick knife dealt with by the magistrates, when he was fined £200.

"In cases with different backgrounds and different circumstances from those to which we have referred, this Court could well take the view that six months' immediate imprisonment could be too long for the carrying of a weapon of this sort. But each case has to be considered in accordance with its own facts. On the facts of this case, which have been shortly summarised, this Court takes the view that the sentence imposed by the extremely experienced judge was perfectly proper and not one with which this Court can interfere."

Appeal dismissed.

5.11   **(x) Grana v. Wilson**

High Court of Justiciary, unreported, July 21, 1988

G. was in the back of a police car. A policeman saw G. pull an object from his trouser pocket and attempt to place it down behind the seat where he was sitting. The object was found to be a knife. G. was later charged with possessing an offensive weapon in a public place and after trial he was convicted. He was sentenced to three months' imprisonment and he appealed against sentence.

In his report the sheriff noted that there was no dispute that the knife was a "Class One" weapon in the same category as, for example, swords and flick knives. It was a type used in martial arts and it was described by the policeman involved with the case as "more or less an unsprung flick knife."

The sheriff described the knife as being in two parts which were hinged to the blade at the end furthest away from the point. When the knife was closed, the two parts of the handle enfolded the blade, one on either side of it. To expose the blade, each part of the handle was folded back in an arc of 180 degrees so that the two parts joined together to form the handle proper. The blade itself was sharp and pointed. The hinges holding the two parts of the handle to the blade were very loose so that the knife could be opened, and the blade exposed, very quickly.

The sheriff cited *Smith* v. *Wilson*, 1987 S.C.C.R. 191, and his own dicta at p. 192 (cited *supra* at para. 5.7). Notwithstanding that the details of the present case differed somewhat from those in the case of *Smith* v. *Wilson*, it appeared to the sheriff that the reasoning expressed in the words cited applied in the present case just as it did in the earlier case.

Lord Grieve

"[Counsel for the appellant] submitted that what the sheriff had really done, was to look at the case of *Smith* (albeit he considered that it was not precisely on all fours with the present case) and reached the opinion that for offences of this nature, namely being found in possession of an offensive weapon in a car, the appropriate sentence, never mind the particular circumstances of the case, was a custodial one. It was said by the Lord Justice General, rightly in the case of *Smith*, that if the Court was to alter the custodial sentence imposed in that case, it would simply be substituting its own opinion for that of the sheriff. That is not the function of the Court of Appeal.

"The sheriff has given his reasons, having regard to the particular facts in this case, for imposing the custodial sentence which he did. We cannot fault this approach and we consider he was fully entitled to take the course which he did."

Appeal refused.

NOTE

J. B. Hill in *Weapons Law* lists (in Appendix 2A) various weapons and describes them: a balisong or Filipino butterfly knife is said to be a knife with the blade stored in a folding two-piece handle which reverses for use with the two halves of the handle held together by a clip. It can be opened at speed by flicking the blade and one half of the handle in a circular movement. It is said to be a type of switchable knife. Grana's knife is a form of butterfly knife.

(xi) Jacobs v. Wilson   5.12

1989 S.C.C.R. 9

J. as found by a policeman at 4 a.m. in a public street. He was shouting abuse and he was brandishing a knife. He was cautioned and charged with a breach of the peace and he replied: "I've been done once already. There's no way I'm getting bottled or slashed again." He was also charged with possessing an offensive weapon in a public place and he replied: "He had a broken bottle. I had to defend myself." The knife was a butcher's knife with a blade of about 10 inches long and between one and one and a half inches wide.

J. appeared in court and he pleaded guilty. He had no previous convictions and the sheriff obtained a social enquiry report.

J.'s solicitor explained in mitigation that his client had drunk too much alcohol and returned home late. In the street where his house was he was chased by two youths and he had run into the house and picked up the knife. He had then run out into the street and the two boys had run off. J. had used the knife as a means of deterrence to frighten the youths away.

The sheriff sentenced J. to three months' imprisonment on each charge concurrently and J. appealed to the High Court of Justiciary against sentence. In his report the sheriff referred to his own *dicta* in *Smith v Wilson*, 1987 S.C.C.R. 191, *ibid.*, at para. 5.7, and, while conceding that the circumstances differed from the present case, considered that the reasoning there applied equally. Imprisonment was thus the only appropriate manner of dealing with this case.

Lord McDonald (at p. 11)

"The sheriff in his report made reference to the case of *Smith v Wilson*, which had been decided on appeal from the same sheriff, in which the appellant, although a first offender, had been given a custodial sentence for possession of an offensive weapon. That sentence was upheld on appeal and the sheriff in the present case, while recognising that it differed in certain respects from *Smith v Wilson*, took the view that the reasoning contained within that case applied in the present case. That reasoning made reference to the frequency with which assaults occur, involving sometimes fatal injuries as a result of the use of knives, and made reference also to warnings which had been given about severe penalties which would be imposed upon persons found guilty of such assaults. He said that in these circumstances it seemed that it was a responsibility of the court to take such steps as it could to deter and punish those who carry or are minded to carry knives as offensive weapons and to demonstrate emphatically that the mere carrying of a knife as an offensive weapon in a public place cannot and will not be tolerated. There were distinguishing features in the case of *Smith v Wilson*, not least of which was the nature of the weapon involved, which was of the type known as a 'flick knife' which could be activated by the pressing of a button so causing the blade to spring directly out of the handle. Another feature was that in that case there was no apparent reason for the appellant to be in possession of the knife other than that he intended to use it somewhere as an offensive weapon. In the present case, as we have said, it was pointed out to us that, although the original acquisition of the knife was said to be for defensive purposes only, that particular need had disappeared by the time the appellant was arrested.

"In our view the sheriff in the present case comes close to suggesting that within his jurisdiction at least in every case where a person is found in possession of what can be regarded as an offensive weapon contrary to section 1(1) of the 1953 Act a custodial sentence is inevitable. He does not say so in terms, but it does appear to us that it is possible to take the view that he has fettered his discretion in some way in this matter. We have decided, therefore, that there is substance in the submission which was made to us by counsel on behalf of the appellant, and that in the circumstances the custodial sentence which was imposed can be regarded as excessive. There is a social enquiry report available to us in which it was pointed out that the appellant would be a suitable subject for community service, and although that was recognised by the sheriff, he did not consider that that was an appropriate course. There was also before him a community service order report indicating that he was suitable for such work and that a suitable work placement was available. We consider, therefore, that in the circumstances of this case that course ought to have been followed rather than the imposition of a custodial sentence in the case of this first offender. We therefore propose to dispose of this case by quashing the sentence of three months' imprisonment and we have in mind to impose a sentence of community service for a period of 120 hours."

Appeal allowed.

(xii) McCabe v. Docherty 5.13

High Court of Justiciary, June 7, 1989

It was reported to the police that M.'s house had been vandalised. Policemen attended there but actually found M. in a public street nearby. He was in a highly agitated condition. The policemen thought that M. was seeking the perpetrators of the damage to his home in order to exact his own revenge.

M. was searched and the policemen found a large knife concealed behind the waistband of his trousers and down the leg of his trousers. The knife was a large kitchen knife with a sharp pointed blade of about eight inches long. M. was cautioned and asked why he had the knife. He replied, succinctly: "Nae [person] puts my window in."

M. pleaded guilty to possessing an offensive weapon in a public place. The defence solicitor explained in mitigation that M.'s house had been vandalised, one of the perpetrators having shouted to M. that he was "dead meat". M. had decided to go to stay at a friend's house and had taken the knife with him for protection.

The sheriff considered a social enquiry report and M.'s previous convictions, being nine breaches of the peace and an assault. He noted in his report that by pleading guilty M. conceded that he had the knife with him with the intention to cause personal injury. He recalled the "innumerable warnings" by the High Court of Justiciary that severe penalties are likely to be imposed on individuals found guilty of assaults with knives and that it had often been said in the sheriff court that the mere possession of a knife as an offensive weapon in a public place was "very likely" to result in a custodial sentence.

The sheriff held that there was in this case no other appropriate method of dealing with M. than by a sentence of six months' detention in a young offenders' institution. M. appealed and in the High Court of Justiciary it was held that in those circumstances the sentence could not be said to be excessive.

Appeal refused.

NOTE
A briefer report of this case is to be found at 1989 G.W.D. 29–1329.

5.14   (xiii) Nolan v. McGlennan

High Court of Justiciary, January 18, 1990

Policemen were called to a public house late one evening to deal with a violent incident. There they were told that N. had a knife with him. They spoke to him and took him to the toilet to search him. He began to struggle but he was restrained. He produced the knife but he tried to put it down the toilet bowl.

N. was charged with possessing an offensive weapon in a public place and obstructing the police when trying to search him. He pleaded guilty. The sheriff had regard to N.'s "appalling record" which disclosed at least 10 charges of assault and sentences of up to nine months for crimes of violence. The sheriff sentenced him to three months' imprisonment.

N. appealed and in his report the sheriff noted that he felt that he would be failing in his duty if he had not imposed a sentence of imprisonment. The ground of appeal that N. had no analogous previous convictions was, in a sense, true; but the sheriff held that the 1953 Act is intended to prevent assault, of which N. had convictions for many.

Lord Wylie
"[Counsel for the appellant] recognised that the sheriff was fully entitled and indeed bound to take into account the substantial criminal record placed before him and as the sheriff points out the appellant has a record of violence which certainly aggravates or might be thought to aggravate the possession of this offensive weapon."

Appeal refused.

NOTE
This case is reported briefly at 1990 G.W.D. 8–418.

(xiv) Gilroy v. Lowe 5.15

High Court of Justiciary, March 27, 1990

G. pleaded guilty to a breach of the peace and possession of an offensive weapon in a public place. The circumstances were that in the early hours of a morning at an all-night bakery, G. became involved in an argument and he produced a flick knife and he "played" with it while *inter alia* issuing challenges to others to fight him.

G. was then the subject of a community service order of which 60 hours remained uncompleted and he had outstanding fines totalling £200. He was sentenced to 30 days' imprisonment on the first charge and three months on the second charge, the periods to run concurrently.

G. appealed against both sentences. In his report the sheriff observed that a quarrel in the early hours, when one of those involved is in possession of such a grossly offensive weapon as a flick knife, are circumstances which all too often preface the ultimate tragedy. The sheriff was of the view that wherever possible the courts should act emphatically to prevent the next stage being reached. To the achievement of that end he considered a prison sentence to be the surest means.

Lord Wylie
"[T]he appellant has an appalling record for a man of 22 and although he now regrets his actions on the night in question, the

circumstances as outlined by the sheriff are of a very serious nature. The appellant has recently been the subject of a community service order which we understand has now been completed, but notwithstanding that, we are quite unable to say that the sheriff imposed sentences which were excessive in the circumstances although we might ourselves have taken a different view if we had had the case before us in the first instance."

Appeal refused.

NOTE
This case is reported briefly at 1990 G.W.D. 19–1064.

5.16   **(xv) Murdoch v. Carmichael**

1993 S.C.C.R. 444

M., an appellant, was convicted of a contravention of the 1953 Act in respect of a knife and sentenced to six months' imprisonment. He appealed to the High Court by stated case.

Held, that although the appellant had a long list of previous convictions, including one for contravention of the 1953 Act, that had not led to a custodial sentence and he appeared to have kept out of trouble for about four years, and that taking these matters into account it was neither necessary nor appropriate for the sheriff to impose the maximum sentence; and appeal against sentence allowed and sentence quashed and sentence of three months' imprisonment substituted.

Lord Justice-Clerk (Ross) (at p. 449)
"The sheriff in his note refers to the appellant's previous convictions and there is a formidable list. Between 1985 and 1988 he had been convicted of offences under the Firearms Act and also convicted of assaults to severe and permanent disfigurement, assault to severe injury, assault with intent to rob, assault, as well as other crimes. He has one previous conviction for a contravention of section 1(1) of the Prevention of Crime Act 1953. This occurred in 1986 and the disposal then was a fine of £300. [Counsel for the appellant] has emphasised that the last conviction is in 1988 and that accordingly the appellant had not had any convictions prior to this time for a period of some four years. In these circumstances he maintained that the sentence imposed by the sheriff was in the circumstances excessive. Although the appellant undoubtedly has a long list of previous convictions, we have come to the conclusion that the sheriff did not perhaps attach sufficient weight to the fact

that he appears to have kept out of trouble for a period of approximately four years. Moreover, although there is a previous conviction for section 1(1) of the Act of 1953, that had not led to a custodial sentence in 1986. Taking these matters into account, we have come to the conclusion that it was neither necessary nor appropriate for the sheriff to impose the maximum sentence in respect of charge (1). We shall accordingly quash the sentence of six months imposed by the sheriff and in substitution for that we shall impose a sentence of three months' imprisonment."

NOTE
The appeal against conviction is noted at para. 3.4.11.

(xvi) McMeckan v. Annan 5.17

1989 G.W.D. 33–1515

M. appealed against a sentence of three months' detention imposed for his second offensive weapons conviction. He already had one previous conviction for each of vandalism and assault.

Held, that it had not been established that no disposal other than a custodial one was appropriate for a second offensive weapon conviction. The detention was quashed and community service for 150 hours substituted.

Appeal allowed.

NOTE
Despite the ambivalence in the decision above, the High Court of Justiciary was clearly influenced by the appellant having a second and a third conviction for offensive weapons: see *Walker* v. *Carmichael,* 1993 G.W.D. 2–101 and *McLean* v. *Friel,* 1992 G.W.D. 24–1367, respectively.

(xvii) Pelosi v. Normand 5.18

1993 S.C.C.R. 45

P., the appellant, who was aged twenty at the time of the offence, was convicted of having an offensive weapon with him in a Glasgow street, contrary to section 1 of the Prevention of Crime Act 1953. He was carrying a knife on his way to a disco. He admitted two minor convictions for breach of the peace. He was sentenced to three months' imprisonment, and appealed to the High Court by note of appeal against sentence.

Held, that the carrying of offensive weapons is something that the courts will deal with severely and that, despite the appellant's limited previous convictions, the magistrate was fully entitled to impose the sentence he did; and appeal refused.

Lord Allanbridge (at p. 46)

"What happened was that at 1.30 a.m. in the morning of 7th September 1991 the appellant was making his way to a disco in Jamaica Street, Glasgow. In Argyle Street he was seen by two plain-clothes police officers to remove a knife from a jacket pocket and place it down the front of his trousers. He was stopped by the officers in Jamaica Street before he reached the disco and the knife was taken possession of. Under caution the appellant said, 'It's only for my own safety.' It is probable, said the stipendiary magistrate, that the knife was moved from the jacket to the trousers in case an admission search was carried out by the disco stewards. The knife was of a kitchen type, approximately eight inches in length with a point and a single-edge tapered blade of approximately four and a quarter inches. The knife was of high-quality German manufacture and was probably of professional standard. At the time of the offence the appellant was employed as a chef.

"The stipendiary magistrate said, in selecting the sentence that he did, that the carrying of weapons and crimes of violence are causing considerable concern. Parliament has increased the maximum custodial sentence [on summary conviction] for a contravention of section 1 of the Prevention of Crime Act 1953 from three months' to six months' imprisonment. In the Glasgow area there have been special articles in newspapers and on television featuring a consultant surgeon from one of the main casualty departments which explain, as we are well aware, the effects of using knives as weapons. This youth was going to a disco routinely armed, as the stipendiary magistrate puts it, or at least armed with a knife and he takes the view that the courts must be seen to be taking a firm line and to be bringing the message home to the public that the carrying of weapons will not be tolerated. We agree with these sentiments. It has been said before in this court, and we say it again today, that the carrying of offensive weapons is something that the lower courts and this High Court will deal with severely. This particular young man has very limited previous convictions [...] but none the less, because of the severe penalties which will and must attach to such offences we are of the opinion that in this particular case the stipendiary magistrate was fully entitled to impose the sentence of three months' imprisonment that he did. The appeal is refused."

Appeal refused.

(xviii) Prior v. Normand 5.19

1993 S.C.C.R. 118

P., the appellant, who was aged eighteen and had only one minor previous conviction (for vandalism), was arrested in the centre of Glasgow one afternoon after a disturbance. He struggled with the police, but did not produce a weapon. When he was searched in the police station a lock knife was found in his possession. When he was asked by the police to account for his possession of the knife, he replied, "You were getting that, you [****]." He was charged with having the knife with him in a public place, contrary to the 1953 Act. He pleaded guilty and was sentenced to three months' detention. He appealed to the High Court against the sentence.

Held, that it must be brought home to the appellant and other persons that the carrying of knives as offensive weapons will not be tolerated by the court, and that in this case, and especially in view of the appellant's reply to the police, the sentence was not appropriate; and sentence quashed and sentence of six months' detention substituted.

Lord Allanbridge (at p. 119)

"The sheriff concluded that the gravity of such an offence was certainly such as to justify a custodial sentence being imposed. We fully endorse that view. The sheriff went on to explain that the appellant did not seek to put forward any justification for having struggled violently with the police who were acting in the execution of their duty and although the lock knife had not been produced by the appellant he had had it with him in a public place, namely the centre of Glasgow in the afternoon. The sheriff explains that there has been increasing concern about violence and the carrying of offensive weapons in the centre of certain towns recently. This has always been a problem in Glasgow. We endorse that view and it has become apparent that the courts must take a severe line with persons who carry offensive weapons in public places. Parliament some time ago increased the maximum sentence for this offence to six months' imprisonment. This young man was given three months' detention. We have carefully considered all that has been said on his behalf by his counsel but we have reached the view that it must be brought home to him and other persons that the carrying of knives as offensive weapons cannot and will not be tolerated by these courts. The reason is obvious. The carrying of such weapons can well lead to very serious crimes being committed, even sometimes, as we are well aware, occasioning death. In this particular case, and especially in view of the appellant's reply to caution and charge by the police, we have decided that three months' detention was not appropriate. We therefore quash it and substitute a sentence of six months' detention."

Appeal refused.

NOTE
Financial penalties were imposed in *Farrell* v. *Allan*, 1988 G.W.D. 16–695 and *Beattie* v. *MacDougall*, 1989 G.W.D. 25–1092, which both involved lock knives but occurred some years earlier than *Prior* v. *Normand, supra*. Detention, however, was upheld in *McVicar* v. *Normand*, 1993 G.W.D. 22–1362, and in *Leino* v. *Cardle*, 1996 G.W.D. 7–382 the sentence of imprisonment arose from having "a spring loaded locking knife."

5.20   **(xix) Noble v. Lees**

1993 S.C.C.R. 967

N., a sixteen-year-old first offender, pleaded guilty to having a knife with him in the street at 1.30 a.m., contrary to s.1 of the 1953 Act. He told the police that he had been assaulted earlier that night by another youth and was searching for him in order to "settle the score", having apparently gone home and armed himself after being assaulted. He was of good character and background and it was represented to the sheriff that he had not intended to use the knife to attack his assailant. The sheriff sentenced him to three months' detention and he appealed to the High Court by note of appeal against the sentence.

Held, that the sheriff had not attached sufficient weight to the fact that the appellant was a first offender who came from a good background and was only sixteen, that, had he been older, a custodial sentence might have been called for, but that it was not necessary in this case if the appellant was agreeable to a community service order; and appeal allowed and sentence quashed and order for 180 hours' community service substituted.

In his report the sheriff stated, *inter alia*:
"The respondent's depute informed me that at about 1.40 a.m. on 27 December 1992 two uniformed police officers of Lothian and Borders Police on mobile patrol in the Bonnyrigg area were approached by a taxi driver who warned them that there was a youth about 500 yards up the road waving a knife about. The police then proceeded to the location indicated by the taxi driver where they found the appellant in an agitated state. They detained the appellant and, on searching him, found a knife in

a back trouser pocket. On being asked about the knife by the police the appellant stated that he had been assaulted by another youth earlier that night and that he was searching for the youth to 'settle the score.' Apparently after the incident in question the appellant had returned to his home at ..., armed himself with the knife and then returned to the place where he was seen by the police. The appellant had no previous criminal convictions.

"The appellant's solicitor drew my attention to the terms of a social enquiry report on the appellant prepared in connection with his appearance on 24 June 1993. I noted that the appellant was 16 years of age, single and unemployed. He came of a good family. I also noted that he had been assessed as suitable for community service and that the report suggested community service as an alternative to detention. Further the appellant's solicitor submitted that the appellant's action had been foolish and rash and stated that the appellant had not left his home with the knife with the intention of attacking his assailant.

"In determining sentence I bore in mind the terms of and suggestion as to disposal contained in the social enquiry report. I also bore in mind the facts that the appellant was a person of hitherto good character and that he came of a good family. However, I also considered that I had to bear in mind the fact that, after a violent incident in which he was involved, the appellant in the small hours went home and deliberately armed himself with a knife before going out again. In all these circumstances it seemed to me that a sentence of detention was necessary and inevitable. Bearing in mind the fact that the appellant had pled guilty to the offence and having regard to his character and circumstances, I felt that I could restrict the sentence to three months' detention."

Lord Justice-Clerk (Ross) (at p. 96)
"This is the appeal of James Robert Noble, who pled guilty in the sheriff court at Edinburgh on a charge of contravening section 1(1) of the Prevention of Crime Act 1953. That was a charge of having with him a knife in a public place without lawful authority or reasonable excuse. He was sentenced to three months' detention in a young offenders institution and it is against that sentence that he has now appealed.

"Today on his behalf [counsel] has immediately conceded that this was a serious offence. There is no doubt that the carrying of knives has become far too common and the court is bound to take a very serious view of anyone who is found guilty or pleads guilty to a contravention of section 1(1) of the 1975 Act.

[Counsel], however, has maintained that when regard is had to the circumstances of the appellant, detention is neither necessary or inevitable, as the sheriff thought. The appellant is a first offender and it appears that what occurred was out of character. He comes of a good family and has support within the family. It appears that on the occasion in question the appellant told the police that earlier that night he had been assaulted by another youth and that he was searching for the youth to 'settle the score.' He had apparently gone home and armed himself with a knife and then returned to the place where he was seen by the police. It was represented to the sheriff on his behalf that his action had been foolish and rash and that, although he had left home with the knife, he had not intended to use it in order to attack his assailant.

"There was before the sheriff a social enquiry report which was in favourable terms. The question which we must ask ourselves is whether it was necessary and appropriate in this case for the sheriff to impose a custodial sentence. We have, with some hesitation, come to the view that it was not necessary in this case to impose a custodial sentence. We feel that the sheriff did not attach sufficient weight to the fact that the appellant was a first offender who came from a good background and who was only sixteen years of age. Had he been older than that, it might well be that a custodial sentence would have been called for, but we feel that the sheriff did not attach sufficient weight to the fact that the appellant is only sixteen years of age. Accordingly, although this offence is undoubtedly a serious one and a custodial sentence would, in ordinary course, have been justified, we have come to the conclusion that it was not necessary to impose a custodial sentence in this case, provided that the appellant is agreeable to the making of a community service order which is the disposal suggested in the social enquiry report. Since the appellant has now indicated that he is willing to comply with a community service order, we shall quash the sentence of detention imposed by the sheriff and we shall make a community service order for 180 hours of community service during the next twelve months."

Appeal allowed.

NOTE
Sheriff Gordon has pointed out that in some cases the personal circumstances of the accused outweigh the gravity of the offence: 1993 S.C.C.R. 969. Such a view is based on *Noble* v. *Lees*, *supra*, and also on subsequent cases, *e.g. Logue* v. *Lees*, 1995 G.W.D. 1–33; and *Dougherty* v. *Lees*, 1995 G.W.D. 10–541. In other cases the deterrent aspect prevails: *e.g. Quinn* v. *Friel*, 1994 G.W.D. 9–539; and *McGregor* v. *Heywood*, 1995 G.W.D. 27–1444.

(xx) Anderson v. Orr   5.21

High Court of Justiciary, September 7, 1994

A. pleaded guilty to a contravention of s.1 of the 1993 Act. He was sentenced to the maximum period of six months' imprisonment. He appealed that sentence on the ground that it was excessive in that there was nothing about the offence in particular which justified the maximum sentence.

Held, the appellant had a bad record which included three assaults and he had indicated that the knife was for his own protection. The sentence was not excessive.

In his report the sheriff narrated the following:

"... about 12 noon on Saturday 29 January 1994 on Grant Street in Inverness there was a confrontation between the appellant and his co-accused on the one hand and two other men on the other hand. During the course of this matter which was not further described the appellant pulled out a knife. One of the opponents took it from him, broke it at a point between the handle and the blade and threw it away.

"The matter was subsequently reported to the police and the appellant was identified, traced, arrested and cautioned and charged making no reply.

"In mitigation [the solicitor for the appellant] advised me that the appellant was 23 years of age, unemployed, in receipt of £36 per week and he co-habited with a female, a child being expected in the near future.

"[The solicitor] then dealt with the previous convictions of the appellant. He stated that he could not disguise his lengthy criminal record but emphasised that he came from an unsettled background where offending was more the norm than the exception.

"He submitted that on a closer examination of the list of previous convictions there appeared to be some abate on the rate of offending and there was a general improvement in his behaviour which perhaps could be traced to the fact that he was about to father a child and that he was in a settled relationship.

"Turning to the offence itself [counsel] emphasised that there was no charge of brandishing a knife and the charge was only with carrying it, notwithstanding the circumstances which had been described. [He] emphasised that he could make no excuse for carrying the knife and that it was simply an aberration on the day.

"Prior to my hearing the plea in mitigation the respondent's depute had placed before me, in a plastic envelope, the broken knife. This was a broad bladed weapon rather similar in shape to a large cake knife but with sharp, not serrated edges.

"In considering sentence I paid careful attention to the circumstances described and the submissions of the solicitor for the appellant. I imposed a sentence of six months' imprisonment which is the maximum under the statute.

"While the background circumstances described are such that [the solicitor for the appellant] was correct in submitting that the charge was carrying not brandishing, they are basically unfavourable to the appellant but the fact that this knife was produced rather than simply found in his possession was a minor not a major factor in the sentence which I imposed.

"In relation to that sentence there were three major factors, two of which are closely related but which form separate considerations in my mind.

"The first factor was the appalling record of the appellant who is a regular offender. If there is any diminution in his rate of offending it is almost imperceptible.

"The second factor was the nature of the offence. Parliament has made it quite clear by the passing of the 1993 Act under which the appellant was prosecuted that there is major public concern in relation to the carrying of offensive weapons and knives are a particular public concern in this respect. I therefore considered the matter to be a serious offence for which imprisonment was the only possible sentence and this frankly and fairly admitted to be correct in the ground appeal, only the length of sentence being attacked.

"The third and final factor which is related to the second concerns the issue of knives being carried in a public place. This offence occurred in the middle of the day in an area near the centre of Inverness. So far as I am aware, from my experience in Inverness Sheriff Court over the years, the carrying of knives is an occasional and not a regular problem so far as the police and courts are concerned.

"It appeared to me, and I stated this when imposing sentence that it was the duty of the court to impose a sentence which would discourage others from committing a similar offence. I therefore stated that I was imposing the maximum sentence as an exemplary sentence. The final factor was probably the most compelling in relation to the length of sentence, but the other two factors were also significant in this respect."

Lord Allanbridge
"We have listened to all that the appellant has said very clearly on his own behalf. We want to make it quite clear, as this court has made it clear time and time again, that the carrying of knives in public places is a very serious offence indeed. It is no excuse,

although it is frequently said to be an excuse, that the weapon is carried for the carrier's self-protection. If that were to be a legitimate excuse then serious consequences could flow from such a practice. This court has made it clear, and we make it clear again in this case, that such conduct will not be tolerated. The offence is carrying a knife without reasonable authority and in this particular case we are quite satisfied that this is a case which was properly dealt with by the sheriff in imposing the maximum sentence, in view particularly of the appellant's very bad record. The appeal is therefore refused."

Appeal refused.

NOTE
   This case is reported briefly at 1994 G.W.D. 33–1943. Sentences of imprisonment were upheld in *Maini* v. *H.M. Advocate*, 1994 G.W.D. 26–1575 and *Rankin* v. *Friel*, 1995 G.W.D. 18–1027. In *Rafferty* v. *Annan*, 1995 G.W.D. 5–244 it was said explicitly that "any offence under the 1993 Act would generally attract a custodial sentence." Whereas in *Anderson* v. *Orr, supra*, the sheriff indicated that the carrying of knives was not a common problem in Inverness. In *Monaghan* v. *Friel*, 1992 G.W.D. 38–2248 it was held that an exemplary sentence was justified because of the prevalence of people carrying knives in the Paisley area.

(xxi) R. v. Norman   5.22

(1995) 16 Cr.App.R.(S.) 848

N. appealed against the sentence imposed in respect of his conviction of two charges of possessing offensive weapons. Police officers attending an incident saw the appellant throw away a broken pool cue and a nasal spray containing a solution of ammonia. The police had received a report of men fighting and on arrival they found five men, including the appellant. N. was sentenced to 18 months' imprisonment.

Held, that the appellant had a previous conviction for having an offensive weapon and he had not taken the warning from it. The sentence was entirely proper.

Ian Kennedy, J. (at p. 848)
   "The legislation in this regard is intended to protect people from the risk that those who go about armed may use weapons that they have. If defendants do not take warnings from one conviction but continue with this sort of behaviour, it is perfectly plain that the court before whom they appear cannot treat the matter lightly."

Appeal refused.

INDEX OF OFFENSIVE WEAPONS